When Peace Fails

When Peace Fails

Lessons from Belfast for the Middle East

THOMAS G. MITCHELL

McFarland & Company, Inc., Publishers
Jefferson, North Carolina, and London

LIBRARY OF CONGRESS CATALOGUING-IN-PUBLICATION DATA

Mitchell, Thomas G., 1957–
    When peace fails : lessons from Belfast for the Middle East / Thomas G. Mitchell.
    p.   cm.
    Includes bibliographical references and index.

    ISBN 978-0-7864-4852-4
    softcover : 50# alkaline paper ∞

    1. Arab-Israeli conflict—1993– — Peace. 2. Middle East—Politics and government—1979– 3. Peace-building—Middle East. 4. Northern Ireland—Politics and government—1994– 5. Peace-building—Northern Ireland. I. Title.
DS119.76.M584 2010
956.05—dc22
                                      2010015571

British Library cataloguing data are available

©2010 Thomas G. Mitchell. All rights reserved

No part of this book may be reproduced or transmitted in any form or by any means, electronic or mechanical, including photocopying or recording, or by any information storage and retrieval system, without permission in writing from the publisher.

Cover images ©2010 Shutterstock

Manufactured in the United States of America

McFarland & Company, Inc., Publishers
   Box 611, Jefferson, North Carolina 28640
   www.mcfarlandpub.com

Table of Contents

Acronyms vi
Preface 1

One • Natives and Settlers Making Peace 5

Part I. The Oslo Process

Two • A Dialogue in Oslo 27
Three • The Peace Process Stalls 48
Four • Camp David 2000 64

Part II. The Northern Ireland Peace Process

Five • The Belfast Agreement 93
Six • The Peace Process Collapses 131
Seven • The Agreement Saved 171

Conclusion 205
Epilogue 225
Chapter Notes 229
Bibliography 247
Index 251

Acronyms

Palestine

DFLP   Democratic Front for the Liberation of Palestine
PFLP   Popular Front for the Liberation of Palestine
PLO   Palestine Liberation Organization

Northern Ireland

DUP   Democratic Unionist Party
INLA   Irish National Liberation Army
IRA   Irish Republican Army
IRSP   Irish Republican Socialist Party
LVF   Loyalist Volunteer Force
NIUP   Northern Ireland Unionist Party
NIWC Northern Ireland Women's Coalition
OIRA   Official IRA
PIRA   Provisional IRA
PUP   Progressive Unionist Party
RHC   Red Hand Commando
SDLP   Social Democratic and Labour Party
UDA   Ulster Defence Association
UDP   Ulster Democratic Party
UKUP United Kingdom Unionist Party
UUC   Ulster Unionist Council
UUP   Ulster Unionist Party
UVF   Ulster Volunteer Force

Preface

This book consists of the stories of two cases of peace settlements that went bad. In one of them, the Middle East, the peace was not recovered. In the other, Northern Ireland, the peace was recovered and power sharing is being implemented between the Democratic Unionist Party and Sinn Fein. Unfortunately, this has occurred at the cost of the fortunes of the moderate parties that first implemented the Good Friday Agreement.

In the 1990s there were prominent peace processes in serial succession in three of the leading conflicts on the international agenda: South Africa, the Middle East, and Northern Ireland. In South Africa the peace process had its initial hiccups and problems, particularly one involving an invasion of Ciskei homeland by African National Congress (ANC) activists. But once negotiations finally began in 1992 — less time than it took from the beginning of the peace process until negotiations commenced than in Northern Ireland — they went forward relatively smoothly and there was no case of a failed peace. Elections in the spring of 1994 began majority rule in the New South Africa. I began work on a comparative study of the peace processes in the Middle East, Northern Ireland, and South Africa in 2001, but soon concluded that the South African case was so different from Northern Ireland and the Middle East as to not make comparison worth the effort. To find a case of failed peace in South Africa one would have to go back to the 1890s and the collapse of the peace settlement that ended the First Anglo-Boer War of 1881. But because historians have reached a consensus that British imperialism was responsible for the breakdown of that peace, a detailed examination here would be a waste of effort.

The conflicts in Northern Ireland and the Middle East involved long terrorist insurgencies that were the subject of peace processes. The IRA's terrorist campaign within the Northern Ireland Troubles lasted from 1971 to 1997 and the PLO waged an ineffective terrorist and guerrilla campaign against Israel from 1965 to 1993. The biggest lesson of both cases is the importance of an effective mediation mechanism for resolving the conflict. When there is no mediation or the mediators are considered too biased and lack leverage over both parties, the mediation and peace process is likely to fail. When both parties in conflict perceive the mediation mechanism as reflecting their needs and the mediators are able to persuade or coerce both parties peace is likely to result.

In addition to both Israel and Northern Ireland being settler societies (the Israelis are also returned natives who returned with the approval of the international community) they are also both siege societies. The Palestinians retained at least the rhetorical and political support of the Arab states if not their military support through the First Lebanon War of 1982. They also had the support of the Soviet Union. After the collapse of the Soviet Union in 1991-92, Iran came to replace it as a leading supplier of weapons and military training to the various Palestinian fedayeen groups. In the United Nations and in various Third World forums Israel was delegitimized. Although Israel has extensive trade tries with the West, most Western European countries could not be counted on to support Israel in a crisis. Only Washington could be counted on. Only Washington mattered.

Both the Irish Free State and the Republic of Ireland refused to accept the legitimacy or legality of the British presence in Northern Ireland. The 26 counties, as republicans referred to the southern entity, never attempted to militarily subvert the North or enforce their constitutional claim on its territory. But the existence of that claim in Articles 2 and 3 served to create a psychological state of siege — a siege mentality. In Northern Ireland this is known as a "bawn mentality" (after the stone towers that protected Protestant farms during the seventeenth-century plantation) and in Israel as a "Masada complex." Both Northern Ireland and Israel have siege myths as their primary political myths: the Siege of Derry story for the unionists and the Masada, Betar, and Tel Hai myths for the Zionists.[1] For the unionists their primary connection was with the British Mainland and London, which many of them came to mistrust after The Troubles began. The main division in unionist politics was in many ways between those who only mistrusted Dublin and those who mistrusted both Dublin and London.

Each case is examined for the negotiations and issues involved in the peace settlement. The narrative then looks at why and how the peace negotiations or settlements came unraveled and the implications for such failures for the future. The conclusion examines how the lessons of Northern Ireland might be applied to the Middle East and the mediation process from Northern Ireland imitated there.

Each case consists of three parts: the initial peace negotiations and the settlement, the initial problems, and the collapse of the settlement. In the Northern Ireland case the third chapter details how the peace was saved in the end. The book consists of eight chapters: a theoretical chapter comparing the two cases in an abstract fashion, three chapters each for each of the two cases, and then a final conclusion. Before the narrative presentation of the two cases there is a chapter that examines theories of mediation applicable to both and a review of the literature connecting the two cases and discussing them as settler societies. The second chapter details the negotiations involved in the early Oslo process from 1993 to 1995 up until the assassination of Yitzhak Rabin. The third chapter covers the Peres government from November 1995 to June 1996 and then the Netanyahu administration. The fourth chapter covers the Barak coalition from its election in May 1999 to the Al-Aksa Intifada and the Taba negotiation. Its focal points are Camp David in July 2000 and the outbreak of the Al-Aksa Intifada in October 2000. The fifth chapter covers the start of the Northern Ireland peace process in 1988 with the Hume-Adams talks to the signing of the Belfast Agreement in April 1998. The sixth chapter is about attempting to make the Belfast Agreement work despite the refusal of the IRA to decommission. It covers the period from the referendum in May 1998 until the collapse of the First Assembly in October 2002. The seventh chapter details the demise of the UUP as the leading unionist party in Northern Ireland. It ends with the successful setting up of the Executive for the Third Assembly in May 2007 after the St. Andrew's summit in October 2006 and IRA decommissioning a year before that. The final chapter, the conclusion, is a list of lessons derived from the cases.

The cases were chosen and the lessons in the conclusion written with future mediation in the Israeli-Palestinian conflict in mind. There are no doubt lessons for other regional or internal conflicts as well — possibly Cyprus or Sri Lanka — but as this author lacks expertise in those other cases he will leave it to others to draw lessons for those situations from the cases presented here.

Few first person accounts for the Northern Ireland case are available at this time. The author only had access to the memoirs of George Mitchell, John Major, Alastair Campbell, and Jonathan Powell. The discussion of Northern Ireland is largely dependent on accounts of the peace process, biographies of David Trimble and earlier biographies of John Hume and Gerry Adams, and accounts of the Drumcree controversy written by journalists. The seventh chapter is very dependent on press coverage of the peace process. The author made two research trips to Northern Ireland, in the summer of 1998 and again in the summer of 2001. But the first trip was dedicated to researching a book on the conflict. Only the latter trip involved interviews for a book on the peace process.

ONE

Natives and Settlers Making Peace

Natives and Settlers

From the seventeenth to the twentieth centuries there was a great movement of colonization and settlement by Britain. It began with the province of Ulster in Ireland and the East Coast of North America. It then expanded to include South Africa, beginning with the Cape Province and Natal, and the northeastern maritime provinces of what would one day be Canada as the loyalist losers of the American Revolution resettled. It expanded to include Oceania — the eastern provinces of what is today Australia and New Zealand. And finally included much of Central and East Africa. Whether ultimately the settlers or the native population would be victorious in the long run depended largely on the rate of immigration to the new colonies and the demographic ratio between the two competing populations. A reversal of the process began with decolonization in Africa starting with Gold Coast (Ghana) in the late 1950s and proceeding to include most of British Africa in the 1960s. But the final stage of resolution began in the 1990s in three settler colonies: in Ulster or Northern Ireland, as the truncated six-county version was known officially; in South Africa; and in Israel and Palestine.[1]

In all three conflicts both the natives and settlers felt themselves to be victims. The natives had grievances over discrimination and harsh treatment at the hands of the settler regimes. And the settlers felt themselves to be the victims of terrorism. In South Africa the negotiations were straightforward and without major complications because of two factors. First, official trade sanctions and unofficial financial sanctions by European banks had left the leadership of the National Party with a foretaste of what they could expect if the conflict and apartheid continued. They opted to negotiate. Second, the African National Congress by eschewing terrorism against whites had avoided the bitterness that is the residue of such a strategy and has been left behind in both Israel and Northern Ireland.

In 1990 the first of a series of academic works linking South Africa, Israel, and Northern Ireland was published. It consisted of a multi-author collection of articles analyzing the internal politics and conflicts in the three countries.[2] In 1992 Irish-Canadian academic Donald Akenson published a comparative treatment of the three societies. Akenson had the religions of the three countries — a Old Testament–centered Biblical faith that saw their own people as a chosen people — as the independent variable that produced similar societies.[3] In 2000 I published my own comparative study, *Native vs. Settler,* of the same three cases and explored them all as examples of settler societies. I rejected Akenson's analysis because Rhodesia was similar in behavior yet lacked the religiosity or the view of being chosen of the other three societies.[4] I compared seven different phenomena for the three cases and believe that they generally stand up today a decade after they were written.[5] In a second comparative book, *Indispensable Traitors: Liberal Parties in Settler Conflicts,* I amplified my analysis of the role of liberal parties in the three cases and also discussed the role of conservative parties and internal settlements in South Africa and Northern Ireland.[6] The same year as my first book was published, a book by British academic Stephen Howe appeared that analyzed Ireland's place within the British Empire and its relationship to it once it gained independence. Howe also included an extensive survey and analysis of Ulster/Northern Ireland and the unionists.[7] The main alternate view of the unionists and Ulster as a settler society was as a transborder frontier society comparable to the Serbs in Bosnia and Croatia.[8] One problem for comparing Ulster with settler societies is the low level of distinction between natives and settlers: unlike Africa or Latin America they are of the same race, and unlike Israel/Palestine they are of the same religion — but different denominations — and speak the same language with the same accents. In Ulster both sides have to magnify small differences (much like Canadians when comparing themselves with Americans).[9] In fact, it was not unknown for loyalist terrorists to mistakenly kill Protestants in the belief that they were Catholics.

Howe cites three different authors using a comparative settler colonialism approach: Ian Lustick, Ronald Weitzer, and Michael MacDonald. Lustick compared Ireland to Algeria (and also Israel), Weitzer compared Northern Ireland to Zimbabwe, and MacDonald compared Ulster to South Africa. Lustick is comparing the politics of decolonization at the metropole level. Weitzer is comparing the issue of internal policing. And MacDonald is looking at settler politics. MacDonald's comparison is almost a throw-away as he makes the South African comparison in a single chapter. In my opinion and Howe's,

Lustick's comparison is the most theoretical and most developed. But unlike me he is looking only at the Jewish settlers on the West Bank and in Gaza as settlers rather than at Israeli Jews as a whole.[10]

In early 2004 I wrote an article analyzing the main features of Israeli politics and comparing them to other societies. I wrote that Israeli politics had six salient features, of which four were typical of settler societies.[11] The two non-settler features are weak coalition governments caused by a multi-party system typical of Latin European democracies like the French Third and Fourth Republics and the Italian postwar governments, and powerful religious parties comparable to system-Islamist parties found in Turkey, Pakistan, and Indonesia.[12] The four settler traits are: a class of military politicians in electoral politics (America, South Africa); parties with paramilitary roots (Northern Ireland); the native question as determiner of left and right in politics (all); and the legalized discrimination between natives and settlers (all). When I compared these to the three settler societies with which Israel shared common traits I found that Northern Ireland was the closest with five out of the six traits, compared with three each for the other two.[13]

Northern Ireland since 1970 has had its own autonomous party system usually consisting of five parties: two unionist, two nationalist, and the non-sectarian Alliance Party. Twice during this period unionist politics has fragmented and splinter unionist parties have appeared on the right in reaction to attempts by London and Dublin to resolve the Irish question in the North. From 1973 to 1979 a splintering process eventually resulted in five unionist parties before three of these disappeared. From approximately 1996 to 2003 a similar process took place in Ulster politics resulting in a total of seven unionist parties before returning to two main unionist parties and a small loyalist party. During this latter period there was one coalition government consisting of two parties, the Ulster Unionists (UUP) and the Progressive Unionists (PUP), from December 1999 to October 2002.[14] At one point in October 2001 the UUP was dependent on delegates from the two nonsectarian parties redesignating from "other" to "unionist" in order to help reelect David Trimble as first minister after he had resigned. This is comparable to Israeli coalitions relying on the votes of Arab parties outside the government for support during a peace process.[15] In the second Assembly election in November 2003 all the new parties were wiped out except for one member of the PUP, leader David Ervine.[16] The Democratic Unionist Party (DUP), which was founded in 1969–71 by the Rev. Ian Paisley, the moderator of the Free Presbyterian Church since 1951, was a religious party as well as a conservative unionist party. Paisley remained head of both the church and the party until late 2007 when members of the church who objected to his power sharing with Sinn Fein forced him to step down as moderator. But Free Presbyterians still play a prominent role in the DUP. Thus the DUP is in many ways like a cross between the Likud and the National Religious Party or Shas.[17]

In 2006 Israeli scholar Guy Ben-Porat published a comparative study of the peace processes in the Middle East and Northern Ireland. He looked at them from the economic and sociological point of view. The first half of the book was a comparison of how imperialism had influenced the development of Irish nationalism and Zionism in the latter part of the nineteenth century and the early twentieth century and contained little that was new. The second half was an examination of how post–Cold War liberalism influenced the development of the peace processes. The most interesting feature was his contrast of the political influence of the business community in Israel compared to the political isolation of the business class in Northern Ireland. Ironically, the latter situation seemed to serve the peace process better as it was useful in the referendum campaign and did not produce a backlash from the unionist Right. Ben-Porat also analyzed the distribution of the "peace dividend" in both cases. He concluded that because capitalists connected with the Labor Party received most of the benefit of the peace dividend, this restricted the amount of political support that the peace process received on economic grounds. He also argued that Palestinians reaped few, if any, economic benefits from the peace process. In Northern Ireland the peace dividend was more evenly distributed, but still too small to keep loyalists on board throughout the process.[18] He did not study the negotiations themselves.

In 2008 Ben-Porat served as the editor for a book of essays resulting from a conference comparing the peace processes in Israel/Palestine, Northern Ireland and South Africa. In the introduction Ben-Porat posited that all three conflicts were protracted ethno-national conflicts involving territorial issues. Because they were protracted they exhibited two characteristics: first, a lack of concern about the ethnic opponent; and second, a zero-sum dynamic that rules out most conventional conflict resolution approaches. Ben-Porat also noted that different parties have different perceptions of success or failure. He claimed that the core issues of these protracted conflicts were sovereignty and territoriality and that they offered two types of solution — partition or power sharing. Echoing the contribution by John McGarry and Brendan O'Leary, he noted that a North-South dimension was needed in addition to power sharing in Northern Ireland because it was a national conflict with extra-territorial dimensions. Because of this consociation was a necessary, but not a sufficient, requirement for peace.[19] He also observed that "spoilers" see peace as a threat to either their economic status or political status or both, and that unequal distribution of peace dividends is a threat to peace.[20]

In this reviewer's opinion, two essays stand out in the collection: that by University of Haifa Professor Benjamin Miller on the state-to-nation balance; and that by Bar Ilan University Professor Jonathan Rynhold on the gaps between the two sides. Miller defined the station-to-nation balance in terms of "the incongruence or congruence between state and national boundaries." He saw large imbalances as destabilizing factors both internally and regionally. Of the three conflicts covered, South Africa had the smallest imbalance and the Middle East had the greatest with Northern Ireland fitting somewhere in between. Miller defines the refugee problem, the settlement problem, and the border problem all as manifestations of this imbalance. Miller sees the Middle East as an inherently unstable region because of the large number of "illegitimate" states (at least in the eyes of their neighbors) in the region such as Kuwait, Lebanon, Jordan, and Israel. And because many Arab states have legitimacy problems many rulers have used both pan-Arabism and the Israeli-Palestinian conflict as means to acquire internal legitimacy and regional hegemony. This in turn has made Israel less willing to make concessions.[21]

Rynhold examined the explanations for the failure of the Oslo peace process advanced by both Liberal and Realist theorists. Rynhold concluded that the Israelis and Palestinians were ripe for negotiation but not ripe for conflict resolution because of the large gaps between their positions on the issues. In his opinion it was the large gaps between the two sides that caused the mistrust rather than the opposite. Rynhold claimed that 75 percent of Palestinian refugees were unwilling to accept coexistence with Israeli Jews under any circumstances and that ten percent of the refugees wanted to return to live in Israel. He claimed that Israel's peace agreements with Egypt and Jordan were agreements based on the 1648 Peace of Westphalia of state sovereignty but that this principle did not apply to the conflict between Israel and the Palestinians. He also claimed that Egypt played a negative role in the peace process by discouraging Palestinian compromises. And he noted that social trust can be built up only during negotiations among near equals, which is not the situation between Israel and the Palestinians. Shimon Peres's expectation that the Islamist threat would prove to be a unifying factor between the two sides turned out to be wishful thinking.[22]

Ben-Porat concluded by noting that the Middle East has seesawed between negotiations and outbursts of violence and is nowhere near a solution. He observed that the positive trends in Northern Ireland are not present in the Middle East and that the peace process did not effect a lasting change in the relations between Israelis and Palestinians.[23]

In the peace processes in both Northern Ireland and the Middle East, it was the native liberation movements in conjunction with outside forces who initiated the peace process. The settlers felt compelled to bow to outside political pressure and go along with outside pressure. In Northern Ireland, although republican opponents dubbed it a partitionist settlement, it was really a power-sharing settlement in which the majority unionists would share power with the minority nationalists within the confines of a partition that had taken place over seven decades before. In Israel the settlement was a partitionist settlement — really a restorationist settlement — with the native liberation movement, the Palestine Liberation Organization (PLO), seeking to restore a partition from 1949, which the Arabs had really refused to accept as final at the time. As a result a second partition had taken place in 1967 leaving the Zionists in control of all of western Palestine of the mandate. In both cases the settlers were being required to give up something tangible for promises of peace.

In Northern Ireland the peace process was really initiated by the Adams-Hume talks between the leaderships of the two main Irish nationalist parties, the SDLP and Sinn Fein. When accord was finally reached in 1993 on the basis for a peace process John Hume approached the Irish government. Dublin then brought in London, which in turn brought in the unionists.

In the Middle East the order was slightly different. The Bush I administration in the person of Secretary of State Jim Baker pressured both the Arabs and Israel to meet at a ceremonial peace conference in Madrid in October 1991. This was a prelude to substantive bilateral and multilateral negotiations in Washington. In order to deal with Israeli sensibilities, the PLO was excluded despite its recognition of Israel's right to exist and disavowal of terrorism in December 1988. The PLO then maneuvered to have itself invited into negotiations by blocking any progress in the bilateral talks in Washington between the Jordanian-Palestinian delegation and Israel. Chairman Yasir Arafat thought that a new Labor government might be persuaded to eventually negotiate with it. He was right.

These two cases are legally different under international law as Northern Ireland is a civil or internal conflict and Palestine is an "interstate" conflict between Israel and the occupied protostate of Palestine.[24] Palestinians sometimes compare their resistance to the resistance against the Nazis in occupied Europe during World War II. But they also compare themselves to the ANC in South Africa — an internal conflict. So that for purposes of bargaining and negotiations theory, both cases can be considered examples of internal conflicts. The Israeli-Palestinian conflict is in many ways comparable to the SWAPO insurgency in Namibia. In both instances the occupier arrived as the result of a defensive war but lost international legitimacy for its rule by a refusal to grant self-determination. Both Israel and South Africa saw the occupied territories as buffer zones to protect against foreign invasions.[25]

The Negotiations

William Zartman has written that a "ripe moment" is necessary to conclude peace successfully in regional conflicts. A "ripe moment" or ripeness consists of three elements: "hurting stalemate," representative parties, and a formula that provides a way out. A hurting stalemate is a situation where neither side is able to force its will on the other side, but both have incentives to negotiate, compromise and end the conflict. Usually this is that the dominant side fears an impending reversal of the balance of power and the weaker side fears the cost to be paid to bring about that reversal.[26]

There was a hurting stalemate in both Northern Ireland and Israel. It was not so much that London feared that the British army would lose its advantage in the Irish conflict, but that it feared the price to be paid on the mainland in terms of British civilian casualties and damages to British cities. Gerry Adams and Martin McGuinness had decided that a united 32-county Ireland was not attainable through armed struggle, but that an end to the armed struggle could improve Sinn Fein's political position both within Northern Ireland and the Republic of Ireland. They just had to gradually convince the Irish Republican Army (IRA) of their insight.

The leadership of no unionist party felt that it had a mandate to negotiate with unrepentant terrorists. Ian Paisley and Robert McCartney, the leaders of the Democratic Unionists (DUP) and the UK Unionists (UKUP), respectively, avoided this by the simple device of leaving the negotiations once Sinn Fein entered. James Molyneaux, the leader of the Ulster Unionists (UUP), evaded this fate by resigning his leadership in 1996. David Trimble, the newly elected leader, avoided this fate by refusing to deal with Sinn Fein negotiators throughout the Good Friday Agreement negotiations. Because a moderate nationalist party, in the form of the SDLP, existed the Good Friday Agreement was possible. After about six weeks of serious negotiations an agreement was reached and signed on Good Friday in Belfast in April 1998.

There was a hurting stalemate in the Holy Land in 1992-93 because of the Intifada and the weakness of the PLO. The PLO was broke and the exiled leadership was losing its control of the liberation struggle to a younger generation within the territories. It needed to catch its breath, refill its coffers, and arrange for the exiled leadership to return to the territories as the exiled ANC had returned to South Africa from London and Africa in 1990. For these purposes Arafat was willing to sign nearly anything that came out of Oslo. Arafat knew that he could later disavow the agreements or demand changes. So he took positions on settlements that were unacceptable to ordinary internal Palestinian leaders. This was a reversal of the usual pattern from Rhodesia, Namibia, El Salvador, and Northern Ireland (in 1974) where internal settlements were reached that gave the internal leaders less than what the external leaders associated with the armed struggle were demanding. In Palestine the external leaders associated with the armed struggle were demanding less than the internal leaders.[27] This is because the internal leaders probably intended to keep any agreement reached.

The Israeli leadership could not simply avoid the Palestinian terrorist leaders by turning to civilian leaders not stained by terrorism, because there simply were not any of any importance who did not recognize the primacy of either Arafat or the Islamists. Like the DUP and UKUP, the Likud and its satellite rightist parties condemned the negotiations and agitated against them. Because neither Yitzhak Rabin nor Shimon Peres completely trusted the PLO they decided to have a five-year negotiating period. If the Palestinians proved to be untrustworthy or too demanding, they would simply shut the process down. But the negotiations created their own expectations. This was especially true outside Israel in the Clinton administration, in the American Jewish community, and in Europe.

In both Israel and Northern Ireland there were negotiations taking place against the background of *dissident terrorism*. The dissident republicans of the Continuity IRA, INLA, and Real IRA carried out bombing campaigns in the cities and towns of Northern Ireland. The Islamists of Hamas and Islamic Jihad carried out bombings, suicide bombings, and drive-by shootings from the start of the implementation of the Oslo agreement. The level of terrorism experienced by ordinary Israelis was much higher during the peace process than before. Rabin's main counter-terrorism strategy consisted of closing down Israel to Palestinian workers after each incident in a bid to both prevent further attacks and collectively punish the Palestinians so that they would operate against the terrorists. This gave control of the pace of the process to the Islamists. The Islamists would remain in control until Ariel Sharon finally broke the Al-Aksa Intifada through a reoccupation of the territories and a policy of "targeted killings" or assassinations of suspected terrorist leaders.

In both Palestine and Northern Ireland the native sides was as badly divided as the settlers — but they were divided in very different ways. In Northern Ireland the support level for dissident terrorism was probably about two percent of the nationalist population or less. The major division within the IRA had been resolved in favor of the peace strategy of Adams and McGuinness. It had resulted in the exit of the Real IRA from the Provisional IRA. The main division was between the Adams-McGuinness leadership of Sinn Fein, which wished to avoid divisions within the IRA by not decommissioning, and the SDLP that wanted the IRA to decommission so as not to endanger the peace process. The SDLP adopted a "plague on both your houses" approach between 1998 and 2005 condemning both the failure of the IRA to decommission and of Sinn Fein to pressure it and the failure of the Ulster Unionists to implement power sharing as if decommissioning had occurred on schedule.

In Palestine the divisions were between the Islamists and their supporters as well as various small "front terrorist organizations" such as the Popular Front for the Liberation of Palestine and its splinters on one hand and Fatah and its affiliated organizations on the other. Initially the balance of power favored Fatah and the PLO. But as settlement continued and the constant closures of Israel to the territories hurt the Palestinian economy the balance began to shift.

In negotiations there is what is known as holding the other side's object of value hostage. This occurs when one side knows what is most important to the other side and exploits it to extract concessions. In Northern Ireland this clearly occurred with decommissioning. The threat of future terrorism tied to the weapons to be decommissioned was the IRA's major leverage over both the unionists and London. So they would not give up this leverage easily or early. Originally decommissioning was supposed to occur before negotiations began, as a precondition, according to the unionists. The Republicans, with the support of the SDLP, rejected this. Then decommissioning was supposed to occur parallel to negotiations. The IRA and loyalists also rejected this. Then the decommissioning was supposed to happen parallel to prisoner releases as an obligation under the Good Friday Agreement. The IRA and loyalists rejected this and Sinn Fein and the loyalist parties claimed that their only obligation was to use their influence — if they failed, they failed.

Because the Ulster Unionists sold decommissioning as one of the main benefits of the Good Friday Agreement along with the changes in the Irish constitution, they were anxious that it actually did occur. Thus the Ulster Unionists took unilateral sanctions against Sinn Fein to force the IRA to disarm. These included banning Sinn Fein from North-South meetings and shutting down the power-sharing Executive. London feared that these moves would provoke a return of the IRA to terrorism, so it pushed David Trimble to constantly take new risks for peace. By taking unilateral measures that failed to have the intended effect, Trimble appeared weak. This caused the balance of power within the unionist community to shift against the agreement and in favor of anti-agreement parties like the DUP, the UKUP, the NIUP, and the PUP. Britain by releasing its leverage from prison ended up paying for decommissioning several times over and in the process weakening the moderate parties.

In the Holy Land both sides had items of value that they exploited but failed to make a tradeoff on. The Palestinians needed an end to settlements and an end to border closings. The Israelis needed an end to terrorism. Neither side was really in a position to grant what the other side needed. Because of Israel's coalition system, settlements were an important concession needed to retain the cohesion of the coalition. This was true of both the Netanyahu and Barak governments. Even Rabin was able to pass the Oslo II redeployment agreement by only a single vote. Arafat could crack down on Hamas and Islamic Jihad, but this made him look weak. So as time went on he cracked down less and less, particularly as settlements and economic problems made the Oslo settlement less and less popular with Palestinians. Arafat's corruption also ended up making the peace process less popular with Palestinians. Israeli citizens ended up paying for Arafat's corruption with their security and lives.

In 2009 three academics and journalists published a comparative study of the history of British talks with the Republicans in Northern Ireland and Spanish dealings with Basque terrorists. The book, *Talking To Terrorists,* was meant to counter the lesson, peddled by both Sinn Fein and British veterans of the Northern Ireland peace process, that talking to terrorists was the solution to all terrorist conflicts. The authors examine four separate episodes of discussions between British authorities and either the IRA or Sinn Fein. They conclude that the first two instances were counterproductive as they gave the impression that Britain was weak and ready to concede power in Northern Ireland if pushed hard enough. They conclude that talking is only productive once the terrorists have decided to give up their campaign and want to be brought in from the cold.[28] This basically comes down again to a perception of ripeness, something that is inherently subjective and hard to judge.

Mediation

Mediation can range from "good offices" where a mediator serves merely as a postman or messenger for two sides that are not communicating with each other to binding arbitration where a mediator serves as a judge of the merits of the cases of the two sides. Binding arbitration involves the parties agreeing before hand that they will accept the arbitrator's verdict and is usually used in labor disputes or interstate border conflicts rather than in civil conflicts. "Mediation is best thought of as a mode of negotiation in which a third party helps the parties find a solution which they cannot find by themselves."[29] In conflicts like those discussed in this book, the mediator typically works with both sides to reach a settlement that is acceptable to both. Chris

Mitchell defined it as "intermediary activity ... undertaken by a third party with the primary intention of achieving some compromise settlement of the issues at stake between the parties, or at least ending disruptive behavior."[30] The mediator does this because he has an interest in resolving or managing the conflict. The interests of all parties must be compatible—if the parties want a resolution and the mediator does not or vice versa, there will be a problem.[31] Mediation has become more common since the end of World War II, probably as a result of decolonization, and even more common and complex since the end of the Cold War. According to one academic observer, "Odds are so heavily stacked against the mediator that any kind of success is not easy to explain—hence the need for intellectual sophistication."[32]

The conflicts in the Middle East and Northern Ireland are similar in that for Washington and London they are the most important conflicts that each has mediated. The United States has been involved in Middle East mediation in the Arab-Israeli conflict since the Eisenhower administration and continually since the Nixon administration in 1969. The Good Friday negotiations and the implementation of the agreement were the final chapter in the "Irish question," which British governments had been trying to solve since William Gladstone was prime minister in the 1880s. The "Irish question" consisted of two thirty- to forty-year conflict-management efforts separated by nearly a half century. In both conflicts both of the two major parties in Britain and America have exploited each country's conflict for its own interest. Randolph Churchill, the politician father of Winston, began the tradition of "playing the Orange card" during the home rule crisis of 1886. His son was involved as colonial minister in the negotiations that resolved the Irish question in the South in December 1921.[33]

Northern Ireland was Britain's longest running military deployment from 1969 to 2007. Ending that deployment, which was so expensive in both treasure and blood, was a prime interest of successive British governments from Harold Wilson to Tony Blair. The conflict was also a problem for Ireland. It was a source of tension with Britain, one of Ireland's closest trade partners, and a source of terrorism and financial corruption in the Republic. Ireland came close to invading Northern Ireland in 1969 before Britain intervened. In 1973 London brought Dublin into the management of the conflict by making it a partner to the Sunningdale negotiations on a power-sharing settlement. Loyalist workers brought down this experiment in May 1974 after only five months, but a precedent for Irish involvement of this ethnic conflict had been established. In 1986 Prime Minister Margaret Thatcher and Taoiseach Garret FitzGerald negotiated the Anglo-Irish Agreement that gave Dublin a formal consultative role in the setting of policies for Northern Ireland. Unionists cried foul and considered Thatcher to be a traitor.

This cooperation led to what I term *dual mediation* in the conflict: each sponsor is the patron of one party to the conflict and both consult to ensure that the interests of both of their clients are represented in the mediation effort. Neither of the two governments provided the actual mediator who oversaw the negotiations. Instead the two governments turned to their mutual friend, President Clinton, to provide a mediator. The *dual mediation* worked because the relations between Dublin and London were at least as close, if not more so, than those between each partner and its Northern Ireland client. Dublin had very close relations with the SDLP, which was almost a northern branch of Ireland's Department of External Affairs, but very strained relations with the IRA, which was illegal in the Republic. Relations between the intelligence agencies of the two governments were somewhere between these extremes.

In the Middle East the United States, as befits an exceptionalist superpower, has always seen mediation as a solo effort. Washington's interest in the peace process is as a means of reconciling popular sympathies on religious and historical grounds among the American population for Israel with extensive energy and economic interests in the Arab world. In the 1950s and 1960s America inherited Britain's role in the Middle East with it eventually inheriting Israel, Egypt, Saudi Arabia, Kuwait, and Jordan as its clients. Since then America has been experiencing its own "moment" in the Middle East. By mediating between Israel and its Arab neighbors Washington has attempted to give some relief to its Arab client regimes who have been criticized by their own populations for not doing more for Palestine and for maintaining close relations with Israel's patron. Initially Presidents Nixon, Ford and Reagan subordinated Middle East diplomacy to Cold War interests. Nixon allowed his national security advisor to undercut his secretary of state in order to embarrass the Soviet Union during the War of Attrition of 1969-70. Henry Kissinger, wearing both hats in Nixon's second term, encouraged Israel to violate the ceasefire at the end of the Yom Kippur War and then used his shuttle diplomacy to facilitate a change of alliances in Egypt and improve American relations with Damascus.[34] President Reagan had close relations with Israel, but was willing to provoke a confrontation with Prime Minister Begin when the IDF undercut American diplomacy.[35]

With the end of the Cold War in 1990, the United States was able to seek a comprehensive settlement that had eluded President Carter in 1977. President George Bush (41) used the Gulf War dividend to force the Arabs and Israelis to attend the Madrid Conference in October 1991. Both Prime Minister Yitzhak Shamir and President Hafiz al-Assad of Syria had to be practically dragged to the conference. The potential for the two-track peace process of the 1990s was only beginning to develop in mid–1992 when presidential politics intruded. James A. Baker left the State Department to lead Bush's reelection campaign anticipating a return. He took Dennis Ross, a top Middle East aide responsible for the 1982 Reagan Plan, with him.

Two of the leading theoretical topics for theorists of mediation are the question of bias or disinterest and negotiating leverage. Professor Sa'adia Touval argues in a study of Arab-Israeli mediation over thirty years that impartiality is not required of a mediator, provided that both parties feel that something is at stake in the negotiation. Each side compares the danger of biased mediation with the alternatives and if the risk of mediation is less or potentially more rewarding accepts it. He claimed that President Carter was biased in favor of President Anwar Sadat and against Begin. This has become much clearer since then. But because Israel had an interest in preserving of its traditional status as America's leading Middle Eastern client, it had an interest in cooperating with Carter at Camp David and beyond. Egypt had an interest in cooperating in order to replace Israel as America's leading regional ally. Out of this Carter was able to fashion a peace treaty.[36]

Touval argues that a group of mediators usually has more international prestige and legitimacy than a single mediator (here he is referring to powers not persons), but that a single mediator is often more effective because he delivers a single message and is not susceptible to splitting or simple mixed messages.[37] But Zartman argues that "mediators must be important/powerful, multiple and coordinated to succeed."[38] Obviously if a mediator is singular he need not be coordinated except with his own government. Mediators can aid in the ripening process by making solutions available that the parties had not considered as well as by offering "side payments" or bribes for peace.[39]

The mediators in the two conflicts took very different strategies to deal with the question of bias. As mentioned previously, London dealt with bias by inviting Dublin into the process as an equal.[40] President Clinton chose to deal with bias by becoming simultaneously both the most pro-Israel and the most pro-Palestinian president in American history. He treated Prime Minister Rabin nearly as a surrogate father. And allowed Prime Minister Ehud Barak full access to him. He made an official visit to the Palestinian Authority in Gaza. He clearly favored Arafat over Netanyahu during his second term. And he promised Arafat that he would not blame him if the Camp David summit failed. But when he perceived that Arafat and the PLO were not interested in peace he broke that pledge.

Every four years American liberals and the Arabs urge Washington to become even handed in its approach to the Arab-Israeli conflict. But they ignore that there are structural constraints on American impartiality. Although Stephen Walt and John Mearsheimer have blamed this on the Israeli lobby — AIPAC and other organizations — it is more based on popular American sentiments based on shared values and history between Israel and the United States.[41] Israel is a democracy with an increasingly free market. During World Wars I and II the Zionists were on the Allied side, whereas the Arabs were either neutral during World War II or sympathized with the Axis powers. During the Cold War Israel was an important American ally whereas the Palestinians and their main Arab allies were Soviet allies. One of the largest religious groups in America, Evangelical Protestants, tends to overwhelmingly side with Israel against the Arabs. Even many Catholics side with Israel. Only Greek Orthodox and liberal Protestant denominations side with the Palestinians. Most American presidents are Protestants — either Southern Baptists like Carter and Clinton, Presbyterians like Reagan and George Bush, or Methodists like George W. Bush. Thus most American presidents are religiously predisposed to side with Israel and have this reinforced by a popular majority in favor of Israel.

It is simpler and more effective to bring in an outside mediating power to balance American bias, than for Americans to eliminate it by themselves. The choice is between bringing in an Arab power or powers and a European power or powers. Before the terrorist attacks of 9/11 it might have been possible to bring in an Arab power, such as Egypt or Jordan, as a co-mediator — but it would have been difficult. Since 9/11 it has become impossible because of increased militancy in the Arab world and increased American suspicion of Arabs and Muslims. The Europeans have a similar structural constraint on impartiality. Europe has a two thousand year history of anti–Semitism, tied both to the traditions of the Catholic and Greek Orthodox churches and to the use by royalty and imperial structures of Jews as financial middlemen and advisors. Western Europe also suffers from colonial guilt over the roles of Britain, Belgium, France, Germany, Italy, the Netherlands, Portugal, and Spain in the Third World. Britain, France, and Italy played major colonial roles in the Middle East and North Africa (Spain played a minor role) and the Netherlands in Muslim Indonesia. There are large numbers of unassimilated Muslim and Arab immigrants in Western Europe. Due to a combination of traditional anti–Semitism, post-colonial guilt and fear of Arab and Muslim unrest, most European governments will naturally side with the Arabs. The European Union provides the Palestinian Authority with much needed economic aid. The European Union also has extensive economic ties with Israel. So bringing in Brussels — the European Union (not Belgium) — would balance the United States and give Washington more leverage with both the Palestinians and Israel.

The other issue is leverage. Leverage is usually a combination of carrots and sticks — bribes and threats. Traditionally the United States has used bribery of both sides along with occasional threats as its main mediating tool. Following the separation-of-forces agreements with Egypt and Syria in 1974, Israel became a major recipient of American military and economic aid. A year later Egypt began receiving economic aid following the Sinai II interim agreement with Israel. The aid to both countries increased following the Egyptian-Israeli peace treaty of 1979.[42] Damascus would like Syria to become a second Egypt, with new modern American tanks, aircraft, and missiles replacing obsolescent Soviet weapons systems. But Bashar al-Assad knows that he will not receive any of this aid unless he reaches a peace treaty with Israel, and if the recession turns into a multiyear depression, Washington will have little foreign aid to spare. Bribery works better with secular military regimes than with Islamist opposition groups or governments.

In Northern Ireland Britain had direct economic leverage over the population in the form of the Northern Ireland budget. Ireland had leverage over the IRA and Sinn Fein through the Republican prisoners in its prisons. But as long as London refused to exercise that leverage, Dublin would not either. Dublin also had leverage through the degree of surveillance that it exercised over republican strongholds in such border towns as Dundalk and the towns of County Donegal. By threatening to raise water rates and other forms of taxation in 2007, London was able to coerce the DUP into recognizing the IRA's decommissioning and force it into power sharing. Because the IRA had finally succumbed to unionist demands over decommissioning, the stick of increased tax rates and Sinn Fein recognition of the Police Service of Northern Ireland was all it took to seal the deal.

In a book on civil conflicts noted negotiations and mediation expert and African conflict specialist I. William Zartman argues that mediation efforts of civil conflicts usually fail for one or both of two reasons. First, the moment is simply not ripe for resolution. Second, the mediator lacks sufficient material and ideological leverage to deliver the two sides. This is especially true of partial mediators not being able to deliver the side to which they are partial. That is why an ongoing material and ideological relationship between the mediator and the conflict parties is important.[43]

He also argues that when the insurgents are challenged by a serious bid for leadership from within their community they may back off from negotiations or not make necessary concessions out of fear of looking weak.[44] Continued Jewish settlement on the West Bank and corruption by the Palestinian Authority combined to allow the Islamists to make a serious bid for power against the PLO. Under these circumstances Arafat felt unable to make important concessions on either the Temple Mount or refugees. This is the best explanation for the failure to make peace at Camp David in July 2000.

So the important question is, were there ripe moments in the Middle East and Northern Ireland that were wasted? Hurting stalemates and representative parties existed in both cases. The only thing that was lacking was a formula. That formula did not arrive in the Middle East until late December 2000 when President Clinton issued his Clinton parameters. But by then he was a very lame duck with very little leverage over the parties. In Belfast a "formula" was fudged in April 1998 but the IRA refused to recognize that it was applicable to it. Sinn Fein also believed that its only responsibility under the Agreement was to go through the motions of attempting to persuade the IRA to decommission (behind closed doors in secret). The SDLP was also half-hearted about criticizing Sinn Fein for this stance. The real ripe moment occurred after 9/11 when the United States pressured the IRA to decommission and the IRA understood that it would have little support among Irish-Americans for holding out. Decommissioning was begun in October 2001 and completed in September 2005. This then created a ripe moment for the DUP as it could now go into government with the Republican Movement without fear of being outflanked on the right and could justify it by saying that the IRA had finally delivered product. All it took was a little bribery and coercion from London.[45]

In the late 1990s, a number of academics at the U.S. Institute of Peace undertook a study of "multiparty mediation," which they define as being either multiparty simultaneously or in serial and involving international or regional organizations, national governments and non-governmental organizations (NGOs). They concluded that in general in mediation timing and ripeness are more important than the identity of the mediator.[46] They conclude that in theory a coalition of multiple great powers should be more effective than a single mediator due to greater leverage, but this assumes that all involved share similar goals and are willing to work together and not at cross-purposes.[47] Earlier they explain the title of their book. "Organizing the diverse third-party peacemaking entities is a lot like organizing cats ... they will do what they choose to do, gazing at your efforts ... with mild curiosity, or simply ignoring you."[48]

The larger the number of mediators the more likely there is to be conflicts among them — both in terms of interests and positions. The former Yugoslavia between 1991 and 1995 is a good example of this — the United Nations, the European Community/Union, the United States, and Jimmy Carter in a private capacity were all involved. There developed turf battles between Brussels and Washington in Bosnia in 1992, with the result that Washington backed off until Brussels had failed. To be successful the multiple mediators must have a shared analysis of the problem and a sense of a common solution or they will simply undermine each other when talking with the parties.[49] When there are too many mediators on the ground at one time, as in the Great Lakes crisis of 1996, forum shopping and mixed messages become common. When there is sequential mediation the diplomatic handoff must be carefully managed or problems will arise. This possibility arose in Northern Ireland when the Irish and British governments changed but was skillfully handled by Foreign Minister Dick Spring — who was a member of both the Reynolds and Bruton governments — when passing on to the Ahern government in 1997.[50]

Mediation is normally a sort of "political triage" dealing with only the most serious problems that are deemed to be solvable. Many important but less immediate concerns may be left to fester.[51] Thus, decommissioning was left for a more definite solution until later. Difficult problems, such as parades, were give to "quangos"— quasi NGOs — such as the Parades Commission to deal with. This might be a solution for dealing with the refugee question or the Temple Mount controversy.

Traditionally the ideal mediator is said to have been an individual who combined regional expertise with the conflict and players with someone with previous negotiations experience. Such a combination is often rare in government outside of long major conflicts such as the Middle East conflict. But a mediator's leverage is hurt if he is perceived as being too independent and not being able to deliver. Coercive mediation — often required if the conflict has not yet reached its "ripe moment"— requires clear lines of authority between the mediator and the institutions required to carry out the threats. This is why Henry Kissinger, who combined negotiations and regional expertise with the backing of the U.S. government, was so effective in the Middle East and Rhodesia from 1973 to 1976. Richard Holbroke was also effective in Bosnia for the same reasons. But even the best mediator can be ineffective when working alone or shrugged off if a player does not want to make peace. This was why Northern Ireland was stalemated for several years — Dublin lacked pressure over the IRA after the British released their leverage from prison — and why the Middle East peace process collapsed.[52]

Oran Young wrote that there are three types of leadership that are important for the creation and management of international regimes. These three types also apply to multiparty mediation as well: first, structural leadership or formal authority to provide leverage; second, entrepreneurial leadership or the ability to present issues in a way that brings parties together; and third, intellectual leadership, using ideas to shape perceptions and attitudes about policy options.[53] I would argue that George Mitchell combined these three qualities both during the original negotiations and then during the implementation review. While the Irish premiers and British prime ministers were able to work well together, they lacked these qualities. They deferred too much to Sinn Fein, rather than successfully building a cross-community centrist coalition of SDLP, Alliance, and the UUP to put pressure on Sinn Fein and the other paramilitaries to decommission. Tony Blair was unable to understand that 9/11 had effectively neutralized the paramilitary option of the Republicans.

The two examples of Yugoslavia and Northern Ireland demonstrate that *dual mediation* is superior to multiparty mediation at least when applied to high priority conflict situations in which the two mediating parties have leverage over the belligerent parties. Like alliance theory, the best mediation coalition is the smallest one that can do the job, which is usually two powers with leverage. But, just as the two governments made use of individuals from Canada, Finland, and the United States, Brussels and Washington can make use of individuals from friendly Arab governments such as Egypt and Jordan — as Clinton used King Hussein during the Wye talks in October 1997. George Mitchell was chosen for the position because he had spent much time in Ireland and was trusted by all the leaders in Dublin, London, and Belfast (except by Paisley and McCartney — who did not want any outsiders involved).[54] King Hussein was trusted by both Netanyahu and Arafat.

Mediation literature refers to ripeness for a mediator as readiness — the moment when a mediator has assembled the requisite resources, political backing and institutional support — both domestically and among coalition partners — to be able to move the negotiation process forward.[55] Mitchell was ready after he arrived in Belfast and the two governments committed to his presence. The two governments were ready from the fall of 1993 when the peace process began. This is in contrast to the United States in the Middle East conflict. Washington was ready from the summer of 1977 to the spring of 1979, from the fall of 1991 to when George Bush the elder left office and from the fall of 1998 briefly and then again from February 2000 to July 2000 and again briefly in December 2000. The hard part of the Arab-Israeli conflict is coordinating readiness and ripeness — it is like coordinating conception in a couple where both partners suffer from fertility problems and have busy schedules. Either Washington, Damascus, Jerusalem or Ramallah was not ready (or ripe) at any particular moment.

Power Sharing/Consociational Democracy

In 1968 Dutch American political scientist Arend Lijphart published his study on constitutional arrangements in the Netherlands.[56] He followed this up with *Democracy in Plural Societies* in 1977 based on the experiences of four Western European countries in the postwar period: Austria, Belgium, the Netherlands, and Switzerland.[57] Lijphart divided societies up into two types: plural, in which no single ethnic group or religion dominated, and nonplural. For plural states *majoritarian democracy* as practiced in Anglo-Saxon countries was inappropriate because it left the minority or minorities permanently outside of power in opposition. In nonplural societies government and opposition usually consisted of loose temporary coalitions of voters — the independent floating vote holding the balance of power. In plural societies party divisions are along ethnic or religious lines. Based on the experience of these four European societies, only two of which were multiethnic,[58] Lijphart came up with a set of formal and informal practices that he termed *consociational democracy* (or consociationalism) suitable for plural societies. These consisted of: proportional representation as the franchise system, enforced power sharing, sectarian or confessional allocation of offices, minority vetoes over certain matters, or weighted majorities necessary to pass certain types of legislature. Lijphart emphasized elite coalitions where elites of the various communities would have friendly relations with each other. Political scientists or mediators designing a new constitution could use these like a pick-and-choose menu.[59]

John McGarry and Brendan O'Leary, consociational theorists who have long written about Northern Ireland and other ethnic conflicts, argue that Northern Ireland is an example of a "pluri-national" society — that is it is a frontier region where the nations of Great Britain and Ireland intersect. Of Arend Lijphart's original four cases, only Belgium is pluri-national according to McGarry and O'Leary, and therefore representative of the majority of cases to be encountered in the Third World and Central Europe. For pluri-national societies power sharing is a necessary part of a solution, but insufficient by itself. A extra-territorial dimension needs to be added so that the national minority feels that its national status is recognized. In Northern Ireland this is the North-South council, similar to — but sufficiently different to be acceptable to unionists — the Council of Ireland from the 1974 Sunningdale agreement.[60]

Duke University Law Professor Donald Horowitz proposed an alternative to consociationalism or other form of power sharing.[61] Horowitz argued that "consociationalism only worked where it was not needed," i.e., in existing European democracies.[62] Consociationalism had a bad record in the Third World and in situations where it was needed to end ongoing conflicts. It failed in Cyprus in 1963, in Lebanon in 1975, in Northern Ireland in 1974. Horowitz's alternate approach, dubbed integrationism, was to manipulate franchise rules so as to force voters to form multiethnic coalitions by requiring the winner of an election to have certain levels of support outside of his home region or ethnic group. The approach was attempted in Fiji and in the Nigerian election of 1979. But because integrationism also failed in Nigeria its record was not really much better than that for consociational democracy.[63]

Various teams of Northern Ireland academic researchers have over the years advocated Belgium as a model for Northern Ireland. The Catholic/Protestant team of Kevin Boyle and Tom Hadden wrote *Northern Ireland: The Choice* with Belgium as the model.[64] The Northern Irish-Canadian team of John McGarry and Brendan O'Leary have been the leading advocates of applying consociationalism to Northern Ireland since the mid–1990s.[65] But unlike Belgium's neat territorial division between French-speaking Walloons and Flemish Flanders (and a tiny piece of former German territory and Brussels) and Switzerland's division into ethnic cantons, Northern Ireland consists of a checkerboard of segregated neighborhoods, especially in Belfast and Derry. Now that Northern Ireland finally appears stable it is being advocated as a model for ethnic conflicts elsewhere from Sri Lanka to Kurdistan and Iraq. Consociational democracy finally appears to be vindicated.

Part I.
The Oslo Process

Two

A Dialogue in Oslo

The Setting: Regional Diplomacy and Israeli Politics 1991-92

In the spring of 1991 following the American victory over Saddam Hussein and the Iraqi army, Secretary of State James Baker decided to make a second attempt at Middle East diplomacy. The first, in 1989, had been in response to the Palestine Liberation Organization's (PLO) acceptance of United Nations Security Council (UNSC) Resolutions 242 and 338, the backbone of the Middle East Peace Process since 1973, and Arafat's renunciation of terrorism. This in turn caused a recognition of the PLO by the outgoing Reagan administration. That attempt failed due to both the indifference of the Israeli government, a national unity government led by Prime Minister Yitzhak Shamir, and the refusal of PLO Chairman Yasir Arafat to condemn a terrorist raid by a PLO terrorist faction, the Palestine Liberation Front, led by Muhammed Zaidan al-Abbas (not to be confused with Abu Mazen). Baker ended his diplomacy in frustration and pronounced a curse on both their houses. In 1990 a right-wing government led by the Likud replaced the national unity government after Labor pulled out and was unable to form a coalition with the religious parties.

In 1991 after several months of coaxing, persuasion, and arm twisting, Baker got the principal players in the Middle East conflict, minus the PLO, to attend an international summit in Madrid on October 31–November 1, 1991. The summit was co-sponsored by the two superpowers, but the Soviet Union hardly had any input as it was more worried about stemming its ongoing collapse as an imperial power. The Madrid summit was a cover for a series of parallel bilateral and multilateral negotiations between Israel and its neighbors. Israel was engaged in bilateral talks with Syria, Lebanon, and a joint Jordanian-Palestinian delegation. Shamir had vetoed any participation by the

PLO in the negotiations. There were multilateral talks on such subjects as water, arms control, economic cooperation, and so forth. At the Madrid summit neither Israel nor Syria appeared very eager to discuss peace and the Palestinians appeared pacific and reasonable by comparison. The Syrian representative held up an old British wanted poster of Shamir, from when he was a Lehi (Stern Group) terrorist, after the Israelis accused the Syrians of supporting terrorism. The Washington talks soon stalemated as: Israel under the Likud had annexed the Golan Heights and did not want to return them to Syria; Jordan refused to make a separate peace deal with Israel until it had made peace with the Palestinians; Israel did not want to give up control of the West Bank to the Palestinians as this would be a violation of the Likud's *Eretz Israel haShlema* (the "complete land of Israel"/Greater Israel) policy; and Lebanon was not really free to negotiate with Israel without Syrian permission.[1]

In February 1992 the Labor Party held its leadership primary, a practice introduced by Labor in the 1970s and soon adopted by the other main secular parties, and for the sixth time since 1974, the two candidates for the party leadership were Yitzhak Rabin and Shimon Peres. The relationship between Rabin and Peres was similar to that between Zachary Taylor and Henry Clay, their American counterparts respectively, except that under the parliamentary system in Israel they ended up not only in the same party but also repeatedly in the same government. Israeli prime ministers unlike American presidents are not totally free to choose their own governments as they must reflect not only their wishes but the main factions in their own party as well as in other parties. Rabin, a former Israeli chief of staff during the Six Day War of June 1967 and ambassador to Washington, narrowly won the first two contests. Peres managed to gain control of the central committee of the Labor Party and win the next three contests. Peres had served as Rabin's defense minister in the first Rabin government from 1974 to 1977 and two years later in his (ghost-written) memoir Rabin accused Peres of being an "untiring intriguer" and attempting to undermine his government at every turn. The contest between the Rabin and Peres camps, a continuation of that between the Allon and Dayan camps that dominated the early Labor Party from 1968 to 1974, kept an entire generation of alternative leaders from developing. In frustration many of Labor's most talented members retired from politics or left the party.[2]

Labor personalized its election campaign around Rabin. In 1967 there was a popular song, *Nasser is waiting for Rabin*; for the campaign this became *Israel is waiting for Rabin* and Labor in all of its publicity material advertised itself as "Labor headed by Rabin" rather than as merely the Labor Party. The public was rather apathetic as yet another campaign was fought over foreign policy issues. Rabin promised to make peace with the Palestinians in between nine months and a year of forming his government and also promised to make peace with Syria without giving up the Golan. Labor's platform in fact stated, as it had in previous campaigns, that there would be no second state between the Mediterranean Sea and the Jordan River. Running for the first time in a national election was the liberal Meretz party formed out of the Mapam, Shinui, and Ratz (Citizens' Rights Movement) remnants that had broke their connections with Labor in 1984 when it formed a national unity government with the Likud. The three parties formed a common alliance to contest municipal elections in 1989 and formalized this into a party in 1992. The Likud was headed again by Yitzhak Shamir, as it had been since 1984, who was the uncharismatic copy of Herut/Likud founder Menahem Begin.[3] Shamir's strategy from 1984 to 1992 had been to stall all peace initiatives while Israel settled the West Bank and attempted to make it unviable as a future Palestinian state.[4]

Labor won 44 seats to the Likud's 32, and Meretz won 12 seats its first time out to make it Israel's third largest party. From 1977 to 1996 the secular center-left and center-right blocs had been within a few seats of each other in the Knesset.[5] In the 1992 election parties of the right actually received more votes than parties of the left, but the cutoff level for entrance to the Knesset for a party had been raised from one percent to 1.5. These wasted votes on the right for parties that did not make the cutoff, such as Tehiya, allowed Labor to form the next government. It was the biggest upheaval in Israeli politics in fifteen years.[6]

Rabin wanted to balance Meretz with a party of the right to keep Meretz from combining with Peres and his followers to defeat him and dominate the government. He negotiated with Rafael "Raful" Eitan's *Tzomet* (Crossroads) party with its eight seats. But Eitan was a supporter of West Bank settlement and refused to accept Rabin's freeze on "political settlements." Rabin made a distinction between "military" and "political" settlements — the former helping to control key terrain while the latter being established to satisfy the national religious right. So instead Rabin was forced to rely on the religious Shas party supported by *mizrahi* Jews from North Africa and the Middle East.[7] *Mizrahi* Jews, whose parents had immigrated to Israel from the Arab countries and Iran, tended to be both more traditional than the *Ashkenazi* European Jews and more nationalistic. They tended to vote for either the Likud or for Shas. Shas was not a national religious Zionist party like the National Religious Party (NRP/Mafdal), but tended to naturally favor the Likud over Labor when choosing coalition partners.[8]

Rabin as a former chief of staff and defense minister from 1984 to 1990, elected to be his own defense minister. This meant that Peres, Labor's number two man, was forced to choose between being finance minister or foreign minister. He had served as finance minister from 1988 to 1990, and as foreign minister from 1986 to 1988. He wished to return to the foreign ministry so that he could attempt a peace initiative in the Middle East based on the Washington talks. Having brought security to Israel in the first half of his political career from 1949 to 1977 as the deputy director and then director of the defense ministry under Ben-Gurion in the 1950s and 1960s and then as defense minister from 1974 to 1977, Peres longed to bring peace to Israel. As prime minister in 1984–86 he supervised Israel's withdrawal from most of Lebanon. In 1986 as foreign minister he negotiated a secret deal with King Hussein of Jordan to hold an international peace conference, but Shamir vetoed the idea and Secretary of State Charles Schultz refused to play his role and introduce it as an American initiative. Having experienced and observed Peres's political entrepreneurship, Rabin was determined to allow him no rope.[9]

At their first meeting following the election and formation of the government, Rabin told Peres that he himself would manage both relations with Washington and the bilateral negotiations with the Arabs. Peres could supervise the multilateral talks in Washington, relations with the Third World, and relations with Europe. Rabin, a former ambassador to Washington and protégé of Henry Kissinger (and Yigal Allon), considered himself to be an expert on American politics and Middle East policy. He wanted to personally supervise the bilateral negotiations with the Arabs so that he could manage the security aspects, which he considered to be paramount. Peres was forced to agree.[10]

The Oslo Channel Develops

Peres's deputy foreign minister was Yossi Beilin, who had been Labor Party spokesman since 1984 and the head of his own *Mashov* (feedback) faction in the party since 1981. Beilin had been a former journalist at the Labor Party newspaper *Davar* and a professor of political science. Beilin tried to forge a "third model" of a career path in Israeli politics to supplement the traditional paths of party *apparatchik* (functionary) and secretary general. In 1984 Prime Minister Peres had organized his own team of young advisors known as the "blazers" for their habit of dressing in blue sports jackets. The blazers included Beilin and Uri Savir, who would become director general of the foreign ministry under Peres. The blazers tended to be well-educated, multi-lingual professionals and academics who were interested in making peace with the Palestinians. Beilin's maternal grandfather had been a fairly important Zionist pioneer and Savir's father Leo was a veteran Israeli diplomat who helped to found the foreign ministry. Since the late 1970s Beilin had been convinced that Israel would have to negotiate with the PLO. He was influenced in this by Loav Eliav, the secretary general of the party in the early 1970s, who resigned to become a leading Israeli dove. Peres throughout the 1980s preferred Amman as a negotiating partner to the PLO, but began to change his mind once Hussein withdrew from supporting Jordan's traditional role in the West Bank in 1988. Rabin would take longer to come around.[11]

At the end of April 1992, during the election campaign, Beilin met with Terje Larsen, the Norwegian head of FAFO (Applied Social Sciences Organization), which was conducting economic research in the Palestinian territories. On June 19, 1992 Beilin met with Larsen, Feisal Husseini (the PLO's representative in Jerusalem), and Yair Hirschfeld (an Israeli academic specializing in Middle Eastern studies and a member of Beilin's *mashov* faction) in East Jerusalem to discuss setting up a back-channel negotiation to parallel the Washington talks. Husseini thought that such a channel could be useful for exploring options without publicly committing either side. Three months later on September 9 Beilin met with his Norwegian counterpart to set up a Norwegian funded back channel. On December 4, Hirschfeld met with Ahmed Qurei, aka Abu Ala, a long-time financial adviser to Arafat in London as part of an academic conference. They discussed the mechanics of setting up the back-channel talks in Norway. In January 1993 Hirschfeld and Ron Pundak, a former student of his and the son of a prominent Danish-Israeli journalist, held their first meeting with a Palestinian team led by Abu Ala.[12]

The talks were held in a country estate owned by the Norwegian government about two hours from Oslo. The talks were "facilitated" by Larsen and his wife, Mona Juul, who was an administrative assistant to Egland in the foreign ministry. The Norwegians provided three things. First, they completely financed the back channel, which when the PLO was strapped for funds and formal funding allocation in Israel would have blown the secret was critical. Second, they provided the venue complete with security, transportation, and meals. Third, they provided a sympathetic ear to the participants and served partially to interpret each side to the other later on in the talks. The Norwegians were essentially providing "good offices" rather than more advanced forms of mediation such as the Americans had provided from 1973 onwards in negotiating the separation-of-forces agreements, the Egyptian-Israeli peace treaty, and ceasefires and a never-implemented peace treaty in Lebanon. The Norwegians did not actively participate in the discussions, nor come up with bridging proposals, nor put pressure on either party to accept the other's proposals. The Oslo talks can be divided into roughly two periods: the unofficial talks from January to April 1993 and the official talks from May to August 1993. The change in status occurred when Uri Savir joined the talks in May, followed by Yoel Singer in June. Neither Hirschfeld nor Pundak were Israeli officials, making it easy for Beilin, Peres, and Rabin to deny that they represented Israel. The talks were always official from the Palestinian side as Abu Ala was a senior Arafat associate and the talks were being coordinated by Mahmoud Abbas, aka Abu Mazen, a founding member of Fatah, Arafat's party, and the future prime minister and then president of the Palestinian Authority.[13]

Beilin did not inform Peres of the existence of the back channel until February.[14] Peres promptly reported it to Rabin at one of their regular meetings so as to avoid the appearance of one of his infamous intrigues. Rabin gave his approval, probably because he did not take it seriously at first and figured that it would keep Peres occupied and away from attempting to interfere with the Washington talks. Rabin asked only to be quietly informed of any progress and that the talks remain secret and unofficial.

The basis for the Oslo talks was the "Gaza first" plan that had been kicked around in various forms since the late 1970s in Israel. The basis for this was that unlike the West Bank, no one in Israel really wanted the Gaza Strip (henceforth Gaza). Measuring 28 miles long and between three and eight miles wide, Gaza was home to more than a million Palestinians in the early 1990s. It consisted mainly of urban slums in three main cities, refugee camps, orange groves, and a small group of Israeli settlements, Gush Katif, in the center. It had no religious or historical resonance for Israelis as it had been inhabited and ruled by Gentiles from ancient times: first the Greek-speaking Philistines, then the Arabs, the Turks, the British, and the Egyptians. Unlike Jordan and the West Bank, Egypt never annexed Gaza. Egypt ruled in Gaza from 1948 to 1967 and Israel ruled from 1967 to 1994. In 1992 Rabin said that he wished it could just sink into the sea. The idea was that the PLO would be offered administration of Gaza and if they behaved and proved capable, Israel would then discuss turning over the West Bank to them. Peres decided as a sweetener he would throw in a city on the West Bank to assure the Palestinians that "Gaza first" would not become "Gaza only." Two cities were discussed by the Israelis: Jenin in the north and Jericho near the Jordan River in the southeast.[15]

The talks in Oslo centered on the modalities of Israeli-Palestinian cooperation until administration was completely turned over to the Palestinians. But the talks in Oslo focused on crafting a Declaration of Principles (DOP) that would serve as the basis for mutual recognition of the PLO and Israel, the establishment of a Palestinian Authority in Gaza and Jericho and a "road map" for future negotiations. The nitty gritty details of administration and Israeli security concerns were discussed in subsequent talks that took place from October 1993 to October 1995. So it took eight months to negotiate in principle the Declaration of Principles and the Gaza first proposal, another eight months to discuss its implementation in Gaza and Jericho, and about another year its implementation on the West Bank. The Israeli foreign and defense ministries conducted the subsequent negotiations.[16]

The motives for Rabin's change in attitude towards the PLO were various. First, as a man of his word he felt embarrassed by his failure to deliver on his campaign promise of cutting a deal with the Palestinians within one year. Arafat helped convince him by deliberately stalling and preventing any progress in the Israeli-Palestinian talks in Washington. All the Palestinian negotiators were Arafat loyalists who took orders from Arafat. At one point an Israeli foreign ministry official sent Peres copies of summaries of the various rounds of the talks with the dates removed. Peres was unable to arrange them in the correct—or any—order because the talks were going in circles. Second, he realized that it was better to reach an agreement with the Palestinians while the PLO was weak because of the financial cutoff experienced as a result of having sided with Saddam in the Gulf War in 1990-91, than to wait until the organization had recovered or been replaced by a more extreme organization such as Hamas. Third, Rabin did not want to rule over Gaza any more and he never committed himself to allowing the PLO to have a state. He figured that he could always halt or even reverse the process if the PLO failed to live up to its end of the agreement. But both Rabin and Peres never thought that the process might have a momentum of its own and that they had already committed themselves in May 1993 when the talks became official. Beilin later admitted that the decision-making process on Oslo was very sloppy and ad hoc. This was mainly because of the desire to preserve the secrecy of the talks. Originally it was anticipated that the results of a deal negotiated in the back channel would be introduced by the official teams in Washington and presented as a result of the official negotiations. Later, it was determined that this would be impractical.[17]

The PLO had gradually realized after its expulsion from Lebanon in 1982-83 that it had no real military option and could only continue its terrorist campaign against Israel, more of a nuisance to the Jewish state than an existential threat, or engage in talks leading to a two-state solution. It took the PLO leadership six years to come to this realization. The problem was that the PLO was deeply divided and the distribution of power within the organization favored the weaker more extremist terrorist factions at the expense of Fatah. For two years, from 1983 to 1985, Arafat played a dance with Hussein around the idea of accepting 242 and allowing Jordan to negotiate on its behalf with Israel. Hussein finally lost his patience and ended the negotiations. Then after the PLO renounced terrorism in December 1988 and accepted a two-state solution officially, Arafat refused to discipline subordinates who made statements that called this change of policy into question.[18] And he refused to denounce the Mahmoud al-Abbas raid on Tel Aviv in 1989 that ended the American-Palestinian dialogue. If one examines Arafat's political career from its beginning as chairman of the PLO in 1969 to his death in 2004, there are two constants. First, was his inability to delegate power and create a rationale decision-making structure. Second, was his inability to distinguish between tactical and strategic decisions. Or more accurately, *all* his decisions were tactical. Arafat was a master of improvisation and a genius at impromptu tactics. But he was incapable of analyzing his situation rationally and dispassionately and acting on the basis of that analysis. In this regard he was the total opposite of Rabin. Arafat would attempt contradictory courses of action simultaneously and see which was most effective.[19]

Rabin would stubbornly stick to a course of action until he was persuaded — by others or by himself— that this strategy was no longer viable and then he would reanalyze the situation and attempt a new course. For both emotional and logical reasons it took the Labor leadership a long time to accept the death of the Jordanian option. They probably went through the various classic stages of dealing with death. Meretz had served a missionary role in convincing Peres that the PLO was the solution rather than Jordan. This was by speaking publicly about such negotiations when the topic was taboo within Labor. Meretz (and its component predecessors) helped to convince those around Peres, who then influenced Peres. Peres then seduced Rabin by allowing the Oslo talks to gain greater status.[20]

Rabin was by natural inclination (and later through friendship with Henry Kissinger when he was ambassador to the United States) a Realist. He thus tended to discount the Palestinians because militarily they were not much of a threat to Israel. As a general he dealt with the conventional threat posed by the armies of the surrounding Arab states: Jordan and Egypt, whom he had fought against in 1948, and Syria, whose forces he faced off against without firing a shot during the Sinai War of 1956. Rabin believed in a forceful response to guerrilla warfare and terrorism, or even rock throwing as evidenced by his infamous order to break bones during the first Intifada. He also did not believe in relying on nuclear weapons for defense, although he had no plans to voluntarily give up those that Israel had. Unlike Peres, who was more oriented towards Europe (he spoke fluent French and was born in Poland), Rabin was oriented towards Washington. Thus he was concerned with keeping Washington happy. He was happy to serve the role of American client state during the Cold War and as the protector of Jordan.[21]

But Rabin's thinking began to evolve during the early 1990s as the result of two things. The first was the Gulf War in early 1991 that eliminated Iraq as a serious military threat to Israel, and thus destroyed the concept of the Eastern Threat (a hypothetical alliance of Iraq, Jordan, and Syria). The second was the collapse of the Soviet Union in December 1991. Within a matter of some ten months the Arabs had lost their main military power and their main external ally. This dramatically changed the strategic balance in Israel's favor. At the same time there was the growing future threat of Islamic fundamentalism (Islamism) and weapons of mass destruction. The revelations about how close Saddam Hussein had been to possessing nuclear weapons before the Gulf War raised the latter threat. The spread of ballistic missiles to Iran, Iraq, and Syria was another worry. The former threat was embodied in Hamas, Hezbollah, and Iran. Rabin saw Israel as having a narrow window of opportunity to make peace on favorable terms before the region returned to being fundamentally hostile.[22]

The talks advanced from personal story telling, to discussion of Israeli and Palestinian politics, to explorations about what each side could grant in exchange for concessions by the other side. Normally the two teams would meet for a weekend of nonstop talks, pausing only to eat and sleep for maybe two-three hours. Then they would report back to their superiors and spend the time until the next session planning for it. The big Israeli concession was made up front when the academics informed the PLO team that Israel was ready to turn administrative control over Gaza to the Palestinians in a very quick fashion.[23]

Neither Hirschfeld nor Pundak had any formal legal training. Abu Mazen had some legal training at the University of Damascus, which was not very helpful.[24] The Palestinians were threatening to end the back channel in the April round unless Israel upgraded the status of its team. Informed of this by the negotiators, Beilin went to Peres who in turn went to Rabin. Peres volunteered to go to Oslo himself, but Rabin did not want to bring in someone from his government. The two decided to bring in Savir. He was informed of the decision on May 14, 1993, and attended the May round of talks in Oslo. After examining the DOP he decided that an expert in international law would have to be brought in. Beilin was familiar with Yoel Singer, a former IDF colonel who headed the defense ministry's legal team and had moved to Washington about a year before Oslo began. Singer had worked on the Taba arbitration talks in the 1980s and was trusted by Rabin. Singer attended the June round of talks in Oslo. He was scathing when he examined the draft

DOP. He compared Hirschfeld and Pundak attempting to write the DOP to two lay people attempting a complicated surgery only to realize in the middle that they were in over their heads. His approach was to engage in a cross examination of the Palestinian team as if he were conducting a pretrial legal hearing. At first they were offended by his blunt manner, but when he explained that Rabin had instructed him to do this they were appeased as they then knew that Israel was taking the talks seriously. He asked probably about between 100 and 200 questions during the June round. Then he returned to Washington to his day job at a top D.C. law firm.[25]

In July a second round was negotiated with the assistance of Singer. In this round the emphasis was on the negotiation of the mutual recognition. Israel had seven demands that Savir negotiated with the Palestinians. The demands were: (1) the PLO recognize Israel's right to exist in peace and security; (2) it would resolve the conflict on the basis of UNSC 242 and 338; (3) it would repeal certain sections of the Palestinian Covenant of 1969 that were contrary to these principles; (4) it would renounce terrorism and cooperate with Israel to ensure its security; (5) it would end the Intifada; (6) it would resolve all outstanding issues with Israel peacefully; and (7) Arafat would negotiate with Israel as PLO chairman rather than as president of Palestine. These were henceforth referred to as the seven points. The last point had been conceded on the Israeli side, that is Arafat's return to Gaza, by Peres in a conversation with Peres in a conversation with Larsen and Juul on July 13.[26] In a final round in mid-August most of the PLO's retractions disappeared. It was then realized that for the remaining details the principals, Peres and Arafat, would have to negotiate by phone.

On the night of August 18-19 Peres negotiated by phone from his hotel suite in Stockholm, where he was on a diplomatic visit, with Arafat and Abu Ala at PLO headquarters in Tunis for seven hours. Rather than one marathon call, it was a series of five shorter calls. The main issues were the status of PLO offices in East Jerusalem and the size of Jericho to be included in the Palestinian area. The latter problem was deferred for the implementation talks. The next day Abu Ala flew in to Oslo from Tunis and Peres went there from Stockholm and the two sides initialed the DOP using the same table that the Norwegians had used in 1905 to sign the treaty on their separation from Sweden. The table had been borrowed from a museum for this purpose.[27]

Peres, Singer, and foreign ministry official Avi Gil then flew off to California to inform the vacationing Secretary of State Warren Christopher and Middle East negotiator Ambassador Dennis Ross that an agreement had been reached with the PLO. The Americans had been informed early on about the back channel, but they had neither requested nor had Israel volunteered any details. But the CIA had learned some details about the back channel through Arab rulers who were briefed by the PLO. Washington dismissed the significance of the negotiations for three reasons. First, because Peres rather than Rabin was in charge they did not take the negotiations seriously. Second, because reports of secret talks were so frequent and so wrong these were dismissed as well. And finally, Washington considered itself to be the indispensable mediator and could not believe that anyone else could perform this function. Christopher was chagrined but not upset by the news of the agreement. He was only too happy to agree to hold an official signing ceremony in Washington in September. The Likud opposition in Israel took the Oslo process very seriously. In a speech to the Knesset on August 30, 1993, Benyamin Netanyahu compared Rabin to Neville Chamberlain, the British prime minister who appeased Hitler at Munich in 1938.[28]

Initially it was agreed that Peres would go to Washington for the ceremony. Then Arafat announced that he would go. This meant that protocol demanded that Rabin go. Peres was furious because he thought that he was being upstaged and left at home. Finally it was agreed that both would attend the ceremony. Peres left Hirschfeld and Pundak off of the invitation list and the two had to fly out privately for the ceremony. The signing was delayed when Arafat demanded that the wording be changed from the "Palestinian delegation" to the PLO. This was penciled in, but Arafat still was not satisfied and so a frantic search began for a printer that could reprint the document with the words added. Rabin's body language reflected his lack of comfort in shaking the hand of the man whom most Israeli Jews considered to be an arch terrorist. Peres was more comfortable with the handshake — he had apparently thought it out ahead of time. Clinton was terrified of being publicly kissed by Arafat. The Washington signing then committed the Clinton administration to the future well-being of the Oslo process and served to rehabilitate Arafat in America.[29]

The DOP committed the two sides to a process, but it was not a peace treaty by any stretch of the imagination. The details of the Israeli withdrawals and security measures still had to be negotiated.

Oslo I

Serious negotiations on the details of the agreement for Palestinian rule in Gaza and Jericho began the following month in Gaza. After the Senior Joint Liaison Committee, headed by Peres and Abu Mazen, held a purely ceremonial meeting in Cairo on October 13, the real negotiations got under way in

Taba. The Israeli team was headed by General Amnon Shahak, the deputy chief of staff, and the Palestinian team was led by Nabil Shaath. Shaath, an economist by profession who had taught in the United States and spoke impeccable English, came across as a Palestinian version of former Israeli Foreign Minister Abba Eban. Shahak looked like a Hollywood version of a war hero. Shaath would later serve as planning minister in the Palestinian Authority and was another close aide to Arafat.[30]

The real difference was over two fundamentally different conceptions of the role of the Palestinian Authority (PA). The Palestinians conceived of the PA, which they always referred to as the Palestinian *National* Authority (PNA), as a probationary state that would operate for five years until the Palestinians established independence. The Israelis conceived of the PA as the body that would implement an updated version of the autonomy proposed for the territories by the Likud government at Camp David in 1978. Under the Likud conception autonomy applied only to the Palestinian inhabitants but not to the territory. Under the Labor conception Israel and the Palestinians would have shared control over the territory during the five-year period. Israel would be jointly responsible for maintaining security with the PA in Gaza, having complete responsibility for "external security." That is Israel would control the borders and entry points into both Gaza and the West Bank. Under the eventual agreement there were seven crossing points into Gaza from Egypt and Israel that were controlled by the IDF. Rabin personally explained the Israeli concept of "external security" to Arafat and justified it as being necessary as the borders between Gaza and Israel were porous. Israel was inclined to let the Palestinians have the symbols of independence—flags, passports, postage stamps, an airline, and so on. while maintaining control over the substance. As Egypt had never even allowed the Palestinians this much during its nineteen years of rule over the Strip, this was still a net improvement for the Palestinians.[31]

Much of the time was spent arguing over the details of security, particularly at the airport at Gaza and in the Palestinian ports. The joint working groups that were created by the two sides handled most of these details. On the Palestinian side the ultimate decision-maker was Arafat. He had a veto over all agreements reached by his negotiating team. On the Israeli side the decision-makers were Peres and Rabin. Rabin set up a team to advise the two of them and oversee the negotiations, but the tough decisions were made by the two of them meeting in private both before and after the team meetings. Rabin and Peres made a good decision-making team because each compensated for the other's weaknesses with his own strengths. Rabin was detail oriented—he concentrated on the trees. Peres was a visionary who concentrated on the forest—the big picture. Rabin worried about the implications of decisions on the security of Israel and Peres worried about their impact on the peace process.[32]

The first real blow that the process suffered, and it was nearly a lethal one, came in late February when an American-born settler at Hebron, Baruch Goldstein, decided to attempt to end the process through an act of terror. Goldstein was a doctor and a reserve captain in the Israeli army. On the morning of February 25, 1994, Goldstein dressed in army fatigues and took an M-16 assault rifle and several magazines with him to the Cave of the Machpela, a shrine associated with Abraham holy to both Jews and Muslims. He walked past the IDF guard and entered the Ibrahimi Mosque and then opened fire on the Palestinian worshipers at prayer. He went through several magazines before he was finally overtaken by the survivors and killed in self-defense. The toll was 29 killed and scores wounded. Some thousand settlers marched in his funeral procession and his grave became a shrine for opponents of the peace process.[33]

The killing sparked rioting throughout the territories and threatened to shut down the peace process. Ross spent fourteen hours on the phone the next day talking to Palestinians, Israelis and Terje Larsen in an attempt to calm the situation. Arafat wanted the Hebron settlers, who were hated by the Palestinian population both for their fanatical bigotry and for the inconveniences that their presence caused for the local population, removed from the city. There were only some 400 settlers in Hebron — most followers of the late Rabbi Meir Kahane, who had founded the Jewish Defense League in Brooklyn in the 1970s before immigrating to Israel in the late 1970s.[34] Some 120,000 Arabs surrounded them. The settlers belonged to two separate organizations, Kach ("thus") and Kahane Chai (Kahane lives), founded by the rabbi and his son respectively, and the first was outlawed by the Israeli government in the mid–1980s as racist. Peres was inclined to go along with Arafat because he did not want to risk a second incident. But Rabin had promised, when the Knesset approved the DOP, that he would not evacuate any settlements during the interim phase but would wait until the implementation of the final status agreement, if that time ever came. Rabin did not want to break his promise and risk his reputation for honesty while the peace process was just getting started. The incident put him psychologically on the defensive with Arafat regarding Hamas terrorism. What the two sides eventually settled for was a temporary international monitoring force made up of Scandinavians and Italians, the Temporary International Presence in Hebron, who kept the two sides apart. This solution took all of March to negotiate. When Israel carried out its first redeployment on the West Bank in late 1995, Hebron was the only city that the IDF did not withdraw from. Instead a solution to

Hebron waited until Benyamin "Bibi" Netanyahu was prime minister and it was his only contribution to the peace process.[35]

There was a second incident in Gaza as the two sides were getting ready to implement the agreement that caused a problem. Mohammed Dahlan, the Fatah security man in charge of Gaza, sent a five-man team into the territory to prepare the ground for the takeover. The men, who were armed with AK-47 assault rifles, began firing into the air in celebration. Israeli soldiers hearing the firing responded and upon seeing the men opened fire killing five. The Israeli soldiers were within their rights under the agreement, but Dahlan was not happy with the decision to go on with the peace process.[36]

The agreement was signed in a ceremony in Cairo on May 4, 1994. At the ceremony Arafat "suddenly" decided not to initial the maps attached to the agreement on a pretext. President Mubarak of Egypt, who was presiding over the ceremony, turned on Arafat furiously and ordered him "sign, you dog." Arafat had staged the incident for the cameras so that he could show himself standing up to Israel and the United States for their rights. The incident had the effect of ending Mubarak's role as a mediator in the conflict. Between 1989 and 1994 Egypt had mediated between the Palestinians on one hand and Washington and Jerusalem on the other in dealing with the conflict. This was a way for Egypt to both improve its standing with Washington and justify the generous financial and military aid that it received and to increase its standing in the Arab world among the moderate countries. Egypt had first mediated during discussion of the Rabin-Shamir plan of 1989 calling for elections in the occupied territories in response to the PLO's acceptance of UNSC Resolution 242 and Israel's right to exist in December 1988. Cairo then played a role in the Washington talks and during the Oslo I negotiations. Now Mubarak had been cowed by Arafat into not crossing him again.[37]

Arafat delayed his return to Gaza from Tunis for two months until July 1, 1994, when he was greeted by a crowd of 100,000 well-wishers. It had probably been forty years since Arafat had spent any time in the Strip. Although Arafat's father was from Gaza, and Arafat at various times claimed that he was born in Gaza (or Jerusalem depending on who was interviewing him), he had actually been born in Cairo and grown up there. He spent time in Gaza only during the 1948 war and in its aftermath when the Mufti, Haj Amin al-Husseini, was attempting to restore his authority in Egyptian-controlled Gaza. Arafat spent the next eighteen months in the city until he relocated his capital to Ramallah on the West Bank where he remained almost until his death. Arafat had operated clandestinely on the West Bank for a few months following the Arab defeat in June 1967 before he was forced to flee, one step ahead of the IDF.[38]

Oslo II — the Interim Agreement

Unlike the Gaza Strip, where the 14 Israeli settlements were located in a bloc — Gush Katif— in the southwestern part near the ocean, the West Bank had Israeli settlements scattered throughout the territory. While Labor was in power from 1967 to 1977, Israeli settlement of the West Bank took place in two main areas. First, in the unpopulated Jordan Valley along the Jordan River settlements were established to establish a security belt that would help prevent terrorist infiltration or the entry of a foreign army into the West Bank. Also the Gush Etzion bloc near Bethlehem, where Israeli settlements had existed in the 1930s and 1940s until the War of Independence, was resettled. Then when the Likud came to power in 1977 the national religious *Gush Emunim* (bloc of the faithful) settler movement was allowed to spearhead the populated areas of the West Bank. Settlers established settlements both in these populated areas between the Arab cities and in blocs along the 1949 armistice line, known as the Green Line for its color on Israeli maps. Gush Emunim had actually started its settlement effort in 1974, but was limited to a few settlements. After the Israeli government created generous subsidies for housing and tax breaks for those living on the West Bank, the settlement blocs were flooded with secular Israelis looking to live the Israeli dream, subsidized by the American taxpayer, in settlement blocs within commuting distance of the major Israeli cities in the coastal plain and Jerusalem. Since settlements were one of the controversial issues deferred until final status talks, security arrangements had to be made to protect them.

Israeli negotiators came up with the concept of dividing the West Bank into three separate areas: Areas A, B, and C. In Area A, the major cities and towns of the West Bank, the Palestinians would be in charge of both civil government and security. In Area B, consisting of some 450 villages and small towns, the Palestinians would be in charge of civil government and the IDF would have the primary responsibility for security, assisted by the Palestinian police. In Area C, consisting of the Jewish settlements and the countryside away from the villages, Israel would be in charge of both security and government. Israel agreed to make three redeployments during the five years in which territory would be transferred to the PA. But Israel deliberately refused to specify the scope of the redeployments. This then became a major area of contention between the two parties and an area of mediation by the Americans. Arafat wanted the three redeployments to consist of thirty percent of the West Bank each, so that when the final status talks began he would control 90 percent of the territory. Israel did not agree to this for two reasons. First, it did not fully trust Arafat and did not know what the security situation would look like in a year, let alone in five years. Second, it wanted to be able to use the territories as a bargaining chip to trade off in the final status negotiations with other difficult issues like refugees, Jerusalem, and settlements.[39]

Israel and the Palestinians set up a number of joint technical committees to deal with the Oslo II negotiations. These handled security, civil government, and elections. But a secret back channel also existed where the difficult issues were handled by the veterans of the Oslo process on both sides. The secret channel began negotiations on January 4, 1995. The Israeli team consisted of Uri Savir, Yoel Singer, General Gadi Zohar, head of the IDF's Civil Administration on the West Bank, and Uzi Dayan, nephew of former Defense Minister Moshe Dayan and himself the deputy chief of staff. The Palestinian team was made up of Abu Ala, Hassan Asfour, both Oslo veterans, General Abdel Razak Yihye, and Hassan Abu Libdeh from the Palestinian Office of Statistics. As with Oslo I all decisions were referred back to Abu Mazen and Arafat on the Palestinian side and an Israeli security team that advised Rabin and Peres, who would make the ultimate decisions.[40]

Most of the negotiations consisted of negotiating the final details of the security measures so that Israel would feel satisfied that its security was not being put at risk. The talks were interrupted several times by major terrorist incidents carried out by Hamas and Islamic Jihad. These incidents highlighted both Israel's perceived need for greater security measures and the ineffectiveness of these measures.

Terrorism and Peace

From the beginning there were terrorist and guerrilla attacks carried out by the Islamists (Hamas and Islamic Jihad). The first occurred in September 1993 within days of the signing of the DOP. The incidents increased after the PA assumed responsibility for Gaza in May 1994. An early pattern was soon established that persisted for the next six years. Israel would tell Arafat and the PLO's negotiators that the PA must confront the Islamists and establish its authority over them. The Palestinians would say that the Israelis had never stopped terrorism when they were in control and that the Palestinian method of talking with the Islamists was much more effective. They claimed that they were having much success eating into the political support of the Islamists based on their political gains at Oslo and in the interim negotiations (Oslo I and Oslo II). Israel after each incident would put pressure on the PA, do its own investigation, and turn over names of those they wanted arrested. Arafat would order a round of arrests and a number of Islamists, often from the political or social wings of Hamas, would be arrested. After a few days or a few weeks they would be quietly released. Arafat made a determined effort only when he felt that his own authority was being threatened, as when his police fired into a Hamas demonstration and dispersed it by force. The Israelis would bring up Israeli history from the 1940s and tell of the *Altalena* incident when the IDF opened fire on an Etzel (*Irgun Zvai Leumi*—National Military Organization underground) arms ship that had broken a UN truce by openly landing arms on a beach in Tel Aviv. The ship, a World War II surplus landing craft, was sunk and several of its crew were killed or wounded. The Labor Party people were saying, "We risked civil war when our independence was at risk, you should do the same." During the first Intifada from 1987 to 1993 172 Israelis were killed compared to almost 300 during the first three years of Oslo "peace" from 1993 to 1996.[41]

Arafat believed in negotiating with the Islamists. He would negotiate with their political leadership abroad, in Cairo, Amman and Damascus. Throughout the six years of the implementation of the peace process he would often compare the Oslo process to the Treaty of Hudaibiya that Muhammed signed with the Jewish Qurayesh tribe in Arabia in 628 AD. The treaty was a ten-year non-aggression pact that Muhammed proceeded to break after only two years. Muhammed told one of his leading followers who criticized the peace that it was an "inferior peace." Shortly after the signing of the Oslo I agreement, Arafat spoke to a crowd of South African Muslims in a mosque in Johannesburg. He made the same comparison. Unknown to him, a South African Jew disguised as a Muslim was in the audience. Arafat's words were recorded and reported to Israel. In April 1998 he told Egypt's Orbit Television that Muhammed had agreed to have his title "Messenger of Allah" removed from the Hudaibiya agreement, and for this reason Omar Bin Khatib and others referred to it as "an inferior peace agreement." He then mentioned that Saladin had considered the agreement that he broke with the Crusaders in 1187 to be an inferior peace. He said that he was only following the example of Muhammed and Saladin. This would be the equivalent of an American politician claiming that he was following the example of Christ and of Lincoln.[42]

Initially Arafat was cautious to make these sorts of statements only in front of closed audiences, but once Benyamin Netanyahu became prime minister in mid–1996 and he perceived how disliked Netanyahu was in Washington, he threw caution to the wind. He then maintained this attitude once Netanyahu was defeated in the next election and replaced by Ehud Barak.

Arafat's attitude towards Israel during the peace process was similar to David Ben-Gurion's attitude towards the British during the 1940s. Ben-Gurion's Jewish Agency during the British mandate was similar to the Palestinian Authority. Ben-Gurion had his own semi-official army, the Hagana, and he was opposed by two Revisionist underground paramilitary groups, Etzel and Lehi. Ben-Gurion used the Hagana to crack down on Etzel in late 1944 and early 1945 after Lehi assassins murdered a senior British official in Cairo in November. Then for a year the Hagana cooperated with the two organizations against the British during 1945 and 1946 before returning to an antagonistic posture. Then in April 1948 the Hagana and Etzel signed a cooperation agreement to fight the 1948 War of Independence. There were a number of Israeli families that had members in both the Hagana and the Etzel.

Likewise, Arafat's attitude towards the Islamists went back and forth during the 1990s until they cooperated in the Al-Aksa Intifada that began in late September 2000. Ben-Gurion used violence from the Revisionists to extract concessions from the British and put pressure on them. He then saved his own army for the battle with the Arabs after the British left. Likewise, Arafat envisioned using the Islamists to soften Israel up and solicit foreign pressure on Jerusalem, while he saved his Fatah/PA army for the confrontation with Israel once the final status negotiations had failed to reach a satisfactory solution. There were Palestinian families that had members in both Fatah and Hamas.[43]

The Israeli public was closely divided down the middle before the Oslo process started, with the 1992 election being decided by a few thousand lost votes. Just as American political commentators speak of "red states" and "blue states" as shorthand for a perceived cultural rift in America between religious traditionalist voters and secular progressive voters, Israeli commentators speak of a Jerusalemite and Tel Avivian or Judah and Israel.[44] The former are Likud and religious party voters who are nationalistic, afraid of the outside world, traditional, and more comfortable in the ghetto. The latter are secular voters from the center-left Meretz and Labor parties who are Western oriented, progressive, not afraid of the outside world, and less nationalistic. The former wanted to expand the "iron wall," to use a Revisionist metaphor introduced in the 1920s and adopted in practice by the ruling Mapai Party in the 1940s, to include the West Bank, Gaza, and the Golan, and use the sword to survive. The latter wanted to tear down the wall, invade the Arab world with businessmen and assimilate into the Middle East on their own terms. This was epitomized in Peres's concept of The New Middle East based on economic cooperation between Israel and its neighbors. Rabin stood between the two groups as a sort of referee. He was a man of the sword who was contemptuous of Peres's castles in the sky and skeptical of the intentions of the Palestinians, but willing to take a chance for peace.

The positive results of the Oslo peace process were in three main areas.

Two. A Dialogue in Oslo

First was the peace treaty with Jordan that was signed in November 1994. It was quickly negotiated by both Peres and Rabin after the DOP and Oslo I had given Amman the political cover to seek a formal separate relationship with Jerusalem after the covert relationship that King Hussein had pursued with Israel since the early 1960s. Second, Israel expanded its diplomatic relations widely in the 1990s both as a result of the collapse of Communism in Europe and as a result of the peace process. Israel opened diplomatic relations not only with numerous former Communist regimes but with a number of Asian countries, and renewed diplomatic ties with African countries that had been broken in the early 1970s when Arab aid and pressure led a number of African countries to break relations with Jerusalem. Third, Israel opened economic ties with a number of Gulf states and North African countries. Most of these relations proved to be short-lived as they ended with the collapse of the peace process a few years later. But most of these benefits were felt by those who were already supporters of the peace process rather than those who opposed it or were neutral towards it.[45]

Israel's main reaction to terrorism coming from the territories, whether the portion administered by the PA or that still administered by Israel, was closure of the territories. On November 25, 1994, a bus in Jerusalem was bombed and so Rabin closed the territories for two weeks. As time went by and terrorism intensified, Rabin would close the territories for longer and longer periods of time. This would create havoc with the Palestinian economy and raise the level of unemployment, and thus create a bigger pool of potential suicide bombers to be recruited by the Islamists. But it was reassuring to the Israeli public who at an emotional level felt that they were hitting back at the Palestinians for terrorism. Arafat also began rounding up Islamists who were tortured and imprisoned. This lowered Arafat's popularity and the less popular he became the more arbitrary and dictatorial.[46]

On January 22, 1995, there was a suicide bombing at the Beit Lid Junction in central Israel that resulted in the deaths of 29 soldiers. President Ezer Weizman called on Rabin to halt the peace process in response until Arafat suppressed Hamas. Under Israeli law the presidency is a non-political ceremonial post and the president is not supposed to take positions on matters of policy. But Weizman had always played by his own rules. As a general and as a minister in the first national-unity government in the 1960s he had been a right-wing Herutnik. Then as the Likud minister of defense from 1977 to 1980 he had championed peace with Egypt. Then he joined Labor in 1985 and became a leading peace activist advocating negotiations with the PLO. But he had always been a political foe of Rabin. So Rabin ignored the call and pressed on with negotiations.[47]

The Oslo II agreement was finally signed in Washington on September

28, 1995. When it came up for a vote in the Knesset it passed by a single vote, 61 to 59. Labor had to bribe a defector from Raful Eitan's *Tzomet* party with a ministerial appointment and his own car in order to win the vote.[48] The Palestinians were eventually convinced to reset their five-year clock from March 4, 1994, to September 28, 1995. Arafat treated this five-year goal as a legal promise for independence, while ignoring his numerous obligations under the agreements to fight terrorism. Five years later the Al-Aksa Intifada began as a cross between the 1936–39 Arab Revolt against the British and the early part of the 1948 war. "If the partners in the peace process do not unite against the angel of death that is terrorism, all that will be left of this ceremony is a souvenir photo, and soon rivers of hatred will flood the Middle East," warned Rabin at the signing ceremony in Washington.[49]

Throughout October 1995 there were large rallies of the political right in Israel consisting of settlers, Likud supporters, and national religious Jews. The protestors bore placards with doctored photos of Rabin in a Nazi uniform and Rabin with a kaffiyeh. Some 30,000 demonstrators attended a rally in Zion Square in Jerusalem on October 5 after the Knesset ratified Oslo II. Nationalist rabbis from the settler movement went farther and declared Rabin to be a *rodef* or "pursuer" who under ancient Jewish law could be killed by any Jew without a trial.[50] The fact that Rabin's peace policy relied on the support of Arab votes in the Knesset made it illegitimate in the eyes of the nationalist right. On matters of great importance to Israel they considered only Jewish votes to be valid. This is similar to the narrow tribal outlook in South Africa among the Afrikaner right that considered the input of English-speaking whites to be suspect. Thus, Rabin was in the political fight of his life.

In January 1995 Netanyahu had organized a joint campaign with other right-wing parties and the settlers. In February 1995 Rabin told Netanyahu to shut up during a debate. "You have never in your life filled any kind of position involving responsibility for security," Rabin told him. Rabin, as a sabra (native-born) Israeli, considered Netanyahu to be an immigrant who spent half of his life abroad. Rabin respected Sharon and Shamir but had nothing but contempt for Netanyahu. Netanyahu was asked by the head of the Shabak, the general security service, to tone down his attacks on Rabin as they were afraid of fanatics going after him. Netanyahu considered it an attempt to shut down his campaign. In October 1995 he was filmed at one rally stroking the red letters of a poster that called for "death to Rabin" in Hebrew and English.[51]

The peace camp in Israel decided to rally public support by holding a mass peace rally in Tel Aviv, the heart of the Labor Party, sponsored by Peace Now, the leading mainline peace organization. Peace Now managed to convince both Peres and Rabin to attend the rally. The two attended and were featured on the stage together where Rabin was even persuaded to sing the "Song For Peace." Moments later, after Peres had already gone home, Rabin was shot in the back from point-black range by Yigal Amir. Amir was a law student at Bar-Ilan University, a university for religious Jews, and right-wing activist who was involved in organizing anti–Oslo rallies. Amir was allowed to get close to Rabin because he was a Jew and his Shin Bet bodyguards were conditioned to see only Arabs as potential assassins. Rabin had been warned by the Shin Ben director of threats against his life, but refused to take the threats seriously by wearing body armor for protection. Rabin died shortly after arriving at the hospital.[52]

Now the peace process would have to survive without its most effective Israeli political supporter. It would have to rely on Shimon Peres, who managed to win only one of the four elections he contested as his party's nominee for the premiership. And that time he won by such a small lead that he was forced to rotate out of the top post halfway through his term. This was not good odds. Yasir Arafat was deliberately kept away from Rabin's funeral for security (as well as political) reasons and he had to pay his respects to Rabin's widow in private a few weeks later. Rabin's funeral was attended by 87 heads of state and government from around the world including many from the Arab world. Jordan, Egypt, Oman and Qatar sent official delegations to the funeral.[53]

Three

The Peace Process Stalls

Peres in Charge

Peres immediately took over as prime minister following the assassination. This was for a number of reasons. First, Peres was the number two man on the Labor Party list in 1992, the run-up candidate in the primary, and the man who had more support in the central committee than any other man or woman. Second, he was the co-architect of the peace process with Rabin and knew the Palestinian track better than anyone else. He also had the international connections in Washington and Europe that other potential rivals lacked. Third, the only possible rival was former Chief of Staff Ehud Barak, who was the interior minister under Rabin at the time of the assassination. Most felt that he was too inexperienced to follow Rabin, but needed to be groomed under Peres. He was named as Peres's successor as foreign minister. Peres, like Rabin before him and Barak after him, took over the defense ministry as well as the premiership.

Before the assassination Benyamin Netanyahu and Rabin were about even in the polls with Netanyahu even being ahead in a few. After the assassination Peres jumped far ahead as he benefited from public sympathy for the slain Rabin. His colleagues urged him to call immediate elections so that he could benefit from this sympathy for the good of the party and the peace process. But Peres was sensitive about his image as a perennial loser in Israeli politics. He had lost in 1977, 1981, and 1988 and won so narrowly in 1984 that he was forced into the *rotatzia* (rotation) scheme with Shamir under which they swapped jobs halfway through the term. Peres did not want to end his political career without being able to say that he had won at least once clearly in his own right. If he was carried into office riding on Rabin's casket he would not be able to make that claim. So he was prepared to lose everything in order to win for himself.

Three. The Peace Process Stalls

In order to win Peres decided that he would have to not only continue the peace process, but also reclaim his early image of "Mr. Security" from the 1950s to 1970s that he had shared with Moshe Dayan. Peres lost this image to Rabin when he moved to the left in the late 1970s and early 1980s. He also decided that he needed to make progress, if not actual peace, on the Syrian track to give Israelis a feeling of security and to compensate for the increased terrorism that had accompanied the Palestinian track. Peres was surprised when Clinton took him aside during the Rabin funeral and told him about the "deposit" that Rabin had left in Washington. Rabin had agreed that he would return the entire Golan in exchange for a full peace with full normalization with Damascus. Peres was surprised by this revelation but told Clinton that he would honor Rabin's promise.

At the end of October 1995, Yossi Beilin concluded a secret agreement that he had been negotiating in a back channel in Stockholm with Abu Mazen. It involved an intact Palestinian state in the West Bank and Gaza, no mass return of refugees to Israel, and having the Palestinians declare the East Jerusalem suburban village of Abu Dis as Al-Quds, the Palestinian capital. Before Beilin could reveal the document to Rabin the latter was assassinated. Beilin had kept the existence of the Stockholm back channel a secret from Peres for two years. He had set it up in Tunis with Arafat, Abu Mazen, and Abu Ala in October 1993 shortly after the Oslo agreement was signed in Washington. Beilin was afraid that the official channels would be too subject to political pressures resulting from continued terrorism, settlement activity, and so on, to be able to deal constructively and imaginatively with the difficult issues such as settlements, Jerusalem, and refugees. The negotiators needed to be shielded from political pressures and inputs. Peres was less than impressed with the achievement. As late as 1997 when Labor was in opposition, Peres was opposed to changing Labor's foreign policy and coming out in support of the establishment of a Palestinian state. Peres concluded that after Rabin's death, without the political cover that Rabin's security credentials provided, it would be easier to conclude an agreement with Syria.[1]

Peres, unlike Rabin, did not see security as the major issue in the negotiations with Syria, but, rather, normalization. Peres wanted to see if Assad was interested in going for an early agreement so he asked Washington to see if Assad would be willing to have a face to face meeting with Peres. Assad considered this to be premature. So Israel began negotiations with Syria with American mediation in December 1995 and Peres called for early elections at the end of May 1996. The process made some slight progress in December and January before becoming bogged down after only three rounds of talks. The negotiations ended in March 1996 in response to the wave of Hamas bombings in Israel in February and March, which Damascus failed to condemn. Peres felt that the negotiations were no longer politically tenable, as the Israeli public had turned against peace with Syria and Assad was unwilling to make any public relations gesture to reassure the Israeli public, and broke them off over this refusal. Damascus had also refused to prevent Hezbollah attacks on Israeli positions in southern Lebanon.[2]

It has been alleged that while Netanyahu was in the opposition he sent signals to Syrian leader Hafiz al-Assad that he should wait until he was elected prime minister as it would be worth his while. The signals were sent by academic Dore Gold, who later became Israeli ambassador to the UN under Netanyahu, through contacts that he had in the United States and Arab world. Netanyahu did not want to give up the Golan and was convinced that Assad did not want normalization with Israel, but would settle for non-belligerency with the Golan becoming a buffer zone became the two states.[3]

In January 1996, Peres gave the go-ahead signal for a plot to assassinate Hamas bomb maker Yahya Ayyash, known to both Israelis and Palestinians as "the engineer" (the word is the same in both languages). The assassination was carried out by an Israeli agent whom Ayyash trusted handing him a cell phone that was booby trapped with explosives. The Shin Bet dialed the number and when Ayyash answered it exploded the bomb with a remote radio signal. But Ayyash had already managed to train at least one replacement "engineer." A crowd of about 300,000 attended his funeral in Gaza and Arafat, speaking at the funeral, called him a "true martyr" and led the funeral procession. Palestinian policemen carried the casket. He also privately expressed his condolences to the family. A month after his death a square was named for him in Gaza. Arafat had just legitimized terrorism in an open fashion. He also exempted families whose houses had been destroyed by Israel from paying any taxes — these were mainly the families of suicide bombers and other terrorists. Hamas responded with five major bombings in Israeli cities in late February and early March: three in Jerusalem, one each in Tel Aviv and Ashkelon. Scores were killed — almost sixty in nine days, Israeli faith in the peace process was severely shaken, and the electoral chances of Peres took a nose dive. Arafat responded with his biggest crackdown on the Islamists to date arresting hundreds.[4]

The *coup de grace* for the peace process took place in April when Peres ordered an invasion of Lebanon in response to increased Hezbollah activity in the south. The operation was codenamed "Grapes of Wrath" by Israel but should have been called "sour grapes." The IDF responded to Hezbollah rockets with counter-battery fire from heavy artillery. One 155-mm shell was a direct hit on a United Nations position where over a hundred civilians had taken refugee from the shelling. Over a hundred were killed. This brought an end to the Israeli operation, an international condemnation of Israel, and a boycott of the polls by Israeli Arabs at the end of May.

Peres refused to make effective use of Ehud Barak, now his foreign minister, in the election campaign. Peres did little to reassure the Israeli public about their security while "Bibi" Netanyahu played to the insecurity and fear of the Israeli public. Peres wanted Clinton to announce that he would move the American embassy in Israel from Tel Aviv to Jerusalem, a pledge that Clinton — like most other candidates — made while running for the presidency, and Christopher was willing to go along with this. National Security Advisor Sandy Berger was unwilling to sign off on this unless it was the only way that Peres could win and was guaranteed to make the difference. Ross and Indyk could not swear to this. American Ambassador Martin Indyk was predicting a narrow Peres victory on the eve of the election.

As the election returns came in on election day it at first appeared that Peres would narrowly retain power. But then as the night wore on Peres's lead evaporated and by the morning when Israelis awoke Benyamin "Bibi" Netanyahu was the winner. Netanyahu won by about 30,000 votes or less than a single mandate; Labor actually outpolled the Likud with 34 seats to 32. He had a solid lead about Jewish voters, but Labor led among Arab voters. The problem was that looking tough for the Jews had cost Peres the votes of thousands of Arab voters who had decided to stay home from the polls. The narrow lead from 1992 had shifted back to the right. It was also the first of three elections held under a new system in which Israelis got two votes — one for prime minister and one for the Knesset. Netanyahu received 50.5 percent of the prime minister's vote to 49.5 percent for Peres. Netanyahu had campaigned on the slogan of "Peace With Security" thereby implying that Labor failed to provide security. He also used the slogan "Peres will divide Jerusalem." And he used a Republican ad specialist to devise a series of devastating ads against Peres. President Bill Clinton stayed up late that evening to watch the returns come in from Israel. He and his advisors were shocked by the result and did not know how to proceed initially with the peace process. The left lost most with Meretz losing two seats.[5]

Guy Ben-Porat, an Israeli academic who investigated the effect of globalization on the peace process, sees Netanyahu's coalition as one of the nationalists and the marginalized — those who had either economic or political objections to the peace process. The peace dividend within Israeli society was not evenly distributed, but rather, was skewed in favor of those well-educated individuals who could benefit from globalization and peace. They were found mostly in Meretz and Labor. Many of the *mizrahim* (Jews from Muslim countries) feared that if Israel withdrew from the territories they would go back to the bottom of the economic ladder. And, of course, many Israelis felt less secure rather than more secure as a result of the terrorism accompanying the peace process.[6]

Clinton had met Netanyahu for the first time in March 1996 when he came to Jerusalem to visit Rabin's grave and confer with Peres on the peace process. He told the opposition leader that Washington would back Israel's battle against terrorism but that Israel must continue to support the peace process. That month Clinton sent letters to Arab letters urging them to crack down on Islamist terror, and he announced the grant of $100 million to Israel to fight terrorism. Netanyahu developed the concept of "reciprocity or mutuality." Israel would support the peace process only so far as Arafat complied with the Oslo agreement. This was a way of dealing with both Arafat's deviousness and Netanyahu's internal critics who were opposed to the surrender of any further territory to the Palestinians.[7]

Benyamin Netanyahu and His Partners

Netanyahu was one three individuals whose personalities were problematic for the peace process. The other two were Arafat and Barak. Netanyahu was closer to Arafat than to Barak in terms of his personality and operating style. Like Arafat, Netanyahu would make mutually contradictory promises to various parties in the hope that he would never have to be held accountable for all of his promises and that he could keep everyone happy. It was this trait that would eventually cost him his support with the electorate, his coalition partners and Washington.

From mid–1996 to 1999 Washington's support tilted away from Israel towards the Palestinians. This was not the first time that the president had supported an Arab leader at the expense of Israel—Carter had had a similar tilt from 1977 to 1980 when President Sadat made his peace initiative. The reasoning was the same—Israel had more than one leader who would support the peace process but the Arab partner was crucial to its success. To a much greater extent than during the Rabin and Peres years, from 1993 to 1996, Washington became an active mediator and referee between the two parties. Realizing that Netanyahu was under pressure, Arafat stopped attempting to restrain the Islamists and relied on pressure from Washington to keep Israel in line. Secretary of State Warren Christopher devoted himself, in vain, almost exclusively to the Syrian track, making humiliating pilgrimages to Damascus in search of a Syrian partner. Dennis Ross, as head of the Clinton peace team consisting of four Jews and an Armenian-American, became Washington's point man in the peace process. Christopher announced that he was leaving his position at the end of Clinton's first term and Washington was alive with speculation as to who would replace him. The leading candidates were: Richard Holbrooke, Clinton's ambassador to Germany and then Assistant Secretary of State for European Affairs, who had negotiated the Dayton Accords in Bosnia in November 1995; George Mitchell, the former majority leader in the Senate and Clinton's contribution to the Northern Ireland peace process since 1994; Senator Sam Nunn of Georgia, a leading Senate expert on foreign affairs; Ambassador Tom Pickering, a career diplomat who lacked political connections; and United Nations Ambassador Madeleine Albright. Albright was initially the dark horse candidate, but she had the support of Mrs. Clinton who shared similar views to hers. Raised in Central Europe as the daughter of a career Czech diplomat, she came as a refugee to America in the late 1940s after her country disappeared after Munich and then after the Communist coup. Her father, Joseph Korbel, became a professor of international relations in Denver, Colorado (and mentor to Condolezza Rice). Educated initially in Switzerland and London, Albright had to make the adjustment to life in America. She worked her way through the Washington foreign policy bureaucracy as an aide first to Senator Edmund Muskie of Maine and then to Zbigniew Brzezinski. A Soviet and East European specialist who spoke Czech, Russian, Polish, and Serbo-Croatian, she was initially content to let Martin Indyk and Dennis Ross handle the Arab-Israeli negotiations while she concentrated on the rest of the world.[8]

Netanyahu's coalition was made up of the Likud, Natan Sharansky's Russian immigrant party *Israel B'Aliya* (Israel in Ascent), Raful Eitan's *Tzomet* (Crossroads) party, the Third Way, a party of Golan Heights settlers, and the religious parties including Shas. Netanyahu was committed to honoring Israel's agreements from the Oslo process, keeping the Golan, retaining—and by stealth expanding—the settlements in the territories, and preserving Israel's good ties with Washington. In practice that meant renegotiating the terms of Israel's implementation of the Oslo accords. Bibi appointed David Levy as foreign minister; Yitzhak Mordechai, a former general who commanded both central and northern commands, as defense minister; Meridor, a future defector from the Likud, as finance minister; and Sharon, thanks to the intercession of Levy, as national infrastructure minister. In 1992-93 Netanyahu had published *Israel's Place Among the Nations,* a standard recitation of the Revisionist-Likud view of history and foreign policy.[9]

Netanyahu was a Likud "prince"—the son of one of the leading Revisionist families in Israel. The princes were the offspring of leading figures from the Etzel underground and Ze'ev Jabotinsky's Revisionist Party and included Benny Begin, Netanyahu, Dan Meridor, Ehud Olmert, and Tzipporah Livni.

Bibi was the son of Benzion, an eminent historian of medieval Spanish Jewry and former editor of the Revisionist newspaper, and the brother of Yonatan, a war hero who was killed in the 1976 Entebbe rescue. Netanyahu became the protégé of Moshe Arens, a defense technocrat who served twice as defense minister and as foreign minister and was Shamir's designated successor as head of the Likud. Arens unexpectedly retired from politics in 1992 following the Likud's defeat in the 1992 election. Netanyahu served as ambassador to the United Nations and deputy foreign minister. Partially raised in the United States he spoke fluent colloquial American English. The following year Netanyahu, with Arens's blessing, beat David Levy and Benny Begin, to become leader of the Likud. Levy was leader of the *mizrahim* (North African and Middle Eastern Jews) within the party and Begin was the geologist son of the founder of the *Herut* (freedom) party that became the main party within the Likud when Sharon merged four parties to create the Likud in 1973. Bibi won double the percentage of his nearest competitor, Levy.[10]

From 1992 to 1996 under Rabin and Peres a further 46,000 settlers moved into the territories for a total population of 200,000 with 50,000 new housing units built. Palestinians were concerned that the Jewish expropriation of Palestinian land continued unabated during the Oslo years. In addition Palestinians lost on average 73 days of work in 1995 and would lose a further 82 in 1996 due to closures. Unemployment had risen from six percent in 1993 to 29 percent in 1996. And average income had decreased by 17 percent. So the average Palestinian had not benefited from the peace.[11]

Arafat's Palestine

Arafat had lived in turn in royalist Egypt, Nasser's Egypt, Kuwait, Jordan, Lebanon, and Tunisia. He had as chairman of the PLO dealt with all the Arab heads of state and foreign ministers so he was familiar with the typical systems of government in the Arab world in both its varieties of monarchial dictatorships and military republican dictatorships. Arafat had learned, and as imitation is the sincerest form of flattery, set himself to flattering his fellow Arab dictators. His rule was based on the security apparatus, which was built out of the various Palestine Liberation Army conventional units and fedayeen guerrilla and terrorist organizations created over the decades of exile. The Oslo accords limited the police Palestinian force to 16,000 members but Arafat soon exceeded that limit with the acquiescence of Rabin and Peres who wanted him to make progress on containing the Islamists. Arafat made no effort to prevent the smuggling of illegal weapons into Gaza and the West Bank or to disarm the Palestinian population as he was required to do under the accords. By late 1994 there were estimated to be upwards of 26,000 illegal weapons in the territories.[12]

He lacked a real modern economy. Arafat, like a typical Arab ruler, began demanding ownership shares in new industrial plants and used both international aid and licenses as a means of buying loyalty for his rule. As long as terrorism continued tourism would not be a viable industry. Many Palestinians were dependent on finding work as migrant day laborers in the Israeli economy as: agricultural workers, construction workers, waiters and kitchen staff, domestic servants and other menial jobs. Palestinians were as dependent as South Africans from the homelands (bantustans) were dependent on migrant employment and Mexico is dependent on American migrant employment. So Arafat was vulnerable to closures.

The PA began receiving generous foreign aid from both America and Europe after Arafat returned to Gaza. But Arafat insisted on using the money as a source of patronage to buy political support and dependence. The *Independent* newspaper of London reported that in 1996 the PA wasted some $323 million to corruption or about half of the amount that the PA received. Suha Arafat, Arafat's wife, was a major stockholder in the *Al-Bahar* (the sea) construction company, which was known by Palestinian wags as *Al-Muheya* (the ocean) because it had its tentacles in everything. The fact that it was known that Arafat's wife was a stockholder might have entered into its clients minds when selecting a company. The PA imported office furniture from Italy through an Israeli company rather than turning to a local manufacturer to supply it and thus provide employment for Palestinians. Congress had many complaints about the lack of visibility in the PA's finances.[13]

Peace dividends were practically nonexistent or negative for the Palestinians. Palestinian unemployment nearly tripled from 11 to 28 percent, in response to Israeli closures in response to terrorism in the spring of 1996. Nearly two-thirds (66 percent) of the Palestinian workforce was either unemployed or severely underemployed. Palestinians saw the closures as a form of collective punishment rather than as a form of Israeli protective measures against terrorism. And real wages declined 38 percent between 1992 and 1994, further weakening support for Oslo.[14]

Arafat remained an outsider dependent on his colleagues from Tunis who had been with him since at least Beirut, if not Jordan and Kuwait. His closest colleagues were Abu Mazen, Abu Ala, Saeb Erekat, and Nabil Sha'ath. Abu Mazen (Mahmoud Abbas) was a former high school teacher in Syria and Qatar who became a close Arafat advisor. Abu Ala (Ahmed Qurei) was from a Jerusalem family. The two were Arafat's closest advisors and he played the two off against one another in order to keep them divided. Abu Mazen, who supervised the Oslo attacks from Tunis, signed the accords in Stockholm, while Abu Ala was excluded. Erekat was the head of the Palestinian delegation to the Washington talks and Nabil Sha'ath was the head Palestinian negotiator and development minister. Erekat was an economist by profession and an American citizen who spoke fluent American English and loved to deal with Americans on an official basis. He lived in Jericho, but his family was from Abu Dis and he lacked any independent power base. But he could talk Arafat into unmaking deals that other Palestinians had negotiated. Arafat's other close associate was Yasir Abd Rabbu, a defector from the Democratic Front for the Liberation of Palestine (DFLP) who set up his own small party, FIDA. His main function was to provide Arafat with Fedayeen backing outside of Fatah. Outside of this, Arafat relied mainly on locals with little independent support and on a few distinguished insiders such as: Feisal Husseini, the son of Abu Musa, the leader of Palestinian forces in 1948, who was killed in battle in April 1948; Hanan Ashrawi, a professor of English at Bir Zeit University from a Christian family; and Sari Nusseibeh, a philosophy professor and son of a former Jordanian defense minister. Arafat soon alienated these prominent locals by refusing to consult with them during the Oslo process, calling them insulting names such as "whore" in the case of Ashrawi, and not giving them the positions that their expertise warranted.[15]

In South Africa there was a similar problem between "insiders" and "outsiders" after the African National Congress's cadre returned from exile in London, Europe, and Africa. The latter also took the main jobs in the new administration at the expense of the "insiders" who had served in the ANC's legal front organization, the United Democratic Front, and in trade unions. But the problem was amplified in Palestine because the period of exile was 45 years compared to 30 years in South Africa and because the insiders and outsiders had different interests. The "outsiders" represented those Palestinians who had gone/been forced into exile in 1948 and who were interested in preserving the right of return to their former homes in Israel. The "insiders" were more interested in establishing an independent state in the West Bank and Gaza. Attempting to reverse the results of the 1948 war would put the goal of an independent state at risk.

As in other Arab countries the press was carefully controlled. The PA's main newspaper was *Al-Haya Al-Jadida* (the New Life). It regularly carried anti–Semitic attacks and incitement against Israel. The Palestinian press engaged in Holocaust denial. At the beginning of December 1997 to mark the fiftieth anniversary of the UN's partition resolution for Palestine, a member of the Palestinian Council declared on PA Television, "Our war with Israel and the Jews has not ended and will not end until the establishment of a Palestinian state on the whole of Palestine." Censorship was strict and works by Palestinian authors from the diaspora who were critical of Arafat, such as Edward Said, were banned. Arafat was alienated from Palestinian intellectuals both among insiders and outsiders.[16]

The Palestinian education system involved anti–Israeli incitement and anti–Semitism with attacks on the Bible and the Talmud. After it took control of the West Bank the PA opened summer camps for teenagers that involved a combination of anti–Israeli indoctrination, rudimentary military training in small arms, explosives, and physical fitness. They were run on the model of the Hitler Youth camps and the Soviet Pioneers.[17]

In October 1994 Arafat appointed his own mufti, or religious leader, for Jerusalem. There was already an existing Jordanian-appointed mufti but Palestinians thereafter ignored him. Preachers at Al-Aksa Mosque began turning in their sermons to Arafat's officials for approval. After Arafat's police killed 14 Hamas activists in the first major clash with the Islamists in December 1994, a pro-Arafat preacher blamed the deaths on Israel. Arafat made false charges at a UNESCO conference in 1995 that Israel was violating Christian and Muslim holy places and restricting the practice of religion. Later in October 2000, at the start of the Al-Aksa Intifada, Ahmad Abu Halamiya called on Arabs to kill Jews throughout the world in a broadcast on PA Television.[18]

Netanyahu and Arafat

Netanyahu did not meet with Arafat until the beginning of September 1996. In the meantime and afterwards his trusted American-Israeli advisor Dore Gold became his liaison with Arafat. Terje Larson would supervise meetings between the two. Both his foreign minister and defense minister also had meetings with Arafat.

At the end of that month, a pattern was developed that would last through Netanyahu's term and beyond. In order to solidify his support on the right, Bibi ordered the creation of a new entrance for the ancient Hasmonean tunnel that ran parallel to the Temple Mount and was about 80 meters long. The Muslim *waqf,* the authority that administered the Temple Mount, had agreed to this in exchange for Muslims being granted permission to pray in Solomon's Stables. A few yards of stone were tunneled through so that tourists could exit rather than having to retrace their steps through the dark tunnel. The new exit opened to the public on September 24. Arafat saw this as a unilateral Israeli change of the status quo. He saw it as an opportunity to send a signal to Netanyahu and shift the balance of power in their relationship. Rumors that Israel was trying to undermine the Temple Mount were sent through Arab Jerusalem. Riots began at the end of September and lasted for three days. There were 57 Palestinians and 15 Israelis killed and hundreds wounded in three days of rioting with Palestinian police, with Arafat's blessing, shooting it out with Israeli soldiers in the streets. Arafat saw several advantages in this course of action. First, he was seen as sticking up for Palestinian rights and demonstrating that the Islamists did not have a monopoly on violence. Second, he was able to make Netanyahu look inept and dangerous in the eyes of America and the world. Third, he destroyed the trust that had been developing between Israeli soldiers and Palestinian police so that the Israelis would be more reluctant to jointly patrol with their Palestinian counterparts in areas under the jurisdiction of the PA. Fourth, it served as a practice run for the Al-Aksa Intifada. After the confrontation, Arafat began importing heavy weapons to equip his police force in violation of the Oslo accords.[19]

As a result of the clashes, Clinton called a summit in Washington and asked Netanyahu, Arafat, Hussein, and Mubarak to attend. Hussein accepted the invitation and Mubarak declined. Ross presided over negotiations that lasted for 40 hours but the only outcome was that Bibi agreed to begin intensive negotiations to resolve the Hebron situation with Arafat. They were to result in the only positive accomplishment for the peace process during Netanyahu's tenure.[20]

The tunnel confrontation also served to sour King Hussein on Netanyahu. During the election campaign Hussein had interfered on Netanyahu's behalf by inviting him to Amman on the eve of the election while declining to extend an invitation to Peres. Hussein feared that Peres would too quickly move forward and conclude peace with Syria if elected. Hussein also may have wanted some payback for Peres's failure to deliver on the international conference in 1986 and for his indiscretions regarding confidential Israeli-Jordanian negotiations in 1993. Hussein would soon regret his decision.[21]

Ross was sent back out to the region and negotiated in a non-stop shuttle for 23 days without being able to reach a deal. Ross then returned in January 1997 and was able to successfully negotiate an Israeli redeployment within the city. The agreement was recorded in three documents: a protocol to implement the redeployment, a "note for the record" prepared by Ross of a meeting between Arafat and Netanyahu, and a letter from Secretary Christopher to Netanyahu. The redeployment split Hebron into two areas: H-2 and H-1. H-1 consisted of 80 percent of the territory of the city and most of the population. H-2 was the area of the Old City with its 400 Jewish inhabitants and 20,000 Arabs. In the course of the second shuttle, Ross began to see Arafat as someone who could not be trusted because he was always asking for more and denying what he had previously said. He saw Netanyahu as being very similar and as a result he lost his temper several times during the two shuttles.[22]

The first of the three Israeli redeployments scheduled to take place under Oslo II was scheduled to occur in March 1997. On March 7, 1997, the Israeli cabinet voted to withdraw from 9.1 percent of the West Bank. Washington was hoping for a bigger withdrawal but settled for attempting to convince him to make a bigger redeployment in the second stage. In preparation for this withdrawal, the cabinet authorized the construction of 6,500 housing units on a hill located between East Jerusalem and Bethlehem known in Hebrew as Har Homa and in Arabic as Abu Ghneim. Two days later Arafat met with Hamas officials in his office in Ramallah and gave them a green light for a terrorist offensive against Israel. Hundreds of Hamas activists were released from Palestinian prisons and on March 21 a Hamas bomb went off in a Tel Aviv café wounding 48 and killing three. Arafat went off on a tour of the Arab world and South Asia and visited Iran for the first time in eight years. Marwan Barghouti of the Fatah Tanzim offered his condolences to the "martyr" who died in Tel Aviv in front of the Palestinian Council to wild cheers. That same month, King Hussein wrote a very critical personal letter to Netanyahu blaming him for the problems with the peace process. Netanyahu wrote back absolving himself and claiming that the process was on the verge of collapse when he was elected and he had made efforts to revive it.[23]

The international press played up the Har Homa construction and Netanyahu and Israel came off looking like the villains. Albright had made an agreement with Clinton when she took the position of secretary of state that she would not come to the Middle East unless the prospects of making real progress were good. This kept her out of the region during her first eight months in office. Ross mediated between Arafat and Netanyahu, while Albright hosted them when they came on visits to Washington. In August 1997 Arafat was photographed embracing a Hamas leader. On September 4 three Hamas suicide bombers detonated themselves in downtown Jerusalem killing five and wounding 181. A scheduled visit to the region by Albright followed soon after this and focused on security aspects of the Israeli-Palestinian relationship. Arafat saw that he was hurt by his green light to terrorism.[24]

The next month Mossad agents were caught trying to poison Hamas leader Khaled Meshal in Amman. They were caught and Israel was forced to provide Hussein with the antidote to the poison and free seventy prisoners including Sheikh Ahmed Yassin, the spiritual leader of Hamas. King Hussein threatened to storm the Israeli embassy in Amman to capture Mossad agents hiding there. Negotiations continued with little progress through the end of 1997. It took pressure from Clinton on Netanyahu to work out the deal. Israeli-British historian Avi Shlaim claims that three days before the assassination attempt, Hamas had offered Israel a thirty-year truce and the offer had been communicated to Netanyahu through Hussein. King Hussein was furious with Netanyahu because he saw him as frustrating his own efforts to build a bridge of peace between Israel and the Arab world. He had harsh words for Netanyahu when the two next met in Washington. As a result of this Hussein allowed Netanyahu's Likud rival Arik Sharon to open a back channel with him via Israeli Druze MK Mjali Wahbah, a former IDF lieutenant colonel.[25]

In a book published in 1993, *Israel Among the Nations*, Netanyahu argued the Revisionist Zionist case for Israel. He argued against the creation of a Palestinian state. In 1997 he won government approval of a plan for a final settlement with the Palestinians that would give them a state in about 40 percent of the West Bank. Israel would keep for itself Greater Jerusalem, the Jordan Valley, the hills east of Jerusalem, essential roads and corridors, and water sources. Netanyahu marketed it as "Allon plus," referring to the 1967 Allon Plan that envisaged returning about sixty percent of the West Bank to Jordan while retaining the Jordan Valley and Etzion Bloc for Israel. But Netanyahu planned to retain about twice as much territory as Yigal Allon did and make peace with the Palestinians rather than with Jordan.[26]

By the end of the summer of 1998 Ross had narrowed the differences between the two sides on the issue of the second Israeli redeployment. With U.S. agreement the Palestinians had accepted that Israel would withdraw from no more than thirteen percent of the West Bank, three percent of this would be nature preserves. Arafat had in turn agreed to submit a new Palestinian Charter for approval by the Palestinian National Council of the PLO. President Clinton felt that the two sides were close enough to call for a summit in October 1998 to be held at the Wye River Plantation where Israeli-Syrian negotiations had been held in 1996. By the spring of 1998 Clinton was no longer taking risks for the peace process as such, but rather to improve his tarnished image as a result of the Lewinsky affair. By that summer Clinton was severely weakened as a result of the affair.[27]

Bibi had lost three senior ministers from the government in the course of a year: Benny Begin in January 1997, Dan Meridor in June, and Levy in January 1998. He would later lose Yitzhak Mordechai in early 1999. Four developments made for a summit and the Israeli withdrawal. First, Washington made clear that it expected Jerusalem to provide the key to progress. Second, May 4, 1999, was fast approaching. Third, Ross had negotiated the basis for a deal. Fourth, Bibi had developed a coalition that would support a 13 percent withdrawal. Just before coming to Maryland for the summit, Bibi appointed his rival Ariel Sharon as the new foreign minister to replace David Levy, who had resigned in exchange for Sharon's support for a 13 percent withdrawal.[28]

In eight days of talks at Wye River an agreement was finally reached. Clinton was absent for most of the time at Democratic fund-raising events for the midterm elections. Most of the mediation was handled by Dennis Ross, Secretary of State Madeleine Albright, and National Security Advisor Sandy Berger. Both Albright and Berger had earlier contemplated issuing a statement that they could not work with Netanyahu. Clinton weighed in during the final two days, pulling an "all nighter" to negotiate the agreement. Netanyahu agreed to pull out of eleven percent of territory and two percent of nature reserves in exchange for Arafat agreeing to call a special session of the PNC to modify the Palestinian Charter and to crack down on terrorism and confiscate illegal weapons. A major sticking point was the Palestinian demand for an Israeli release of Palestinian "political" prisoners. Arafat wanted a thousand prisoners released — all of them imprisoned for political offenses. Netanyahu wanted to release only 500 and refused to release either Hamas prisoners or those with "blood on their hands"— those directly involved in the murder of Israelis. The Americans suggested that they split the difference. Netanyahu agreed provided that he did not violate existing Israeli policy. In a move worthy of Arafat, Netanyahu tried to arrange a pardon for convicted American spy Jonathan Pollard, who had spied for Israel, as part of the arrangement. CIA Director George Tenet threatened to resign if this went ahead and so Clinton vetoed the release. Netanyahu was forced to sulk home without Pollard as political cover. For Clinton and the Americans Wye River was good preparation for Camp David two years later. For Sharon it was a trying experience to have to sit at the same table with a man he regarded as a war criminal, and probably the same was true for Arafat. The two spoke to the Americans referring to the other only in the third person. A dying King Hussein played an important supportive role near the end of the negotiations, but did not take an active part in them. He did meet with the three leaders and was briefed by Clinton. His main contribution was to urge Clinton to stay firm and let Netanyahu walk out if necessary. Hussein attended the signing ceremony for the agreement in Washington on October 23, 1998, in his last public gesture for peace. He died of lymphoma cancer in Amman in early February 1999. The summit resulted in a major break of trust between Washington and Jerusalem.[29]

Unfortunately, the agreement was never fully implemented, as right-wing defections from the government caused Netanyahu to call for early elections on January 4, 1999. Elections were scheduled for May 17. The IDF withdrew from a further nine percent of the West Bank in November and some 250 Palestinian prisoners were released —150 of them ordinary criminals. The government had given its approval to the agreement negotiated by it by a one-vote margin: six to five with three abstentions.[30] On November 24, the PA inaugurated its airport at Rafah in Gaza near the Egyptian border. In December Clinton made a triumphal official visit to the PA and Israel. The PNC passed by voice vote Arafat's decision to remove offensive clauses from the Palestinian Charter, but the Charter was never republished in amended form. Israel threatened to stop implementation of all of its agreements unless the PA agreed to five Israeli demands. First, the PA must stop threatening to unilaterally proclaim a Palestinian state. Second, it must stop demanding the release of prisoners guilty of violent political offenses. Third, it must mount an operation under American supervision to seize illegal weapons. Fourth, it must furnish a definitive list of Palestinian police, who can number no more than 30,000. And finally, it must furnish the first report of the committee on incitement to violence.[31]

Negotiations and progress in the peace process were on hold until after Israel held its elections for prime minister and the Knesset and formed a new government. As in 1992 this meant that much of the year was wasted due to domestic Israeli politics. The candidate of the center-left for the premiership was Ehud Barak, who had started the Oslo process as chief of staff and then become interior minister under Rabin, foreign minister under Peres, and then Labor Party leader in early 1997. Barak would be the third difficult personality to have an adverse effect on the peace process. Barak was a highly intelligent, renaissance man who in addition to being Israel's most decorated soldier, had a degree in economic engineering, was an accomplished classical pianist, and repaired watches and clocks as a stress-relieving hobby. His problem was that he was not shy about letting people know that he was more intelligent than they were, which in most cases was true, and that he was a poor listener. In a profession where he could rise because of his merit and did not have to suffer fools, he never learned how to suffer them. He also expected that others should accommodate his political needs without expecting that the reverse was true as well.[32]

The Clinton administration clearly favored the election of Labor, running as One Israel — an alliance of Labor with David Levy's Gesher list and a list of religious doves. Clinton "loaned" Barak three senior figures from his 1992 presidential campaign, and a number of Democratic fund raisers raised money for the Barak campaign in the United States illegally. This was facilitated by the fact that many of the top fund raisers in the Democratic Party were Jews. Barak outspent Netanyahu by a wide margin. James Carville said that Clinton received regular updates on the course of the Labor campaign. State Department personnel regularly furnished the Washington media with stories about Netanyahu's deficiencies so that in Israel an appearance of a crisis with Washington existed.[33]

But the decisive factor was not money, or American interference, but Bibi's personality and record. Most Israelis no longer trusted Netanyahu and they still wanted the peace process to continue, but at a slower pace. The fact that Barak ran as Rabin's heir made him a comfortable alternative for most Israelis to both Peres and Netanyahu. He was seen as not another schemer or an impractical dreamer but as another Mr. Security.[34] His attempt to complete Rabin's dream would destroy that image within two years.

Four

Camp David 2000

Barak's Two Decisions

Barak was elected prime minister with an appreciable margin — 56 percent to 44 percent — over Netanyahu, but his One Israel party received only 26 seats. Along with Meretz's nine seats this gave the peace camp a combined total of only 35 seats, far too few for a coalition government by themselves. The Likud was reduced to 19 seats. Barak could either go for a national unity government with the Likud and a few religious parties and thus forego any more peace agreements, or he could build a broad coalition without the Likud. Barak chose the latter option giving him more of an option for negotiating peace. The government included all the major parties, except Likud, such as Shas with 17 seats, the National Religious Party, Meretz with 10, Natan Sharansky's *Israel B'Aliya* Russian immigrant party, the Center Party with six seats, and a few smaller religious parties. The coalition controlled 73 seats giving Barak a comfortable margin to survive no-confidence votes and prevent blackmail by any single party. The coalition was presented to the Knesset in July.[1]

Barak's next decision was almost as crucial to the peace process: with whom would he attempt to make peace first? He had three options. He could either attempt to wrap up the Palestinian track and conclude an agreement with Arafat before the five year clock ran out, or attempt to first negotiate an agreement with the Syrians, or negotiate on both tracks simultaneously. Barak, like every prime minister before him since 1967, ruled out the last option of a comprehensive peace. Both the Israeli public and the Israeli elites lacked trust in the Arabs and thus wanted to retain territory while testing the *bona fides* of their peace partners. The Arabs since 1967 had always attempted to impose a comprehensive peace through the United Nations while Israel had attempted to negotiate peace directly with its neighbors one at a time. Now that Israel had peace treaties with Egypt and Jordan, only the Palestinians, Syria, and Lebanon remained and the latter could not really negotiate separately from Damascus.

Barak, like Rabin and Netanyahu before him, opted for the Syrian track first. This was for several reasons. First, Syria was a much greater military threat to Israel than the Palestinians. By eliminating Syria as an active enemy, Israel would be faced with only a terrorist threat that was manageable. Whereas if Israel made peace with the Palestinians but not with Damascus, it would still have to maintain a large military and defense budget and Damascus could always reopen the Palestinian track through support for the Islamists and the nationalist rejectionist organizations such as the PFLP, DFLP, PFLP-GC, and so forth. Second, during the election campaign Barak had promised to withdraw Israeli troops from southern Lebanon. He could not safely do this without Damascus cutting off its aid to Hezbollah. Third, Barak like Rabin preferred dealing with a fellow career military officer like Hafez Assad than with a terrorist leader like Yasir Arafat. Assad since 1974 had built a reputation for keeping any agreements that he reached with Israel, whereas Arafat had continually violated the Oslo accords. Fourth, if Barak reached peace agreements with Syria and Lebanon, the Palestinians would lose their last major Arab allies and would be forced to rely on distant Iran. They could more easily be squeezed during the final peace negotiation. Fifth, the Syrian track was considered by most Israeli decision makers to be simpler than the Palestinian track.[2]

But not all Israelis agreed with this decision. Both Ami Ayalon, head of the Shin Bet internal security service, and Shaul Mofaz, the chief of staff, spoke to Ross and asked him to try to convince Barak to negotiate first with the Palestinians. Both were aware of Palestinian anger that was building due to continued Israeli settlement activity, incitement by Arafat and Hamas, and the thought of being put on the back burner. Two months earlier Mofaz had endorsed the decision by Barak to deal with the Syrian track first. With Mofaz, who served as Likud defense minister under Sharon, this might have been an attempt to have the negotiations with the Palestinians explode for political reasons, while precluding a successful negotiation with Syria. Mofaz claimed that the Palestinians were ready for an agreement and he did not want to miss "a historic opportunity."[3]

Barak was faced with two ticking clocks. First was the five year clock from May 1994, which had been reset to start ticking from September 13, 1995. Second was the clock on Clinton's second term in the White House. Clinton had been a reliable friend to both Israel and to Barak's mentor, Rabin. In the summer of 1999 it was still not known who Al Gore's Republican opponent would be the following year. But with Clinton having been impeached and acquitted there was the possibility that the American public was suffering from Clinton fatigue and might elect a Republican in November 2000.

Negotiations over the Golan Heights did not get started until December 1999. This was largely because American Jewish businessman Ron Lauder, who served as an intermediary for Netanyahu with Assad in the summer of 1998, had convinced both Netanyahu and Barak that Assad was willing to settle for a return to the international border of 1923 (see below). It took half a year for the Syrians to disabuse Israel of this notion. This involved a trip by Dennis Ross to Damascus to meet with the Syrians. By then Assad was dying of cancer and was visibly weaker. His energy was devoted to ensuring the succession of his son Bashar, an eye surgeon by profession who was married to a British woman. During the 1980s there had been a failed coup attempt by Assad's brother Rifaat, who was banished to various diplomatic postings abroad.[4]

The problem with the negotiations was twofold. First, Assad demanded a return of Israel to the June 4, 1967, border with Israel. This was a problem for Israel for a number of reasons. First, Syria had conquered territory along the Israeli side of the international border in fighting between 1949 and 1967. Thus, Assad's demand violated the rationale behind the Arabs' demand that Israel return to the 1967 lines. Syria would be allowed to retain territory conquered by force. Second, Syria wanted access to Lake Kinneret (the Sea of Galilee), which served as Israel's main source of fresh water for its population. Israel risked putting its source of fresh water at risk to Syrian blackmail or sabotage. The other main problem was that there was no precise marking on the ground of where the ceasefire line was on June 4, 1967. The international border between mandatory Palestine and French Syria was well marked on maps as were the demilitarized zones. So even if Jerusalem accepted in principle the return to the June 4, 1967, line it would still have to negotiate the actual line with Syria. Also the timetables for withdrawal of the two sides were very different.[5]

Although Syria was willing to make allowances for Israel's security needs, it wanted all security measures negotiated to be mutual and equal. Thus, any demilitarized zone on the Syrian side had to be matched by a zone of similar dimensions on the Israeli side. This meant that Israel could not rely on having the Golan demilitarized without leaving much of the eastern Galilee demilitarized as well. Assad was also unwilling to make any of the dramatic public relations gestures for the Israeli public that Sadat had made in November 1977 by coming to Jerusalem or that King Hussein had made. With a powerful Golan lobby having arisen in Israel since the initial negotiations between Israel and Syria in 1992, this was crucial. In 1992 a group of Labor

Party members living on the Golan formed their own list and ran in the Knesset elections. In 1996 this Third Way party ended up joining the Likud coalition. A million new immigrants from the former Soviet Union thought that Israel was quite small as it was and did not think that it could afford to give up more territory.[6]

For Assad the negotiations and their result were about honor and showing the correctness of his defiant stand towards Israel over the decades. Israel had agreed to give the entire Sinai back to Egypt because it was both less strategically important than the Golan or West Bank and because Sadat was the first Arab leader to make peace with the Jewish state. Now Assad wanted to demonstrate that he had gotten more than Sadat had by forcing Israel to withdraw from territory allotted to it under the international border. He wanted to prove that he did better than Sadat and Hussein had done by holding out.[7] For Israel to satisfy Assad's concept of honor meant surrendering strategically vital territory and risking its water supply. Barak told American ambassador Martin Indyk that he could not honor Rabin's "deposit"—the promise to return all of the Golan.[8]

Negotiations opened in Shepherdstown, West Virginia in January 2000 after preliminary discussions had been held in Washington the previous month starting on December 15. Involved on the Israeli side were Barak, Foreign Minister David Levy, former Chief of Staff Amnon Shahak, Attorney General Elyakim Rubinstein, and Reserve General Uri Saguy, a former head of military intelligence. Barak, Shahak and Saguy had all dealt with the Golan professionally in the past during previous rounds of peace talks. The Syrian delegation was also high-powered and included Foreign Minister Farouk al-Sha'ara; his deputy, Majid Abu Saleh; former Syrian army commander Yusef Shakkour; and several other generals as well as several senior diplomats. The State Department mediation team was headed by Madeleine Albright and included Dennis Ross, the senior Middle East negotiator; Ambassador to Israel Martin Indyk; Gamal Helal, Ross's Arabic translator and cultural expert; Jonathan Schwartz, the deputy legal advisor to the State Department; National Security Advisor Sandy Berger; NSC Middle East specialist Rob Malley; and several others from the NSC.[9] The talks soon reached an impasse over the issue of the border along the Kinneret. Syria withdrew its negotiators so that Assad could concentrate on the transfer of power. Barak met with Clinton and convinced him to meet with Assad in Geneva in March in an attempt to revive the negotiations. Barak carefully rehearsed with Clinton what he wanted Clinton to tell Assad about Barak's new offer, which involved a swap of a strip of Israeli land along the Golan instead of the land that Assad wanted along the Kinneret. Barak had written out a script for Clinton. Barak had seen polls from Israel that indicated that the public was opposed to a complete withdrawal from the Golan and Barak was afraid to risk his reelection. Barak wanted the land swap so that he could include a strategic road within Israeli territory. But Assad was not interested in land swaps.[10]

Assad took the offer seriously and brought along a full complement of negotiators and rented out 135 rooms in the Intercontinental Hotel in Geneva to allow them to work. But when Assad, who was visibly wasting away from the effects of the bone cancer, met with Clinton at the hotel on March 26 and discovered that Barak was not willing to give him the return to the June 4, 1967, line, he refused to even allow Clinton to finish making his presentation of the offer. He gathered up his negotiating team and flew home to Damascus. He died on June 10, 2000, apparently from a heart attack as a result of the cancer. Israel would have to await the consolidation of power under Bashar before it would be able to return to peace negotiations with the Syrians.[11]

Successful peacemaking in the Middle East requires both Israel and the Arabs to take risks. Sadat took a risk when he came to Jerusalem in 1977. Israel took a risk when it gave back the Sinai to Egypt in 1982. On the Syrian track neither Assad nor Barak was willing to take risks and the talks collapsed. Would the Palestinian track be any different?

Barak and the Palestinian Track

Barak had spent nine months on the Syrian track and had nothing to show for it. It was nine months that he could ill afford to lose. When the Syrian track collapsed in late March 2000, Barak had less than ten months left until Clinton left office to deal with the Lebanese and Palestinian tracks. Barak decided to go ahead and pull Israeli troops out of Israel's security zone along the Lebanon border where they had remained since the rest of the IDF had withdrawn from Lebanon in 1984. Sixteen years later the last Israeli troops pulled out of Lebanon in May 2000. Israeli troops in Lebanon would no longer be hostage to Syrian pressure ploys, but northern Israeli towns like Metulla and Kiryat Shemona. would be vulnerable to shelling from across the border from Hezbollah.

While the Israeli army was busy withdrawing from Lebanon, its diplomats were busy renewing negotiations with the Palestinians in Stockholm, Sweden on final status issues. Stockholm was the first of three major negotiations that Israel conducted with the Palestinians on final status issues; the other two venues were Camp David, Maryland, and Taba, Egypt.

Initially things did not go well between the Palestinians and Barak. This was for a number of reasons. First, Barak failed to put any limitations on settlements and allowed all settlements approved under the Netanyahu government to proceed. In September 1999 he visited the large West Bank settlement of Ma'ale Adumim and assured them that every house built would remain "part of the state of Israel — forever — period." More settlements were built by the Barak government than by the Netanyahu government — probably because Barak was not as provocative in where he built the settlements and Washington felt more constrained about criticizing Barak. Second, Barak did not always deliver on his promises. In the spring of 2000 he offered to deliver three villages near Jerusalem, including Abu Dis — which had been slated to be the Palestinian capital under the Beilin-Abu Mazen understanding — to the Palestinians. But then Arafat either permitted or encouraged widespread Palestinian rioting on May 15, Nakba Day — which commemorates the birth of Israel as a disaster for Palestinians. This was just as the transfer was coming up for a vote in the Knesset, so the Palestinians sabotaged the deal. Third, the Palestinians felt slighted that Barak chose to negotiate first with Syria and Washington put all of its mediation efforts into that negotiation. They suspected that if Barak had reached a deal with Assad, he would then have refused to negotiate further with them on the grounds that the Israeli electorate would not be able to absorb two peace agreements, with the territorial concessions involved, in such a short period of time. Fourth, Barak wanted to skip completely the third redeployment under Oslo and roll it into the final settlement talks. Coming after three years of stalling by Bibi, this simply looked like more of the same. Barak acted as if he were coming to power in June 1996 after Peres, rather than in July 1999 after Netanyahu, and did not process how Netanyahu's tenure affected the Palestinian perception of Israel.[12]

The negotiations with the Palestinians on a final-status agreement began in January 2000. They consisted of two channels, like the negotiations under Rabin in 1993: an overt official channel and a secret back channel in a suburb (Harpsund) of Stockholm, Sweden. In the official talks Israel was represented by Oded Eran, a fluent Arab speaker from the foreign ministry. Because he was from the foreign ministry and not a former general or intelligence professional, the Palestinians thought that he was a lightweight and did not take him seriously. His interlocutors were Saeb Erekat and Yasir Abd Rabbu. Abd Rabbu was considered by Israelis to be a radical and a hardliner rather than a moderate. His function in the PLO was to make it look like Arafat had multiparty support as he was originally from the Democratic Front for the Liberation of Palestine, a rejectionist organization based in Damascus, and headed his own small political party.

In the secret back channel Shlomo Ben-Ami, the minister for internal security, and Gilead Sher, an attorney who was close to Barak, faced Abu Ala and Hassan Asfur, both Oslo veterans. The first meeting took place in Jerusalem on May 5, before moving to a Galilee kibbutz and then to Stockholm by May 10. In the first meeting, Abu Ala agreed to give up four percent of the West Bank, while Ben-Ami reduced Israel's territorial demand to between 8 and 10 percent of the West Bank. It appeared that a compromise could be reached between four and eight percent. Abu Ala, per instructions from Abu Mazen, refused to discuss numbers of refugees but insisted on the right of return. The Palestinians also insisted upon the Jordan River as Palestine's eastern border with no Israeli military presence. The opening Israeli position, quickly abandoned, was similar to the 1967 Allon Plan that had guided the Labor Party for two decades. Ben-Ami insisted on Israel maintaining a presence in the Jordan Valley for up to 20 years and keeping three large settlement blocs near the Green Line.[13]

Following the Nakba Day rioting in which four Palestinians were killed and some 200 wounded along with eight Israeli soldiers, the talks came to an end on May 17. The Nakba Day riots were the result of a competition between Marwan Barghouti's Tanzim organization, part of Fatah, and Hamas to each show that it was the more militant in confronting Israel.[14] The two teams made progress in a number of areas. But by mid–May 2000 word of the channel was beginning to leak, as had been the case with Oslo, and Barak was coming under attack from members of his coalition over reported concessions that Israel had made to the Palestinians. In the Knesset on a no-confidence vote a majority of Shas MKs along with the National Religious Party voted against the government. This was a warning to Barak that these parties, plus Sharansky's *Israel B'Aliya*—Sharansky was critical of the Abu Dis deal — might soon bolt from the government. The Israelis reported that the Palestinians wanted to move forward only on secondary issues, whereas the Israelis wanted to advance on the primary areas of disagreement (settlements, borders, refugees). Abu Mazen, who competed with Abu Ala and intensely disliked Asfur, helped close the Stockholm channel down because he was upset that Arafat had approved it without his knowledge. Yasir Abd Rabbu was also upset that Stockholm was taking place behind his back and so he resigned in protest.[15]

During the late spring and summer of 2000 the Clinton administration was forced to make some tough decisions about its Middle East policy. Both the Palestinians and the Israelis thought that Ross's step-by-step shuttle diplomacy method had run its course. The Palestinians were beginning to backtrack on policy positions that they had taken in the secret channel. Barak was experiencing coalition problems and needed to make decisions quickly. Barak preferred a summit so that he could either force Arafat to make concessions and reach a final agreement with Israel or expose him as an extremist. He also thought that he could survive politically better with a high-stakes summit than with a series of endless non-reciprocated concessions. Ross, knowing that Arafat was a procrastinator who always put off hard decisions until the last minute, wanted to schedule the summit in August, just before the five-year limit for a final settlement was set to expire. But Clinton wanted to get the summit done before the political conventions of the two parties in August. He did not want to appear to be playing politics with the peace process. The primary foreign policy figures in the administration were divided over the utility of a summit. Albright was worried that Arafat had done nothing to prepare his people for the compromises required by peace and never spoke about Israel in terms of moral legitimacy. Sandy Berger wanted the bottom lines of both sides nailed down before a summit in order to know if the situation was "ripe" for a solution. He wanted some indication that the summit might succeed before he would give his approval. Martin Indyk thought that step-by-step diplomacy had run its course and wanted to up the ante. Ross was willing to go along with what Barak wanted.[16]

Barak was receiving intelligence about Palestinian preparations for another intifada and wanted a chance to expose Arafat as an extremist before it erupted.[17] In the period preceding Camp David II Barak spoke of reaching peace with Arafat or exposing him as if they were equally satisfactory outcomes in his view.[18]

Throughout May and June 2000 Tom Friedman, the *New York Times* columnist and former Middle East correspondent who had close ties to all the parties, kept up a series of columns calling for the convening of another Middle East peace summit. In one column he gave his opinion as to the parameters of an agreement that was likely to come out of the summit. Friedman was co-founder of a Conservative Jewish synagogue in Bethesda, MD with Dennis Ross, the lead American peace negotiator.[19]

June was a month of preparation for the summit and decision. Albright traveled to the Mideast twice and was told by Barak that the pressure-cooker atmosphere of a summit could produce an agreement. Albright was skeptical. When she returned to Jerusalem the second time on June 27 she arrived to witness the meltdown of Barak's coalition. Natan Sharansky had already given Barak notice four days before that he intended to withdraw *Israel B'Aliya* from the coalition. Foreign Minister David Levy publicly came out against a summit before meeting with Albright. The next day when she went to Ramallah she received more opposition. "There was no question that Barak wanted a summit. We were running out of time ... we needed the 'pressure of a summit' to get it done.... There is also no question that Barak did not want a summit.... He was objecting on the basic fact that he wasn't in charge of the schedule," Albright explained to Swisher years later.[20] By the time that Barak arrived in Washington for the summit, Shas and the National Religious Party had also withdrawn from the coalition and Levy refused to accompany Barak as part of the Israeli delegation. Shas voted against the government in a preliminary vote for new elections on June 7. Shas withdrew because Barak refused to provide a list of his "red lines" (bottom lines) to Rabbi Ovadia Yosef, Shas's spiritual leader. Attempts to bribe the party with offers of new funding for its religious school system failed. Barak now had a minority coalition composed of Labor, Meretz, and the Center Party that controlled 42 seats. There was no "plan B" if the summit failed.[21]

The PA leadership went to Washington on June 15. Arafat was in a bad mood and started out by criticizing Barak for his failure to stop building settlements, for not carrying out the third withdrawal, and other Palestinian complaints. Clinton mollified him by showing sympathy for his complaints, but without making any firm commitment — a typical Clinton ploy. Arafat gave his ideas for solving the remaining final status issues. Clinton promised Arafat twice, once after Arafat asked for this reassurance, that he would not be blamed if the summit failed.[22]

Clinton did not believe that the chances of success for the summit were good — or at least that is what he wrote in his memoirs after the fact. But he was afraid that the Middle East peace process would collapse without it. The unilateral Israeli withdrawal from Lebanon had weakened support from the Palestinian public for the peace process. They were upset that they had received so little from the negotiations whereas Hezbollah had never negotiated and received a complete Israeli withdrawal. This, combined with Israeli settlement activity and official PA incitement, produced a volatile mixture that threatened to explode either with or without a summit. Clinton issued an invitation to the two sides to attend a summit at Camp David on July 4. That weekend his senior foreign policy staff spent the weekend at Camp David in preparation for the summit. The summit would begin on July 10 and continue until Clinton departed for a G-8 summit on July 19.[23]

In 1991 the U.S. Institute of Peace, a governmental think tank in Washington, convened a three-day seminar to discuss the history of American mediation in the Arab-Israeli conflict and generate lessons. The seminar produced the following six basic guidelines:

- Successful mediation requires tedious, prolonged pre-negotiation to narrow the agenda.
- Choose a venue for negotiations that is conducive to unpressured, informal discussions.

- Keep in mind that leverage or pressure is of little value until the process is well advanced and the parties can "smell agreement."
- Do not become involved in Israeli internal politics. Deal with the Israeli prime minister as the ultimate decision maker.
- Try to base the negotiating process on already accepted guidelines, for example UNSC Resolutions 242 and 338 and the Camp David agreements.
- Avoid public rejection by the parties of U.S. ideas or proposals.[24]

Camp David II July 10–23, 2000

Rather than discussing at length in chronological order the course of the negotiations throughout the summit,[25] I offer a summary of the mechanics and procedures of the summit and discuss how they might be improved upon for the future.

The basic way the summit functioned was to have separate multinational teams of Americans, Israelis, and Palestinians discussing the three main final status issue areas: borders and settlements, Jerusalem and refugees. There was no official agreed record as there was at Camp David I in 1978, because after two days the Americans gave up any pretense of trying to be neutral and became basically persuaders for the Israelis. Progress was made in all three areas but in widely different degrees — the least progress was made on the refugees issue and the most on Jerusalem. Barak and Arafat did not take part in the daily discussions, but met only once during the summit and then did not discuss anything of substance.

The Israelis and Americans attempted to engage in traditional "bazaar-style" negotiations in which both sides would begin with unrealistic opening positions and then narrow the gap between them by gradually making a series of better offers to the other side until agreement was reached. But the Palestinians refused to go along with this type of bargaining. They, like Egypt and Syria before them, believed in issuing a basic territorial ultimatum or guideline and then negotiate about the details of implementation once the Israelis had agreed to their basic position. Like the Arab countries, Arafat wanted a return to the June 4, 1967, borders — basically the Arab interpretation of UNSC Resolution 242. He also wanted Israel to recognize a theoretical right of return for all the Palestinian refugees from 1948 and 1967 and their descendants. The Palestinians made their biggest concession on Jerusalem when they accepted the Israeli principle that Jewish neighborhoods would become Israeli and Arab neighborhoods would become Palestinian. But Arafat rejected all attempted compromise offers on the subject of the Temple Mount (*Har haBeit, Haram al-Sharif*).[26]

There were a number of factors that contributed to the failure at Camp David. First, the American delegation was top-heavy with American Jews including: Secretary of State Madeleine Albright, National Security Advisor Sandy Berger, Ambassador to Israel Martin Indyk, Middle East negotiator Dennis Ross and his assistant, Aaron Miller. In the modern Middle East Arabs and Muslims have been infected with European anti–Semitism since the 1930s when the Nazis first became involved in the region. Many Arabs take it as an article of faith that Jews control America through the media, Hollywood, and campaign financing. Clinton's choice of foreign policy advisors seemed to confirm this belief. Second, because the summit was such an important political event with consequences for the fall elections many non-foreign policy political appointees were present. This meant that time was wasted and focus was lost. Third, there was inadequate preparation ahead of time. Clinton and his advisors did not know what the bottom lines of the two sides were. This meant that they were in a bad position to mediate because they did not know what the overlapping area for compromise was on each issue. Fourth, both sides were weak and did not believe that they could make certain compromises. Barak was worried because he had a minority coalition and would have to sell any agreement to the remaining members of his coalition, to the religious parties and/or to the Likud. Barak remembered the fate of Rabin. Barak was willing to take risks, but he had to be sensitive on certain issues such as the Temple Mount. Arafat was worried about the falling popularity of the Fatah government, which although it did not have to face new elections needed a certain base level of support among Palestinians. Arafat was worried about what other Arabs and Muslims would say particularly regarding Jerusalem and refugees. In light of the subsequent Hamas electoral victory in the January 2006 election this fear was probably not misplaced. Fifth, although Clinton read several chapters from William Quandt's book *Camp David: Peacemaking and Politics* and Indyk prepared a special study for Clinton on Camp David I, the Americans were unwilling to copy the successful procedures from that summit. Instead of remaining neutral and helping the two sides to narrow the gap, the Americans became persuaders for the Israeli positions and thereby lost their moral influence with the Palestinians. At one point Clinton spoke very harshly to Abu Ala, at the suggestion of American Arabic interpretor Gamal Helal, thereby causing Ala to withdraw into himself for the remainder of the summit. Abu Mazen had also withdrawn because he interpreted American interaction with Mohammed Dahlan, who was hosted at the White House, as support for him for the succession. Thus, he too shut down leaving Arafat without the counsel of his two main moderate supporters. Sixth, Arafat continued to play his advisors off against one another producing fear, wariness, and jealousy. Arafat himself was in a sulk when he arrived and his mood never improved throughout the summit.[27]

Because Barak had not thought through or rehearsed his bargaining positions he was caught off guard when the Arabs in the borders committee refused to make counteroffers. It was this failure, more than anything else, that doomed the summit to failure. For some thirty years the two sides had been involved in an elaborate process of internal bargaining between moderates and hardliners who did not take into account the needs of the other side. This had produced the Allon Plan, named after former 1948 General and Foreign Minister Yigal Allon, which called for a partition of the West Bank between Israel and Jordan with Israel retaining between one-third and forty percent along with the Golan Heights and part of the Sinai. The harder alternative to the Allon Plan was: the Dayan Plan, which called for a functional partition of the West Bank between Israel and Jordan with Israel maintaining security control and the Jordanians maintaining political control. Neither of these two versions of the Jordanian Option was acceptable to King Hussein of Jordan. The Likud initially wanted to annex all of the West Bank, then at Camp David I settled for autonomy (for the Palestinian population not the territory) and after Oslo for a Palestinian state on about 40 percent of the West Bank. During this same time the PLO offered Israel the "democratic secular state," which would be neither democratic in the Western sense nor secular. Later the Palestinians after 1988 adopted the policy of "two states for two peoples" but with the borders and other details not up for negotiation. Only in 1993 did the two sides begin negotiating with each other. Initially this resulted in agreements that were very biased in favor of the Israeli positions, but which Arafat had no intention of fulfilling. It might have been easier and wiser to have had the moderate extremes on both sides — Likud and Hamas — negotiate with each other if either really valued peace enough to sacrifice for it.

Since 1937 the Palestinians have had a double-track approach to the Arab-Israeli conflict. On the one hand they have attempted repeatedly the military option, either by themselves or by proxy through the Arab states. They tried this in the Arab Revolt 1936–39, the 1947–49 war, the June 1967 war, the War of Attrition from 1967 to 1970, the October 1973 war, the 1982 war, the Intifada 1987–93, and the Al-Aksa Intifada 2000-present. Parallel to this the Palestinians have attempted to win diplomatic terms for themselves not through negotiations with Israel, but through the Arab League, the Non-Aligned Movement, and the United Nations. The idea was to use numbers and oil diplomacy to pass resolutions that were hostile to Israel on peace terms and then insist that these terms constituted an "international consesus." These terms would be presented to Israel on a "take it or leave it" non-negotiable basis. The 1974 Arab summit in Rabat passed a resolution adopting the

Palestinian "phase strategy" that called for the Palestinians to use any territory liberated from Israeli control as a base for the liberation of the entire territory of the state of Israel. At the time this was denounced by rejectionists as cover for a Palestinian diplomatic strategy to replace armed struggle. But the wording of the resolution made clear that this was not the case. Because Israelis were well aware of the phase strategy they rejected any peace terms offered by the Palestinians as insincere.[28] This made Israel appear intransigent to Western publics that were not familiar with the history of the dispute.

In Israel UN General Assembly resolutions are ignored and Jerusalem has used its influence with Washington to ensure that Security Council resolutions, which Israel does accept as being binding, reflect Israeli interests. Since 1973 the basis for the Middle East peace process has been UNSC Resolutions 242 and 338; as 338 merely calls on the parties to open negotiations on the basis of 242, it has been basically 242 — passed in November 1967 — that has been the basis for negotiations. At Camp David II there were three different interpretations of 242 present. The Arab interpretation was that the future borders of Israel must be the June 4, 1967, lines. The Israeli interpretation was merely that it had to return some, but not all — and not even on all fronts — of the territory conquered in the June 1967 war. The American interpretation was that the majority of the territory would be returned so that the weight of conquest would not be reflected in the new borders and that it was binding on all fronts. The reason for this discrepancy is the deliberate ambiguity of the wording of the resolution that refers to the "non-admissibility of the acquisition of territory by force," "secure and recognized borders," and withdrawal from "territories occupied in the recent conflict." The language was carefully negotiated by London, Washington, and Moscow so that it would be acceptable to both Israel and the Arabs. Israel accepted the "non-admissibility" language because it came in the preamble, which in UN resolutions has no binding effect. Often in Israel it is printed without even the text of the preamble. For years the PLO refused to recognize 242 both because it was not explicit enough for them and because it referred to the Palestinians only in terms of refugees and not in terms of a people with national rights.[29]

When the Palestinians look at diplomacy in the Middle East conflict they look at the problem as dating back to 1948 and that their compromise has been to accept only 22 percent of the territory of the former British mandate in Palestine. Israel argues that by refusing to negotiate from 1948 to 1967 the Palestinians lost any right to negotiate about what happened before 1967 and that any compromise should reflect that the Palestinians were part of the Arab side that forced the war through its actions and lost. Many Israelis also argue that because the West Bank was illegally occupied by Jordan from 1949 to 1967, Resolution 242 does not apply to it as it was "unassigned territory" legally belonging to nobody since 1948 when the British mandate ended. This means that until there is a peace agreement the Israeli occupation remains legal. The American State Department has never accepted this argument, but many American jurists have accepted it. Traditionally Congress has been much closer to the Israeli position, the State Department has been close to the Arab position, and the White House has been somewhere between the two.[30]

Arafat and Barak had never gotten along or trusted each other. But this does not necessarily preclude being able to negotiate peace. At Camp David I, Menahem Begin and Anwar Sadat did not get along. Sadat, like Peres, was a visionary, whereas Begin, like Rabin, was a details man obsessed with security and legality. Sadat was angry that after having made his bold gesture of a trip to Jerusalem and a speech in the Knesset Begin refused to negotiate peace on his terms. This was gotten around by Ezer Weizman, who had good relations with Sadat and other Egyptians, going to meet with the Egyptians and explain Israel's position. It took another seven months of negotiations after the conclusion of the summit to sign a peace treaty. This could have worked at Camp David II. Generally the Israeli and Palestinian teams had good working relationships. Abu Ala and Asfur had been negotiating with the Israelis throughout the Oslo process. Ben-Ami and Sher had negotiated with Abu Ala at Stockholm, and Shahak had negotiated with the Palestinians in the Oslo II negotiations and with the Syrians. The problem was that Arafat was not willing to make fundamental compromises — he had not prepared his public for the necessity of making these compromises, in fact he had always downplayed the importance of the peace process when speaking in Arabic.[31] Barak's problem was that he was unwilling to listen to advice from others. He still thought of himself as a general in uniform who made the decision after listening to what others thought.[32]

On the sixth day of the summit the Israeli delegation proposed that the inner Arab neighborhoods of Jerusalem would be autonomous and provided services by the Palestinian state, but under Israeli sovereignty while the outer Arab neighborhoods of Kfar Aqab, Kalandia, and Beit Hanina would be under Arab sovereignty. On the territorial question Israel was seeking 10.5 percent of the West Bank so that the settler blocs would be under Israeli sovereignty and 80 percent of the Jewish settlers on the West Bank would be included in these. Rabin had contemplated giving back only 70 and 80 percent of the West Bank — the Allon Plan plus — to Palestine. The Israelis tried to work through Mohammed Dahlan and Mohammed Rashid, "the two Mohammeds," and through the Americans to get Arafat to make a counteroffer that would enable serious bargaining to begin.[33]

The next day Barak began retreating slightly from the Israeli offer and offered only 88.7 percent of the West Bank instead of 89.5 percent and only one village instead of three. Clinton blew up at Barak with some pent up hostility over Geneva. "I can't go see Arafat with a retrenchment. You want to present these ideas directly to Arafat ... you go ahead and see if you can sell it. There is no way I can. This is not real.... I went to Shepherdstown and was told nothing by you for four days. I went to Geneva and felt like a wooden Indian doing your bidding." Clinton ended by shouting, "I simply will not do it."[34]

The next day Ross proposed to the Israeli team that they modify their Jerusalem offer to give the Arabs sovereignty over both the Muslim and Christian Quarters in the Old City and custodianship over the Temple Mount. After discussing the American ideas with Barak the Israelis presented a modified version to the Palestinians: less Palestinian responsibility over the inner neighborhoods and continued Israeli sovereignty over the Christian Quarter. The Palestinians gave no official response to either the Israeli or the American proposals. The Palestinian delegation was divided: those with the least weight, Dahlan and Rashid, were the most open to compromise; Akram Haniya and Yasir Abd Rabbu were the most hardline, and the rest merely tried to guess where Arafat stood on any issue and agree with him.[35]

Barak then agreed to go down to Israel annexing nine percent of the West Bank, with a one percent swap north of Gaza; the Palestinians would get seven out of eight of the outer neighborhoods, plus both the Christian and Muslim Quarters in the Old City and police powers, planning, zoning, and security in the inner neighborhoods.[36] In reality Barak felt constrained by what the Israeli public would accept Israel offering. He was probably fishing for an American proposal, like the Clinton Parameters of December, that he could present to the Israeli public as an ultimatum that Israel must accept.

On the ninth day of the summit all the senior American team members agreed that Clinton must put pressure on Arafat to bargain seriously — to engage the Israelis with counteroffers. Otherwise, Ross felt that Clinton was entitled to blame Arafat for the failure of the summit because he had not made a good-faith effort. Barak told Ross emotionally, "Arafat was never serious, never a partner." Barak said he would probably have to go into a national unity government, if he was not already too weak politically for that. In desperation Clinton, who was about to depart for the G-8 summit in Okinawa, phoned a number of Arab and Muslim leaders to put pressure on Arafat. But because he was unwilling to divulge the details of the offers most of them naturally refused to help by second-guessing Arafat. President Ben Ali of Tunisia and King Abdullah of Jordan agreed to urge Arafat to defer on Jerusalem — make an agreement that would leave the Jerusalem issue to be tackled later.[37]

Yossi Ginossar, Rabin and Barak's link to Arafat, went to see Arafat in his cabin. He found the Palestinian leader paralyzed — or feigning — with fear about making any concessions on Jerusalem. He told Ginossar that the Jewish Temple had not even been in Jerusalem, but rather had been in Nablus — thus confusing the Jews with the Samaritans. Arafat considered himself an expert on monotheistic religions — Judaism and Christianity as well as Islam, when in reality he knew only about a few rituals. This had the effect of putting off the Americans — even Egyptian born Gamal Helal, the translator. The problem is that in the Koran and Haditha Jerusalem is referred to only by inference as the far mosque that Mohammed traveled to in his night journey on his magical steed. Thus for a Muslim, and Arafat as a young man associated with the Muslim Brotherhood in Egypt, Jewish claims are irrelevant. Christians can understand and accept the Jewish claims because they are part of the New and Old Testaments of the Bible. Thus Helal, a Christian, was personally offended by Arafat's claims — and as an American he was not forced to accept Arafat's claims of religious knowledge at face value.[38]

Clinton departed for Okinawa and the summit continued for three days awaiting his return. But without Clinton there little was accomplished: Albright lacked the detailed knowledge to be taken seriously by the two sides and Ross was considered biased by the Palestinians. Arafat, in fact, asked Clinton to fire Ross as a mediator before Camp David. The more flexible Palestinians were prepared to continue discussing issues, but the Israelis were not happy with this because they knew that the Palestinians would simply pocket any concessions that they made while Arafat would cancel any concessions made by his side.

The Americans, upon Clinton's return on the evening of the thirteenth day, began focusing on bridging proposals for Jerusalem. By then Barak had retrenched and was unwilling to grant the Arabs any sovereignty within the walls of the Old City. But Ben-Ami told Erakat that they were willing to make special arrangements for the Arab quarters in the Old City that in practice amounted to the same thing as in the inner neighborhoods. On the Temple Mount Israel offered the Palestinians "religious sovereignty" — daily control — and they would retain the remaining sovereignty. The Palestinians countered by offering that neither side should have sovereignty. But Ben-Ami insisted that Israel must have some sovereignty. After Camp David, Israel was to change its position and accept no sovereignty, but by then the Palestinians had also changed their position and insisted on sovereignty. The Americans ended up offering the Palestinians several options for the Haram al-Sharif/Temple Mount. The Arabs could have sovereignty over the surface of the Mount, and thus over the two mosques, while Israel would have sovereignty over the substructure. Or, neither side would have sovereignty and either the United Nations or God would have sovereignty.

Much of the post-summit controversy has focused on the territorial differences or on Jerusalem. This is understandable: there were no maps of the various offers produced at the summit so subsequent maps were made from memory and were not authoritative. And many people have conflated the Clinton Parameter offer on territory with the Camp David position. Jerusalem was the focus because it is such an emotional issue that people beyond the actual parties to the conflict feel they have a stake in. But the real issue that precluded any agreement at the summit was refugees. The Palestinians insisted that Israel recognize a theoretical right of any refugee to return to Israel. The negotiators said that only a small portion of these would actually return. But the Israelis were not about to fall into this trap. Israel has always refused a right of return to every refugee and insisted that it have a veto over returnees so that only a limited number have been allowed to return for the purposes of family reunification. An unlimited return would swamp the Jewish state and make it a binational state in which the Jews would soon lose their majority. It was an attempt at politicide through the womb. In the 1995 Beilin-Abu Mazen agreement the Palestinians agreed that there would be no right of return to Israel. Even if there had been agreement on the other issues, the refugee issue prevented an agreement at Camp David and again at Taba in January 2001. By 2003 the Palestinians had changed their mind again and the 1995 position on refugees was reproduced in the Geneva Accord. But for Arafat this probably was just a device to prop up the Israeli left and embarrass the Sharon government that he would not feel bound by if the Israeli government suddenly decided to accept it.[39]

It was almost inevitable, given the huge gaps between the positions of the two sides, that they would fail to reach a solution in only two weeks of bargaining. Egypt and Israel required sixteen months of negotiations to reach a peace treaty in 1979 and this was despite the fact that Israel had agreed to return all of the Sinai to Egypt before the negotiations really began. Based on the greater importance and sensitivity of the West Bank to Israel in historical, religious, and security terms than the Sinai and the much greater demonization of Arafat within Israel it was inevitable that it would take even longer for the two sides to reach a peace agreement. In 1999 this author predicted to Condolezza Rice that Clinton would engage in a high-profile peacemaking effort and would fail for this very reason. Barak wanted Camp David to be a trap for Arafat; Arafat wanted to survive the trap rather than make peace. So Arafat rejected the Israeli offer on the issue of Jerusalem rather than on the issue of the refugees, because he would have the widest possible Arab and Muslim support on Jerusalem.[40]

The main fault of Arafat is that despite a number of meetings between Israeli and Palestinian officials during the period after Camp David from July to September 2000, there was no high level attempt to reengage in negotiations. There was also the decision by Arafat to engage in another intifada, the Al-Aksa Intifada, as a means of softening Israel up so that new concessions could be extracted. Arafat, who fundamentally misunderstood Israeli politics, did not realize that even if this worked with Barak, which it did, it would merely restore his previous image as a terrorist leader and make him unfit for Israel as a peace partner in the eyes of the Israeli public. Barak also failed to realize that any concessions made under fire would erode support for a deal among the Israeli public. Barak also gave the IDF a free hand to put down the AAI by force, without understanding that this paid into Arafat's hand by increasing his support among Palestinians and abroad. By the time he had the IDF under control Arafat had lost control of the Intifada. Israeli minister Anton Lipkin-Shahak saw Arafat as riding a tiger from which he could not safely dismount.[41]

The main mistake of Clinton was to wait until days before Christmas 2000, five months after Camp David, to come up with his bridging proposals instead of either offering them at the summit or immediately afterward. On Jerusalem the American proposal was close to the Palestinian proposal made at Camp David. On the territorial issue Clinton split the difference between Israel and the Palestinians and offered Arafat between 94 and 96 percent of the West Bank (the difference is because Israel does not count the Jerusalem municipality as part of the West Bank whereas the Palestinians do count all of the Palestinian portions of the city as part of the West Bank). He also offered the Palestinians an additional 1–3 percent of Israeli land as compensation, so that in reality the Palestinians would be getting up to 99 percent of the West Bank's acreage outside of Jerusalem. Israel would also provide Palestine with a guaranteed passage between Gaza and the West Bank. On Jerusalem Israel would have full sovereignty over Jewish neighborhoods and the Palestinians over Arab neighborhoods, with the Palestinians having the choice on the Haram mentioned above. Clinton favored Israel on most security issues giving Palestine sovereignty over its airspace, but requiring it to reach an agreement with Israel that accommodated the training needs of the Israeli Air Force. Israel would be allowed to maintain its early warning stations on the West Bank with dual manning, with the situation to be reviewed after ten years. The IDF would be positioned in the Jordan Valley for six years. There would be no right of return of Palestinian refugees to Israel. And the signing of an agreement would terminate all claims between the two parties and end the hostilities.[42]

Israel accepted the Clinton Parameters after two days of debate, with reservations that were within the scope of the parameters. Clinton had given the two sides five days to reply. Barak made his announcement of acceptance on Israeli television on Christmas Day. The Palestinians came back with a "Yes, but..." answer with so many reservations (territory, time frame, refugees) that the net effect was a rejection of the parameters. But Clinton refused to say so openly at the time. He wanted the process to continue.[43]

There were some differences within the American team on the parameters primarily on the territorial issue. Rob Malley, Gamal Helal, and Aaron Miller thought that the Palestinians were entitled to 100 percent of the West Bank, so that any land swaps in compensation for territory annexed by Israel should be on a 1:1 basis. Malley and Helal believed that this was an issue of fairness. Miller pragmatically believed that since the other Arab states had either received (Egypt, Jordan) or were demanding (Syria) a 100 percent return of territory, Arafat or any Palestinian leader could not afford to settle for less. There were no differences on refugees and the differences on Jerusalem and security were minor. Ross wanted the deal to reflect what both sides needed for the deal to stick, not what they wanted or felt entitled to.[44]

But their differences could easily have been hashed out between the president and his principal Middle East advisors in a day at Camp David or the White House. So it was merely a matter of taking a day out when all of the principals would meet together within weeks of the end of the summit. Had this happened, the Al-Aksa Intifada probably would not have been avoided, but it would have been much clearer exactly what Arafat was rejecting and he would not seem to be benefiting from violence when the Clinton Parameters were eventually released. Instead Clinton left it to the two parties to substantially narrow the gap before he would call a second summit. Needless to say, a second summit was never called.[45]

The Al-Aksa Intifada

Over time Arafat was steadily militarizing his police force. Most of the members of the police force had some sort of military/paramilitary training as they came from either the brigades of the Palestinian Liberation Army stationed in the Arab countries prior to 1982 or from Fatah. By the spring of 2000 he had organized the police force in Gaza into a 12,000 man division complete with military academies, and battalion commanders and others had been trained in courses around the Arab world in Algeria, Egypt, Libya,

Morocco, Yemen and Pakistan. By then he had also established the nucleus of a navy, an air defense arm, and an air force. The goal was an armed force of 100,000. By then the total number of security personnel, all ostensibly police, was 45,000 or ten times the ratio of police to population as in the United States. They had some 40,000 illegal weapons beyond those allowed by Oslo. In many ways the PA was repeating what the Hagana/Palmach had done in 1945–48 and what Fatah itself had done in Fatahland, Lebanon in 1980–82. In April he gave orders to senior Fatah members Mohammed Dahlan and Marwan Barghouti to prepare for a return to terrorism against Israel. Israeli military intelligence, Aman, had predicted in March 2000 that a new Intifada would break out if the peace process failed or in order to advance their cause.[46]

By late May 2000 Arafat had equipped much of his "police" force with armored personnel carriers armed with machine-guns and mortars, illegal under the terms of the Oslo accords. During the May Nakba riots Tanzim had taken the lead away from the police in fomenting violence.

In late July the Palestinian security forces began training exercises in which they practiced to assault Jewish settlements with infantry forces equipped with APCs and snipers. Arafat figured that the United States and Israel both needed the peace process too badly to complain about this violation of the Oslo accords. At the same time the PA began stocking up on emergency food supplies and hospitals began stocking up on blood and on medicines, in some cases taking them off the shelves for consumers. Petrol was stockpiled along with other basic commodities at both the national and institutional levels. The PA's ministry of supplies conducted a series of meetings with large wholesalers to discuss what supplies needed to be stockpiled. On July 24, 2000, near the end of the Camp David summit, PA Minister of Information Hassan Kashef wrote an article in *Al-Ayyam* calling for a national campaign to prepare to defend the state that would be proclaimed on September 13. He listed basic food supplies that every family should stockpile. He also called for the PA to adopt a strategy of guerrilla warfare. The PA seemed to have learned the lessons of 1938-39 and of 1948 and intended to be prepared for a new war of liberation.[47]

On the night of July 3–4 the PLO's Central Committee had voted to declare a state on September 13, 2000, no matter what the state of the negotiations were. This was a year after the Sharm al-Sheikh summit and was the goal set for negotiating a final settlement. Before he left for Camp David, Arafat met with Fatah commanders to discuss the military consequences of the expected failure of the summit. In late July, antitank ditches were dug and trap holes were dug under major roads and filled with explosives. From mid–September onwards policemen began infiltrating in increasing numbers in Area B portions of the West Bank that were under Israel's security umbrella.[48]

On Friday July 21 the Imam of Al-Aksa Mosque gave an inflammatory sermon in which he declared that it was the duty of Muslims to liberate all of Palestine as it had been liberated from the Crusaders. "It should be clear that Palestine is not owned by the Palestinians. It ... belongs to all the Muslims.... Any permanent agreement with the disbelievers is void automatically. The permanent agreement means the cancelling of jihad, which can never happen.... What a great treason is going on in Camp David." Three days later, Ikrama Sabri, Arafat's handpicked mufti of all of Palestine issued a series of *fatwas* that would have undercut Arafat's ability to reach a compromise even if he wanted to. He issued a *fatwa* (binding religious opinion) against the acceptance of compensation by Palestinian refugees. He declared Palestine to be a sacred *waqf*—Muslim land held in trust by the Muslim community—that could not be traded by anyone.[49]

As soon as he returned from Camp David, Arafat asked the League of Ulema of Palestine for a similar *fatwa* to that issued by Ikrama Sabri. He received an even stronger *fatwa* that rejected compensation for refugees, that declared all of Palestine—from the Mediterranean Sea to the Jordan River—to be a *waqf* of Muslims, that the liberation of Jerusalem was a sacred duty, and that jihad (in the meaning of holy war) was the sacred duty of every Muslim. He had ensured that he could not negotiate a peace treaty even if he wanted to.[50]

PA officials began a campaign of religious incitement against Israel. Abu Ala told the PA's newspaper, *Al-Ayaam,* that the Israelis declared their desire at Camp David to demolish the Al-Aksa Mosque, a complete lie. Near the end of Camp David the PA media began a campaign of incitement that continued until the outbreak of the Al-Aksa Intifada in late September. In August the PA ordered all teenagers sent to military summer camps for indoctrination and paramilitary training. There they were indoctrinated with pre–1988 PLO ideology of liberating all of Palestine. Arafat also let dozens of Islamist terrorists, jailed at the insistence of Israel, released on extended vacations. [51]

An interview with a "senior administration official" quoted in the *New York Times* in August stated that a final settlement had to be negotiated by the end of September, as the Barak government would not survive long once the Knesset reconvened in October. This gave Arafat the impression that the pressure would be off of him after that so he hardened his position. Ross returned to the Middle East on August 17 to explore the possibility of Arafat and Barak meeting with Clinton at the UN in September during its new session. Barak said that a summit was possible only if Arafat softened his positions. Ross found no ground for progress by the end of August. Shlomo

Ben-Ami went to Egypt to hear new ideas on Jerusalem from Foreign Minister Amr Musa. The "new idea" was that Israel abandon Jerusalem as "the idea of partial or shared sovereignty is contrary to international law and Egypt cannot agree to that."[52]

During the UN millenium session in September 2000, Arafat by chance found himself alone in an elevator with Barak and his wife. Arafat, trying to play cute, asked Mrs. Barak if she knew who that man next to her was. The two did not exchange a word. Arafat hardened his position on Jerusalem so as to discourage any further attempts at settlement by Clinton. But Arafat was warned very sternly by the Clinton administration not to even think about declaring independence. Barak invited Arafat to his home on September 25 and the two talked for about 45 minutes and the two talked, but no progress was made. Barak phoned Clinton and told him that he would go beyond Rabin, Clinton's hero and Barak's mentor, in making peace. Israelis claimed that Arafat never mentioned Sharon's upcoming visit to the Temple Mount during the meeting.[53]

Arafat took a decision to embark on a liberation struggle, a new intifada, without first declaring independence. After all, he could always argue that the PLO's declaration of independence from November 1988 was still in effect. His goal for the first phase was to break off the peace process with Israel while retaining links with the United States. This would allow Arafat to use Washington to restrain Jerusalem from crushing the intifada at the beginning. He hoped to use the intifada to spark a regional Arab-Israeli war, as in 1948 or 1967, but if no general war ensued he would continue the intifada until pressure from Washington and the Israeli population forced Barak to sue for peace on Palestinian terms.[54]

With elections looking like a sure thing for the winter of 2001 or before, Netanyahu and Sharon began jockeying for position within the Likud. Sharon decided that an "inspection visit" to the Temple Mount would go down well with Likud primary voters when it came time to vote for the Likud leadership. Sharon asked Ben-Ami, the internal security minister, for permission to visit the Temple Mount on September 28, the weekend before *Rosh HaShana,* the Jewish new year. Ross appealed to Ben-Ami to forbid the visit. But Ben-Ami and Barak were afraid that to refuse a permit would make them look weak and hurt them in the general election. Sharon would talk about every Jew's right to visit Judaism's holiest site. Ben-Ami phoned Jibril Rajoub and arranged the visit. Rajoub stipulated only that Sharon not attempt to enter either of the mosques on the Mount. Ben-Ami conveyed this condition to Sharon and he agreed and the permit was issued. For Rajoub and Arafat it was a godsend — it gave them a pretext for the intifada, and eventually its name, that ordinary Palestinians and Muslims around the world could rally to while those in the West and even in Israel might hold Sharon responsible.[55]

Hostilities actually began the day before Sharon's visit with an attack on a settler convoy on the West Bank and then on the morning of the visit with an attack on an Israeli jeep patrol by Palestinian police. Before that a Fatah-affiliated Islamist group had been coordinating rock throwing at an IDF post at the Netzarim junction in Gush Katif in Gaza since September 17. The idea was to estrange relations between the IDF and the PA security forces before the intifada broke out. But both the Mossad and Israeli military intelligence (Aman) came to the conclusion that the outbreak of the Intifada was spontaneous rather than planned.[56]

The Sharon visit lasted about 45 minutes and consisted of Sharon accompanied by five Likud MPs and dozens of elite police officers. He was met on the Mount by a crowd of hundreds of Palestinian demonstrators accompanied by Palestinian MKs. The crown shouted various slogans including: "Sharon is a murderer"; "We won't forget Sabra and Shatilla"; "With blood and with fire we'll free Al-Aksa." The last was a modification of a Jewish slogan from the mandate period. The Palestinians threw stones and the police fired rubber bullets, no one was killed and about 30 policemen were lightly wounded along with about 15 demonstrators, and MK Ahmad Tibi broke his arm. Five protestors claimed they were hit by rubber bullets. [57]

Rajoub was disappointed by the turnout. After the visit ended he held a meeting with key Fatah figures. They began spreading the rumor that a massacre had taken place on the Haram and riots soon swept the Old City and spread to Rachel's Tomb in Bethlehem, to Hebron, and by October 2 to other sites throughout the West Bank. In that first week five Israelis and more than sixty Palestinians were killed. At Jacob's Tomb in Nablus the Palestinians desecrated a Jewish shrine and then turned it into a mosque. Eleven Israeli Palestinians were killed by live ammunition by Israeli police when the rioting spread to Israeli towns in the first two weeks of October. After this the Al-Aksa Intifada, as it was soon dubbed by the PA, ended within Israel but the moderate Israeli Arabs were outraged enough that they stayed home during the next election and the nationalists voted for Arab parties. Albright called a meeting with Arafat and Barak in Paris and both promised to end the fighting. Arafat refused to sign his agreement with Barak and insisted that it be signed at Sharm al-Sheikh. Beilin explains this as Arafat wanting to give Mubarak a forum. The fighting soon resumed, as it did after another meeting with Clinton in Sharm al-Sheikh. Clinton set up George Mitchell, fresh from his triumphs in Northern Ireland in 1998-99, to head a commission on the causes of the violence. It consisted of former Senators Mitchell and Warren Rudman and European and Muslim representatives. At the second meeting Sharon attended along with Barak and the latter offered him a post in a national emergency government. Sharon agreed on condition that Barak take all the Israeli offers to the Palestinians off the table, which Barak refused to do. In Paris Albright ordered the gates of the U.S. Embassy closed in Arafat's face so that she could talk to him when he walked out of the meeting. This only encouraged him to escalate the violence. By late October the intifada was militarized with the Tanzim and PA security forces taking a greater role. There were daily attacks on Israeli settlements and sniping on Jerusalem suburbs.[58]

For the three months between the beginning of the Al-Aksa Intifada and the Clinton Parameters the two sides continued to meet and the Israelis offered minor concessions on the Temple Mount and refugee issues while the Palestinians stayed pat. Israeli elections were announced in November for February 2001. After the American election in November 2000, Ross warned Arafat that Bush would probably win the election and that in the new year Arafat would have to deal with both Sharon and Bush. But Arafat, with his Arab dynastic understanding of politics, thought that George W. Bush would be like his father in his Middle East positions and would be more sympathetic to the Palestinians than Clinton was. This was because of the Bush family's oil ties to Saudi Arabia and George H. W. Bush's pressure on Shamir in 1991 during his presidency. Arafat's understanding of American politics was even shakier than his understanding of Israeli politics.[59]

Taba was the site of Israeli-Palestinian negotiations from January 21 to 27, 2001. Ben-Ami headed the Israeli team, which consisted of Yossi Beilin (refugees), Gilead Sher, Amnon Shahak, and Yossi Sard, while the talks were supervised from Jerusalem by Barak and Peres. The Palestinian team consisted of Abu Ala, Saeb Erakat, and Nabil Sha'ath. The Palestinians were divided among themselves as to whether or not they had rejected the Clinton Parameters or merely modified them. But the Palestinians refused to make any major concessions on either Jerusalem or refugees. Saeb Erakat admitted that Arafat was not eager for an agreement. And Barak had told Clinton by phone on New Year's Day that he had no intention of concluding a peace agreement before the election in February. After a week the Israeli delegation withdrew as they saw no prospect of an agreement and their continued presence would be an electoral liability to Barak and Labor. Miguel Moratinos, the former Spanish ambassador to Israel served as the European Union's representative at the talks. He observed but did not mediate. Taba would go down in the mythology of the Israeli left as a great missed opportunity by Israel. Martin Indyk, who was briefed by the Israeli negotiators, believes that the two sides may have been closer than at Camp David but were still far apart.[60]

But Arafat was still waiting for Bush. Bush, Dick Cheney, and Colin Powell were briefed by Clinton, Ross, Berger, and Albright during the transition briefings not to trust Arafat. President George W. Bush told Martin Indyk in March 2001, "Clinton and Barak were ... desperate to make a deal. They made Arafat an incredible offer but he turned them down and resorted to violence. The Israelis elected Sharon. Now there's nothing to be done because Arafat already rejected an offer that Sharon is not going to repeat. There's no Nobel Peace Prize to be had there." The Mitchell Commission issued its report at the end of April 2001 and Bush did not tackle the Israeli-Palestinian issue until 2003, when he did so mainly as cover for the invasion of Iraq.[61]

Conclusion

Israeli academic and peace process veteran Itamar Rabinovich divides the Western reactions to Camp David II into four schools: orthodox, revisionist, deterministic, and eclectic. The orthodox school consists of the Clinton administration and the Barak government and Israeli Arabists such as Barry and Judith Rubin, and Danny Rubinstein. They both blame Arafat for the failure of the summit. The revisionist school consists in Israel of veterans of the peace process from the Israeli center-left such as Peres, Ron Pundak, and Uri Savir. It also consists in the United States of Rob Malley and Hussein Aghi, and Clayton Swisher, with the latter being the most articulate spokesman. The Israeli revisionists have a vested interest in protecting themselves from fallout from the failed peace process and possibly sour grapes that Barak excluded them from its final phase. The American revisionists are interested both in correcting errors made in American mediation and in balancing the record by spreading out the blame. Swisher does a very credible and valuable job of pointing out errors in American mediation, but he has a definite pro-Palestinian bias. The deterministic school consists of the Israeli right and their American Jewish supporters. They are interested both in "protecting" Israel from future peace processes with the PLO and with clearing the reputation of the Likud after the Rabin assassination. Their most elegant spokesmen are Israeli-American journalist Yossef Bodansky and Israeli academic Efraim Karsh, based in London. But Rabinovich also puts Henry Kissinger into this category. The eclectic school finds multiple causes for the failure. Its leading spokesmen are Dr. Menahem Klein and Yossi Beilin, as well as Gilead Sher, Barak's negotiator at Camp David and Taba. French journalist Charles Enderlin would also fit into this category.[62]

This author fits into the eclectic category because I have taken elements from all the three other schools. When I first read Bodansky's account three years ago I found it interesting, disturbing and ordered a copy. It was easy to dismiss it because of its lack of sourcing, but I found in re-reading it in tandem with Karsh's fully-sourced account that it was entirely consistent. My only qualification is that the deterministic school sees Arafat as a brilliant mastermind, whereas I, like the Rubins, see him as the supreme opportunist. I believe that initially he attempted to appease both the Islamists and Israel and play them off against one another. But when the combination of his regime's corruption and Israeli pressure made this impossible he sided with his own past, his people, and the Islamists against Israel. It may be that the deterministic school is correct about Arafat. But in the end it makes little difference if the orthodox or the determinist camp is correct — the end result is the same: Arafat was unsuitable as a peace partner for Israel.

Swisher makes valuable points, but they should be used to improve future performance at future summits rather than to assess blame. Swisher ignores all of Arafat's activities before Camp David and whitewashes his actions after. I find him much more convincing when dealing with the Syrian track than with the Palestinian track. I think he goes beyond Malley and Aghi's account, which merely seeks to balance the record. I have not read either Pundak or Peres and so cannot comment on them further other than to state that they both have vested personal interests in taking the positions that they do.

Part II.
The Northern Ireland Peace Process

FIVE

The Belfast Agreement

The Origins of the Peace Process

The Northern Ireland peace process that resulted in the Good Friday or Belfast Agreement of April 9, 1998, began almost a decade earlier, predating the end of the Cold War. Two separate processes started off in 1988 that culminated in the formal start of the peace process over five years later. The first was the Hume-Adams talks that lasted from January to September 1988. This was a semi-formal series of organized discussions between the two main Irish Catholic or nationalist parties in Northern Ireland, the Social Democratic and Labour Party (SDLP) led by John Hume and Sinn Fein led by Gerry Adams. The two parties exchanged position papers and engaged in a series of organized discussions over the nature of the British presence in Northern Ireland and the nature of the Northern Ireland conflict. Sinn Fein, which everyone but its own officers considered to be the political wing of the Irish Republican Army (IRA) terrorist group, argued that it was the British imperialist presence in Ireland that caused the conflict. The SDLP asserted that it was the division between the two ethno-religious communities in Ireland, the pro-British Protestant unionists and the Catholic Irish nationalists that resulted in the conflict.[1] Unless the unionists could be persuaded to agree to a united Ireland it would not occur. The two parties were unable to reach agreement after more than eight months of discussion but the two leaders agreed to stay in touch.

Simultaneously the SDLP was engaged in a series of discussions with the two main unionist parties, the Ulster Unionist Party (UUP) and the Democratic Unionist Party (DUP) of Ian Paisley — also known as the Paisleyites — in Germany. Both of these talks resulted in further discussions that eventually served as the basis of the peace process. Northern Ireland Secretary Peter Brooke, from an established Ulster family — the Fermanagh branch had provided the province's third prime minister, Sir Basil Brooke (later Lord Brookeborough) who ruled from 1943 to 1963 and had a reputation for inflexibility and bigotry — arrived in Northern Ireland in July 1989. During 1990 he signed off on renewed secret contacts between MI5 (the internal counter-intelligence and anti-terrorism service) and the IRA as long as they were deniable. In November 1990 he gave a speech in his Westminster constituency on the British mainland in which he stated, "The British government has no selfish strategic or economic interest in Northern Ireland: our role is to help, enable, and encourage." The statement was solicited from him by John Hume in order to prove its point from his 1988 discussions with Sinn Fein. Brooke's semantic signals to Republicans during his three-year tenure were a repetition of previous British policy from the 1970s. Merlyn Rees made similar statements in the run-up to the 1975 IRA truce.[2]

Brooke initiated a series of discussions among the four main constitutional parties in Northern Ireland — the SDLP, the two unionist parties, and the nonsectarian bicommunal Alliance Party of Northern Ireland — in March 1991 that lasted for four months until early July. The British and Irish presses both blamed the unionists for the collapse of the talks. The talks continued under Brooke's successor, Patrick Mayhew, in the summer and fall of 1992 before ending on November 10 with no result. The talks were conceived by London as a means of keeping pressure on Sinn Fein by giving the British an alternative to a settlement with the Republicans. Some progress was made, but Dublin refused to amend its constitution as the unionists were demanding. The second round of talks resulted in some serious discussion between the parties on power-sharing and North-South relations, but ultimately the priorities of the SDLP and the unionists were too far apart with the former content to hold back until the Republicans were willing to make peace. Hume introduced a scheme of governing the province through six commissioners: one from each of the main communities, one from Dublin, one from London, and one from Brussels.[3] The unionists were not impressed. The importance of the Brooke-Mayhew talks is twofold. First, it initiated the three-strand arrangement that was used in the Good Friday Agreement. The first strand was arrangements within the province. The second strand was North-South ties between Northern Ireland and the Republic. And the third strand was East-West ties between Britain, Northern Ireland and the Republic. Second, it began the rise in importance of David Trimble who headed the third-strand team for the UUP. Trimble had a falling out with "liberal Unionist" Ken Maginnis who feared that Strand 3 would just give Dublin another chance to tighten its contacts with London and through London influence events in Northern Ireland. UUP leader James Molyneaux, Reg Empey, and Jeffrey Donaldson were the Strand 1 team. Reg Empey would eventually become the leader of the UUP after Trimble resigned in 2006. Donaldson was Trimble's most important internal foe within the UUP from 1998 to 2003.

Ken Maginnis joined Chris and Michael McGimpsey in the Strand 2 talks. Trimble impressed Michael McGimpsey with his ability to think quickly on his feet and analytically. The Unionists came out of the talks with some credit, but the two governments later used Unionist submissions in the Mayhew talks as the basis for the Framework Documents of February 1995.[4]

The unionists wished to end the role of formal Irish consultation in the administration of Northern Ireland through the conference secretariat near Belfast at Maryfield, Northern Ireland that resulted from the Anglo-Irish Agreement of November 1985. The unionists had been content to accept direct rule from London in March 1972 in order to avoid both a united Ireland and power-sharing. The nationalists were not happy with direct rule but preferred it to the autonomy of Stormont rule from 1922 to 1972. Unionists and loyalists combined in a workers' strike to topple the Sunningdale power-sharing experiment in early 1974 that involved the SDLP, a breakaway faction of the Ulster Unionists led by former party leader Brian Faulkner, and Alliance. The loyalists and the IRA had both worked separately to topple the new power-sharing executive that lasted in power for five months.

Sinn Fein began competing against the SDLP in provincial local and assembly elections in 1982. They had dramatic gains in the 1983. Prime Minister Margaret Thatcher of Britain negotiated the Anglo-Irish Agreement with Taoiseach (Prime Minister) Garret FitzGerald of Ireland in 1985 as a means of making the SDLP more competitive with Sinn Fein in Northern elections. The unionist community was outraged by what they considered to be a betrayal by their champion and reacted with a series of strikes and protests that resulted in the collapse of the assembly in 1986. The unionists suddenly had an incentive to enter into power-sharing discussions with the SDLP in order to free themselves from the Anglo-Irish Agreement and the danger of eventual joint sovereignty or even a united Ireland.[5]

The Political Parties

The common point in these various initiatives was the SDLP, which had connections with the Irish government in Dublin and with the two main Irish political parties, Fianna Fail and Fine Gael, with the unionists and Alliance, and with Sinn Fein. The SDLP was created in August 1970 by the merger of two small left-wing nationalist parties, and an independent former member of the Nationalist Party, Austin Currie, with three independent members of parliament from the Northern Ireland parliament (Stormont) who had been members of the Northern Ireland Civil Rights Association (NICRA). Gerry Fitt had been appointed leader because he was the party's only Westminster

MP and thus its link to the wider world. John Hume, the most dynamic and outspoken of the three NICRA independents, became deputy leader. The SDLP quickly became the successor to the Nationalist Party, which had served as the ineffective opposition party in the Stormont parliament from 1925 to 1970. It disbanded in October 1970. In a "coup" in 1979 Hume ousted Fitt as leader and Fitt resigned from the party. Hume was more "green"—more of a nationalist—while Fitt was more "red." Fitt wanted to improve the condition of Catholics within Northern Ireland whereas Hume wanted to do away with Northern Ireland peacefully by persuading the Irish and British governments to "persuade" the unionists to accept a united Ireland. But Hume, unlike Adams, was opposed to the use of violence to achieve this—he thought it both immoral and counterproductive. While the unionists generally disliked socialists, they had even less time for a united Ireland and so were suspicious of Hume.[6]

The creation of the SDLP had followed by four months the creation of the nonsectarian Alliance Party in April 1970 and preceded the formation by Paisley of the Protestant Unionist Party—the forerunner of the DUP—in 1971. Paisley had split the unionist community by running against Unionist leader Terence O'Neill in 1969. So between 1969 and 1971 a new political party system for the province was created. This combined with Northern Ireland's autonomous self-rule status within the United Kingdom from 1922 to 1972 gave Northern Ireland a character in between that of the *dependent settler colonies* ruled from a colonial metropole and the *independent settler colonies* ruled by the local settlers as in Israel, Rhodesia, South Africa and the United States.[7]

The Northern Ireland conflict began in late 1968 and early 1969 when unionist mobs and police reservists—the B Specials—reacted with violence to protest marches by the NICRA and student groups aimed at ending institutional discrimination against Catholics in housing, employment, and voting. In August 1969 London deployed the British army to Northern Ireland to restore order. Although they were initially welcomed by the nationalists and even republican communities, this welcome lasted for only about six months. In December 1969 the IRA split into two separate wings, the Official IRA led by the existing leadership that wanted to emphasize political action and the Provisional IRA led by traditionalists who wanted to emphasize military action. The British had a problem distinguishing between the two different organizations. By the end of 1970 the need to uphold the existing Unionist order in Belfast and the province, combined with rough counterinsurgency methods imported from colonial conflicts, created an opening for the Provisionals—better known as the Provos to their supporters and to the British as PIRA—to instigate an insurgency in February 1971 to drive the Brits out. The Official IRA — better known to all republicans as Stickies or Sticks — were forced to follow suit. In May 1972 the Official IRA declared a unilateral ceasefire and got out of the military business permanently as its members became involved in criminal activity or politics as first the Republican Clubs and then the Workers' Party. A militant faction broke away from the Officials in 1974 to form the Irish Republican Socialist Party (IRSP) with the Irish National Liberation Army (INLA) as its armed wing. The INLA was especially dangerous from 1979 to 1989 until internal feuds rendered it largely ineffective. The Workers' Party, created in 1982, was competitive with the SDLP and Sinn Fein only in local council elections and only for about a decade. The IRSP was never an effective political party and served only as the public relations wing of the INLA, as Sinn Fein had served for the IRA before 1982.[8]

The IRA originally broke up over two issues in 1969-70: the inability of the IRA to defend republican ghettoes against loyalist attacks in August 1969 and the Officials' desire to end the policy of abstention that prevented successful candidates from taking their seats in either the Irish Dail at Leinster or the Stormont parliament. For the traditionalists this was nearly a sacred principle. In 1983 Sinn Fein Vice President Gerry Adams defeated President Ruari O Bradaigh (Rory O'Brady) in a reversal of this same principle and forced the traditionalists to leave Sinn Fein. Henceforth, Sinn Fein would take its seats in Leinster and eventually in Stormont, but not yet at Westminster in London. Until recently — after the ceasefires — most Sinn Fein officials were former IRA members who took up a party role after either their release from prison or becoming too old for the armed struggle. Both Gerry Adams and Martin McGuinness, the party president and deputy president and head negotiator, are both reported to have been former heads of the IRA, although Adams refuses to admit to ever having been an IRA member. Adams first ran Bobby Sands, the leader of the IRA prisoners in the Maze Prison, in a by-election in 1981 when Sands was on hunger strike. Sands won the election but died soon afterwards. His election agent then ran in a second by-election and was reelected. In 1982 Sinn Fein began competing with the SDLP on a regular basis in local, assembly, and parliamentary elections.[9]

The loyalists were much slower to become politically active. Although the Ulster Volunteer Force (UVF) was founded as the terrorist revival of a mainstream unionist organization of the 1910s in 1966, it did not really develop a political party until 1978. The Ulster Defence Association (UDA) was founded in 1972 as the union of a number of neighborhood defense organizations in the loyalist areas of Belfast. It also developed a political branch in 1978. But neither of these two parties — the Progressive Unionist Party (PUP) for the UVF and the Ulster Democratic Party (UDP) for the UDA — was really organized and effective until the early 1990s, a decade behind Sinn Fein. Most unionists regarded the loyalist paramilitary organizations more as fronts for organized crime and psychopaths than as defenders.[10] They regarded the British security forces — the army and the Royal Ulster Constabulary (RUC) — as their real defenders. So the UDP after having marginal success in local elections went out of business in late 2001; the PUP continues in existence today but has been reduced to a single member of the assembly (MLA).

For the conflict overall the IRA in particular and the republicans in general were responsible for the greatest number of casualties — about 60 percent compared to 30 percent for the loyalists and 10 percent for the security forces. But the revival of the UDA with a new leadership led the loyalists to actually surge ahead of the IRA/INLA in the death toll in 1992–94.[11]

Northern Ireland politics is treated by the local, Irish, and British presses as two separate two-party contests: between the UUP and the DUP for the unionist electorate and between the SDLP and Sinn Fein for the nationalist electorate. Alliance, which polled nearly 15 percent of the vote in local elections in the mid–1970s, had been reduced to between 5 and 6 percent during the 1990s. Alliance is competitive only in the Greater Belfast area around Belfast Lough and is a thoroughly middle-class party with a leadership and electorate made up of educated professionals. Its support is based on both people from a mixed-religious background and from moderate liberals from both communities who regard themselves more as Northern Irish than as nationalist or unionist. The party refuses to define itself as either unionist or nationalist, although most nationalists see it as the liberal wing of the unionist community as do some unionists.[12] Sinn Fein is a working-class party and the SDLP is a middle-class party. Among unionists the Ulster Unionists are more of a middle-class party and the Democratic Unionists more of a working-class party but class lines have blurred among the unionist electorate since the mid–1980s. Formerly the UUP's leadership came from the gentry and business classes, but David Trimble effected a takeover by middle-class lawyers in the 1990s. The UUP was always a "broad tent" party like the Democrats and Republicans in the United States.[13] The DUP began as the political arm of Ian Paisley's Free Presbyterian Church in the early 1970s, but soon attracted an urban working-class base to augment the rural religious supporters. Paisley had remained party leader for over 35 years and his will was party policy. His deputies were Peter Robinson and Nigel Dodds.[14]

After the implementation of the Anglo-Irish Agreement the SDLP stabilized its lead over Sinn Fein with the former receiving between two-thirds and sixty percent of the vote and the latter between one-third and forty percent. Sinn Fein support actually dropped as a result of the agreement. By the late 1980s Gerry Adams realized that the armalite was actually interfering with the ballot box portion of the combined Republican strategy. Either deliberate policy or indifference and incompetence by poorly-trained volunteers often resulted in civilian casualties during IRA operations. These casualties resulted in many potential Sinn Fein voters voting for its rival. This combined with British successes against the IRA due to the deployment of the Special Air Service to the province in 1976 and improved intelligence led him to conclude that the armed struggle was a stalemate. He concluded that the British army was not prepared to leave Northern Ireland unilaterally.[15] Therefore, to have anything to show for twenty years of terrorism he needed to improve Sinn Fein's political standing. He could do this only by ending the armed struggle. But if he was to copy the Stickies without ending up like them, he needed to bring a large majority of the Republican Movement along with him. Adams came from the republican aristocracy — one of the few traditional republican families that had been active in the struggle since the early 1920s. These families tended to intermarry. Adams is the nephew of a former IRA chief of staff and his father was sentenced to hang by the British in 1942 for a shooting incident. Adams's mother is a Hathaway from another traditional IRA family. As a result of his background, Adams joined the IRA as a youth of sixteen in 1966 — before the split. McGuinness is from a non–IRA family and actually joined the Stickies before switching to the Provos several months later. Both were quite conscious of the fate of the Stickies. They needed several years to consolidate their control of the Republican Movement before they could implement their strategy.

The unionists had been largely unresponsive to new British initiatives since the collapse of Sunningdale in 1974. James Molyneaux took command of the Unionists in 1979 and owed his longevity as leader —16 years when he was voted out of power — because Paisley did not perceive him as a threat. Paisley saw his role as the conscience of unionism. He did not crave power for himself, but moved against any Unionist leader whom he perceived as too liberal. He had forced four leaders out of power: Terence O'Neill in 1969, James Chichester-Clark in 1971, Brian Faulkner in 1974, and William Craig in 1977. Paisley regarded power sharing with nationalists as anathema and threatened any Unionist leader who attempted to prove him wrong.[16]

Hume-Adams and the Joint Declaration

Hume and Adams remained in touch and renewed their talks in 1993. Adams had not changed his mind about the British but had changed his perception of the armed struggle. Hume and Adams began working on a draft of a joint declaration that they wanted Dublin to introduce to London to serve as the basis of a peace process. Hume went to Dublin and asked Taoiseach Albert Reynolds to begin a peace process with Prime Minister John Major. Hume refused to enter into what he termed an "internal settlement" with the unionists that left out Sinn Fein and a North-South dimension.[17] It was this refusal that served as the basis both for the collapse of the Brooke-Mayhew talks in 1992 and for the renewal of the Hume-Adams talks. Hume saw the failure to include the extremes as one of the main lessons of the Sunningdale experiment.

Albert Reynolds, a former businessman who was a pragmatist, replaced Charles Haughey as Taoiseach in February 1992. Reynolds was from Co. Longford, which was closer to Ulster than to Dublin. Haughey was noted both for his corruption and for playing the "green card" on Northern Ireland. When the New Ireland Forum produced a report in 1983 with three separate alternatives to the status quo on the island (a unitary United Ireland, a federation, and joint British-Irish sovereignty), Haughey played up the most nationalist of the three choices for party political reasons although the SDLP and the opposition Fine Gael party were supporting joint sovereignty.[18] John Major replaced Margaret Thatcher in December 1990. Reynolds and Major liked each other and felt free to speak frankly with each other without worrying about disturbing either their personal or their professional relationship. Major invited Reynolds to visit him in London about two weeks after he was elected and both agreed to do everything they could to end the conflict in Northern Ireland. Major won a surprising extension of his term as prime minister in his first Westminster election in April 1992. This gave the two more time to work together. In that same election Gerry Adams lost the West Belfast Westminster seat that he had held to Dr. Joe Hendron of the SDLP. Two months later Adams associate Jim Gibney told a Republican crowd at the annual Bodenstown, Co. Kildare Wolfe Tone commemoration that peace would have to precede a British departure from Northern Ireland. This was a hint of future Sinn Fein flexibility.[19]

Although the two governments had had their differences over Northern Ireland over the decades, they had cooperated much more often than they had feuded. In 1973-74 they had cooperated in negotiating the power-sharing initiative at Sunningdale, in 1985 they had negotiated the Anglo-Irish Agreement, Ireland's *Garda Siochana* (police force) had cooperated with the RUC, and both forces' special branches traded intelligence on a regular basis. Articles 2 and 3 of the Irish constitution still constituted a legal claim by Dublin to the territory and population of Northern Ireland, and were an object of intense resentment by the unionists. But Dublin had never attempted to enforce its claim and as The Troubles intensified during the 1970s most Irish really did not want a united Ireland. Dublin wanted to see an end to discrimination *and* to conflict in Northern Ireland. During the early 1970s London instituted a number of social, political, legal, and policing reforms in Northern Ireland that eliminated the most egregious forms of discrimination.[20] After that the conflict became largely a matter of republican extremists attempting to do away with a polity that they regarded as illegitimate and loyalist extremists attempting to restore the *status quo ante*. London and Dublin were willing to cooperate on administering the province because ultimately neither one relished the prospect of governing the province alone.

During the early 1990s as a loyalist offensive led to an escalation of the conflict in Northern Ireland, the IRA went on a bombing offensive in England. In April 1992 a bomb at the Baltic Exchange in London killed three people and did more property damage than all the IRA's bombs from 1969 to that point. There would be major bombs the following year and in 1996. These gave London an incentive to end the conflict.[21]

In September 1992 James Molyneaux led a Unionist delegation down to Dublin to meet with Reynolds. Trimble was included in the delegation. The Unionist team was impressed by Reynolds, but the taoiseach was unwilling to amend the constitution at that time. Shortly after that Trimble was part of a Unionist delegation that met with Dublin peace activist Chris Hudson. The other team members were the McGimpsey brothers and Ken Maginnis. Trimble spent the time discussing music with Hudson's wife. Eventually Hudson became a go-between between the UVF terrorists and Dublin during the peace process.[22]

During 1993 the peace process came together out of the constitutional talks, the Hume-Adams initiative, London's back-channel with the Republicans, and the intergovernmental relationship. Major insisted that all parties to the peace talks commit themselves to exclusively peaceful means. Reynolds agreed to this. Hume, who was conducting parallel talks with Reynolds, insisted that London become a persuader for a united Ireland with the unionists. Major absolutely refused to do this. The overt talks never reconvened in 1993 because the two sides had talked themselves out in 1992. They would meet with London but not with each other.

During 1993 the conflict accelerated with the IRA returning to its bombing campaign in Britain. The loyalists also stepped up their activities causing the IRA to start targeting loyalist targets. After January 1993 loyalists were gunning for all members of the pan-nationalist front: Sinn Fein and SDLP officials, the Gaelic Athelic Association and even Irish government officials. October 1993 turned out to be the bloodiest month in 17 years — since 1976.

On October 23 an IRA bomber attempted to blow up the UDA high command, which usually met in a room above a fish shop. The UDA was not meeting at that time and the bomb went off prematurely killing the bomber and nine innocent civilians. Gerry Adams carried the coffin of bomber Thomas Begley, which gave little credibility to his claims of no relationship with the IRA. The UDA retaliated a few days later with an attack on a packed bar in the Catholic village of Greysteel, near Derry, and killed eight people. Six individual Catholics were killed in individual incidents. Twenty-three people were killed in the space of a week. Businesses in Belfast were deserted after dark as people stayed home out of fear. The killings caused revulsion among most ordinary citizens and led Major and Reynolds to speed up their contacts. This was after Major slowed them in reaction to an IRA bombing in Britain.[23]

Hume came under severe criticism both from unionists and from members of his own party for his continued meetings with Adams. The two had come up with a joint draft of a declaration that they presented to Dublin through Martin Mansergh, the Fianna Fail expert on Northern Ireland who was that rare thing in either part of Ireland, a Protestant republican. In February and April 1993 Mansergh met with McGuinness and Aidan McAteer in a monastery in Dundalk. The Republicans wanted a guarantee that Irish unity would occur within a particular timeframe, but also played lip service to the principle of consent. The Irish government refused to provide this guarantee and soon Sinn Fein's attitude hardened and refused to consider any changes to the 1992 text.[24]

Hume's deputy, Seamus Mallon, was particularly opposed to the meetings. He thought it pumped up the images of both Hume and Adams and the expense of emphasizing the differences between the two parties particularly on the question of violence. Hendron was also very critical and wondered aloud if Adams was not just using Hume for his own ends. John Taylor of the UUP referred to "the SDLP and its friends the IRA" in a parliamentary debate. Hume was also criticized by the Fine Gael opposition in the Republic, the SDLP's former partner in the New Ireland Forum. The criticism, Hume's career of hard work, little sleep, and drink led to his hospitalization for exhaustion.[25]

Northern Ireland Secretary Patrick Mayhew attempted to balance pro-nationalist statements with pro-unionist statements emphasizing the principle of majority consent (the unionist veto in nationalist parlance) and no Republican role in negotiations while the IRA continued with violence. But these pro-nationalist statements went too far for even Alliance leader John Alderdice who accused the Conservatives of trying to kick Northern Ireland out of the Union "through the back door." This criticism apparently provoked

Mayhew into declaring in April that there would be no joint authority in Northern Ireland. But the *Shankill People,* a loyalist newspaper, wrote of "a community in retreat which feels itself being squeezed physically, territorially and culturally."[26]

On October 29, 1993, Major and Reynolds met at a European summit meeting at Brussels to discuss Northern Ireland. Throughout the following fourteen years European summits became a convenient means of meeting for either prime ministers or foreign ministers of the two governments, usually without arousing much publicity. Their common membership in the European Community/Union since 1973 had brought the two governments closer together since 1973. The two prime ministers issued a public statement that "new doors could open" if violence was given up. Trimble at this point was still thinking of a military solution rather than a political solution to the conflict. Trimble was chosen by his party to respond to the statement. He said that Hume-Adams were now completely off the agenda.[27]

The following month Major suffered another blow when journalist David McKittrick of the Independent Group of newspapers revealed the existence of a secret back-channel between London and the Republicans. This provoked anger not only, predictably, from the unionists but also from Reynolds as well. He had been straightforward with Major about his dealings with Hume and indirectly with Adams. Reynolds expected the same courtesy from Major, who in turn was afraid of jeopardizing his link with the Republicans. The British government tried to play down the import of the back-channel and said that all messages were consistent with their public statements. Sinn Fein published its own version of the secret correspondence, which differed in many ways with the London version, and claimed that it had begun in 1990 and not 1993 as claimed by London. Peter Brooke later confirmed that the back-channel had begun in 1990, thereby contradicting the account in Major's memoir. Major claimed that the correspondence began with a Sinn Fein plea for help in ending the conflict secretly. McGuinness denied having sent such a message. It appears that this message was sent by one of the back-channel conduits, Brendan Duddy.[28] The back-channel consisted of three phases: 1990 to February 1993; February to early November 1993; and then a short period in November. During the first phase the British were actively courting Sinn Fein by sending nineteen messages and receiving only one reply. During 1993 Sinn Fein became very interested when London mentioned the possibility of a meeting and messages were exchanged on a weekly basis on average, but London was reluctant to hold a meeting while IRA violence continued. In November 1993 the dialogue came to an end as it was publicly revealed and as London refused to hold a meeting with Republicans as long as violence continued. The revelations seriously compromised London's credibility, particularly with unionists.[29]

As a result of the back-channel coming to an end, London decided to concentrate on working with Dublin to draft a joint declaration that would serve as the framework for the launch of a peace process. The British had received two draft texts from the Irish in 1992, and both had the fingerprints of Hume-Adams all over them and were completely unacceptable to the British as they were too one-sided. A third draft in September 1993 was little better. After a cabinet meeting on November 23, Major decided to present Reynolds with his own draft.

Major and Reynolds met for a summit at Dublin Castle in early December after Reynolds rejected a British draft on November 29. The summit began with an hour-long private meeting between the two prime ministers in which they both vented their frustrations and anger with each other. Reynolds was probably angry over Major's holding out over the back-channel and over Major's rejection of all of the drafts. And Major was angry over the one-sided nature of the drafts and the foot-dragging on the talks process. Reynolds later told an aide, "It went all right — I chewed his bollocks off and he took a few lumps outa me." Major characterized it as "the frankest and fiercest exchanges I had with any fellow leader in my six and a half years as prime minister." By lunch the two were talking about sports instead of politics. By the end of the summit they had knocked out the basic principles of the declaration and civil servants finished drafting the language for the declaration within two weeks.[30]

On December 10 the Combined Loyalist Military Command (CLMC), which controlled the UVF, UDA, and Red Hand Commando, handed a copy of a six-point communique to BBC security correspondent Brian Rowan with the loyalist terms for a peace agreement. The peace could not threaten Northern Ireland's position within the Union or result in joint sovereignty for the province. The communique was published. It was an unnecessary step — the Joint Declaration that was released at a joint press conference at Downing Street in London on December 15 had already taken into account unionist concerns. The twelve-article declaration consisted of carefully crafted wording that recognized the Irish right of self-determination without giving up the unionist veto. This was done by declaring that Irish self-determination had to be exercised separately in both parts of Ireland — the Republic and Northern Ireland. All parties would be allowed into negotiations if they gave up violence and agreed to using only completely nonviolent means. This principle was later enshrined in the Mitchell 6 principles that all parties to the all-party talks had to swear to.[31]

Reynolds wanted to show to unionists that he was not trying to impose joint sovereignty on them. To do this he engaged with both Alliance and with Molyneaux via Archbishop Robert Eames, the head of the Church of Ireland — the second largest Protestant church in Northern Ireland — who was eager for peace. Molyneaux had direct input into paragraphs three to six of the Downing Street Declaration. Loyalist paramilitary leaders also had input through the Rev. Roy Magee, who later played a major role in bringing about the loyalist ceasefire.[32]

Dual Mediation

The subsequent peace process that stemmed from the Downing Street Declaration and lasted for fourteen years consisted of *dual mediation* by the two governments with support from a number of other governments and individuals including Washington, Ottawa, and Helsinki. The two governments issued a series of three documents over a five-year period that served as setting the framework for the peace process: the Downing Street Declaration in December 1993; the Framework Agreements in February 1995; and the Heads of Agreement in January 1998. The two governments after the second document decided to integrate Washington, Helsinki and Ottawa into the process by appointing a three-man international commission to write a report on the issue of decommissioning. The Clinton administration became involved and played a major role to the point that Washington became nearly a third, but not equal, partner with Dublin and London.

Washington made three major contributions to the peace process (in decreasing order of importance): the loan of former Senate Majority Leader George Mitchell for five years to play various roles in the peace process; the invitation of the parties to the annual St. Patrick's Day party at the White House in mid–March from 1994 to 1998 and President Clinton making phone calls during the final day of the Good Friday Agreement negotiations; and the issuing of visas to Gerry Adams and Joe Cahill of Sinn Fein in 1994 and 1995 against the strong advice of the British government. After the first Adams visa controversy in early 1994, Northern Ireland policy passed from the hands of the State Department to the National Security Council where it was handled by National Security Advisor Tony Lake and his assistant Nancy Soderberg, the former aide to Senator Edward Kennedy. At one point four or five NSC staffers were working fulltime on Northern Ireland. Clinton made the big decisions himself after consulting with his advisors. Clinton raised the Adams fundraising visa request in a 1995 meeting with Lake. Clinton was in favor of granting the visa. Niall O'Dowd, the Irish-American publisher of the

Irish Voice, faxed a notice of a Sinn Fein fundraising event in London from the British press to Soderberg. This demonstrated the hypocrisy of the British request — Adams could already legally raise money in Britain. Major was upset that Clinton never demanded anything in return from Adams for the visa. But Clinton was careful to coordinate with both Dublin and London on his moves and never differed from both of them at the same time.[33]

Clinton had several motives for supporting the Northern Ireland peace process. First, he had a personal interest as he had ancestors from both sides of the religious divide and he had been a young Rhodes scholar in Britain during the early days of The Troubles. Second, Irish-Americans had played a major role in his nomination and election in 1992. He wanted to repay them, fulfill his campaign promise to get involved in the peace process, and ensure their support for his reelection. Third, Northern Ireland was his biggest foreign policy success in 1995-96 as Haiti was not much of a success and Bosnia was still unsettled in 1996.[34]

"Would we have had a ceasefire at all without American support?" mused Reynolds. "Maybe we would have, but I have my doubts...." Sinn Fein could compete with Britain on an equal basis in Washington. Partially in order to counteract this, Reynolds urged Vice President Gore to make contacts with unionists to balance unionist perceptions of the Clinton administration. As a result of an invitation from Gore, UUP MPs David Trimble, Ken Maginnis, William Ross, and Jeffrey Donaldson, who was then party secretary, went to the White House on September 21, 1994. Gore assured them that the White House did not have a political agenda for Northern Ireland but just wanted to move the peace process forward. By 1996 the Americans were seen by Unionists as more balanced than they had been during the early peace process.[35]

After the negotiation of the Good Friday (or Belfast) Agreement in April 1998 the American role reduced dramatically. George Mitchell presided over the review of the agreement in the autumn of 1999 and successfully mediated an agreement between Sinn Fein and the Unionists for the setting up of the Executive in the absence of an IRA decommissioning. After this the American role was much reduced. Under President Bush the State Department Planning Committee monitored the progress of the peace process and facilitated by meeting with the various parties.

Between the two governments the parties involved were the two prime ministers, the foreign ministers and the staffs of their respective foreign ministries and cabinet offices. The two governments frequently held meetings at European Union meetings. Later after 1999, summits were held every few months to deal with new crises in the peace process as events dictated. The approach "worked" for two reasons. First, there was an ongoing commitment to it that transcended individual governments and parties. Second, the two governments were closer to each other than they were to their respective clients. Both felt a commitment to ending the conflict in Northern Ireland. The series of documents jointly drafted allowed the two governments to shift the "tilt" of the process to one side or another as events dictated. The Framework Documents favored the nationalists. The Heads of Agreement were much more oriented towards the unionists. The former helped to keep the Republicans on sides during the process until Adams and McGuinness were able to dominate the Republican Movement. The unionists were able to sell the more "orange" Heads document to their followers.[36]

Two academics described the role of the two governments as "partners in the peace process on a permanent and institutionalised basis to engineer a political settlement. The partnership was durable and strong enough to survive mutual suspicion, differing emphases and personality clashes." Gradually the relationship between the two governments was transformed from one of competition to one of cooperation. The governments repeatedly emphasized that there was no Plan B. Only the two governments were authorized to introduce an alternative plan, leaving the parties the choice of either working within the framework or facing an uncertain future in the political wilderness.[37]

The European Union had little direct impact on the peace process. Indirectly, by changing the Republic's orientation away from narrow nationalism starting in 1973 it made it easier for Dublin to give up pushing for a united Ireland and cooperate with London. Between 1994 and 1999 the European Union provided about 375 million Pounds Sterling of economic and social funding for Northern Ireland — or about three weeks worth of subsidy at the rate that London provided. But European Union meetings were a handy venue for the prime ministers or foreign ministers of the two governments to meet.[38]

Foreign experts (such as Americans, Canadians, Finns, and South Africans) were usually regarded by either the governments or the parties as biased towards one side or the other. They had to walk a fine line between being acceptable to the two governments and being independent. Originally the unionists regarded George Mitchell as pro-nationalist and the Republicans regarded John de Chastelain as pro-unionist. Eventually the two sides became disabused of these initial impressions.[39]

The Republican and Loyalist Ceasefires

Initially the loyalists reacted by saying that they would react by ascertaining if the Union was safe, if no special deal had been made by London, and if the Republicans would react favorably but they retained the right to respond to republican terrorism in 1994. The Republicans initially ignored the declaration. This led to a ugly spat, possibly staged, between Washington and London over a visa for Gerry Adams to visit the United States and speak at an academic forum on the Northern Ireland conflict.[40] The State Department supported London while the National Security Council lined up with the White House to back the visa. Clinton had made promises about actively backing a peace strategy to Irish-American activists during the 1992 campaign and Irish-Americans (that is those of Catholic Irish ancestry as opposed to the Scotch-Irish Protestants) overwhelmingly backed Clinton during the primaries and the general election as a result. Clinton, who wanted a second term as well as peace in Northern Ireland, decided to take a risk for peace and reward his Irish-American backers. Most Irish-American members of Congress supported granting Adams the visa. Reynolds and Hume were also in favor of the visa. Soderberg and Lake advised Clinton that the visa would help give Adams leverage over the IRA in getting the paramilitaries to approve a ceasefire. Major later complained that Adams took a tough anti–British line during his visit and criticized the unionist veto.[41]

In March 1994 the IRA fired a number of mortar bombs at Heathrow airport. The bombs did not explode — forensic examination showed that they had been tampered with so that they would deliberately not explode. The firings occurred in three sets of four bombs each two days between each firing. The tubes had been buried in empty ground near the airport and fired by a timer. The IRA seemed to be sending a very subtle message to Major that it was still a dangerous organization but that it wanted to talk.[42]

Molyneaux was under pressure within his own party to simply ignore the declaration or write it off. Paisley and his deputy, Peter Robinson, then came to Downing Street to complain to Major that since the declaration there had been 74 bombings, 75 shootings and nine murders. Major was not impressed by Paisley's histrionics. Seamus Mallon, Hume's deputy and the future deputy first minister, called the declaration "the best thing in Ireland in 150 years." Apparently, his placing it above the Irish independence struggle of 1919–21 did not endear him to republicans. Sinn Fein's leadership pressed for a meeting with Major or the British, which the latter refused as long as their armed struggle continued. Dublin was requested to get Adams and McGuinness to provide them with any questions that they might have about the declaration. Adams provided a list of twenty questions, only one of which related to the actual text of the declaration. Major interpreted the other 19 as attempts to reopen bargaining on the Republican agenda. London responded to the questions in May.[43]

Adams and McGuinness were busy selling to the ordinary IRA volunteers the idea that a united Ireland could be achieved through the pan-nationalist alliance of Sinn Fein, the SDLP, Dublin and the Irish parties, and Irish America all working to corner the unionists and pressure Britain. The New Irish Agenda, founded in 1991 by Irish-American journalist Niell O'Dowd, was the organizational arm of the American branch of the alliance.[44] Adams sold the visa as a major victory over Major and the Brits. Adams's technique throughout the peace process was to tell the Republicans that he was lying to the British, Dublin, and the unionists and tell everyone else that he was lying to his own followers if they questioned him closely. There was an internal Republican strategy document that was leaked to the media. In the document the acronym TUAS appeared. Adams told reporters and Dublin that it stood for Totally Unarmed Strategy whereas he told Republicans that it stood for Tactical Use of Armed Struggle. This became most acute after the Good Friday Agreement was signed and Adams had to justify Sinn Fein taking its seats in a new Stormont and in a government similar to that set up by the Sunningdale process in 1974. This is why Seamus Mallon dubbed the whole peace process "Sunningdale for slow learners." Mallon was also referring to the unionists who had worked to destroy the power-sharing government.[45]

David Trimble began to get the feeling that Major would eventually lose the next election and that it would be smart for the Unionists to forge ties with Labour as well as with the Tories. Since the UUP was created early in the twentieth century it had fallen under the Conservative whip, and Trimble would continue to support Major in key votes after he was elected party leader in the summer of 1995, but he wanted to be ready for the eventuality of Labour returning to power. Laboor had a similar arrangement with the SDLP and had a clear nationalist bias in its policy on Northern Ireland. Tony Blair, before he was the leader of the Labour Party, invited Trimble to his office for a discussion on the Prevention of Terrorism Act. This led to a second meeting between Molyneaux, Trimble, Blair and Labour leader John Smith in which Molyneaux alluded to the good relations that he had had with Jim Callaghan. Smith said that as someone from the West Coast of Scotland he understood unionists. It was all coded language hinting at a possible future rapprochement between the two parties. It also demonstrated Trimble's quick rise in the party. Blair later visited Trimble at his Lurgan office in Northern Ireland on December 13, 1996, during a trip to the province. The RUC told Blair that they expected a major IRA bombing before Christmas. Blair found Trimble to be very closed off and hard to talk to during the visit.[46]

By the summer there was increased speculation about an IRA ceasefire coming soon in reaction to the declaration. The organization had declared a 72-hour Easter truce. This was a buildup to a longer truce. The Republicans decided to go out with a bang during the summer. They began targeting

Protestant-owned pubs in North and South Belfast, something that they had not done since the 1970s. They also targeted a number of leading loyalists including the Rev. William McCrea, the DUP member of parliament for mid–Ulster, who escaped unharmed from an attack on his home on July 10. The next day they killed Ray Smallwoods, leader of the small loyalist Ulster Democratic Party, affiliated with the UDA. This left Gary McMichael, son of founder John, in charge of the party. Gary McMichael was forced to leave Northern Ireland for several days in August after the RUC warned him that he was being targeted by the IRA. Gary was at a disadvantage as a leader of a paramilitary party like the UDP because unlike his father and Smallwoods, or the leaders of the rival PUP, he had had no operational experience as a terrorist. They then killed two UDA men in South Belfast two weeks later. David Ervine, the PUP leader, figured that the Republicans wanted to call a ceasefire while the loyalists continued revenge killings and looked bad in front of the international media. This is a tactic that the IRA would deploy repeatedly during the peace process. The IRA held an Army Convention at Letterkenney, Ireland in July. The Convention, a meeting of all IRA volunteers, was the highest authority in the IRA. It outranked the twelve-man Executive and the seven-man Army Council that ran the organization on a daily basis. There Adams and McGuinness won approval for their peace strategy by keeping the volunteers in the dark. By the beginning of August the British ambassador to Dublin was reporting to Major that the IRA would be on ceasefire by the end of the month. During August American ambassador to Dublin Jean Kennedy Smith, the sister of Senator Kennedy, fought hard to get a visa for Joe Cahill, an old IRA man. Cahill had been sentenced to hang in 1942 along with Gerry Adams's father and was a founder of Irish-American Northern Aid (NORAID) in 1970 and thus was known to the IRA's traditional American supporters. Reynolds called Soderberg 48 hours before the ceasefire was scheduled to go into effect to lobby for the Cahill visa. Clinton granted the visa with British approval and the next day the IRA went on ceasefire. On August 31 the IRA declared a ceasefire effective from midnight that night. The word permanent did not appear in the IRA's announcement to the press, instead it was described as "a complete cessation." Paisley warned that this wording was deliberate and that the ceasefire would not last. Cahill toured Irish America meeting IRA supporters and explaining the reasons for the ceasefire.[47]

The Republican propaganda machine orchestrated victory celebrations in West Belfast and throughout Northern Ireland to give the impression to both nationalists and unionists that they had won their "long war." Ordinary republicans were happy to cooperate as most were glad that the war was over. This was similar to Belgrade organizing victory celebrations five years later in the Serbian capital to convince ordinary Serbs that they had won the war against NATO. The most gullible in this exercise were ordinary working-class loyalists who have little trust in the British government and have an inferiority complex vis-à-vis the republicans. Loyalists had over the decades been ignored by the UUP and exploited by Paisley and the DUP. The politicized loyalists in the leadership ranks of the two loyalist parties understood what the IRA and Paisley were doing in glossing over the reality of the IRA's strategic defeat, but ordinary apolitical loyalists did not.[48]

The loyalist paramilitaries waited on hold for six weeks to ensure that no guarantees had been made to the Republicans regarding the province's future. On September 8 the CLMC issued another six-point statement to the media. They wanted to establish that the IRA's ceasefire was permanent and they wanted to see if the INLA would also go on ceasefire. On September 10 McMichael of the UDP and Hugh Smyth of the PUP met with officials from the Northern Ireland Office in Belfast. They were given answers to their six points. The NIO had no information on the INLA and speculated that it might be waiting to see how the loyalists responded to the IRA ceasefire. Then on October 10 the UDA prisoners issued a statement urging a ceasefire. Two days later the leaders of the three main loyalist paramilitary groups met in Belfast and agreed on the wording of a communique announcing a ceasefire. The following day the announcement was made by the CLMC, with seven senior loyalist political figures appearing before the media to make it along with an apology of "true remorse" for all the innocent victims of the conflict. The paramilitaries were in retrospect condemning their own policy of targeting nationalist civilians in reprisal for IRA actions. The IRA never issued an apology. Being "historically correct" means never having to say you are sorry.[49]

Throughout the peace process the paramilitary organizations had four bases of strength or support on their side: First, the respective traditions that they represented in their respective communities. It was for this reason that the organizations were conservative about choosing their names: Irish and republican for the republicans and Ulster for the loyalists. The original loyalist paramilitary organization, the UVF, deliberately went back a half-century to resurrect a name that was rooted in the unionist mainstream. Second, close links with paramilitary political parties (Sinn Fein, PUP, UDP). Third, core support in ethnic ghettoes especially in housing estates (housing projects). Fourth, the paramilitaries had a capacity to threaten and deliver violence — at some time or another all the paramilitary organizations on ceasefire broke their ceasefires.[50]

The British responded to the ceasefires with their own program of demilitarization, a key Republican demand. Within six months of the IRA ceasefire five army bases had been closed and the Belfast Civilian Search Unit had been abandoned. Between 1995 and 2000 a further 41 out of 105 army bases and installations had been closed and the army announced that it planned to reduce the remaining number to "no more than twenty."[51]

Decommissioning and Negotiations 1995–1997

Both the British and Irish governments had meetings with Sinn Fein soon after the IRA ceasefire went into effect. In late October Reynolds conducted the first meeting of the Forum for Peace and Reconciliation in Dublin. The Forum was attended by the constitutional parties from the Republic, by the SDLP, by Sinn Fein and by Alliance. The unionist parties boycotted the Forum. They had their own Forum for Political Dialogue in Belfast, which soon became a "unionist talking shop." This was a means of ushering Sinn Fein into political life and the mainstream.[52] Part of Adams's strategy was to have Sinn Fein compete in elections in both the Republic and Northern Ireland and then sell this to ordinary Republicans as the means to bring about a united Ireland. He would use pressure from Sinn Fein inside the coalition in the Republic to force the South to work towards unification. Adams has at various times hinted at 2016, the centenary of Patrick Pearce's declaration of the 32-county Irish republic at the Dublin Post Office in April 1916, as being the time by which a united Ireland might be achieved.[53]

A big roadblock to the peace process came in the issue of decommissioning. The unionists, not eager to engage with the Republicans and not trusting them, wanted the IRA to disarm in a verifiable manner as a confidence-building measure (CBM) that would give the unionist community confidence that the IRA had no plans to return to terrorism or guerrilla warfare in the future. The tradition of republicans had always been one of "dumping" arms after an unsuccessful conflict as with the Fenians in 1867, the IRA after the Irish civil war in 1923, and the IRA in 1962 after the border campaign. The IRA equated public disarmament with surrender and this was deeply offensive to the volunteers because they contended that they had not been defeated. For the unionists a demand to decommission provided an easy way to avoid having to meet and negotiate with Republicans. Initially Dublin went along with London on its demands for prior decommissioning but it soon relented when it saw that the IRA had no plans to disarm. In Washington in March 1995 NI Secretary Patrick Mayhew announced three conditions on decommissioning that all the paramilitaries would have to meet before being included in negotiations. These were: (1) agreement to decommissioning in principle; (2) arranging a means of decommissioning acceptable to the two governments; (3) the surrender of at least some "product" (arms and/or explosives). These three conditions became known as Washington 3, which usually referred to the third demand in particular. These were announced in response to intelligence that the IRA was still recruiting, training, collecting intelligence on targets, and carrying out punishment beatings and kneecappings. The previous month the United States hosted a conference on economic initiatives and investment in Northern Ireland and the six border counties in the Republic. In January 1995 Clinton "strong-armed" Senate Majority Leader George Mitchell into becoming his special advisor on economic initiatives to run the conference as he retired from the Senate. After the conference Mitchell agreed to stay on until the end of the year to help wrap up some economic matters. But Clinton had other plans for him.[54]

In November 1994 the government of Albert Reynolds in Dublin fell when Reynolds refused to allow a pedophile priest to be extradited to Northern Ireland for trial. As a result Tanaiste (Deputy Premier) Dick Spring decided that his Labour Party would switch its allegiance and form a coalition with Fine Gael and another small party, the Democratic Left, which had split from the Workers' Party in 1992. It consisted of former Marxist members of the Official IRA. But instead of being sympathetic to the Republicans they regarded them as old enemies. Taoiseach John Bruton was regarded as so sympathetic to unionists that his opponents referred to him as "Unionist John." After being elected Unionist leader in September 1995, Democratic Left leader Proinsas de Rossa was the first party leader that Trimble met with. It was a deliberate signal to Sinn Fein that he would allow republicans into government if they decontaminated themselves first.[55]

Just before Christmas 1994 a group of Young Unionists, the student branch of the UUP, met at a restaurant in the student union of Queen's University, Belfast to plot the overthrow of Jim Molyneaux. They agreed upon the strategy of using a "stalking horse" candidate — an unknown party member who would demonstrate the weakness of the leader by gaining an unexpected number of votes. The strategy had worked against Thatcher in 1990. Lee Reynolds, who unknown to the rest was a member of the UDP, agreed to be their horse.

The two governments released their *Frameworks* document on February 22, 1995, three weeks after excerpts from it had appeared in the London *Times*. It was a very "green" document with a long list of areas that the North-South body under the Strand 2 negotiations would have responsibility over. Many regarded it as a prototype united Ireland and for the second time under his leadership Molyneaux faced the charge that he had been too trusting of London.

Shortly thereafter the leadership challenge to Molyneaux was made by Reynolds who received only 88 votes to Molyneaux's 521. Trimble had not been behind the challenge and in fact attempted unsuccessfully to persuade Reynolds to withdraw his challenge. Soon Molyneaux was visited by a delegation of party senior members that it was time for him to go. Then on June 15 former Unionist Robert McCartney embarrassed his former party by beating the UUP's candidate in a by-election in North Down following the death of Independent Unionist Jim Kilfedder. Although Robert McCartney had once been a fierce critic of Paisley, the DUP refrained from running its own candidate in order to give McCartney a free shot to embarrass their rivals. The North Down constituency is unique in Northern Ireland, more like South England then the rest of the province. It is the only constituency in the province that the Conservative Party has even a prayer of winning (a prayer, not a real chance) and the Alliance Party is strong there. McCartney's victory was blamed on Molyneaux. Finally on August 28, a day after his seventy-fifth birthday, Molyneaux resigned as leader of the Unionists.[56]

On July 11, 1995, David Trimble became the most recognizable Unionist after Molyneaux by being filmed in a "victory jig" at the end of Drumcree I.[57] From 1995 to after the turn of the millenium a number of contentious parades during the marching season from April to August became proxy battle grounds between Republicans on one hand and members of the Orange Order and other loyal institutions and loyalist paramilitaries on the other. The most contentious march of all was the annual parade from the Drumcree Presbyterian Church outside Portadown down the Garvaghy Road, a nationalist area in the unionist town in North County Armagh. Portadown is a town where the UVF and later the breakaway Loyalist Volunteer Force (LVF) was very strong and where the nationalists suffered from discrimination. The local residents committee chose Brendan McKenna, knowing full well that the Orange Order would refuse to meet with him as he was convicted of blowing up the British Union hall in town. Trimble, whose constituency includes Portadown, negotiated the right for 500 members of the Orange Order to march down Garvaghy Road in silence but not to march back. At the beginning of the march Trimble grabbed Paisley's hand and seemed to dance a "jig" of triumph. In reality he was attempting to prevent Paisley from beating himself to the cameras. While it had the effect of alienating Trimble from nationalists, it made him a hero to ordinary Unionists.[57]

On Friday, September 8, 1995, Trimble was elected the new leader of the UUP on the third ballot with 58 percent of the vote. He had led all three rounds of balloting among the initial five candidates. The candidate with the fewest votes was eliminated after each round, but Ken Maginnis who came in third in the second round also pulled out. The media's candidates were John Taylor and Ken Maginnis. Maginnis was a former major in the Ulster Defence Regiment from Fermanagh who had very good relations with local

Catholics and with the leadership of the SDLP. He led the "liberal" wing of the UUP and was supported by the McGimpsey brothers. Taylor was the former minister of the interior at Stormont and had barely survived an assassination attempt by the Official IRA in January 1972. He was considered a centrist and Trimble was considered to be the candidate of the right. Trimble had the most organized campaign — organized by his aide Steven King and by wife Daphne. His victory took all the "experts" in the media and in London, the NIO and Dublin by surprise. The election took place in the Ulster Hall where Randolph Churchill had first played the "Orange card" with the slogan "Ulster will fight and Ulster will be right" back in 1886.[58]

In the summer of 1995 Mitchell travelled to Belfast and London for two weeks and began meeting with British officials and local politicians. He also read up on the conflict and asked a number of questions of Tony Lake and Nancy Soderberg, both of whom he had known for several years from politics. The two of them had also traveled to London and been snubbed by Sinn Fein, which refused to meet with them after it was reported from Washington by the *Irish Times* that they were coming with fresh ideas and "to knock heads together." On September 1, 1995, the British and Irish governments had reached a decision that decommissioning would proceed in parallel with negotiations, but Dublin soon backed out after Hume indicated his opposton. In late November there was a public disagreement between Irish Foreign Minister Dick Spring and Irish Prime Minister John Bruton during a visit by them to London just as Clinton was flying to London on the first of this three Irish presidential visits.[59]

In November 1995 Mitchell was asked by the two governments if he would be willing to head up an international commission to come up with a solution to the problem of decommissioning and negotiations. The commission, later known as the International Body on Decommissioning or Mitchell commission, consisted of three members each chosen by one government: Mitchell chosen by Clinton and acceptable to London; General John de Chastelain, former head of the Canadian army, chosen by London; and Harri Holkeri, former prime minister of Finland, chosen by Dublin. The commission gave the governments a way of attempting to find an acceptable solution to the problem that they could disavow if they did not like it. Dublin wanted direct American involvement and chose its timing carefully so that London was afraid to offend Clinton during his visit. The British were caught off guard but liked Mitchell's performance up to then.[60]

The commission went to Northern Ireland and interviewed all the parties to the conflict as well as members of the British security forces and the Irish Garda. Based on the input of the nationalist parties and the RUC the

Mitchell commission concluded that decommissioning before negotiations would not work. Major had already told Mitchell that he would have to reject the report if they said this, so they suggested the holding of elections as a means of building legitimacy for negotiations. This would be acceptable to Major as it would allow Sinn Fein to claim an electoral mandate. They also recommended conducting decommissioning in parallel with negotiations. The commission also recommended six principles of nonviolence that the parties to negotiations would be required to swear to before being admitted. The report was made public on January 23, 1996. The previous day Major had received his copy of the report. He stood up in parliament and announced that elections would be held in June 1996 for a Forum that would negotiate a new dispensation.[61]

Adams and McGuinness had lost control of the IRA. Several active service units (ASUs) had opposed the ceasefire in August but went along with it. The two "battalions" of the South Antrim "Brigade" were particularly opposed to the ceasefire. The South Antrim battalions began preparing for a return for war in the late fall of 1995 by preparing a massive truck bomb that would be used in London. The IRA's Executive voted 11–1 in January to call an Army Convention for March. Adams had the Army Council meet at the end of January and unanimously vote to end the ceasefire. On February 9, 1996, the IRA detonated the bomb at the Canary Wharf in the Dockyards section of London that killed two, wounded about a hundred, wrecked scores of buildings causing approximately 100 million pounds of damage, and temporarily wrecked the peace process. Adams did not know about the bomb ahead of time — or so he claims — but did know that the ceasefire was in trouble. He telephoned Nancy Soderberg at the NSC shortly before the ceasefire was broken to tell the administration that it was about to be broken. The call had been sanctioned by the Army Council of the IRA to prevent Adams from losing credibility in Washington. Adams soon returned to his previous status of *persona non grata* in both Britain and Ireland. But he was still welcome in America, if not at the White House. But his supporters in Congress felt betrayed and Niall O'Dowd condemned the bombing in an editorial in the *Irish Voice*. Adams was allowed to visit America on a February visa that had already been issued and Clinton carried out a previously scheduled meeting with him, but Adams was pointedly not on the invitation list for the March 1996 St. Patrick's Day party at the White House as he had been the previous year. Clinton claimed that he had Hume's blessing for allowing Adams into the United States after Canary Wharf.[62]

Major claimed that the bombing harmed Sinn Fein's credibility in both Ireland and America. Major thought that the bombing was either carried out by opponents of peace within the IRA or intended to soften up London before negotiations. The IRA would wait until both the governments in Dublin and London had changed before declaring another ceasefire. That would take about another seventeen months of armed struggle. Most of that occurred in Britain, including a massive bomb in the center of Manchester that wounded 200 but killed nobody and a mortar attack on a British army base in Germany in June. That month the IRA also killed Irish Garda Jerry McCabe during an "unauthorized" robbery in the Republic. But the IRA carried out a very successful and daring bombing at Thiepval Barracks at the British army's headquarters in Lisburn. The year ended with a death toll of 22 due to political violence, up from nine the year before. The IRA was responsible for eight of the deaths, the INLA for six, and loyalists for five.[63]

Sinn Fein and its sympathizers blamed Major for the IRA breaking its ceasefire. Their logic was that Major was deliberately slowing down the process because his government was dependent on the nine unionist votes at Westminster. Therefore the unionists could blackmail Major and force decommissioning on him. If the IRA resorted to violence at the drop of a hat it did not mean that military weapons were dangerous in IRA hands but that Major did not want peace. Infallible republican logic![64]

The IRA's 1996-97 campaign was different from its 1971 to 1994 campaign in two key respects. First, it was centered primarily in Britain rather than in the province. Second, the casualty rate was very low — the IRA actually killed more people during its ceasefire from August 1994 to February 1996 than it did when it was officially off ceasefire from February 1996 to July 1997. In the second half of 1996 the IRA lost two bombing teams in England, bringing its campaign there to a virtual halt. In July six men were arrested in south London. And in September a second five-man team was arrested during police raids on London. Both teams belonged to the South Armagh Brigade, which had the best bomb-making skills in the IRA and whose people had the technical skills to both manufacture the bombs in either Northern Ireland or England and find employment in England as welders or truck drivers. And its bombs were always reliable.[65]

On February 29 the two governments agreed on June 10 as the date for negotiations to begin following new elections for the Forum at the end of May. Sinn Fein would be allowed to compete in the elections but not participate in the resulting negotiations until the IRA returned to ceasefire. In the election a "topping up" feature was added in which the top ten parties were each given an extra two seats each. This was designed to ensure that the two loyalist parties were represented and had a "mandate" to participate in negotiations. The UUP won 24 percent of the vote, the SDLP 21 percent, the DUP nearly 19 percent and 15 percent for Sinn Fein. This was a record showing for the Republican party. While Trimble won 46 percent of the unionist vote, Paisley and other rejectionists won 43 percent. Overall, the UUP did quite well compared to the SDLP, which lost ground to Sinn Fein. Many of its voters were first time republican voters who wanted to encourage the party to pursue peace. The other nineteen percent of the vote went to the nonsectarian Alliance Party (about a third) and Women's Coalition, Robert McCartney's UK Unionist Party (UKUP), the two loyalist paramilitary parties and the tiny Labour Party of Northern Ireland. After the assembly election two years later, the Women's Coalition and PUP were reduced to two seats each, the UDP was eliminated from the assembly, the UKUP broke up into two separate parties, the tiny Labour Party disappeared, and the SDLP surpassed the UUP with the most first-preference votes, but not the most seats.[66]

The first several weeks of the negotiations were spent debating over the ground rules that the two governments offered and the unionists rejected. These were based on the Anglo-Irish cooperation since 1985: the Anglo-Irish Agreement, the Joint Declaration, and the Frameworks Document. The DUP and UKUP (which operated as a satellite of the former party throughout the negotiations) opposed Mitchell as chairman because he was partly of Irish-American background, although a Lebanese-American couple had raised him. The UUP refused to go along with this, allowing Mitchell to remain as chairman. These two "rejectionist" unionist parties were the only parties out of the ten that objected to having Mitchell chair the talks. No one objected to De Chastelain and Holkeri. Mitchell was forced to sit in a hotel room for two days while the two governments decided what to do.[67]

The talks were nearly killed in their infancy by Drumcree II. In July 1996 RUC chief Hugh Annesley initially prohibited the Orange Order from marching down the Garvaghy Road, but then faced with some 10,000 unionist demonstraters backed by loyalist paramilitaries Annesley backed down on the morning of July 12 and forced the march through the nationalist area. This led to widespread rioting throughout the province by nationalists, which had been proceeded by the erection of hundreds of roadblocks by loyalists. Hundreds of homes and vehicles were burned and thousands of visitors left the province and more cancelled their reservations, crippling the tourist industry. The worst rioting was in Derry where the police saw the worst rioting since the early 1970s. Police estimated that some 2,000 petrol bombs were thrown. The Kellyhevlin Hotel in Enniskillen was destroyed by a vehicle bomb that exploded in front of it injuring 17 people. The police estimated that some 24,000 petrol bombs were thrown throughout the province and police used 6,000 plastic baton rounds ("rubber bullets"), the most used since the hunger strikes of 1981. Brid Rodgers of the SDLP reported that "[t]he events of that day had the same effect on the Nationalist community as Bloody Sunday" (in January 1972). One republican rioter in Derry was killed when he was accidentally crushed by a police vehicle, and 149 police officers and 192 civilians were injured; 39 police homes were attacked and 28 police families were forced to move permanently to avoid the risk of future retaliation. A senior RUC officer to justify the force's actions claimed, "We were on the brink of all-out civil war.... We kid ourselves that we live in a democracy. We have the potential in this community to have a Bosnia-style situation." And a senior Presbyterian minister dubbed Drumcree "Northern Ireland's Chernobyl." Clearly The Troubles were not yet over. In parade disputes throughout the peace process both sides sought to emphasize their victimhood and communicate their fears to their supporters in the province. But Sinn Fein's communication skills far outclassed those of its Orange Order opponents.[68]

Billy Wright's Mid-Ulster UVF was responsible for the murder of a Catholic taxi driver who had just graduated from Queen's University three days previously. His unit had been responsible for some twenty deaths in the Mid-Ulster area during the 1990s. Trimble had met briefly with Wright in a bid to avoid violence. This was severely criticized by both nationalists and by his unionist opponents who thought that he was providing the Republicans with cheap ammunition. Trimble displayed some hypocrisy by meeting with Wright and not with Brendan McKenna of the Garvaghy Road residents committee and he justified this by saying that the UVF was on ceasefire but the IRA was not and the PUP was involved in the talks while Sinn Fein was excluded. The UVF might have been on ceasefire but Wright clearly was not. Trimble was severely criticized by the SDLP for his attitude towards the various paramilitaries. The loyalist politicians regarded Trimble's attitude towards them as less hypocritical then that of most unionist politicians.[69]

But the loyalists' ceasefire could be as tenuous as that of the Republicans. The Mt. Vernon UVF branch was guilty of a range of ceasefire violations throughout the 1990s and as late as April 1997 was plotting something as major as a bomb attack on the Sinn Fein office in the town of Monaghan in the Republic.[70]

In the summer of 1996, as a direct result of Drumcree II, representatives of both the business community and trade unions in Northern Ireland formed the G7 as a pressure group. The business community in Northern Ireland, unlike in Israel, was politically independent and not connected to any of the political parties. As a result its initiative was perceived as nonpartisan and accepted by the public as was the idea of a Belfast-Dublin economic corridor. In the summer of 1994 the Confederation of British Industry published a paper arguing that peace could radically improve the economy of Northern Ireland. This optimism eventually became a self-fulfilling prophecy. The business community preached that violence was a luxury that the province simply could not afford. In the summer of 1998 the G7 would be involved in preventative mediation between the Orange Order and the Garvaghy Road Residents Committee that helped to reach a compromise in Drumcree IV.[71]

The talks really just marked time for a year from June 1996 to July 1997 while the two governments waited to see if the Republicans would restore their ceasefire and Sinn Fein waited for elections in the summer of 1997 to see if the two governments would change. In May Tony Blair led New Labour in a crushing defeat of the Conservatives. In those same elections Sinn Fein increased its vote to 16.1 percent and then in local elections a month later to 16.9 percent — within striking distance of the SDLP and ahead of the DUP. The nationalists won a combined total of five out of 18 of the province's Westminster seats. And in the local elections the unionists lost control of Belfast City Council for the first time. Sinn Fein attempted to appoint convicted IRA bomber Siobhan O'Hanlon as its office manager at Westminster with 24-hour access to the House of Commons. Offices, however, were denied to abstaining members of parliament and the Conservatives made sure that this rule was not changed. Elections took place in Ireland in June 1997 with the result that the Fine Gael-led coalition was replaced by a Fianna Fail coalition headed by Bertie Ahern. Ahern's father was an old IRA man who had been involved in the Irish war of independence and then the civil war. Ahern was a career politician who had been close to Haughey.[72]

The IRA Army Convention was held in October 1996 and elected a new Executive that had ten out of its twelve members opposed to Adams political strategy. Adams remained in control of the Army Council, but would have to tread carefully. The dissidents in the IRA had failed in their one clear chance to defeat Adams.[73]

Adams held secret talks with the British government under both Major and Blair to arrange the entry of Sinn Fein into the talks process. By the second half of June Blair was starting to think heavily about how to move forward in Northern Ireland. On June 24 he met with Trimble, John Taylor, and Ken Maginnis from the UUP and Hume from the SDLP. Trimble claimed he had not been allowed to see the negotiations document — but was still opposed to it. Maginnis underlined to Blair how deep the mutual suspicions were and told Blair that he had personally met people that he knew from intelligence had tried to kill him. Trimble told Blair that Hume would never cut his ties to Adams and McGuinness.[74]

On July 9, 1997, Mo Mowlam sent a letter to McGuinness spelling out in detail the terms of the two governments for Sinn Fein's entry into the talks.

Both premiers insisted that the IRA would have to go back on ceasefire first, but Blair was willing to allow Sinn Fein back into talks without a long sanitizing period. Sinn Fein would be allowed back into talks six weeks after an IRA ceasefire if it agreed to decommissioning. London also agreed to participate in confidence-building measures to parallel decommissioning and agreed to parity of esteem in cultural matters. London also agreed to an end date of May 1998 for the negotiations. By the end of June Sinn Fein had worked out a deal with senior Irish civil servants for a ceasefire that involved the early release of IRA prisoners in Irish prisons. Dublin also made a series of promises to Sinn Fein regarding its entry into the talks and Irish politics that amounted to a rebuilding of the pan-nationalist alliance.[75]

The IRA announced a second ceasefire on July 20, 1997. The CLMC had managed to keep the mainstream loyalist paramilitary organizations on ceasefire throughout the IRA's renewed period of armed struggle from February 1996 to July 1997.

At this point London's position was that decommissioning must occur during negotiations. But this was complicated by Dublin telling Sinn Fein that there was no need for actual decommissioning during negotiations but a need only to agree to it in principle. A UUP delegation met with Blair who admitted to them that he could not deliver Dublin on decommissioning. Blair told Trimble that decommissioning was only symbolic, whereas the real problem was what the Republicans would do when Sinn Fein realized that the peace process would not result in a united Ireland. Blair's private secretary, Alastair Campbell, came away from the meeting with the impression that Trimble could not control his own party, a very worrying sign. Maginnis, who Campbell perceived as one of Trimble's political enemies, was "the ranter," whereas Jeffrey Donaldson was quietly menacing. Donaldson complained to Blair that it was always the Unionists who were called upon to make the sacrifices for the sake of the peace process. "We understand these people [Republicans]. They will go back to violence any time they feel like it."[76] On July 28 the talks adjourned until early September. Mo Mowlam, the new Northern Ireland Secretary appointed by Blair, monitored the IRA ceasefire and reported back to London that it held. The DUP and UKUP exited the talks permanently in July, before the recess, in anticipation of the admission of Sinn Fein. Only four of the nine parties voted to admit Sinn Fein and accept the plan of the two governments for substantive negotiations to begin in September: Alliance, the Women's Coalition, Labour, and the SDLP; the two loyalist parties abstained, and the three mainstream unionist parties were opposed. George Mitchell was of the opinion that leaving the talks was a major strategic error by the rejectionist unionists and that if they had remained the talks never would have succeeded. The first order of business on September 9 was getting the Sinn Fein delegates to affirm to the Mitchell Principles. When Sinn Fein went into negotiations the U.S. federal government halted the extradition of six IRA fugitives to the UK for trial on the advice of Secretary of State Madeleine Albright that it would advance the peace process. In early September 1997 a Sinn Fein delegation made a five-day trip to the United States and met with National Security Advisor Sandy Berger and Senators Ted Kennedy, Chris Dodd, Robert Toricelli, and Alfonse D'Amato — representing the four states with the largest proportions of Irish Catholics in their populations. McGuinness flew to California on his own and met with three of the fugitives to brief them. While in San Francisco he was feted by Mayor Willie Brown.[77]

Shortly after agreeing to a second ceasefire in July 1997 there was a major showdown within the IRA leadership between the Army Council, controlled by Adams and McGuinness, and the Executive, controlled by the traditionalists. Some of the latter suspected McGuinness of having supplied the intelligence to the Special Air Service (SAS) that resulted in two IRA active-service units being wiped out at the Loughgall Police Station in 1987.[78] The Executive, which has theoretical seniority over the Army Council, voted 10 to 1 that acceptance of the Mitchell Principles went against the IRA's constitution. Adams claimed that signing the Principles was just signing another piece of paper that did not mean anything. In early October 1997 the IRA held another General Army Convention to decide between the two bodies. The Council carefully choreographed the transportation to the Convention so that all of the opponents of Adams's political strategy — some 20 to 30 delegates — arrived together after all of the other delegates had arrived. The other delegates were warned to expect a possible coup attempt by the Executive. The Executive spokesman, Michael McKevitt, spoke along with a few others. Adams had promised the commander of the Belfast IRA, Brian Gillen, a seat on the Army Council if he supported him. The four motions by the Executive were all voted down and then a motion granting special dispensation for the Stormont delegates of Sinn Fein to sign the Mitchell Principles was passed. Adams had won with comfortable 60 to 70 percent majorities.[79]

On October 23 the new Executive of the IRA met and six of its members resigned. These included McKevitt, the quartermaster general of the IRA who was in charge of all of its explosives and arms, and many of the engineering department and the quartermaster department followed their leaders into exile. Within weeks the leaders had formed their own paramilitary organization, which predictably they called Oglaigh na hEireann or Irish army, the same title that the IRA and the army in the Republic used. The media branded them the Real IRA. McKevitt had some ideological weight as he was the partner — and later husband — of the sister of Bobby Sands, the IRA hunger striker and martyr. By the late winter and early spring of 1998 the Real IRA had joined with the other two dissident organizations, Continuity IRA and the INLA, to began a series of vehicle bombings in the town centers of Protestant market towns across the province. The three organizations would pool their resources to steal vehicles, build bombs, and then transport them into place. Their premier effort was actually a bomb in the South Armagh Protestant town of Markethill in early September 1997 when the Real IRA was still part of the Provos. The bomb, planted outside the RUC station devastated the town center but failed to injure any policemen. This, like the murder of two RUC constables in Lurgan in June, was designed to drive the Unionists out of the talks. Initially the RUC ascribed the Markethill bombing to the Continuity IRA but the bombing fit the later pattern used by the Real IRA. So some in the RUC and some journalists believe that it was really the work of the Provos and was authorized. Trimble at the time had no doubt it was the work of the Provos and attempted to have them expelled from the talks. But he later changed his mind and conceded that it was probably Continuity IRA that was responsible although possibly with encouragement and assistance from the South Armagh Provos. [80]

Continuity IRA was the armed wing of Republican Sinn Fein, the organization formed by Ruari O Bradaigh after Adams took control of Sinn Fein in 1983. The Provos had warned him at the time not to attempt to form his own armed wing. But when the IRA went on ceasefire in 1994 he felt entitled to do so. A number of dissident IRA members were recruited and formed Continuity IRA. The group was believed to have carried out the bombing of the Killyhevlin Hotel in Fermanagh in 1996, but never officially claimed credit for the bombing. The organization was by itself incapable of sustaining an armed struggle. It accused the Provos of destroying one of their bombs in the Republic before it could be brought North.[81]

Trimble had been careful to build bridges to New Labour by attending its annual conference at Blackpool, England in October 1996. Through a Dublin intermediary he arranged a series of private meetings with Ahern in Armagh before the Irish general election to convey to him unionist fears of a future Fianna Fail government. Without making any explicit promises Ahern was able to mollify Trimble. Blair did likewise by making a speech in Belfast on May 16, 1997 — one of his first after being elected — in which he spoke to a unionist audience and spoke in favor of the consent principle. "But none of us in the hall today, even the youngest, is likely to see Northern Ireland as anything but a part of the United Kingdom. That is the reality, because the consent principle is now almost universally accepted ... so fears of betrayal are simply misplaced. Unionists have nothing to fear from a new Labour

Government." Both Trimble and Hume reacted positively to the speech — a quite difficult feat — letting Blair know that he had hit just the right note.[82]

Trimble had decided to remain in the negotiations thanks partly to the advice of a rather unique advisor. Sean O'Callaghan was a repentant former IRA man who had joined the organization in the early 1970s in Dublin and served a few years. He then quit and after a complete change of heart decided to rejoin the IRA to serve as a Garda informer. During the 1980s he served and worked his way up the IRA hierarchy to head of Southern Command, the leader of the IRA's support network outside of the North and the border counties. In 1990 he went to prison for his previous offenses including the murder of a policeman in Northern Ireland. When he emerged at the end of 1996 he got in touch with Ruth Dudley Edwards who put him in touch with Trimble. O'Callaghan advised Trimble that Sinn Fein's whole political strategy was based on a complete unionist walkout from negotiations that would leave them free to negotiate a solution with London. O'Callaghan advised him that neither Adams nor McGuinness had had much contact with unionists and neither was a super strategist. In order to avoid this potentially devastating outcome, Trimble decided to remain. Trimble saw his personal political mission as forcing unionists to make tough choices in order to secure the Union. This was his first tough choice. O'Callaghan would remain a member of Trimble's inner circle of outside advisors that included Queen's University Irish studies professor Paul Bew, former Workers' Party strategist Eoghan Harris, and Edwards, an Anglo-Irish historian from Dublin.[83]

Drumcree III was relatively peaceful as the Orange Order agreed to back down from their demands so as not to give a propaganda advantage to the nationalists as Sinn Fein was about to enter the talks. No march took place along the Garvaghy Road — in fact 1996 would be the last time that the Order marched down the road for at least a decade. Martin McGuinness publicly opposed the Orange Order's right to march at Drumcree in 1997 but privately he worked behind the scenes to tamp down republican reaction in the area. Billy Wright had gone to prison in March 1997 for threatening a local woman who then testified against him in court. On December 27, 1997, he was murdered in the Maze Prison by two INLA prisoners while awaiting transport to the visitation area to see his girlfriend. The INLA had been involved in a number of assassinations of leading loyalist figures such as Johnny McKeague, leader of the Red Hand Commando, over the years. The circumstances of his murder are still being investigated today. There are allegations that the British Prison Service colluded in his death as he was considered a threat to the peace process. Wright's death caused his breakaway LVF faction to go on a killing spree of Catholics over the New Year's holiday in retaliation. Although Mo Mowlam was able to keep the UDA prisoners in the Maze from doing anything foolish by visiting them, the LVF and INLA engaged in a series of tit for tat killings during January 1998. The UDP was forced to "voluntarily" withdraw from the talks for a month after the RUC named the UDA as responsible for one of the murders.[84]

The following month it was Sinn Fein's turn to be suspended, for two weeks or six negotiating days, for the IRA's involvement in the murder of a UDA leader in South Belfast and a Catholic drug dealer. During 1996 the IRA had murdered several alleged drug dealers under the cover name of Direct Action Against Drugs. Mowlam acted on the advice of the RUC, which named the IRA as responsible for the murders, to suspend Sinn Fein. Ironically it occurred just as the talks moved to Dublin; the UDP had withdrawn as the talks moved to London. Sinn Fein brought legal action against the decision in an Irish court and Dublin provided Mitchell with free legal counsel, but Sinn Fein soon dropped the action—which was unlikely to go anywhere in any case—when assured that if the ceasefire was restored and maintained it could return.[85]

On the same day that Sinn Fein was ejected, a bomb planted by either Continuity IRA or the Real IRA ripped through the center of Moira near the RUC station, a town not far from Trimble's home in Lisburn and the home of Jeffrey Donaldson. Three days later a bomb devastated the town center in Portadown. The dissidents were attempting to blow up the talks.[86]

The Good Friday Agreement

The two governments published their *Heads of Agreement* document on January 12, 1998. It was based on the progress that had been made since the substantial negotiations had begun in October 1997. One day each week was devoted to each of the three strands. This kept the parties focused on the topic at hand. *Heads of Agreement* laid out the broad parameters for a final agreement. In Strand 1 this was a power-sharing Executive and an Assembly. In Strand 2 there was to be a North-South council tied to the Assembly and the Dail in the Republic and a limited number of areas for cross-border cooperation between the two states on the island. In Strand 3 there was to be an East-West council consisting of representatives from the Westminster parliament and the Dail and Senead in the Republic. The *Heads* document was rooted in the principle of consent and thus was a major defeat for Sinn Fein and a major victory for Trimble and the UUP.[87]

In March 1998 Mitchell sat down and worked out a schedule for the remainder of the negotiations. Allowing for a month-long referendum campaign and election campaign for the Assembly, Mitchell calculated that he would need two weeks of serious hard negotiations to wrap up the agreement. Earlier Blair had stated that the negotiations would wrap up by the end of May 1998. The Republicans had demanded finality to the process and Blair simply used the expiration date for the legislation authorizing the negotiations as an end date. He originally put down Easter Sunday as his final deadline, but then moved it back to Holy Thursday April 9, so that he could have some wriggle room to have the negotiations spill over into the Easter weekend. This would also allow the new Assembly to be sworn in before the marching season began in earnest, with the potential for another confrontation at Drumcree. Mitchell then cleared the schedule with the two governments, with Trimble and with the other parties. Everything was in place by March 24.[88]

In reality the final negotiations were a series of sub-negotiations conducted by a limited number of parties on each topic. The Strand 1 arrangements on power-sharing were mainly negotiated between the UUP and the SDLP, with some input from Alliance. Sinn Fein deliberately excluded itself by insisting on a 32-county republic, a strategy designed by Adams to appease the IRA so that it would accept the resulting agreement. During the final two weeks the SDLP refused to meet with Sinn Fein on Strand 1 issues, as they figured that then was a bit late and the Republicans had missed the boat. Sinn Fein turned in its proposals on the three strands only on March 24, 1998.[89] Prisoner release and decommissioning was mainly negotiated between the three paramilitary parties and the British government. Strand 2 was mainly negotiated between the two governments, the SDLP and the UUP. Strand 3 was mostly negotiated between the two governments based on the skeleton from the Brooke-Mayhew talks. Earlier the principle of *sufficient consensus* had been adopted that stated that at a minimum decisions had to be acceptable to the two governments, and a majority from each community. This prevented small parties from having a veto over the process while giving the two governments and the largest party from each community a veto.[90]

Alliance played three main roles throughout the negotiations. First, it was the advocate and originator of many key concepts such as power sharing, integrated housing and education, and civic society. Second, it served as a bridge builder between unionists and nationalists and at times passed along messages from one side to the other. Third, it served as the policeman of the talks by supporting the temporary expulsion or suspension of parties whose paramilitary branches had broken the ceasefire. The governments wanted to maintain standards of conduct but did not want to risk alienating any key actors and thereby losing an agreement. As the party's reward for this watchdog function it saw its share of the vote shrink throughout the early peace process to an average of 5.6 percent of the total vote from 1994 to 1999, compared to 8–9 percent a few years earlier.[91]

Five. The Belfast Agreement 127

During the final week of the negotiations both Blair and Ahern flew or drove up from their respective capitals to participate and help wrap up loose ends. Ahern was forced to return from his mother's funeral in Dublin to Belfast to negotiate — he could easily have refused. Blair spent nearly three days straight living at Castle Buildings, an office block in the Stormont complex where the negotiations were taking place, and surviving on bacon sandwiches, chocolate bars and tea. "As soon as Tony Blair arrived — they came in a bit like the A-Team — it changed the whole thing," claimed Alliance leader John Alderdice. Clinton had spoken to several of the parties during the St. Patrick's Day party in Washington immediately before the final negotiations began. He also made several phone calls during the night of April 9–10 to reassure and persuade the parties. He spoke with the two prime ministers, with Trimble, and with Adams twice. Blair prematurely announced an agreement as a means of deterring potential wreckers among the Unionists. On the final day Trimble slept soundly for five hours. Alderdice noted, "Trimble was calm — his attitude was 'I've done my best.'" Trimble phoned Mitchell at 4:45 P.M. to announce, "We are ready to do the business."[92]

The most contentious points were the number of cross-border agencies, the prisoner releases and decommissioning. Blair and the Unionists cut down the original list of joint agencies supplied by Dublin and Hume considerably. Trimble threatened to walk out of the talks if the original list remained intact. When the SDLP was asked for their justification for the list it explained that Northern nationalists needed to have some hope that their aspirations would one day be successful. As their aspiration was for a united Ireland the argument carried no weight with any unionists. Blair sympathized with Trimble's complaint after glancing at Dublin's shopping list. Ahern made quick concessions on this, possibly due to his fatigue and grief after attending his mother's funeral in Dublin. The revised list was negotiated among the two governments and the UUP. The SDLP would then demand payback in the Strand 1 talks for its refusal to stand firm on Strand 2. Ahern nearly came to blows with Trimble, whom he regarded as appallingly rude. It was probably the effect of a lack of sleep on both politicians.[93]

Prisoner releases was a hard sell for the unionists and particularly for the emotional unionists in the DUP, UKUP, and UUP. But for the rational Unionists represented by Trimble, Maginnis, Taylor, and the McGimpsey brothers it was understood all along that this would occur at the end of the process. Prisoner releases were implicitly — but not explicitly — linked to decommissioning by the two-year frame that both were supposed to take place within. Decommissioning was fudged within the final agreement as the paramilitary parties merely pledged that they would use their influence to persuade the paramilitary organizations to decommission within two years. Jeffrey Donaldson, the member of the UUP talks team representing the right wing of the party, decided to reject the agreement at the last moment. He justified his rejection in terms of the language on decommissioning, but John Taylor feels that he was really motivated by an unwillingness to forgive the IRA for its murders of relatives of his who were serving in the RUC. David Kerr, a Trimble aide, felt that Donaldson figured that unionists would turn against the agreement and that he did not want to go down with the ship alongside Trimble. Subsequent events tend to support this analysis but this does not rule out Taylor's contention as being a contributing factor.[94]

In the end Trimble and the other Unionists were persuaded to sign based on a side letter from Blair. Blair promised that if decommissioning did not occur as per the agreement, and the SDLP did not support Sinn Fein's rejection from the Executive, he would support the Unionists by having the decommissioning portion of the Good Friday Agreement changed through legislation that would support the exclusion of the offending parties from the Executive. It also said that "the decommissioning process" should commence immediately. In effect this applied only to Sinn Fein as the two loyalist parties were too small to worry about participating in the Executive. The side letter was a proved technique from the Middle East peace process having been used as part of the Sinai II and Israeli-Egyptian peace treaties to cover difficult issues and "bribes" to the respective parties in military and economic aid. But it failed to satisfy Jeffrey Donaldson. Trimble's future would hang on Blair's willingness to honor his commitment. Trimble had complained to Blair aide Jonathan Powell that his whole party leadership was in revolt against him.[95]

Sinn Fein was unhappy with the final agreement as they thought that the Unionists had gotten their way and the Republicans had nothing to show. Blair went through a list of nationalist gains with Sinn Fein. Adams claimed that they would not be able to sell the Agreement to their followers. But this might well have been acting to see if they could sway Blair into making last-minute concessions to them. At 11:30 P.M. Thursday night Blair called Clinton and asked him to be ready to make persuasion phone calls to Adams, Hume, and Trimble. Clinton made those extended phone calls including two to Adams. Clinton told Blair, "Hell, I'd rather be on holiday with Kenneth Starr (the special prosecutor whose investigation led to Clinton's impeachment) than hanging out with these guys."[96]

Some have criticized Trimble for spending so much time on Strand II issues at the expense of Strand I. There is some justification for this view. Trimble was dealing with the ghost of the Council of Ireland from Sunningdale and his fear that Paisley would do to him what he had done to Faulkner. Ahern and Hume may have strategically played to this fear by deliberately overloading the list of joint bodies so that Trimble would spend his time negotiating with Blair and Ahern over this rather dealing with the Strand 1 arrangements for power-sharing. Having conceded the principle of power sharing, Trimble seemed to be less concerned about the actual details. Others think that he might have anticipated a time when unionists were actually a minority within Northern Ireland and wanted to protect them by granting the nationalists essential equality so that the unionists could have the same status either in Northern Ireland or in a future united Ireland. But it seems more likely that Trimble was attempting to make Catholics comfortable within the Union and convert them from nationalists to Unionists (or at least Alliance supporters). Trimble also later claimed that he was stuck with the basic position on Strand 1 that the UUP had carried over from the Brooke-Mayhew talks into the Mitchell talks in 1996. But Trimble concedes that he should have worked harder on the details of the prisoner release scheme.[97]

Decommissioning was another issue altogether — the issue that would occupy Trimble's entire term in office as first minister and his subsequent time as party leader. He concedes that the Belfast Agreement (as it is formally known) was not perfect. He was of the opinion that the Republicans were then transitioning from violence to constitutional politics. He thought that Blair's letter would give him nine or ten months to solve the problem before the Executive would come into being. He was essentially making a gamble that he could solve the problem with Blair's help.[98]

Strand 1 called for an Assembly with 108 members, six in each of the 18 Westminster constituencies, elected by proportional representation — single transferable vote (PR-STV) for a term of five years. The UUP had wanted five-member constituencies (90-member Assembly), but the PUP wanted a sixth member to ensure that it would be represented. Gary McMichael of the UDP wanted five-member constituencies with a top-up as in the Forum election to ensure that the UDP would be represented. The PUP got its way, but not the UDP.[99] From the Assembly a power-sharing Executive of 10 members would be formed on a proportional basis using the d'Hondt mechanism in which each of the four largest parties would chose an office with the largest party starting first. Normally this would give the two largest parties three seats each and the two smallest (of the four) two seats each.[100] The Executive would be presided over by a first minister and deputy first minister, the former coming from the largest party and the latter coming from the largest party of the other community. In practice they were actually more like co–first ministers than like superior and subordinate. All parties were forced to register as either unionist, nationalist, or other. All measures needed to have majority support from both of the first two groups to pass. This rendered non-sectarian parties like Alliance and the Women's Coalition legally inferior, something that may have helped contribute to the demise of the latter party after it failed to win any seats in the Second Assembly. The agreement also embodied the concept of *parity of esteem* between the two communities so that legally there were no longer a majority and a minority community but two majority communities. This is a recognition of reality — in 60 percent of the province (west of the Bann River) nationalists are the majority and unionists are only a majority in the eastern two counties (Co. Antrim and Co. Down).[101]

Britain would retain control over security arrangements such as the British army, policing, and prisons. All security prisoners imprisoned for offenses related to The Troubles from organizations on a recognized ceasefire would be released within two years of the agreement being approved by referendum, thus by May 2000. All paramilitary organizations that had a party that signed on to the agreement were supposed to decommission their weapons during this same two-year period.

Strand 2 called for Ireland to change Articles 2 and 3 of its constitution so that they could no longer be interpreted as making a legal claim on the territory of Northern Ireland. Taoiseach John Bruton had already agreed to do this when he was in office. Irish nationality was made a voluntary privilege rather than a forced condition.[102] A North-South council would be created from members of the Assembly and Irish parliament with its decisions subject to approval by both bodies. An agreed list of joint cross-border authorities were to be created to manage specific duties. Strand 3 called for a similar East-West council to be created between Britain and Ireland to manage the relationship between the two islands, the Channel Islands and the Isle of Man.[103]

One Blair biographer allows that the situation was indeed ripe for peace and that if Major had been reelected in 1997 he well may have negotiated the Belfast Agreement instead of Blair. But Mitchell claimed that the Agreement would not have been possible without both Blair and Ahern. Despite Blair's rhetoric of feeling "the hand of history" on his shoulder, he in reality shook off the hand of history by rejecting the history of failed peace attempts that had dogged the country from Gladstone to Major. The Belfast Agreement was the greatest accomplishment of Blair's first term and helped to win him a record-breaking reelection in 2001. But a *Washington Post* headline on the day after the Agreement gave the Clinton administration's take on the deal: "Clinton's support played a major part in clinching the deal."[104]

Six

The Peace Process Collapses

The Referendum Campaign

The first task after the participants returned from vacation was to gear up to campaign for a "yes" vote in the Referendum to be held a month after the Agreement was signed. This was a tricky process because the Unionists, loyalists, and Republicans all had to convince their respective constituencies of different, indeed opposite, things. The loyalists and Unionists had to convince the unionist community that the Union was safe and that in effect they had won the war while the Republicans had lost. The Republicans had to convince the republicans that they had won — or at least not lost — and that the Agreement was an assured route to a united Ireland and the 32-county republic that Patrick Pearse had proclaimed in Dublin on Easter 1916. Gerry Adams's logic was that the higher nationalist birthrate would allow demographics to make the nationalists a majority by the provisions for a border poll in the Agreement. He also argued that Sinn Fein's status as the only all-Ireland nationalist party on the island would facilitate this process by working to make Dublin a persuader for Irish unity. In reality the Agreement did not change London's policy on the future of Northern Ireland. Since 1949 it had been conditional upon a majority of the province's inhabitants favoring the Union. The two governments had to play their parts in convincing the different publics of these opposite viewpoints. The way this was done was for the two prime ministers to campaign in their respective ethnic areas in the North, while the governments released prisoners temporarily to attend Sinn Fein and loyalist rallies.

The appearance of such celebrities as the Balcombe Street Gang — the IRA unit that had been behind a series of horrific bombings in England in the 1970s — at a Sinn Fein Ard Fheis and of Michael Stone, a celebrated UFF assassin who attempted to murder Adams at a nationalist cemetery in 1988, at a UDP/UDA rally at Ulster Hall in Belfast helped to convince the paramilitary communities that the Agreement was a good thing. But the prison releases and the triumphalist attitudes of the Republicans and loyalists had the opposite effect on mainstream unionists. The unionists were nearly as shocked by Stone's appearance as they were by the Balcombe Street Gang. Early polls show a majority of unionists prepared to reject the Agreement. Blair aide Jonathan Powell was convinced in early May that the "yes" vote would win the referendum, but that a "no" vote would prevail among unionists, thus undermining the Agreement.[1]

Secretary of State "Mo" Mowlam had let IRA prisoners out of the Maze Prison to appear at the Sinn Fein Ard Fheis without notifying Blair first. As a result both Trimble and Blair were angry with Mowlam. Trimble felt only contempt for Mowlam whom he regarded as biased towards the nationalists, vulgar, and lacking a knowledge of basic details. He bypassed her during the Good Friday negotiations and would continue to do so until she was replaced by Blair the following year. Mowlam may have innocently not realized the import of what she was doing or possibly wanted to show her irritation with Blair for sidelining her during the negotiations. Stone's arrival at the Ulster Hall rally was neither organized nor anticipated by the UDP. UDP leader Michael Stone later admitted, "It was a total screw-up which did us no good.... Stone's presence in the Ulster Hall was an own goal.... Tactically it was a disaster, there's no question of it."[2]

Trimble's strategy for procuring a "yes" vote was based on three points. First, as he was a controversial figure among unionists, he would allow Blair and former Prime Minister Major to do much of the campaigning for a "yes" vote. He would appear together with one or the other in territory where he was personally unpopular. Blair and Major appeared together at a question and answer session before a group of university students. Blair devoted much precious time campaigning before large audiences. Focus groups showed the British the concerns of unionists and in response they came up with a five-point pledge of assurances about the status of the province, prisoner releases, and North-South bodies.[3] Second, Trimble would make a major effort to convince "garden center Prods," who normally did not participate in elections to come out and vote to ensure the Union and the peace. Trimble's longterm project for unionism was based on cutting the UUP's ties to the Orange Order and attracting these same "garden center Prods" to join the UUP and help transform it. Trimble was so busy and imperiled within the party over his decade of leadership that he never had a chance to implement his project. But the project was based on a false premise. "Garden center Prods" rejected unionism and Ulster politics in large part because of the sectarian nature of politics. They saw elections as little more than tribal headcounts. So if they decided to rise above their apathy, why would they get involved in a party with a very sectarian past and present instead of opting for nonsectarian parties like Alliance and the Northern Ireland Women's Coalition?[4] Third, when polling showed that the 18–24 year old group was the largest group of undecided voters it was decided to appeal to this group through rock concerts.

Tim Atwood, a SDLP activist and brother of SDLP MLA Alex Atwood, knew Irish rock star Bono. Bono had campaigned in the past in support of the fight against world hunger and against AIDS and supported the peace process. Atwood was easily able to convince him to give a benefit concert in Belfast on behalf of the "yes" campaign. A local Protestant band, Ash, was lined up to open the concert for Bono and give the rally an ecumenical or nonsectarian character. Tickets were given to both parties to distribute to their supporters, but because the UUP was so unorganized the tickets ended up being distributed through schools and youth organizations. At the rally, on the eve of the Referendum both David Trimble and John Hume appeared on the stage alongside Bono and Bono grasped their arms and raised them above the crowd to wild cheers from the audience. It was the high point of the campaign.

Ads were carefully placed in newspapers read by unionists, particularly middle-class unionists and "garden center Prods" such as the *Belfast Telegraph, Ulster Newsletter,* and the *Daily Telegraph*. But no significant media outlet opposed the Agreement and all three provincial daily newspapers editorialized in support of the Agreement. This is in contrast to Israel. Israeli researcher Gadi Wolfsfeld found that "the Israeli media played a mostly destructive role in the Oslo peace process, while the news media in Northern Ireland was more positive." The British advertising giant Saatchi and Saatchi designed the Yes campaign's posters free of charge. Civil society largely ran the Yes campaign in Northern Ireland.[5]

Trimble appeared on political programs and talk shows on Ulster Television (UTV) and BBC Northern Ireland, the province's two television networks, to sell the Agreement. Trimble also appeared accompanied by Blair or by pro-unionist Labour MP Kate Hoey, whose family was from Nothern Ireland and who had previously campaigned on behalf of opening up the province to Labour Party membership with Robert McCartney. As McCartney was the star of the No campaign along with Paisley, she was particularly effective as a counter to him. Trimble was also tipped off about a controversial ruling prohibiting the Drumcree procession to march along the Garvaghy Road that July by the Parades Commission, a new "quango" body created the previous year to deal with controversial parades. The tipster was a member of the Commission, Glen Barr, who was opposed to the Agreement but who was loyal to Trimble as a result of their joint work against Sunningdale in 1974.

Blair then was able to persuade the Commission head, Alistair Graham, whom he knew slightly, to delay publication of the decision until after the Refendum. Graham actually delayed it until after the Assembly election as well.[6]

The "No" campaign against the Belfast Agreement was launched shortly after Easter from the Dundela House, the DUP headquarters in Belfast. The campaign was run by the two unionist parties that had boycotted the peace negotiations — the DUP and the United Kingdom Unionist Party (UKUP) of Robert McCartney. Robinson ran the campaign for the DUP and there was quite a bit of friction between the UKUP leader who ran his own party as a "one man band" and Robinson, the deputy leader of his party, who was responsible for party administration. The DUP later estimated that the government and the business community between them spent between three and four million pounds sterling on the "yes" campaign compared to 87,000 pounds spend by the DUP to oppose it.[7] Needless to say, these traditional unionists did not coordinate with anti-agreement republicans. In addition the Confederation of British Industry all but endorsed the Agreement and warned of the dire economic consequences of a "no" vote. And President Clinton promised $100 million in economic aid as a bribe to bolster the Agreement.[8]

The Referendum took place on May 22, 1998, on a 32-county basis, the first consultation across the entire emerald isle since 1918. With a 81 percent poll — the highest in Northern Ireland's eighty-year history — 71 percent voted yes and 29 percent no. In the Republic with a much lower turnout there was an outstanding 95 percent yes vote in favor of changing the constitution. The Referendum did not record votes on an ethnic basis in Northern Ireland, but polling data have given estimates of about 96 percent of Catholics voted in favor of the Belfast Agreement, whereas only a slight majority of Protestants, estimated at between 55 and 57 percent, voted yes. Nationalist turnout at 95 percent was much higher than the unionist figure of 70 percent. Nationalists felt empowered by politics, whereas many unionists felt resigned to accepting their fate rather than actively shaping it. The only Westminster constituency that voted no was Ian Paisley's constituency in North Antrim with a 55 percent No vote. The referendum had the effect of extending the ownership of the peace process beyond the two governments to include the various Yes parties, civil society, and the main paramilitary organizations. It also gave some moral and democratic legitimacy to the GFA.[9]

About ten days after the referendum Blair visited Stormont on June 2. Adams brought some senior IRA people with him to meet Blair and informed him that they were members of a local residents committee opposed to Orange Order parades. John Hume told Blair that Sinn Fein could turn violence off and on like a tap. Trimble told Blair that the Parades Commission, which ruled on routes for controversial parades, was "damaged goods." When Blair was trying to reassure a DUP delegation about decommissioning a fire alarm went off and Deputy Leader Peter Robinson joked that it was a lie detector. Blair laughed nervously.[10]

A month later the North held its first Assembly election on June 25. Ken Maginnis was appointed the campaign manager for the Unionist campaign. Trimble was carefully coached by Eoghan Harris, a presenter at RTE Irish Television, on how to improve his speaking style. He was also given a female assistant, Jane Wells — a public relations expert — who carefully selected shirts and ties for him that would show up well on camera and made him wash his hair regularly. The election resulted to a return to the usual turnout figures with a 69 percent participation level. The "garden center Prods" had returned to their apolitical lifestyles and were loath to come out again. They will probably be coaxed back out of their gardens only for border polls on the constitutional future of the province. The UUP ended up the winner with 28 seats, but had its lowest number of first preference votes — fewer than the SDLP received; next was the SDLP with 24 seats; the DUP had 20 seats, and Sinn Fein 18 had 17.6 percent, its highest figure so far. Of the smaller parties Alliance received six seats, the UKUP five, the United Unionists three, the PUP two and the Women's Coalition two. The United Unionists consisted of three anti–Agreement Ulster Unionists who ran as independents and then formed a faction together after the election. The UKUP soon split with Robert McCartney being left as its sole MP, while the other four split off to become the Northern Ireland Unionist Party. Within the "unionist" group in the Assembly 30 — the UUP and the PUP — were pro-Agreement and 28 — the DUP, UKUP/NIUP and United Unionists — were anti–Agreement. Six unionist parties received 384,000 votes compared to 389,000 votes for non–unionist parties (nationalist and nonsectarian parties). It was the first time that the unionist sector did not constitute an absolute majority in an election.[11]

This gave Trimble only a thin two-seat majority on important votes in the Assembly. He was dependent on the votes of the PUP and so could not afford to push the loyalist paramilitaries too hard on decommissioning. He also could not afford to lose any of his party's Assembly members to the opposition. He was in the same tight situation that the Rabin government had been in on the Oslo II vote.

There were more than the usual post-election recriminations as the two camps wanted to blame each other for the party's poor performance. Jeffrey Donaldson publicly blamed Ken Magginis for the losses during a public television interview. This earned him Maginnis's eternal contempt and an angry rebuttal. Several UUP seats were lost to nationalists because of the large number of competing unionist candidates simply split up the unionist vote and left the SDLP or Sinn Fein with a majority.[12] The UUP, with its lack of a centralized party machinery, has also been much worse than the DUP in managing its vote within individual constituencies so that first preferences would be wasted on a single candidate rather than equally divided among two. The SDLP also has this problem compared to Sinn Fein. Thus, both the DUP and Sinn Fein are able to maximize their votes in terms of seats won. Sinn Fein could also count on a large number of Republican activists to turn out during the campaign and to help get out the vote on election day — and to vote repeatedly in the name of those who don't vote.[13] The DUP could also count on a large number of volunteers from Paisley's Free Presbyterian Church.

The UDP did not manage to secure a single Assembly seat, a portent of its later demise in three-years time. This left it with no reward for having supported the peace process, a major drawback in dealing with people used to immediate gratification of their needs. The UDP suffered from two basic problems. First, unlike the PUP its voters were dispersed across the eastern half of the province and not concentrated in a single constituency. Second, in the UDA's heartland in the Shankill area of West Belfast six unionist parties fought for one unionist seat and the UDP candidate, double-murderer John White, came in last. Leader Gary McMichael ran in Lagan Valley and lost to a UKUP candidate. This left it with two councilors in Belfast and two in Lisburn. The PUP had a safe seat for David Ervine in East Belfast and Billy Hutchinson was competitive for the moment in North Belfast. The UDP also was not as successful in distancing itself from its paramilitary organization as was the PUP. The PUP was ideologically more socialist than the UDP and this held some danger for it as most loyalists were not socialists. In Belfast it could hope to attract the votes of the children whose parents voted for the Northern Ireland Labour Party in the 1960s. But as the Union appeared less secure many of the voters for the two loyalist parties would drift to the DUP in future elections leaving the UDP without a consituency and the PUP restricted to East Belfast.[14]

Many anti-agreement unionists saw the loyalist parties as the creatures of the Northern Ireland Office and the media as a means of giving respectability to the loyalist terrorists. They point out that Billy Hutchinson and John White, leading spokesmen for the PUP and UDP respectively, were convicted murderers. This attitude was most common among conservative UUP members and UKUP members, whereas the DUP tended to embrace some loyalist terrorists for tactical reasons. One writer complained that between the emergence of the PUP and 2007, its military wing, the UVF, carried out a dozen murders.[15]

Until the next Assembly election was held in five years, Trimble would have to attempt to get the IRA to decommission and state that the war was over so that he could retain the support of his party caucus. In the meantime he would also be forced to fight off challenges to his leadership by Jeffrey Donaldson and others in the Ulster Unionist Council (UUC) a 860-member body that acted as the party's central committee.[16] On April 18 the UUC had voted to approve the GFA by a vote of 540 to 210 or a 2.5:1 ratio; a week earlier the party executive had voted to support the Agreement by a vote of 55 to 23 or roughly the same ratio.[17] The strange thing about the UUC is that due to the unique ties between the UUP and the Orange Order, which go back to the former's origins a century ago, it included members who were not necessarily party members — and might in fact even be members of rival unionist parties like the DUP and UKUP. Over the next four years Trimble would face thirteen separate leadership challenges in the UUC. Like the IRA when it was attempting to assassinate Thatcher, Trimble's rivals only had to be lucky once and Trimble would be forced to step down as party leader.

Three days after the Assembly election IRA members burst into the house of Michael Donnelly, a former Republican internee who had called the Agreement a "sell-out," and tried to kidnap him. Donnelly and his son drove off the attackers. Even though the attackers' blood was left at the house no one was arrested. Within days the names of the attackers were widely known in Derry. This was the first of many attempted kidnap-murders carried out by the IRA in the years following the GFA.[18]

Forcing Decommissioning

Republicans started out with a nearly absolutist position on decommissioning at the time of the Agreement. The IRA issued a statement that it was not a party to the Agreement, and therefore was not bound by it. Grafitti in republican ghettoes in the North was even more blunt: "Not one bullet, not one ounce." As republicans considered decommissioning to be the equivalent of surrender, this was in effect a republican translation of the unionist cry "No surrender!" issued by the defenders at the Siege of Londonderry in 1688 and repeated by unionist politicians such as Edward Carson and Ian Paisley on a regular basis in the twentieth century. Sinn Fein's position was that they could not deliver decommissioning, at least for present, and that the Belfast Agreement obligated them only to make their best efforts — it did not actually require decommissioning. "Trust in rust" was the paramilitary maxim regarding decommissioning by loyalists and Republicans alike.[19] At various times Dublin, London, and the SDLP had all supported the unionists demands for decommissioning, but as time went on and the Republicans stubbornly refused to decommission, the others dropped their demands.

The Good Friday Agreement itself had no enforcement mechanism — no sanctions specified for violators of the Agreement. A party could be expelled from the Executive for noncompliance, but this would require cross-communal support: in practical terms the SDLP had a veto over any attempts by the Unionists to force the decommissioning provisions down the throats of the Republicans. This was why Tony Blair gave the UUP his side letter on the day the Agreement was signed. Absent British support for fulfilling the side letter and expelling Sinn Fein, the Unionists had two main mechanisms for sanctions against Sinn Fein. First was refusing to set up the Executive or collapsing it once it had been established by Trimble resigning as first minister and thereby causing the collapse of the Executive. The second was by threatening the North-South Ministerial Council, under Strand 2, which was of importance to nationalists but not to unionists.

The most obvious mechanism for coercing decommissioning would have been to refuse to release the prisoners of any group refusing to decommission. With the same time frame for prisoner releases as for decommissioning, this was implied linkage within the Agreement. But when the British passed the necessary legislation for prisoner releases in parliament, they did so in a clumsy fashion that made it into a "time off for good behavior" scheme rather than connecting it to observance of the Agreement. While release was conditional on good behavior after release and violators could — and were — (be) returned to prison to fulfill the remainder of their sentences, this was on an individual rather than a collective/organizational basis. Once the problem became evident Blair refused to introduce legislation to correct the deficiencies of the original legislation thereby raising suspicions that he feared provoking the IRA because of a fear of its return to operations in Britain. Realist theory in international relations holds that a country's first priority is to ensure the protection of its own citizens. When one takes into account that neither the British elite nor the British public considers the unionists to be really British — they are considered a strange species of Irish — then this behavior was and is entirely predictable.

But why the unionist emphasis on decommissioning in the first place? There are several reasons for this. Most fundamentally it is a confidence-building mechanism (CBM) caused by the lack of trust between the two communities. Decommissioning is the equivalent of a notorious womanizer surrendering his "little black book" to his wife when he gets married. This does not remove the possibility of his cheating on her in the future, but it makes it more difficult and removes a certain degree of temptation. Likewise, the IRA could always acquire new arms and explosives in the future either from rogue states or friendly terrorist movements or from the open arms market. But intelligence that they were doing so would give a warning to the

British and Irish security services that they were planning to go back to war. With their arsenal intact there would be no warning. Second, the arms could be used as a form of blackmail to force either the unionists or London to do the bidding of the Republicans. Nowhere in Europe or the West was an armed faction allowed into democratic institutions. Third, Unionists saw the Agreement as a balanced compromise with unionists receiving changes in the Irish constitution, decommissioning, and the end of the terrorist war in exchange for power sharing, early prisoner releases, police reform, and the North-South Ministerial Council. By refusing to decommission the IRA was subsequently modifying the terms of the Agreement. With support for the Agreement at 55–45 percent in the unionist community any de facto changes in the terms of the Agreement eroded support for it. Fourth, for many anti–Agreement unionists the failure to decommission became a focus for all of their emotional rejection of the Agreement.

Unionism like republicanism was going through a crisis in the 1990s. Unionism had always been divided between "rational unionists" and "emotional unionists." Rational unionists focused on details, tradeoffs, and possible alternative courses. Emotional unionists focused on all the things they did not like and played upon them. Emotional unionism had much in common with the dynamics of the secessionists in the antebellum South or the right in Israel. It was backward looking rather than future oriented like the Trimbistas in the UUP. The split ran down the middle of the UUP. Most, six out of ten, of the UUP's Westminster caucus was anti–Agreement. Trimble refused to purge his opponents within the party and his only sanction was to prevent anti–Agreement members of parliament special dispensation to run for the Assembly as well as Westminster.

The Republicans were going through a similar process, made more difficult because it was a covert process rather than an overt process. Whereas Trimble attempted to conduct an honest debate with his opponents within his party and the wider unionist community, Adams and McGuinness used stealth, manipulation, and deceit to outmaneuver their opponents. This is why their approach was initially more rigid and accommodative but ultimately more successful. Adams and McGuinness had merely to tell Republicans what they wanted to hear until it was too late to do anything different. Ultimately it would be changes in the international political climate in America and the West caused by the Al-Qaeda attacks on September 11, 2001, that allowed or forced decommissioning to go ahead.

Trimble was constantly forced to make promises that hurt him in the long run in order to win in the short term. Before the Good Friday Agreement was negotiated his wife Daphne told him that in her opinion he would always win just enough support to keep fighting while the opposition would likewise win enough support to keep going. Trimble was also burdened by the knowledge that every marching season he could suddenly see all of his careful planning go awry because of an incident when Orange members and loyalist thugs intoxicated with liquor and rhetoric might go too far. As a result Trimble was always tough during the marching season and conciliatory during the fall and winter.[20] He refused to establish the Executive in July 1999, but did in November. He collapsed the Assembly by his resignation in July 2001, but agreed to a deal in October. But Trimble also collapsed the Assembly in February 2000, due to a promise he made to the UUC when he won its approval to go into government with Sinn Fein before decommissioning. And he resigned in October 2002 in response to revelations of a Sinn Fein spy ring within Stormont.

Trimble and Adams were the two indispensable actors in process once the Agreement was signed. Adams (and McGuinness) were necessary to keep the Republican Movement in line. Trimble was necessary to keep the Unionists in the process. Deputy UUP leader John Taylor was ambivalent about the Agreement and was too old to take over the leadership from Trimble. Presumably if Trimble had been killed in a car accident or plane crash or developed a terminal illness, leadership would have devolved to a member of the party's liberal wing such as Ken Maginnis or one of the McGimpsey brothers or Reg Empey. But it is doubtful that any of them could have received approval from the UUC or maintained it in the face of opposition from the anti–Agreement wing of the party. In the 1995 leadership election Maginnis came in third, just one vote ahead of the fourth-ranking candidate. Trimble was elected with the support of what latter became the anti–Agreement wing, because of his performance at Drumcree that year. In any case, Maginnis retired from parliament in 2001. He then restricted himself to a council seat.[21] Only Trimble was able to continually pull "a rabbit out of the hat" year in and year out.

Among the SDLP leadership no single leader was indispensable. While Hume played a major role in initiating the peace process and selling it during the Referendum campaign, he, like Adams and Paisley, declined to serve as leader in the Executive of his party. Seamus Mallon, the deputy leader of the SDLP, became the deputy first minister serving alongside Trimble in the Assembly and Executive. Mallon and Hume both retired together in 2001 after the collapse of the Executive. Mark Durkan, a former assistant to and protégé of Hume, became the new party leader of the SDLP. But by then the pattern of the SDLP's response to the decommissioning crisis had been well established. It was to condemn both the IRA's (and loyalist paramilitary organizations') failure to decommission while equally condemning any moves by the UUP to coerce the Republicans to decommission. Just as Hume and Mallon retired, Sinn Fein bypassed the SDLP in local elections to become the largest nationalist party.

Normally the press in Northern Ireland and abroad would refer to Sinn Fein, the SDLP and the UUP as being pro-Agreement parties and the DUP as an anti–Agreement party. But in reality it was nowhere this simple. Both the DUP and Sinn Fein were ambiguous in their attitudes towards the Agreement. The DUP condemned the GFA as a sell-out for unionism and a corrupt bargain with bloody terrorists, but they were quite happy to assume their seats in the Executive. Sinn Fein supported its own interpretation of the Agreement that did not require the IRA to decommission according to the GFA's May 2000 deadline. The UUP was not ambiguous, but was divided down the middle with a 53 to 47 percent majority for the Agreement. Only the SDLP was unambiguously in favor of the Belfast Agreement. So in reality the math was 1.5 parties in favor and 2.5 opposed, rather than three in favor and one opposed.[22]

Trimble's future really depended on his forging a cross-community center bloc consisting of the UUP, the SDLP, Alliance, and the NIWC. This in fact is what Arend Lijphart and other writers on consociationalism recommend — a multiethnic coalition at the elite level. Northern Ireland's proportional representation — single transferable vote (PR-STV) system with its multiple votes in fact is designed to create just such coalitions. If the party leadership in each of these parties had urged their supporters to transfer their surplus votes to pro-Agreement centrist parties across community lines a viable center could have been created. In the 1998 Assembly election just over a third — 36 percent — of lower-transfer votes from UUP voters went to the SDLP, and fifteen percent of UUC members said that they would be willing to vote for SDLP candidates. [23]

Trimble later blamed the SDLP for the failure to forge such a coalition.[24] In fact Hume seemed to be more sympathetic to Adams's difficulties with the IRA than with Trimble's difficulties with his right wing. Due to personality differences more than differences on the issues, Trimble and Mallon, the two co–first ministers, did not get along very well together.[25] When Trimble brought down the Executive in February 2000, Mallon resigned. But because his resignation was not officially presented to Speaker Alderdice, it was simply ignored by the Alliance Party and the Unionists when the Executive was revived in May.

Few voters transferred votes across community lines, at most voters from the nonsectarian Alliance and Women's Coalition would do so and voters from the sectarian center parties would vote for Alliance candidates. But it was much more common for Unionist voters to use their surplus votes on behalf of DUP candidates and for SDLP voters to use their surplus votes on behalf of Sinn Fein. David Vance also complains that DUP voters tended to use their lower preference votes for UUP candidates rather than for UKUP candidates, who were also anti-agreement. This was probably a matter of habit. In any case, the NIUP and UKUP failed to win any seats in this local election.[26] West of the Bann River and in Counties Antrim and Down, away from Greater Belfast, Alliance and NIWC candidates were simply not viable, so the vast majority of voters simply stuck to their traditional pattern of trying to keep candidates from the other community out of office.[27] This sectarian pattern was simply too ingrained to break without a major effort, and decommissioning prevented the two sectarian centrist parties from coming together to forge that coalition. With both leaders afraid of losing ground to the extremist parties on their flanks — or to the rejectionists within their own party in the case of Trimble — they were in no position to make concessions that might lose them votes within their own sectarian bloc. The best time to forge this coalition would have been in 1998 during or immediately after the Referendum campaign, but Trimble did not make the effort. After the Assembly election it quickly became difficult and then impossible once Trimble refused to establish the Executive in the spring and summer of 1999.

The Fight to Establish and Maintain the Executive 1998–2001

As soon as the Assembly election was over and the Assembly was sworn in during a largely administrative meeting on July 1, Trimble had to worry about the annual Drumcree confrontation in his constituency. This author was in Northern Ireland during the 1998 marching season and remembers the press coverage. The area around the Drumcree Church looked like a movie set from a film on the First World War. The British army had called in earth-diggers to build a set of trenches to keep the protesters separated from the lines of police and army troops set to enforce the Parade Commission's decision to ban the march. It was a nightmare for Trimble as any incident could spark a major confrontation that could cause his Assembly caucus to further split and leave him with a minority in the Assembly. For five days running there was a violent confrontation between the police and the Orange-loyalist protesters. Sixty four members of the force had been injured by slingshot launched ball bearings, fire bombs, and fireworks. Catholics and Protestants clashed in the streets in North Armagh. Many police families were forced to evacuate their homes after being forced out by neighbors and loyalists. Over a thousand Orangemen had besieged the village of Dunloy by manning roadblocks on all the access points to the village.[28]

On the morning of July 12, the day of the traditional Orange Order marches commemorating the Battle of the Boyne in 1689, two men from the UVF firebombed the home of a mixed couple in Paisley's hometown of Ballymoney in North Antrim. The couple's three youngest children, aged eight, nine, and ten, were burned to death in their bedroom before the fire department could put out the blaze. The family had only returned from England, where they had fled to two years earlier, six days earlier. It was a loyalist housing estate marked with red, white, and blue curbs and the UVF as the paramilitary organization that ran the estate would not tolerate the presence of the family.

The murders were front page news across the province. Many commentators connected the Orange Order to the climate of violence that had allowed such murders to occur. Like the Rabin assassination three years earlier, those who associated with the organization of the murderers were implicated as well. The Rev. William Bingham, a senior figure in the Order, preached a sermon that Sunday "No road is worth a murder." Trimble made a point of attending the funeral service for the Quinn children at the Catholic church in Ballymoney. Trimble and Mallon issued a joint appeal for the Orange Order to call off its protest. Trimble issued his appeal as the local member of parliament rather than as first minister. The Orange Order in shame called off its protest and the Drumcree confrontation quickly petered out for that year. In October 1999 the driver who brought the two petrol bombers to the housing estate was convicted of three counts of murder and sentenced to life in prison. The following year his conviction for murder was reversed on appeal and he was sentenced to 14 years for manslaughter. The two actual murderers remained at large.[29]

The UDA did not formally participate in Drumcree IV, but the Red Hand Defenders was used as a cover name for dissident loyalists from both the UVF and the UDA who participated at Drumcree in backing up the Orange Order. Over the next three years it would be used as a cover name in claiming responsibility for several sectarian murders. In November that year the Orange Volunteers emerged as another dissident loyalist group. In reality the name was just a flag of convenience for UDA hardliners in the SE Antrim Brigade.[30]

On August 15, 1998, a massive bomb ripped through the market town of Omagh in Co. Tyrone in the west of the province. The bomb killed 29 (not counting a pair of unborn twins) and wounded some 200, many quite seriously. It was the single most deadly bombing in the history of The Troubles.[31]

The bombing, according to the police investigation afterwards, was the work of the Real IRA, with assistance from the INLA. The INLA stole the car that was used to transport the bomb and the Real IRA built the time-detonated bomb and phoned in the bomb warning. Either through incompetence or deliberately the location of the bomb was misreported so that the police actually herded people into the path of the bomb in an effort to get them away from it. The dead included visitors from Spain and the Republic and over half the victims were Catholics. This prevented a loyalist reprisal killing in response to the bomb. Both Blair and Ahern rushed to the hospital to visit victims of the bombing and Blair was visibly upset by what he had seen.

The bombing was condemned by all shades of opinion in the province and abroad leaving the dissident republicans very isolated from public opinion. Even Ruari O Bradaigh of Republican Sinn Fein and Gerry Adams of Sinn Fein rather hypocritically condemned the bombing. Special anti-terrorist legislation was passed in the Westminster parliament and Dail allowing for conviction of terrorists upon the testimony of police officials. This would allow for the conviction for membership in a paramilitary organization even if there was little evidence that would normally be sufficient for conviction. As a result both the Real IRA and the INLA shortly after the bombing publicly went on ceasefire. Continuity IRA remained on armed struggle but was the least able of the three dissident republican terrorist organizations to continue that struggle. The Real IRA later went on a bombing campaign in London in 2000 but accomplished very little. The ceasefire caused several of the hard men in the RIRA who had come over from the Provos to either retire from terrorism or go abroad. The organization was forced to actively recruit new members in the Republic and this allowed both the Garda and the Police Service of Northern Ireland, as the RUC was renamed, to infiltrate the organization with informers. Arms-purchase stings were perpetrated against the RIRA resulting in several arrests. The organization was soon no real threat but more of a nuisance. The INLA was so weakened after some fifteen years of internal feuds that it offered little to the RIRA. Between the three organizations there were perhaps fifty to seventy-five active members and they regularly cooperated with each other in the spring and summer of 1998. Omagh changed all that.[32]

Omagh had done for the republican dissidents what the Quinn children did for the Orange Order — temporarily defanged them. The Real IRA and its 32-County Sovereignty Committee were ostracized in the republican ghettoes of the North and its members were forced to retreat across the border into the "wild west" frontier town of Dundalk, just over the border from Newry. Bernadette Sands-McKevitt quickly became a forgotten figure in nationalist politics.

"Mo" Mowlam wanted to go back on vacation in Greece immediately after Omagh. She flubbed the press briefings after the bombing, which helped the Tory press in Britain to equate the Real IRA with the Provos. Already a month before Blair had decided that she was not really up to the job of Northern Ireland Secretary as she could not handle the unionists or the civil servants (whom she gratuitously insulted) properly.[33] Her days were numbered.

With his extra-parliamentary threats removed on both flanks, Trimble could now concentrate on finding a solution to the problem of decommissioning. Before the Assembly election the two governments had contemplated immediately forming a shadow-Executive and then after a few months devolving power to it. But because of Trimble's narrow majority in the unionist group in the Assembly, this was no longer a viable option. He refused to form an Executive with Sinn Fein, while the SDLP refused to exclude the Republicans. In early September Trimble was taken aback when Blair advised him to develop a good personal relationship with Adams. In October 1998 a *Belfast Telegraph* survey of the Assembly team revealed that nine members would vote against Trimble if he attempted to go into government with Sinn Fein before decommissioning had begun. This meant that Trimble had to tread carefully. That same month a group of leading businessmen from the province toured North America to drum up investment in Northern Ireland. On November 25 there was a lot of tension between Trimble and Deputy First Minister Seamus Mallon at their first meeting with Blair at Stormont when he came for a visit to get the process back on track.[34]

In December 1998 Trimble and Hume were jointly awarded the Nobel Peace Prize for that year for their efforts to bring about the Agreement. In Oslo Trimble delivered a speech written for him by Eoghan Harris full of quotes from such figures as Irishman Edmund Burke, the child of a mixed marriage, as well as from international figures like American Cold War diplomat George Kennan and Israeli novelist Amos Oz. Trimble also admitted that Northern Ireland had often been a "cold house for its Catholics." He also warned against appeasement by quoting Kennan. The quote seemed like it was more directed at Dublin and London than at history students. His comments did not go over well with public opinion in Ireland, particularly among the chattering classes in Dublin. In Belfast the fact that he had been awarded the prize in the first place was taken as proof by his opponents in the DUP and UKUP that he was being paid off for selling out Ulster. The year ended with the UKUP splitting after four of its five MLAs refused to sign a pledge to resign their seats if Sinn Fein went into government without decommissioning. Trimble regarded McCartney as his most dangerous opponent, and this seriously defanged him. Conor Cruise O'Brien had also published his memoirs and called for unionists to negotiate their way into a united Ireland from a position of strength. This was a severe shock to the party as O'Brien had been the party's best-known spokesman outside of the province.[35]

A week after Trimble and Hume received their Nobel Prizes at Oslo the first physical act of decommissioning occurred. The Loyalist Volunteer Force (LVF), created as the Mid-Ulster branch of the Ulster Volunteer Force (UVF) split from its parent organization following Drumcree II in 1996, had not been one of the loyalist organizations recognized to be on ceasefire by the Northern Ireland Office. It was similar to the dissident republicans and therefore its prisoners were not eligible for early release under the GFA. Desiring to release its prisoners, the LVF put itself in touch with De Chastalain's decommissioning body. On December 18 the LVF handed over nine guns, 350 bullets, two pipe bombs and six detonators to the Independent International Commission on Decommissioning. The guns were all either antique rifles from the original UVF (World War I vintage) or homemade sub-machineguns that did not function well. But De Chastalain had them cut up with diamond-studded power saws that created lots of sparks and had the whole exercise filmed for television news. Trimble was happy to recommend the LVF's prisoners for early release as he had proved that the belief that terrorists never surrender their weapons was a myth.[36] The LVF was more of a drug distribution gang than a paramilitary movement but it was a welcome Christmas present for Trimble and the UUP.

The first real attempt by the two governments to get the Assembly up and running—a function that the two governments would perform repeatedly over the next eight years—came in the early spring of 1999, following the trek to Washington for the annual St. Patrick's Day party. In late March prolonged talks on decommissioning and the Executive were held at Hillsborough Castle outside Belfast by the two governments for all the parties. This was after the UUP had warned in January that a failure by the IRA to decommission could lead to a renegotiation of the Agreement. That same month the party whip was removed from a UUP MLA who opposed UUP policy. Sinn Fein positioned itself for a failure by warning that no decommissioning could occur before the creation of the Executive, and possibly not even after it was up and running. But Adams admitted to Blair for the first time that he knew that there would eventually have to be decommissioning. Trimble insisted that several acts of public destruction of increasing quantities of weapons would be necessary. The next day, March 30, Adams and Trimble together calmly told Blair that they were far apart on decommissioning. Adams said that the IRA could not decommission as a precondition for Sinn Fein joining the Executive. Blair thought that Sinn Fein was "pathetic."

The next day Ahern told off Sinn Fein for "buggering about" and keeping Blair tied down at Hillsborough while he had a war to fight in Kosovo. The following day two senior Unionists complained to Blair secretary Alastair Campbell about Mowlam. Maginnis said she did not understand Unionists at all and John Taylor called her a liar. That same day the British woke Clinton up at 5:30 A.M. Washington time to call Adams on decommissioning, but Adams refused to take the call because he was too busy giving a history lesson to Blair. National Security Advisor Sandy Berger was very angry with Adams over this incident.[37]

A draft agreement was produced calling for the nomination of the Executive followed by decommissioning and then by the Executive going to work. The two governments called for decommissioning to take place in the framework of a public day of reconciliation that would serve as a catharsis for the society with ceremonies of forgiveness. The draft was shown to the IRA, which promptly rejected it. Leading Belfast Republican Brian Keenan told a crowd at Inneskeen in the Republic, "If it fails, it fails." He was referring to the Agreement. Sinn Fein formally rejected the draft on April 13. It was clear which portion of the Republican Movement was in charge when it came to decommissioning.[38]

The next major initiative took place in July. On June 30 a UUP delegation told Blair that it has to be "jump together"— product delivered by the IRA while the Executive is set up. The UUP considered Adams promise to eventually decommission to be a "post-dated check." "We give them a whole load of cash now, but we have to wait to get anything in return," explained Reg Empey. Trimble told Mallon and Blair that he was afraid that once the Executive was set up the IRA would not deliver and Blair would refuse to kick Sinn Fein out of it. Mallon told Blair that he thought that Trimble was constantly afraid of Paisley and McCartney. Trimble said that even if public opinion went along with "jumping first" the Ulster Unionist Council would not go along.[39]

The two governments produced a two-page document called *The Way Forward* that called for devolution to take place on July 15 followed by decommissioning to begin and be completed by the May 2000 deadline. The UUP rejected the document. "No guns, no government" had become the new UUP slogan and mantra. The murders of two drug dealers in Co. Down in May and June, allegedly by the IRA, did not produce any great trust in the IRA's intentions by unionists. On June 17 former IRA informer Martin McGartland was shot and severely wounded at his home in north-east England by IRA assailants. In January Republicans had murdered Eamon Collins, a former IRA intelligence officer who had written his story, *Killing Rage,* after he quit the organization. Collins insisted on living in South Armagh despite being ordered out of the area by Republicans. Mo Mowlam refused to rule the attack on McGartland a violation of the IRA's ceasefire, probably at the behest of Blair. This only increased her unpopularity with unionists.[40]

The IRA seemed to be intent on functioning as it wished no matter how much this might inconvenience Sinn Fein. The IRA had a very narrow definition of ceasefire that prevented it from attacking members of the British security forces. But informers and severe critics from within were considered to be fair game. The IRA still did not accept that British law applied to republican areas, despite what Sinn Fein may have signed up to in the Belfast Agreement. At the end of the month Charles Bennet, allegedly a low-level security force informer within the IRA, was found dead within West Belfast. Four days before the FBI had arrested three Irish citizens in Florida for planning to illegally export small arms to Northern Ireland. The arms were purchased in the United States but their importation into Northern Ireland without a permit was illegal under British law. The arms being bought were pistols and sub-machineguns that were more useful for assassinations and punishment shootings and robberies than for fighting the British. They were smuggled into Northern Ireland by the Belfast Brigade of the IRA. The IRA was rapidly being transformed into a criminal organization.[41]

On the day appointed for the establishment of the Executive, July 15, only the nationalist parties and Alliance turned up. The unionists boycotted the event and after an all-nationalist Executive was nominated it was ruled to lack sufficient cross-community support by Speaker Alderdice and promptly collapsed. At this point Deputy First Minister Mallon announced his resignation from his post. Had Trimble not decided to boycott the event he could easily have been destroyed by the revelations about IRA activity that came at the end of the month. Adams and McGuinness were furious about amendments to a Westminster bill on Northern Ireland, and the SDLP — taking its cue from Sinn Fein — was furious as well. A week later the IRA issued a statement that was a veiled threat to return to violence. Blair saw Sinn Fein as a mirror image of the IRA: both were certain that the other would not deliver on its commitments. McGuinness claimed that Blair and Trimble had more influence over the IRA than either he or Adams had.[42]

Drumcree V in July 1999 was the most peaceful yet since the protests began. Only 25 police officers were injured compared to 76 injured and one killed the year before, and only one baton round was fired compared to 823 in 1998 and thousands in 1996. But Blair alienated the leaders of the Orange Order who thought that he had promised that the march would be allowed to go down the Garvaghy Road. Because the Orange Order refused to meet with residents of the Garvaghy Road the Parades Commission again banned the march and the Order thought that Blair had broken his "promise." In reality Blair had merely voiced an aspiration that he thought the march should go down the road and he wished it to be able to do so.[43]

In October the UUP held its annual party conference at the Killyhevlin Hotel in Fermanagh, which had been bombed three years earlier by the Continuity IRA. This followed the release of the Patten Commission report on the future of policing in Northern Ireland on September 9. Trimble had rashly predicted publicly that all of the speculation about the contents of the report would prove unfounded. If anything, the actual report was worse than the speculation as far as unionists were concerned. There were five main features of the report that were objectionable to unionists. First, the name of the RUC was formally changed to the Police Service of Northern Ireland (PSNI). Technically the name was changed to PSNI (incorporating the RUC) but the latter portion was never used except on formal occasions. Second, the cap badge was changed so as to embrace neutral symbols such as the flax flower, rather than just the old crown and harp. Third, in future recruitment an equal number of Catholics and Protestant applicants would be recruited until the number of Catholics on the force was proportional to the general population. Fourth was the use of local policing boards to supervise the force to which Sinn Fein members could be elected. Fifth, all national symbols were to be removed from all police stations including the Union Jack flag. The three symbolic features were more important to unionists than the more substantial worry that a criminal organization might be able to control the body meant to keep it in check.

Anti-agreement unionists did not consider Patten to be independent, but rather a creature of the British government. He was also considered a hypocrite for advocating the depoliticization of policing while creating policing boards manned by politicians. Policemen killed during The Troubles were regarded as martyrs and heroes by the mainstream unionist population who identified with the RUC in a way that it did not identify with the loyalist paramilitaries. And the renaming of the force was seen as a major Republican victory.[44]

Trimble had left the management of Patten to Ken Maginnis, who specialized in security affairs. Maginnis recommended a particular candidate, P.D. Smith, to the board as the Unionist nominee who did not consider himself bound by Unionist policy. The other members were from Britain, the United States, and the Republic. Trimble never expected the government to adopt the Patten Commission's recommendations completely. These revelations hurt Trimble badly among ordinary unionists and added to his reputation as a detached intellectual more interested in opera and history and obscure legal arguments than in the issues that mattered to ordinary Ulstermen.[45]

Eoghan Harris wrote two long letters to Trimble two days after Patten was released advising him on what to do. Harris wrote that the police could probably live with the report and that he should not attempt to politicize the issue. This would only make nationalists more suspicious and hard to work with. He also saw nothing wrong with the new name, which used the province's formal name rejected by many nationalists in everyday use.

On September 26 Trimble convened a secret meeting of his Assembly team at a hotel at Glasgow Airport to hear three speakers: Harris, Belfast writer Malachi O'Doherty, and Queen's University Irish studies Professor Paul Bew. The three spoke to the Assembly members of their analysis of where the Republican Movement was at that point in time. Bew and O'Doherty limited themselves to objective analyses, but Harris launched into an attack on the "no guns, no government" policy.

A month after Patten was released the party held its annual conference at the Killyhevlin Hotel, the site of the CIRA bombing in 1996 and not far from the site of a Provo atrocity in Enniskillen in 1987. Trimble had been impressed enough with Harris's performance in Glasgow that he invited him back for an encore performance before the entire party. Harris delivered his famous line. "The IRA is like a kid who wanted a bike for Christmas. The bike is a united Ireland. They didn't get the bike. At least let them keep the stickers." By stickers Harris presumably meant the symbology that unionists were so worried about. He also declared that it was the British government's job, and not the job of the UUP, to see that the IRA eventually decommissioned. Trimble himself hinted that he was about to give up his "no guns, no government" policy by speaking of "jumping together," "choreography," and "sequencing." By this he meant that he might set up the Executive, but that decommissioning had to follow shortly afterwards. His device for ensuring that it would was a post-dated letter of resignation lodged with the party president. If by the date on the letter decommissioning had not occurred he would resign.[46]

What prompted this change in thinking from Trimble? Trimble and Adams were in similar situations. Each had to deliver something that was very difficult for their respective constituencies to accept and neither was fully in control of the situation. Both were taking risks — Trimble with his political future and Adams with both his political and physical futures. If Trimble miscalculated he could be out of a job, but it was unlikely that someone would be so vengeful as to kill him once he was out of power. With Adams it was different as the Provisionals took their oaths very seriously and were prepared to use violence to enforce them. Trimble had to find a way of forcing Sinn Fein to force the IRA to disarm. Both had to ascertain the ultimate intentions of the other and if deemed to be sincere, help the other through a judicious mixture of pressure and inducement.

On September 6, 1999, George Mitchell began a Review of the workings of the Agreement, as specified for in the GFA, under the sponsorship of the two governments. Like the original peace negotiations, the initial going was very slow and made little progress. One UUP negotiator later said of McGuinness, "[H]is mind is stuck in gear at 1972. He hasn't realised that the world has moved on." Nationalists also saw their Unionist counterparts as backwards looking. Both sides stressed their limited room to maneuver. One observer characterized Mitchell's handling of the review as being "like adding Prozac to the tea." In other words he lulled the two sides into relaxing their guards.[47]

As the review was proceeding Blair recalled Mo Mowlam to London against her will and replaced her with his close friend and political ally, Peter Mandelson. Mandelson as both a homosexual and a Jew was a bit of a stretch for most unionists, but few knew of his sexual orientation and unionists were pro-Israel. More than this, they were ecstatic to be rid of Mowlam whom they regarded as both pro-nationalist and vulgar. Trimble did not like Mowlam because of her lack of grasp of detail. He tended to ignore her and deal directly with Blair instead.[48]

On October 18 the venue for the Review shifted to the American ambassador's residence in London, an old mansion. That month the European Court rejected McGuinness's claim that Sinn Fein was being discriminated against by being denied House of Commons facilities while maintaining its refusal to take its seats at Westminster. On November 17 in a press conference Gerry Adams for the first time publicly acknowledged that Sinn Fein had a responsibility to bring decommissioning about. Trimble told a different press conference at Castle Buildings that Sinn Fein had a legitimate right to pursue a united Ireland by peaceful means. The next day the IRA issued a statement that it was appointing a representative to interact with General de Chastelain's Independent Commission on Decommissioning. To former Republicans like Anthony McIntyre this was a sign that the IRA was serious about decommissioning. The following day Trimble called a meeting of the UUC to repeal the "no guns, no government" policy for November 27. On November 23 NI Secretary of State Peter Mandelson awarded the George Cross to the RUC for bravery. This went a long way towards canceling the negative symbolic aspects of Patten. The UUC decided to back Trimble's new policy by a vote of 480 to 329. This was 58 percent of the party and the high point of Trimble's leadership. When Trimble announced the decision to the press he stated simply, "Now its over to you, Mr. Adams. We jumped, now you follow." Two days later the Executive was formed. The next day devolution was repealed at midnight and power sharing returned to Northern Ireland after 25 years. McGuinness had given vague assurances to the UUP that if the Executive were set up at the beginning of December that the IRA would begin decommissioning by the end of January to be completed within four months.[49]

Trimble apparently had not thought through the implications of going into government with Sinn Fein fully. One of these was that Sinn Fein would have its choice of two posts in the Executive under the d'Hondt system. Trimble seems not to have reached agreement with any of the other parties over what posts they would choose. He should have been able to reach agreement with the SDLP, if not with the DUP as well. Reg Empey became minister of Enterprise; Michael McGimpsey took over the position of Culture, Arts, and Leisure; and Sam Foster, a former B-Special reserve policeman loyal to Trimble, became minister of Environment. Brid Rodgers of the SDLP became minister of Agriculture; Durkan became minister of Finance; and Sean Farren took over Higher and Further Education (vocational schools and universities). For the DUP the two ministerial positions were reserved for its two competing crown princes: Peter Robinson at Regional Development and Nigel Dodds at Social Development. For Sinn Fein Martin McGuinness took on Education and Bairbre (Barbara) de Brun Health. The discretionary non-security bloc grant from London was largely (60 percent) in the hands of the two Sinn Fein ministers while the UUP controlled very little of the budget! Plus the education of their children would now be in the hands of an unrepentant former terrorist — something that almost gave unionists apoplexy! And the ministry of Health was the largest employer in the province with its multiple hospitals and clinics.

When McGuinness moved to abolish the 11-plus exam that all students were required to take in order to determine their future educational needs, middle class parents of both communities were upset. McGuinness, a high school dropout who became an apprentice butcher, was reacting to his own experience. Had Trimble carefully coordinated the offices that would be selected rather than just the ministers, he could have saved himself from another loss of esteem in the eyes of the unionist public. But Trimble did not realize that under Northern Ireland's new power sharing system he did not have policy powers comparable to the prime minister in London or in the old Stormont. Ministers had autonomy within their own ministries so as to prevent a return to majoritarianism.[50]

On December 13, 1999, the North-South Ministerial Council held its first meeting in Armagh, an appropriate site as it was the ecclesiastical capital of the island with both the Catholic Church and the Church of Ireland having their headquarters there. De Brun spoke in Irish about the importance of the NSMC in bringing about a united Ireland — fortunately for the unionists they could not understand what she was saying. This was the third all–Ireland body in twentieth-century Irish history but the first to actually meet. The Government of Ireland Act (1920) had called for the establishment of a Council of Ireland, this was in order to facilitate the anticipated partition of the island — but it never met. The Sunningdale Agreement of 1973 also called for a Council of Ireland but the power-sharing government was destroyed by a loyalist workers' strike before the Council could be implemented. Later Minister of Regional Development Reg Empey (UUP) was the first minister to go to the Republic on North-South business. This was reassuring to unionists who could trust him not to cook up a plan with Dublin to bring about a united Ireland.

On December 17 the British-Irish (East-West) Council had its inaugural meeting, this being the last part of the GFA machinery to go into effect. After the meeting Bertie Ahern called on all the paramilitaries to assist in "decommissioning the word decommissioning. Get rid of it!" Meaning that the only way to get rid of the issue was to do it. That same month the Irish cabinet formally amended Articles 2 and 3 of the Irish constitution by a declaration after a ten-minute discussion at the regular cabinet meeting. Having already been approved by the referendum in May 1998 this was not controversial, Dublin was merely waiting for the implementation of Strands 1–3 of the Agreement in the North before moving ahead with its obligations. The modifications never became an issue in Irish election politics partly because the two main parties pursued a bipartisan approach to Northern Ireland.[51]

During 1999 over 230 pipe-bomb attacks were carried out by loyalists, most of them by the UDA's youth wing, the Ulster Young Militants. Most of these attacks were against Catholics or mixed families living in Protestant areas, either in rural Protestant towns or in Protestant housing estates. Intraloyalist violence also increased. The first intraloyalist incident was a UDA attack on a UVF bar in May 1996. Bloody encounters between rival flute bands occurred during an Apprentice Boys march in Derry in August 1997, resulting in "Brigadier" John Gregg of the SE Antrim Brigade losing an eye. Loyalist violence was approaching the level of intra-INLA violence in the 1980s. The relative political success of the PUP compared to the UDP also exacerbated tensions between the two paramilitary organizations. By late 1999 27 UDA members had been killed by the UVF, more than were killed by republicans according to a pamphlet authored by UDP politico John White.[52]

On September 14, 1999, Johnny Adair, commander of C Co. of the UDA's Shankill Brigade, was released from prison as part of the GFA. He was very bulked up from working out and using steroids that had been smuggled into prison. White, who was an alleged cocaine and Ecstasy dealer nicknamed

"Coco" in grafitti, became a mentor to Adair. The UDA "brigadiers" met with De Chastelain in January 2000 but nothing came out of the talks. Adair emerged as the moderate because he wanted a UDA decommissioning event in order to put pressure on the IRA. Adair began painting curbstones in West Belfast to mark C Company's territory. In January 2000 a feud broke out in Portadown between the LVF and the UVF. Adair and C Co. sided with the LVF as Adair had befriended Billy Wright while the two were in prison together.[53]

When Trimble went into government with Sinn Fein he left a postdated letter of resignation dated February 4, 2000, with UUP President Josiah Cunningham that would go into effect if decommissioning had not occurred by then. There was a week's grace authorized by Cunningham before the letter went into effect. Both governments, Sinn Fein and the SDLP, were aware of the existence of the letter but not the exact date for its going into effect. Only on January 27 did Trimble reveal the letter's date to Mandelson. Trimble was in effect playing a version of the game of "chicken" by taking control out of his own hands. Sinn Fein seemed to believe that once the institutions of the Agreement were up and running, Trimble would lack the nerve to interrupt them. The letter was meant to dispel that belief. Gerry Adams went to Washington in January and met with President Clinton, Secretary of State Madeleine Albright, and National Security Advisor Sandy Berger at the White House. They all stressed the need for IRA decommissioning.

London, Washington, and Dublin — especially the latter — put great pressure on Sinn Fein to get the IRA to decommission. De Chastelain's report on decommissioning was due at the end of January and if he had nothing positive to report it was likely that the Executive would collapse. On February 1, De Chastelain turned in his report to the government. The text was made public two weeks later and made clear that the IRA had conceded nothing. Sinn Fein Vice President Pat Doherty told reporters "no, no, no" when asked if decommissioning would occur soon. The UUP had scheduled a debate on the report for the day after it was turned over to the government. Seamus Mallon said during the debate that only two questions to the IRA were relevant: "Will you decommission?" "If you will decommission, when will you do so?"

For two months the Assembly held sessions on mundane topics dealing with agriculture, education, and tourism, etc. The power sharing government was held up as a model in conflict resolution for other national and regional conflicts. But under the surface there was great tension. Trimble forbade Sinn Fein ministers from traveling to Dublin on North-South business as a sanction until decommissioning occurred. On February 2, 2000, Secretary of State Peter Mandelson met with President Cunningham about the letter. Mandelson feared that if Trimble resigned he might not be able to get the government up and running again because of defections in the Assembly to the anti–Agreement camp by UUP MLAs. A UUC meeting was scheduled for February 12 and Mandelson did not want Trimble to have to face the Council without having either resigned or the government having been suspended. On February 3 Ahern and his top aides jetted to Cornwall where they met with Blair for two hours in a futile attempt to resolve the crisis.

During the final week legislation was introduced into the Commons to suspend the institutions. The IRA issued a statement on February 5 denying that it had ever agreed to decommission. And it made clear that it would not do so at anyone else's dictate. So on Friday February 11, 2000, in the afternoon Mandelson transferred power from Belfast back to London. A second De Chastalain report issued that same day was even bleaker than the first about the chance's of decommissioning occurring in the near future. This was the day before the UUC was scheduled to meet. Northern Ireland's latest experiment in power sharing had lasted even less time than Sunningdale — 72 days to be precise.[54] And de facto the IRA had conspired with the Paisleyites and the anti–Agreement emotional Unionists and Trimble himself to bring down the Assembly. It was a replay of 1974 but under very different circumstances.

In early 2000, Brian Keenan, adjutant or number two man in the IRA, traveled to Colombia to found a joint IRA/FARC training camp. Jim Monaghan, named by Peter Robinson in the Assembly on May 8, 2001, as the IRA's director of education, accompanied Keenan. He had developed the IRA's series of homemade mortars and would be one of the "Colombia Three" arrested in Bogota for entering the country illegally.[55]

The next three months were spent forging a new compromise on decommissioning while the institutions remained frozen. At the UUC meeting on March 25, 2000, the Rev. Martin Smyth, MP for Belfast South, made a leadership challenge to Trimble and received 43 percent of the vote. Asked before the meeting if Smyth was a "stalking horse" one wag replied that he was more like a "stalking donkey" and Taylor dismissed him as a "carthorse." The size of Smyth's vote was a rude shock to Trimble — an aide had estimated that the outcome would be 70 percent to 30 percent, three times the margin that Trimble actually received. Trimble later admitted to journalist Frank Millar that if Donaldson had immediately followed up with a challenge of his own or replaced Smyth he might very well have toppled him, but Donaldson lacked the killer instinct. He was more interested in harassing Trimble and making his job impossible than he was in actually replacing him. He was an Ulster

Unionist version of Paisley in this respect. But the UUC did pass a resolution prohibiting Trimble from going back into the Executive until the RUC name was restored to the PSNI. It was another futile gesture. After the vote Trimble muttered to aide Dennis Rogan, "We're in damage limitation mode now. I mightn't be here next year. As the IRA said about the Brighton Bomb, 'We only need to be lucky once.'"[56]

Trimble had brought some of this on himself by stating during a press conference in Washington for Clinton's final St. Patrick's Day party that he might again go back into government before decommissioning had occurred if he had "good reason" to believe that it would occur soon after. He repeated the offer twice, so it was not a case of his merely misspeaking. At this point his nationalist partners in Dublin and Belfast were ready to sacrifice Trimble rather attempt to force the IRA to deliver "product."[57] The SDLP seemed to be a victim of "Stockholm syndrome." It was identifying with its armed captors rather than with its unarmed Unionist associates. Sinn Fein referred to all attempts to make the IRA live up to the Republican Movement's commitments as "saving Dave." As if it were possible to save the peace process without "saving Dave" or delivering product. This caused journalist Frank Millar to ponder in print, "Has David lost the plot?" He thought that Trimble might be preparing to deliberately split his party as Brian Faulkner did in January 1974.[58]

Dublin's efforts were focused on finding an alternate means of putting the IRA's arms "beyond use" other than physical destruction that might be acceptable to both the IRA and the Unionists. Mandelson had become as nearly alienated from the nationalists, and in particular the Republicans, as Mowlam had from the unionists. Mandelson especially disliked McGuinness, whom he regarded as a bully, who had the habit of poking him in the chest during moments of tension. McGuinness also treated him as stupid—too dense to understand the simple point that Sinn Fein was trying to make. But Mandelson did allow that McGuinness was a very effective negotiator. Republicans had observed that there was a keen rivalry between Blair's chief of staff, Jonathan Powell, and Mandelson. So the Republicans decided to whenever possible work through Powell. Powell would often travel to either the Republic or Northern Ireland to meet with Provo leaders in an attempt to work out alternative modalities of decommissioning. Northern police insisted on being kept informed of his travels so as to not risk his accidentally being arrested or surprised at a roadblock and having the details of his business exposed in the media. London and Dublin worked out a deal with the IRA while Trimble and the UUP were kept out of the picture. Their only input would be a thumbs up or thumbs down on the final deal.[59]

After traveling to both Dublin and Belfast in April, Blair scheduled a high-stakes summit at Hillsborough Castle for May 5 to put remaining issues plaguing the peace process to bed. The summit coincided with the election of a new mayor in London and because incumbent Ken "Red Ken" Livingstone looked certain to beat the New Labour candidate, Blair's spinmeisters focused press attention on Belfast as a diversion. Negotiations went on for two days — thirty hours. During the first morning Blair took John Taylor aside for a private conversation. He asked Taylor what the Unionists needed in addition to a resolution on decommissioning. Taylor replied that they needed only two things. First, legislation to ensure that all ministries be required to display the Union Jack. Second, the retention of the "crown and harp" on the badge of the new police service. Blair replied that Mandelson's reserved powers should be sufficient to cover the flying of flags on specified dates and that the badge was a matter then being debated in parliament. The IRA agreed that it would coordinate with the IICD to have agreed international figures conduct inspections of its arms dumps to ensure that no access was being granted. This would occur within (an unspecified number of) weeks of the Executive being reestablished on May 22, 2000, according to an IRA statement of May 6 that Blair thought was a bit "watered down."[60]

Because Patten claimed that the RUC would be subsumed into the new policing service, the formal name of the force was specified as: The Police Service of Northern Ireland (incorporating the RUC). The final cap badge ended up including the crown and harp along with a number of other symbols including the shamrock and the flax plant. Mandelson ordered that all flags be flown on a specified list of 17 holidays from seven different government buildings and departmental headquarters and police stations. These dates included the Queen's birthday to the annoyance of nationalists. Anti-Agreement unionists had focused almost entirely on symbolic issues related to police reform such as the name and symbol rather than substantial issues like mandatory parity in recruiting or an overall reduction in the size of the force. As a result Trimble was desperate to keep RUC in the name.[61]

By the end of June former African National Congress (ANC) Secretary General Cyril Ramaphosa and former Finnish President Martti Ahtisaari had conducted their first inspection of "a number of arms dumps" (believed to be at least three) in the Republic and ascertained that devices were in place to ensure that any unauthorized tampering would be detected. They then reported this to the IICD. This was initiated as a confidence-building measure (CBM). Ahern seemed to be happy with this as having disposed of the issue but both Blair and the Unionists did not consider it to be a final substitution for decommissioning.[62]

A meeting of the UUC was held on Saturday May 27, 2000. Before the meeting Sean O'Callahan spoke to various Council members in small groups around Belfast and told them that as a former senior IRA member from a republican family he interpreted the IRA's statement as an admission that the war was over. Trimble won a vote to reenter government with Sinn Fein by a margin of 53.75 percent to 46.75 percent. The anti–Agreement faction had conducted a sophisticated anti–Trimble campaign for two weeks prior to the vote and was surprised when Trimble was once again victorious. One thing that made the outcome of votes difficult to predict is that nearly every time there was about a third of the Council that refused to commit itself before the vote. Thus, the other two-thirds appeared to be evenly divided before the vote — one-third pro- and one-third anti–Agreement. In a press conference after the vote Trimble remarked, "As far as democracy is concerned, these folk ain't housetrained yet." This remark was very upsetting to nationalists and especially republicans who took it as a literal comparison with dogs. But many of those offended had remained silent about continued IRA murders, punishment beatings, and the long refusal to decommission. Devolution of power to Belfast returned on May 29, 2000.[63]

Loyalist Feuds 2000–2003

July brought a return to the annual confrontation at Drumcree. Loyalist terrorists from the LVF and Johnny Adair's C Company of the UDA showed up to back the Orange protesters. Adair had benefited from the early release scheme of the GFA. Portadown Orange leader Harold Gracey refused to condemn Orange violence because he said that Adams never condemned it — he was wrong Adams condemned other people's violence as at Omagh. But the provincial Orange leadership led by Grand Master Robert Saulters condemned the violence. The violence was at lower levels than in previous years, but unlike 1999 the police were required to use their two Belgian water cannons — in light spray mode rather than at full force. Life in much of the province was again interrupted for several days and many who could afford to do so took their vacations abroad or in the Republic during the Drumcree period. Tourism continued to suffer as a result of the protests.[64]

The final prisoners were released in accordance with the GFA in July. On August 19 the UDA staged a provocative parade on the Shankill with some people carrying LVF banners. The UFF/LVF alliance was seen as a threat by the UVF. This alliance came about because Johnny Adair, leader of UDA C Company (C Co.) in the Lower Shankill, was an admirer of Billy Wright. Following Wright's assassination LVF prisoners were moved into the UDA wing of the H block in the Maze Prison. Adair became friendly with a number of senior members of the LVF before he was released in July 2000 after having served five years of a sixteen-year sentence. Members then assaulted the Rex Bar, a UVF stronghold and UVF houses.[65]

The feud resulted in seven killed and over 300 families forced to relocate from their homes because they were in territory claimed by the rival organization to that which they supported. It was similar to the republican feuds between the two rival wings of the IRA and between the Stickies and the INLA a quarter century before in 1975. Troops were deployed to the Shankill Road area of West Belfast for the first time that they had appeared in Belfast streets in two years. As a result the Northern Ireland Office finally recognized the UDA as being officially off ceasefire — a year after they began a pipe-bombing campaign to intimidate Catholics out of Protestant areas across the province. Johnny Adair was ordered back to prison by Peter Mandelson after Chief Constable Ronnie Flanagan provided him with intelligence on Adair's responsibility for the feud. Police found weapons and ammunition in the charred remains of John White's firebombed office. But he was not charged. Adair credited the decision to reimprison him with saving his life.. Sean O'Callaghan unsuccessfully attempted to mediate between the two loyalist organizations on behalf of Trimble.[66]

British troops were deployed to Coleraine and Carrickfergus because of the feud. In late October the feud migrated to North Belfast. . In the first week of November there were four feud murders in four days. Loyalist sectarian attacks on Catholic targets of opportunity occurred throughout the feud. On November 22, 2000, a truce was announced after nine people had been killed. In December 2000 the IRA shot a Protestant taxi driver in retaliation for loyalist attacks on Catholics.[67]

There were several sectarian killings of Catholics in the summer of 2001 that were attributed to the UDA by the police. Throughout the year sectarian attacks on Catholics living in Protestant towns increased. In response republicans attacked Orange parades in North Belfast in July 2001 with two blast bombs and 263 petrol bombs during the sectarian riot that followed. Rioting had begun in North Belfast on June 19, 2001, and continued on a nightly basis through late September — aided by the long daylight hours in the far north. The Holy Cross Catholic girls primary school, located within the loyalist neighborhood of Glenbryn, was the target of intimidation by loyalist residents who spat on and hurled obscenities at the young girls walking to school. This was in itself a reaction to republican intimidation of loyalist residents in the neighborhood but boomeranged against the loyalists in the national and international media. On October 12, 2001, Northern Ireland Secretary John Reid officially declared the UDA to be off ceasefire, a reality that everyone else had been aware of for at least six months. A few weeks later a teenage loyalist was killed when his own blast bomb exploded prematurely as he prepared to throw it. Another loyalist was run down on his bike by a Catholic mother in a car after he threw a rock into her windshield.[68]

In November 2001 the UDP was disbanded by the UDA. It had not held any constituency meetings in the two years before its disbandment. For all practical purposes its four councilors functioned as independents. Because the UDP lacked a fulltime staff, it failed to register as a party to contest the 2001 local election and its candidates had to run as independents. It was replaced by the Ulster Political Research Group (UPRG) in which John White played a prominent role until his expulsion from the organization. The UPRG in reality played the same role for the UDA that Sinn Fein played for the IRA before 1981.[69]

In January 2002 thousands attended Belfast rallies against sectarian killings after a young Catholic postman was murdered by the UDA under the cover name of Red Hand Defenders. He was killed as he delivered mail in a loyalist housing estate. Adair was released from prison for the second time on May 15, 2002. In July Drumcree VIII passed off peacefully for the first time since 1994. In August 2002 Andre Shoukri, the head of the UDA in North Belfast, defended sectarian killings in a press interview. On September 25, 2002, the UDA Inner Council announced the expulsion of Adair and John White. Adair had not only openly aligned himself with the LVF, but he also attempted to assassinate Jim Gray, leader of the East Belfast UDA.[70]

In November 2002 a feud broke out between the mainstream UDA and the LVF after an LVF member with links to Adair was murdered. On December 26, C Co. murdered the nephew, Jonathan Stewart, of a UDA man who had clashed with Adair. Stewart's girlfriend's father was an Adair supporter. By January 2003 this feud had expanded to include Adair's C Co. against the mainstream UDA. That month Adair was reimprisoned — for the third time in a decade — for criminal activities including drug dealing. On January 31, 2003, John Gregg, a prominent UDA leader from East Belfast, and his number two man were assassinated by C Co. The UDA quickly opened an office near Adair's house in the Lower Shankill and C Co. men began reporting to the office to turn in weapons and cash in exchange for pardons. Early the next month Adair's family and the C Co. leadership were driven out of the Shankill by the mainstream UDA. The police escorted them to the ferry in Larne where they boarded and went into exile in Scotland. The UDA then reorganized that year and moved back into the more political role that it had fulfilled from 1994 to 2000. On February 22, 2003, the UDA announced a year ceasefire, which it then renewed in 2004. In the spring of 2005 the UDA began removing many of the physical markings from loyalist ghettoes such as painted curbstones and flags.[71]

But the UDA faced two main problems in fulfilling this political role. First, unlike the PUP, the UDP had its supporters scattered throughout the province and lacked sufficient concentration to win Assembly seats. Second, the UDA had a much more criminal role than the UVF and often ignored the advice of its political advisors.

Deterioration 2000-2001

John Hume announced in August 2000 that he would give up his Assembly seat in the near future. He ended up retiring from politics when his term in parliament expired in 2001. And UUP President Josiah Cunningham was killed in a car accident that same month removing one of the few figures respected by all factions and someone who understood the party's finances. The following month the UUP lost a formerly safe Westminster seat in South Antrim when the DUP's the Rev. William McCrea beat UUP candidate David Burnside. The low turnout — 43 percent — suggested that many middle class voters did not bother to vote in a contest between two anti–Agreement candidates and many in the pro-Agreement camp were glad that Burnside had lost. But Trimble dutifully canvassed for the party candidate, after his own candidate lost to Burnside in a nomination contest, and seemed to enjoy himself. He ascribed the loss to reaction to the implementation of the Patten Report. Most observers saw this as a setback for the peace process.[72]

October saw the second inspection of IRA dumps by the international inspectors and the murder of Real IRA member Joseph O'Connor in Belfast. The IRA had also been implicated in the May murder of a drug dealer in South Belfast by RUC Chief Constable Ronnie Flanagan in June. At the beginning of the month Trimble warned his critics at the party's annual general conference. "Stop undermining the leadership of this party," he warned. They did not listen and three weeks later challenged him again in another UUC meeting. At the meeting Trimble announced that he would prohibit Sinn Fein ministers from participating in NSMC meetings until such time as the IRA decommissioned. He had cleared this with Blair earlier. When the votes were counted Trimble had again won, but by a narrower margin — 445 to 374 (54 percent to 46 percent) — than in the previous vote. His safety margin was slowly evaporating.[73]

Sinn Fein did not withdraw from the Assembly but took Trimble to court over his latest sanction in December. The loyalist feud finally was declared at an end after four months. President Clinton visited Ireland for his third and final official visit in December. He began his visit in Dundalk, home of the RIRA, where he make some anemic remarks criticizing the organization that were not helpful to Trimble. While he was in Belfast a resolution of the contested 2000 American election occurred, pushing Clinton's visit off the front pages in both America and the province. The trip served as a grand tour of one of his foreign policy triumphs before he returned, much too late, to negotiating peace in the Middle East. By December Seamus Mallon was starting to become more difficult as he became worried that Sinn Fein would soon overtook the SDLP by outflanking it as the "greener" or more nationalist party. In January 2001 the court ruled that Trimble had acted illegally as no sanctions were specified in the GFA. Trimble lodged an appeal but was forced to remove the sanction. De Chastelain had issued a pessimistic report on the prospects for decommissioning the month before. In 2000 there were 262 punishment beatings and shootings by paramilitary organizations.[74]

The new year began with Peter Mandelson, for reasons unrelated to his performance in the province, being replaced as Northern Ireland secretary with John Reid. Reid was a Catholic from western Scotland where there were still sectarian tensions similar to those in Northern Ireland. Trimble hoped that this would make Reid more even handed in dealing with the Ulster situation, but Reid acted as if he already understood Ulster politics based on his own experience in Scotland. This, combined with the difficult personalities of both Reid and Trimble and made worse by the pressure that the latter was under from anti–Agreement unionists, served to make Reid a poor replacement for Mandelson as far as the Unionists were concerned.[75]

On January 18 Ian Paisley told Blair that Trimble was "going down the tubes" and that London had better get used to dealing with the DUP. Blair finally became worried that without actual decommissioning Trimble was dead politically and without him there would be no peace process. Blair tried to persuade both Dublin and Sinn Fein that electoral disaster for Trimble would not be good for them. Soon after this Blair met with Chief Constable Ronnie Flanagan and Lieutenant General Alistair Irwin, the new commander for Northern Ireland. Blair wanted to be able to offer Sinn Fein something on demilitarization in exchange for decommissioning but would defer to the two of them on security grounds if they thought it too risky.[76]

In May Trimble lodged another postdated letter of resignation, this time with Assembly Speaker John Alderdice, dated July 1. This was one year after the Republicans said they would begin decommissioning. For his own political survival Trimble was forced to hold the entire process at ransom in order to force the Republicans to begin delivering product.

In the June 2001 Westminster election that reelected Blair by a record margin, the UUP lost three seats — two to nationalists and one to the DUP — while both the DUP and Sinn Fein made major gains at the expense of the

SDLP. The UUP's results would have been even worse but a de facto alliance between the UUP, Alliance, and the Women's Coalition allowed Sylvia Hermon to win Robert McCartney's North Down seat.[77] After the election the province's 18 Westminster seats were redistributed as follows: UUP 6 (9); DUP 5 (3); Sinn Fein 4 (2); SDLP 3 (4). The political center seemed to be shrinking. The UUP's share of the vote province-wide was 26.8 percent compared to 22.5 percent for the DUP, 21.7 percent for Sinn Fein and 21.0 percent for the SDLP, while Alliance — which normally polls low in Westminster elections — received only 3.6 percent.[78] In the local government elections held the same day Sinn Fein surpassed the SDLP for the first time and confirmed its status as the leading nationalist party. In the local election the UUP received 154 seats and 23.0 percent of the vote, the DUP 131 seats and 21.5 percent, Sinn Fein 108 seats and 20.7 percent, the SDLP 117 seats and 19.4 percent, and Alliance 28 seats and 5.1 percent.[79]

Before the election Trimble discussed a possible election pact with Alliance leaders Sean Neeson and David Ford. No agreement was reached because the UUP saw a pact as a one-way street: Alliance should stand down in all those constituencies where the UUP would benefit from this, but the UUP refused to give Alliance a clear shot in East Belfast and South Antrim, where its candidates had polled well in the past. Despite the failure to reach a formal pact, Alliance refused to run candidates in many constituencies where SDLP and pro-Agreement UUP candidates appeared to be in trouble. And in other constituencies where the Alliance ran candidates its electorate switched to support the UUP candidate anyway. The level of cross-community, other than in traditional Alliance areas, was very low despite an appeal by Trimble to Catholics to support pro-Agreement candidates. As the SDLP considered itself to be the only authentic pro-Agreement party among the Big Four, it did not encourage this among its voters. At best most SDLP voters would give their lower preference votes to Alliance, at worst they would vote for Sinn Fein to keep unionists out of office.[80]

Sinn Fein's gains were a real threat for Trimble, because even if the UUP beat the DUP and remained the largest party in the next Assembly election, Sinn Fein was likely to emerge as the largest nationalist party and thereby nominate the deputy first minister. The unionist electorate would not tolerate a Sinn Fein deputy (co–) first minister while the IRA still retained its arsenal. If he remained in office in that situation there would be major defections to the anti–Agreement camp and Trimble would lose his majority in the Assembly. This made Trimble even more determined to go through with his threat to resign. Trimble made these points to Blair in a meeting at 10 Downing Street.[81]

Following the election the British Tory press began calling on its party to make Trimble its new leader. Trimble was the first Unionist politician since Edward Carson during World War I to have support on the British mainland. While it was unlikely that the Conservatives would have elected him their leader, they probably could have found him a safe constituency in England and made him the party spokesman on Northern Ireland. But Trimble wanted to raise his youngest child in the province and to see through his projects of reforming the UUP and saving the Agreement. As long as he had a chance to accomplish those he would not resign.[82]

Trimble resigned on July 1, 2001, while on a trip to the Somme battlefield in France to commemorate the dead from Ulster in that battle in World War I. This gave Secretary of State Reid six weeks to either get Trimble to withdraw his resignation and be reelected by the Assembly as first minister or call new elections. The result was that the two governments held another all-party summit at Weston Park in England to discuss the situation. The DUP boycotted the summit as it did not want to be associated with any bribes that were made to Sinn Fein in order to get it to decommission. Jeffrey Donaldson joined the UUP's negotiating team for the first time in two years. The two governments published a report in which only one of the twenty topics covered related to weapons. Blair was attempting to bribe the IRA into delivering by promising a general amnesty on all crimes committed during The Troubles, so that all IRA on-the-runs (fugitives) could return to Northern Ireland without fear of facing prison. He also made concessions on policing boards to Sinn Fein.[83]

Because the crisis was not resolved by mid–August when the time limit expired, Secretary Reid used a technicality and "suspended" (also known as parked) the Assembly for a day on August 10 in order to restart the six-week clock. The negotiations took place against the background of bitter sectarian rioting in North Belfast that occurred on a nightly basis for some two months. Unionists suspected paramilitary involvement by both sides in the rioting and there were calls to return released prisoners to prison for violating the terms of their release. Although geographically isolated this rioting was comparable to the rioting that had accompanied the Drumcree protests from 1995 to 2000 around the province. During the next six weeks two events had a major effect on the process.[84]

On August 13, 2001, three Republicans were arrested at Bogota airport by Colombian authorities for traveling on false passports. It was alleged that they were in the country to pass on their technical expertise in making homemade mortars and "bunker buster" bombs to the rebel FARC (Colombian Revolutionary Armed Force) that was trying to overthrow the government. They had been under surveillance since entering the country and had been observed in the rebel "demilitarized zone." Initially Gerry Adams denied any knowledge of the three men. But it was soon established that one was a former IRA prisoner, another a well-known Republican and the third was Sinn Fein's representative in Havana. PSNI Chief Ronnie Flanagan said that he thought that the three might have gone to Colombia without the knowledge of Adams. After their identities were revealed in the press, Adams then claimed that they were there merely to observe the peace process in Colombia between the government and the rebels. He never explained why it was necessary for them to travel on false passports.

The U.S. State Department considers FARC to be "narco-terrorists"—terrorists who use the cultivation and sale of cocaine as a means of financing their war. As cocaine smuggling to the United States is a major issue in both American domestic and foreign policy, this served to alienate the new administration from Sinn Fein. Previously the Bush administration had thought merely that Clinton overindulged the parties in Northern Ireland in order to solve a dispute that had little relevance to American interests. But they were willing to continue backing the peace process at a much lower level. The arrests were well publicized in the American media, which hurt Sinn Fein with its traditional Irish-American base. This threatened to have a major impact on its fundraising efforts in America. It also became a major domestic issue in Ireland as the country appeared likely to face new Dail elections in the next year.[85]

On September 11, 2001, approximately 2,750 people were killed in New York City by two hijacked aircraft crashing into the Twin Towers in Manhattan. Suddenly terrorism became even less reputable in America than Communism had been during the Cold War. That afternoon, Richard Haas, the head of policy planning at the State Department and the Bush administration's liaison in Belfast, met with Gerry Adams. He had been scheduled to discuss the Colombian escapade with Adams. In very stern language he explained to Adams that the administration was now dividing the world into those who favored terrorism and those who opposed it. The only way that Sinn Fein could show that it was in the latter group was by having the IRA promptly begin decommissioning, as it was required to do under the Belfast Agreement. Adams understood that groups like NORAID would now be under increased government scrutiny.[86] In addition, ordinary Americans simply stopped donating to organizations like Sinn Fein that were affiliated with terrorism.

On September 23 Reid signed a second one-day suspension order in order to give the parties more of a chance to work things out. He justified it with the changed circumstances following 9/11. For Blair there was no question of expelling Sinn Fein from the Executive and he made that quite clear to Trimble. Trimble's attitude towards Blair had changed in the last year and he was no longer so deferential towards the Labour leader. He saw clearly that Blair was ready to sacrifice him in order to keep Sinn Fein on board and the IRA's guns silent. The threat from the two governments was that if devolution returned it would not be the devolution from 1974 to 1998 but rather something much closer to joint authority. It would be an enhanced version of the Anglo-Irish Agreement arrangements.

On October 18 Trimble's three ministers in the Executive resigned. On October 22 Adams announced that the IRA was about to decommission. The following day the IRA announced that it had put "beyond use" a quantity of arms including small arms, ammunition, and explosives. The IRA had finally jumped. Trimble was able to take credit for finally compelling the IRA to do what it had sworn it would never do. But because the first decommissioning event by Republicans was so opaque, a poll by the *Belfast Telegraph* showed that 52 percent of Protestants did not believe that any decommissioning had occurred.[87]

On Friday, November 2, 2001, a vote was held in the Assembly to reelect Trimble as first minister and Mark Durkan, the new leader of the SDLP, as deputy first minister. The vote was 72–30 in favor, but within the unionist group 30–29 against. Trimble had attempted to win the vote without members of the "other" group redesignating as unionists. Two Ulster Unionist MLAs, Peter Weir and Pauline Armitage, defected and voted with the DUP. Armitage was upset over the fate of the RUC and Weir over the failure to decommission. Trimble asked both Alliance and the Women's Coalition to have members redesignate to save the Agreement, but probably not with much conviction as he himself thought it was "tacky." Ford did not like the idea and there was much opposition from within party ranks. Finally on November 6, without approval from its membership, half of Alliance's six MLAs redesignated — it was voluntary — after being asked to do so by Reid along with the Women's Coalition's two MLAs. The latter party had one redesignate as a nationalist and one as a unionist in order to maintain balance. Alliance made clear to Trimble that this was a one-time effort and that he could not expect them to rescue him in the future. In exchange Alliance won a promise of a review of the Agreement that would examine its categorization into three categories, one of which did not count in any important votes.[88]

Weir was expelled from the party and Armitage was suspended as a result of their failure to vote with the party. They eventually left to joint Donaldson in the DUP in the summer of 2003. The DUP took the government to court for holding the vote after the end of the suspension period. It went to the House of Lords where the DUP lost by a 3:2 ratio. The year had been the most violent in the province since 1994.[89]

The First Assembly continued functioning relatively smoothly for eleven months. On St. Patrick's Day 2002 there was a break-in at the Special Branch (police intelligence) office at the Castlereagh Police Station. It emerged that the codes of many informers had gone missing as well as personal information on their handlers. Many Special Branch officers were forced to relocate at great expense to the state for their own safety. The police's whole informer network also seemed at risk — not an empty threat considering the attempt on the life of McGartland in England, and the murder of Eamon Collins, who was merely critical of the IRA. Although some people, including Jonathan Powell, Blair's chief of staff, initially were inclined to believe that it was an inside job by rival intelligence officers, an investigation by John Chilcot of the Northern Ireland Office put the blame squarely on the IRA. As a result the IRA carried out a second act of decommissioning in April 2002 but received little political bounce from it. The police sought the extradition of a former American chef who worked in Castlereagh and who had ties to prominent Republicans. His ex-girlfriend was brought in for questioning. The IRA soon denied any involvement in the burglary and the process survived but was considerably weakened and therefore more vulnerable to subsequent episodes of misbehavior.[90]

In early 2002 Alex Maskey, a longtime Sinn Fein councilor in Belfast became the first Republican Lord Mayor of Belfast after Alliance supported his election as a reward for IRA decommissioning and promises of further decommissioning in the future. This was a means of demonstrating Alliance's independence of the UUP after redesignating in November. But the IRA was still gathering intelligence on the movements of leading Conservative politicians in Britain. This was probably both in order to retain a breakout option if necessary and in order to keep the paramilitaries "gainfully employed." In the spring 2002 Irish general election Sinn Fein expanded its base in the South. Rioting in Belfast in the summer of 2002 indicated widespread loyalist dissatisfaction with the GFA.[91]

The continuing activity of the IRA, both criminal and terrorist, had severely stretched Sinn Fein's credibility in the unionist community. Then on October 4, 2002, police arrested Denis Donaldson, the head of Sinn Fein's office in the Assembly, on the grounds that he was running a spy ring in the Assembly. The police made a number of dramatic raids on Sinn Fein offices and on private homes and were filmed carting off computers for examination. As a result of this Trimble resigned as first minister and the First Assembly was permanently parked on October 14. The UUP and Alliance were in favor of excluding Sinn Fein from the Executive and the SDLP seriously discussed the option but decided not to — they probably feared that the nationalist electorate would punish them for doing so.[92]

The Assembly spy ring remained murky as several years later in December 2005 it emerged that Donaldson was in actual fact a British agent. He admitted this in a Sinn Fein press conference and pronounced "the so-called Stormontgate affair" a "sham and a fiction."[93] No charges were ever issued and the statute of limitations was allowed to expire. Donaldson held a press conference, organized by Sinn Fein, and confessed that he had been a British agent for years after having been blackmailed by the British. Donaldson then retired to a small remote cottage in rural Co. Donegal where he was murdered by a shotgun blast from unknown assailants after the location of his cottage was revealed. While it was clear that he was murdered for political reasons by republicans, it remained unclear if his assassins were dissident republicans, former IRA prisoners — or their relatives — who thought that information that he revealed led to their arrest, or whether it was in fact an authorized "hit" by the IRA.[94] In April 2009 the RIRA claimed credit for the assassination of Donaldson.

It is quite possible that Donaldson was spying on other parties at Sinn Fein's orders while keeping his British handlers informed. The fact that no one was ever prosecuted just means that because of Donaldson's role as a double agent, it would have been difficult to prove in court whom he was spying for. It should not be taken as proof of his innocence. BBC security correspondent Brian Rowan later claimed that the source of the information that led to the police raid was a second informer that the British had within the Republican Movement.[95]

On October 17, 2002, just after direct rule had been restored, Blair gave a speech in Belfast in which he declared that retention of their arsenal by Republicans was counterproductive because it produced unionist distrust. He also declared that if direct rule became permanent, it would not result in a strengthening of Irish influence. He wanted to remove any incentive for Sinn Fein and the IRA to not cooperate with the peace process. From the point of view of Trimble and the UUP, it was the most pro-unionist speech that Blair had made since May 1997 when he reassured them that the Union was safe.[96]

Trimble was convinced that the British were writing him off and were "briefing against him." Blair aide Jonathan Powell admits that this was true of John Reid and the NIO, which was convinced that Paisley would be a better bet as a unionist leader. But Powell claims that Blair stayed loyal to Trimble to the end. Sinn Fein had already perceived Trimble as "damaged goods" and were urging Blair to drop him in favor of a peace with the DUP. This may have been because they thought that having Paisley as their unionist interlocutor would make the battle for public opinion in America and Britain easier to win. It may also have been because they did not want the governments compensating Trimble for concessions that he made — it was all right, nay mandatory, to compensate the Republicans, but that was another matter. But the problem was that Blair and Powell both underestimated unionist dissatisfaction with the execution of the Agreement and the opaqueness of decommissioning.[97]

As 2002 ended it was a mixed legacy. The Assembly had collapsed, but the IRA was finally beginning to decommission. Most unionists favored a return to devolution — by nearly a 3:2 ratio. They had no trust in Sinn Fein and also thought that the SDLP was an unreliable partner because of its willingness to tolerate the IRA's activities. If the two governments were to save the Assembly and the peace process they would have to hold new elections soon. But Trimble and the UUP were likely to lose any such elections because of public opinion in the unionist community towards the way the peace process had gone. It was seen by most unionists as rank appeasement by the two governments — and the SDLP and even by Trimble — of the Republicans. The Republicans had proved that they still were not house trained yet as they left a trail of messes from Colombia to Castlereagh to the Assembly.[98]

Alliance general secretary Stephen Farry published an article in 2002 in which he analyzed the problems with the Assembly. He saw four main reasons for the problematic implementation of the Agreement: First, the deep divisions within the UUP and the failure of the pro–Agreement Unionists to give it vigorous support; second, the inability of the paramilitary organizations to keep their ceasefires and decommission; third, the perception of a moral vacuum in the implementation of the GFA; finally, the institutionalization of sectarianism in the Agreement. In Northern Ireland as in other conflicts, entrenchment of group identity has deepened divisions and fuelled ethnic conflict. Alliance recommended replacement of the double ethnic veto with weighted majorities.[99]

But German ethnic conflict specialist Stefan Wolff argues that it usually takes generations rather than years to move away from traditional patterns of prejudice and mistrust in conflict-torn societies. He also argued that periodic attempts by Blair to periodically rescue the GFA have taken away control and responsibility from the local politicians. This has given them a convenient scapegoat to blame for the resulting failures. Wolff also feels that the two governments should have called a new Assembly election in August 2001 rather than extending the six-week period. This would have altered the balance of power among the political parties and possibly resulted in a new dynamic.[100]

In a post–peace process analysis written in 2007 Peter Mandelson argued that Blair largely kept Sinn Fein in the process after 1997 by making promises that he knew he could not keep in the belief that "process was policy." Blair was like a juggler who was alright as long as he could keep all of the balls in the air. After the Good Friday Agreement, Jonathan Powell promised Republicans that there would be further concessions in exchange for IRA decommissioning. The Republican response was to ask him if these would be related to a united Ireland. So both sides were deceiving themselves.[101]

SEVEN

The Agreement Saved

To Elect or Not to Elect?[1]

As 2003 began there were two questions that needed to be resolved that would determine the future of the peace process. First, would Assembly elections be held as scheduled in May 2003, five years after the last election? Second, would the two governments set up an objective independent commission to monitor paramilitary activity in the province as Trimble had called for throughout 2002? The future of the process seemed to ride on the response of the two governments to these two questions. Even if they managed to restore devolution to a power-sharing Executive in Belfast, without fresh elections the parties would lack a democratic mandate and Trimble's situation within unionism would deteriorate. But if a fresh major act of decommissioning did not occur in a transparent fashion, then Trimble would probably lose the election within unionism and the Democratic Unionist Party would emerge as the largest unionist party. Ian Paisley would have seen off another potential reformer — the fifth in his long career. The three other major parties pushed for fresh elections in the inevitable consultations that were held in Belfast and London. The DUP was eager to demonstrate objectively that it was the major force within unionism and be able to call the shots. Sinn Fein wanted to consolidate its victory over the SDLP in 2001 and establish itself as the new main nationalist party in the province. This would also make Martin McGuinness or Gerry Adams the new deputy first minister with a veto over the new unionist first minister — whether that was Trimble, Paisley or Peter Robinson, Paisley's deputy. And the SDLP feared that the longer elections were delayed the bigger the gap between itself and its Republican rivals would grow.

But if the two governments would surrender a bit of control over the process and give Trimble the commission that he wanted — that he needed to survive — he might be able to tough out elections and maintain a small majority. Trimble persuaded the British to give the commission teeth by allowing it to have access to classified security information from the two governments. And so at a meeting in Dublin in January 2003 the British Northern Ireland hands were able to convince their Irish counterparts to set up an International Monitoring Commission that would issue "yellow cards" (warnings) and "red cards." The former might include suspension of allowance payments for MP/MLA offices at Westminster and/or Stormont and the latter would mean expulsion from government.[2]

In the three sovereign capitals involved in the peace process — Dublin, London, and Washington — there had been discussion over the future of unionism and the process. Many were convinced in all three capitals that Trimble was "clapped out" — yesterday's man — and that they would all be better off giving the DUP a chance to rule. Their hopes were placed not on another candidate within the UUP — for there were none — or on Paisley, but rather on Peter Robinson. Robinson had been regarded as a closet pragmatist eager for a role in government since the 1980s.[3] It was the old De Gaulle in Algiers or Nixon in China syndrome: only the authentic established conservative can afford to make major revolutionary concessions to his opponents and survive. Tony Blair did not buy this logic and still felt some residual loyalty for the man who had risked his political future for peace. Elections would be held, but they would be held in the friendliest possible environment for Trimble and the UUP.

The Irish were hoping that they could get the IRA to issue a statement that the war was over that would reassure unionists in the absence of major decommissioning, which they believed was unlikely. The Irish reported that senior Sinn Fein figures had been making the rounds of units in the field in the winter of 2003. Sinn Fein agreed to a month's delay in scheduling elections at a meeting at Hillsborough in early March. The UUP wanted to see the new commission proposals enshrined in Westminster legislation. Whereas Sinn Fein acquiesced in the existence of a commission, they wanted it administered by Stormont where it would be subject to cross-community consensus and hence SDLP fears of electoral retribution if action were taken against Sinn Fein.

The next meeting took place at Hillsborough on April 7-8. It encompassed both a busy meeting between the parties and a Bush-Blair summit. The United States and Britain had jointly gone to war against Iraq in March and Blair was attempting to sell Bush on the necessity of reviving the Middle East peace process as a diplomatic accompaniment to the war. He was demonstrating for Bush the Northern Ireland peace process as a model for how peace could be achieved between Israel and the Palestinians. After asking many questions about how the process worked in practice, Bush promised Blair that he would devote the same energy to the Middle East that Blair devoted to Northern Ireland. This produced a number of nervous giggles among Blair's staff (either because they knew that this was a Texas tall tale or that they believed that he might be sincere). But the language from the IRA proved to be less than adequate — as had always been the case in their statements. And so little real progress was made.[4]

The two heads of government, Ahern and Blair, were supposed to return to Hillsborough on April 10. But because the IRA's language was so inadequate, Blair refused to publish any concessions on policing and demilitarization. This ended up saving Trimble as any concrete language would have demonstrated that the Republicans were once again getting something for nothing. This would have confirmed unionist fears that the peace process was about appeasement rather than negotiations and mutual concessions. The only concession from the IRA was to guarantee a third decommissioning act in the near future. By then this was almost politically worthless for Trimble. On April 23 Blair pointedly asked the IRA three questions at a press conference. First, did the IRA intend to cease all activities such as intelligence gathering, targeting, and punishment beatings that were inconsistent with the GFA? Second, did the IRA intend to decommission all of their arms? Third, when they said that they would not undertake any activities inconsistent with the GFA did this mean that the war was over? The IRA was furious at having to clarify their communiqués — even though they had demanded the same thing of the two governments in 1994.

The Republicans wanted their reward (Assembly elections) even though they had failed to deliver on arms or a statement. Trimble feared that Dublin would pronounce their performance satisfactory and then demand that elections be held. But Blair was backing Trimble up for a change. Trimble suggested to Adams that they take a break until the fall and then try again. On May 1, Blair decided to call off elections. He was severely criticized for this by the other parties — particularly by nationalists and their sympathizers who dubbed it a "colonial exercise" in not wanting the "wrong result." In the Republic those polled blamed both the IRA and the unionists but thought the latter more responsible for the mess. This seems to illustrate the results of a nationalist educational system.[5]

In late May 2003 an internal Ministry of Defence memo was leaked to the press showing reduction of the Royal Irish Regiment from its present level of 14,800 troops to 5,000 by 2007, provided that the threat was sufficiently lowered so that demilitarization could proceed. This meant losing many jobs that Protestants depended upon to make ends meet and making them feel less safe. Trimble went to 10 Downing Street to protest. Jonathan Powell, Blair's chief of staff, said that the cuts were news to him. Trimble was eventually given reassurances that no definite plans had been made regarding the long-term future of the army in Ulster.[6]

The anti–Agreement figures within the party remained unimpressed and in June mounted another leadership challenge to Trimble led by Donaldson. Trimble easily survived by 440 to 369 votes (54 percent to 46 percent). Donaldson saw he had no long-term future in the party but was not ready to leave quite yet. Along with Martin Smyth and David Burnside he resigned the UUP whip at Westminster on June 23. Overnight this made the UUP the smallest party in the Commons along with the SDLP. Trimble was not just going to sit idly by and let the party collapse. He referred the matter to a 14-strong officer team of the UUP, which in turn voted 5–2 to refer it to a disciplinary committee. The committee then ruled that their memberships should be suspended until they returned to the party whip. The three dissidents took the matter to court and two weeks after their defection, the court ruled that the disciplinary action was illegal. This then put the question of holding elections on hold at least until October, although Trimble did continue to meet with Adams throughout the summer.[7]

Donaldson scheduled a UUC meeting to consider the matter on September 6. He hoped to effectively limit Trimble's leadership of the party. Trimble won the vote by a margin of 55 percent to 45 percent. It was a slight improvement (13 votes) over the previous vote in June and for the first time Donaldson was heckled at the meeting. This demonstrated to the NIO, Dublin, and Adams that Trimble still had value as a negotiating partner. But by the fall of 2003 polls were showing that two-thirds of unionists were opposed to the Agreement.[8]

The legislation authorizing the continuance of the GFA political apparatus, which meant the salaries to Assembly members, was set to expire on November 1. NI Secretary Paul Murphy, who had replaced Paul Reid in October the previous year, did not want to face a hostile Commons and request a renewal of the legislation without elections with all of the province's parties and the Tories opposing him. The Conservatives had recently begun to abandon Trimble for the DUP. Trimble met with Ahern in Dublin on September 15 and told him that he needed an "act of completion" by the IRA if he was to survive in the election.[9]

The various parties then began choreographing an elaborate political ballet in which the IRA would decommission further, another "end of war" statement would be issued by the Republicans, the creation of the IMC would be announced, and a date for new Assembly elections would be announced. The whole idea was to hold elections in circumstances that would be most favorable for Trimble.

In practice the choreography went terribly wrong because the IRA wanted to show that it was upset over being dictated to. After the announcement of new elections was made, General de Chastelain held a press conference. He announced that the IRA had made a third decommissioning event in recent days and that it involved more arms than in the previous two. He also announced that it involved light, medium, and heavy arms and both weapons and explosives. Other than that he was sworn to secrecy by the IRA and could not reveal any more. The IRA did not issue a schedule of future decommissioning events or when it planned to complete decommissioning. Trimble had previously sent a memo to De Chastelain's office explaining that the event had to be as transparent as possible with photographs, lists of weapons destroyed and a schedule. But De Chastelain did not consider Trimble to be in his chain of command and he simply ignored the memo. He considered his relationship with the paramilitary organizations to be more important. The IRA statement was in Republicanspeak and Adams complained about the International Monitoring Commission not being authorized in the Agreement.[10]

Trimble would now go into an election in a month's time without having gotten what he needed from Republicans. He later admitted in an interview with journalist Frank Millar that hubris was responsible for his plight. "Unfortunately, the truth is worse, its more a case of hubris, that we saw Blair and Ahern fail in March and we were tempted into thinking maybe we could do it better ourselves. And I can't say that we did it much better. So it was more a case of hubris in that sense," admitted Trimble.[11]

When the election was held on Wednesday, November 26, 2003, it confirmed the fears of Trimble and the UUP. On a 63 percent poll of the nearly 1.1 million eligible voters in the electorate, the DUP emerged as both the largest unionist party and the largest party in the Assembly with 30 seats (up 10 from 1998) and 25.7 percent of the first preference votes. Sinn Fein gained six seats to emerge with 24 seats and 23.5 percent of the vote. The UUP actually managed to gain a seat over its performance in 1998 to end up with 27 seats and 22.7 percent of the vote. But Sinn Fein actually received more first preference votes than did the UUP. The SDLP trailed with 18 seats, down five from previously, and 17.0 percent of the vote. Alliance through the miracle of PR-STV managed to hold on to their six seats despite winning only 3.7 percent of the first preferences. Robert McCartney's UKUP was reduced to a single seat after he came in fifth among unionists in North Down with the dissidents having been eliminated and the PUP's Billy Hutchison lost his seat in North Belfast so that the party retained only leader David Ervine's seat in East Belfast. And there was a single Independent. Starting in 2001 a person's religious affiliation was a better indicator of his likely party support in elections than it had been before the election. This demonstrated that the conflict was transformed and not ended.[12] In essence the DUP had sucked up the vast majority of anti–Agreement sentiment in the election away from the minor parties that had received it in 1998 while the UUP had held its own, and the two nationalist parties had switched places from 1998. The UKUP would continue on as a party for another four years before dissolving — after McCartney lost his seat in the 2007 Assembly election — but it was on its death bed for that whole time.[13]

Paisley now had a majority of the unionist seats in the Assembly. This was in some ways a blessing for Trimble — with Sinn Fein the majority nationalist party it would produce the next deputy first minister. Trimble would not have to face the political nightmare of having to form an Executive with Martin McGuinness as his co-equal deputy first minister while the IRA still retained its weapons. Now if the two governments wanted to get the institutions up and running again they would have to negotiate with Paisley and his team and deal with his critique of the Belfast Agreement. Trimble admitted that he had really lost his majority among unionists in October 2001 when he lost the Assembly vote to be reelected first minister after having resigned in July. He was then forced to rely on Alliance to get him reelected by redesignating as unionists. Trimble admitted at the time and afterwards that this was a "tacky" maneuver. But he blamed it on two UUP MLAs who did not live up to their pledges and voted against him and the party.[14]

In the 2003 Assembly election the UUP was able to retain its share of the vote by drawing support from Alliance voters. Many gave their first preference votes to Unionist candidates and then used their lower preference votes for Alliance candidates. Supported by some bitter pro-Agreement Unionist voters who refused to vote for the DUP, this enabled Alliance to retain its six seats. But this worked only in the Greater Belfast Area from North Down to South Antrim and East Antrim where Alliance was strong. This portended a possible future unionist realignment where many former UUP supporters defected permanently to the DUP and were partially compensated for by former Alliance voters.[15] Unionist voters as a whole tended to be partisan voters loyal to either the UUP or the DUP, with the latter increasingly winning new voters, the small unionist floating vote, and the voters from smaller unionist parties as well as the supporters of those UUP figures who had defected to the UUP.[16]

In December 2003 Donaldson along with two other MLAs (Donaldson had been given special dispensation to run for the Assembly while retaining his Westminster seat because the party needed all of its heavy hitters) defected to the DUP.[17] This increased the latter's majority in the Assembly from 30 to

27 to 33 to 24. This also made the DUP the largest Northern Ireland party in the House of Commons with six MPs to the UUP's five. Donaldson would soon find that he would be just one of many competing for the future leadership of the party along with Peter Robinson and Nigel Dodds, instead of being the heir apparent as he had been in the UUP. Paisley also would not tolerate attacks on his leadership of the party.[18]

Research showed that approximately 20,000 voters across the province switched parties from the SDLP to Sinn Fein in the November election. One local party worked blamed the loss on tribalism. "The fact is that hanging tough has never been more attractive. Unfortunately the Good Friday Agreement has made tribalism respectable." Predictably, the outgoing party chairman blamed the unionists. "Nationalism is now moving towards Sinn Fein in greater numbers as a consequence of our unionist partners not selling the project better," he said. "Nationalists are beginning to recognize that there now appears to be an emerging unionist monolith, that our political problems started away back in the 1960s with nationalists saying we are no longer going to take the diktat of unionism," explained outgoing SDLP chairman Alex Atwood. The SDLP election theme of stopping the DUP was not designed to either win unionist cooperation nor to emphasize differences with Sinn Fein. The slogan played into the hands of the SDLP's Republican rivals who could credibly argue that they had more experience confronting unionists. Unionists on the other hand felt that any nationalist gain was their loss and wanted to unite in order to better confront their foes. The other gain by Sinn Fein was due to first-time voters who were attracted to the more dynamic appeal of the Republicans.[19]

The weakness was built into the structure of the Belfast Agreement. Because of nationalist criticisms of the majoritarian nature of Unionist rule from 1922 to 1972 under the old Stormont parliament, the system of double majorities was built into the Agreement. A much better system would have been to simply require numerical super-majorities of X amount (60 percent, two-thirds, 70 percent, etc.) for certain types of votes. This would have ensured that this legislation would have required at least some cross-community support from the other ethnic community to pass. But the nature of tribalism, particularly among siege societies — especially settler siege societies — was that they considered any majority that relied on native support as illegitimate. This was the case in South Africa where Afrikaner nationalists even considered illegitimate majorities that relied on English-speaking whites. This was also the case in Israel where the Likud and the parties to its right considered the Oslo agreements compromised because they relied upon the votes of Israeli Arabs.[20]

It is a rule of experience in ethnic disputes that if consociational solutions are applied and they are too rigid in terms of ethnic mechanisms they can worsen the problem. Such was the case with Cyprus in the early 1960s. Consociational solutions had worked best in European societies, where critics claimed that they were not really needed.[21] Northern Ireland was a critical test case for consociational democracy because for the first time it was being applied to a situation after decades of war where it had not been in place previously. If it succeeded it could serve as a model for conflict resolution in other ethnic conflicts around the globe. But if it failed it would pose severe questions about the utility of consociationalism as a conflict-regulation mechanism outside of Western Europe.[22]

After the election, the two governments met together to reassess the situation. Their strategy of building peace from the center had failed. Blair was depressed and skeptical about Paisley ever doing a deal with Sinn Fein. Trimble was bitter and blamed his fate on the British. Blair wanted to force Paisley into either making a deal with Sinn Fein or rejecting one in a fashion that would make him seem unreasonable. Trimble wanted new elections as early as the spring of 2004. But the UUP could triumph only if Paisley appeared unreasonable to the unionist electorate, and he was determined not to fall into this trap.[23]

Failed Negotiations and Decommissioning at Last

In January 2004 Ian Paisley announced that he would not be running for reelection for the European parliament. Since elections had begun in June 1979 Paisley had regularly topped the poll, proving to be the most popular unionist. He was then followed by John Hume. This seemed to many to be the beginning of a phased retirement for Paisley who was then 78. But others speculated that the DUP was merely planning on running two different candidates in the election. The previous month the Irish *Sunday Business Post* ran a piece on the two "DUP cardinals" who would compete to replace the Protestant Pope, Peter Robinson and Nigel Dodds. The paper seemed to feel that Robinson would be a better selection for nationalists as Dodds still remained a fundamentalist Protestant at heart. The following month, February, Hume announced that he also would not seek reelection to the European parliament, which effectively meant his retirement from politics as he had already retired from Westminster and as party leader. The Irish press was divided about his legacy and could not decide if he would go down in history as another Parnell or another Redmond. Henry McDonald faulted him for not vigorously challenging Sinn Fein after 1994 once the peace process had developed. And Suzanne Breen called him wise to retire when he did and not risk a defeat at the hands of Sinn Fein candidate Bairbre de Brun. She called De Brun "dead cert" to win the seat in June. Prof. Sydney Elliot, a professor of political science at Queen's University who specialized in provincial politics, called a Hume victory in the June elections the last chance of the SDLP to stage a revival.[24]

When the European election came in June 2004, Jim Allister, the DUP candidate, received nearly twice as many votes as the Ulster Unionist candidate. Sinn Fein's Bairbre de Brun beat the SDLP candidate by nearly 57,000. Even though the third MEP elected was Jim Nicholson from the UUP, elected on the third count with 16.6 percent of the vote, the election demonstrated the collapse of the center parties as the extremes triumphed. Nicholson had only 3600 votes ahead of Martin Morgan of the SDLP, who had 15.9 percent of first preference votes. Morgan was the mayor of Belfast, certainly a high-visibility position. Allister had 32 percent and De Brun 26.3 percent of the vote.[25]

But before this in late February 2004 the PSNI stopped a van that contained four suspected IRA men and a prisoner, Bobby Tohill, who had moments before been kidnapped from the Kelly's Cellar pub in central Belfast by the four men. He was beaten with iron bars (or police batons — accounts vary) and was probably being driven to a location to be tortured and executed. A police vehicle rammed the van and arrested the men. Presumably the pub was under surveillance based on intelligence. Tohill gave an interview to the press in which he claimed that the IRA wanted to kill him. Tohill was a former INLA member who joined the Real IRA after the INLA went on ceasefire following the Omagh bombing. He required 98 stitches to deal with the damage from the beating. The four suspects were taken to Maghaberry jail in Co. Antrim and requested to be housed in the Republican wing while they awaited trial. The RIRA spokesman said that the group's prisoners would simply ignore the men and avoid interaction with them.[26]

Adams and Sinn Fein went into spin mode and blamed the whole incident on "securocrats" in the police. Both mainstream unionist parties used the incident as a basis for not negotiating with Sinn Fein. Ian Paisley, Jr. claimed that the arrests "vindicated our stance that we cannot go into government with Sinn Fein while the IRA exists." Trimble said that he might pull out of the talks if the issue were not resolved by some sort of sanction against Sinn Fein. He said that Sinn Fein should be expelled until the IRA ceased all paramilitary activities. Taoiseach Bertie Ahern said that he would raise the issue with Martin McGuinness when he met with him. And Irish Justice Minister Michael McDowell was critical of the IRA. As a result of the incident, the *Irish News* ran a three-page article highlighting IRA ceasefire violations since the signing of the Belfast Agreement. These included eleven murders, two abductions and a major robbery as well as a kneecapping.[27]

In the review the DUP, UKUP, and Alliance all demanded radical changes to the Good Friday Agreement. Both nationalist parties refused to accept any sort of change. The DUP proposal was for the Assembly to be reorganized on the committee system, with no Executive and a series of separate committees responsible for running the various government departments in Northern Ireland. The plan also called for allowing a supermajority of 70 percent to substitute for the simple majority in each community on key votes. And the DUP wanted the Assembly reduced from 108 members to 72 members or four instead of six members from each of the 18 Westminster constituencies. This would incidentally harm both the nonsectarian Alliance and the two centrist sectarian parties. Deputy leader Peter Robinson pledged to share power with Sinn Fein once it gave up its criminal and paramilitary connections, that is, once decommissioning occurred and the IRA disbanded. An editorial in the normally pro-UUP *Belfast Telegraph* called for a serious examination of the merits of the DUP proposals. Trimble rejected the DUP plan on the sensible grounds that the problem was with Republican conduct and not with the Agreement.[28] Roy Garland, a UUP MLA with connections in the loyalist paramilitaries and a regular column in the *Irish News,* hailed Robinson's recent remarks on power sharing as evidence that the DUP was finally facing reality. He speculated that this was the result of the positive influence of Desmond Boal, a leading figure in the early DUP in the 1970s.[29] Because of this impasse and the Tohill incident the February 2004 London review of the Agreement looked certain to go nowhere. The two governments were essentially in stall mode.

In late February the UDA announced that it was once more on ceasefire, for the first time since mid–2001 when it officially went off ceasefire and withdrew its support for the GFA. But PSNI Chief Constable Hugh Orde linked the organization to more than fifty punishment attacks and several murders. It was implicated in the recent murder of Catholic James McMahon, which was purely a sectarian killing. But if it did stick to its ceasefire it would remove one source of problems for the police and the Northern Ireland Office.[30]

At the end of February South Antrim MP David Burnside, a former leading Donaldson supporter, called on Trimble to step down as party leader. In late January, UUP defectors to the DUP Peter Weir and Arlene Foster published statistics that they argued proved that the UUP had lost a whole generation of Young Unionists who had all either joined the DUP or dropped out of politics. Ten of the eleven Young Unionist chairmen since the signing of the GFA had left the party along with 15 of the last 17 chairmen of the Queen's University Unionist Association. The majority had ended up in the

DUP. In March former UUP leader Jim Molyneaux also called on Trimble to step down as Unionist leader. Molyneaux said he feared that the party would never win another election in his lifetime (he was then 84) unless there was a major change in the party's policy. Molyneaux said that he would back Reg Empey for the party leadership if Empey would put his name forward. Many Trimble opponents had spoken of Empey as a leader who could unite both wings of the party. Burnside himself refused to put his own name forward. Trimble rejected the calls to resign and said that it was his "duty" to remain as party leader. Others spoke of a combined leadership of Empey and Burnside. It was almost as if the UUP was forced to adopt the Belfast Agreement's mechanism of co-leaders in order to maintain peace. An unknown Ulster Unionist, David Hoey, an Apprentice Boy and business consultant from Coleraine and former aide to Burnside, challenged Trimble for the leadership as a stalking horse for Burnside. At the party's annual conference, Trimble easily retained his leadership with nearly sixty percent (59.8 percent) of the UUC vote compared to 21.6 percent for Hoey and 17.6 percent for Portadown businessman Robert Oliver. Trimble was fortunate in facing a divided opposition. But leadership contests in the UUP were increasingly becoming analogous to fighting over the best deck chairs on the *Titanic*.[31]

In an editorial in the Belfast *News Letter* it was suggested that the reformist Unionists in the UUP and the nationalists in the SDLP had more in common with each other than they with their fellow unionists and republicans. It suggested that they explore how they could better cooperate for peace rather than fighting each other and trying to outbid their rivals on the ethnic (orange or green) card.[32] However, the time for this cooperation was when both parties were electorally strong and not fighting for their lives after having been ousted in their respective communities by their more extreme rivals in the Assembly election of 2003. And the article made no mention of Alliance, nor of how this cooperation should take place.

On Saturday, March 13, 2004, Alliance leader David Ford told his party's annual general conference that if the two governments were unwilling to confront Sinn Fein over IRA activity they should simply close the review down. "But this time [the Tohill kidnapping], with no clear rulebook, only the governments can take action," asserted Ford. "If they aren't prepared to do so, they ought to be honest and announce that they are shutting down the review." Ford said that hardly a day went by without one of the two governments insisting that paramilitary activity must come to an end. "They tell us that the IRA is inextricably linked to Sinn Fein," he recalled. "The Minister of Justice in Dublin tells us that Sinn Fein is funded by criminal activity, and compares republicans to Nazis, and the Taoiseach does not disagree. And what actions do the governments take? What sanctions have they applied against a party they clearly regard in default of its negotiations? Well none actually," he concluded frankly. "To lecture republicans in the media and then negotiate with Sinn Fein as if it was an ordinary democratic party is to emphasize the weaknesses of the two governments." Ford had just explained why it took fourteen years and the near destruction of two centrist parties to conclude peace in Northern Ireland. "Make no mistake: there must be reforms or there will be no agreement," he told the audience to cheers. "Reform is the only realistic pro-Agreement position." [33]

The next day Jim Cusack, the respected security correspondent, ran a story in the *Irish Independent,* the leading anti–Provisional paper in the Republic, naming the seven members of the IRA's Army Council. Among the seven he named were: Gerry Adams, Martin McGuinness, and TD (Irish MP) Martin Ferris. Days later Chris Thornton, the security correspondent of the *Belfast Telegraph,* wrote a story naming Gerry Adams as the author of an article for *Republican News* in 1976 that ran under the pseudonym "Brownie" in 1976 in which he stated "I'm an IRA volunteer." Research proved through personal facts in the article that the author could not be Sinn Fein spokesman Richard McAuley, who had claimed credit for the articles. Justice Minister Michael McDowell acted as the "hit man" for the Irish coalition government in going after the Republicans. In his first attack he stated, "Hitler was elected Chancellor of Germany but would anyone in their (sic) right mind call him a democrat?" He thus disposed of Sinn Fein's claim that it could do as it wished because it had a popular mandate. Sinn Fein responded to the attack by saying that they were part of a long republican tradition. "Let me say clearly that republicanism does not speak in muffled voice through a balaclava. Republicans don't break drug addicts' legs with baseball bats; finance their political campaigns by organizing major crimes; shoot car thieves in the knees and ankles or plant bombs to kill civilians at Enniskillen, Omagh, the La Mon hotel, or Manchester, Birmingham and Canary Wharf," replied McDowell. This was part of a four-month long campaign by the Irish government to pressure the Republicans into giving up paramilitarism and criminal activity. This was partly in order to advance the peace process and partly to ward off future demands that they form a post-election coalition with Sinn Fein. The coalition had been reelected in June 2002, but there was always the chance that some event might provoke fresh elections in the near future. Around this same time rumors had surfaced that Freddie Scappaticci, the former deputy leader of the IRA's infamous "nutting squad" that tortured and interrogated suspected informers within the organization, was himself a senior British agent within the IRA. After months of denials after initially being named in the press in May 2003 as "Stakeknife" he finally admitted that he was "vulnerable" to claims that he was the prize British agent. The following month he fled to Italy.[34]

The talks really went nowhere because of breaks for St. Patrick's Day, Easter, the European election and finally the July marching season while the two governments essentially waited for the report of the IMC on paramilitary activity in April. Trimble had left the review in March in protest over the Tohill incident. The International Monitoring Commission issued its first report on April 20, 2004. Because the report was very critical of the IRA, Gerry Adams declared the peace process to be "in deep crisis" three days later. Paul Murphy applied financial sanctions related to party financing through the Assembly to both Sinn Fein and the PUP.[35] Because of the significant gaps between the parties, the governments were only too happy to take the breaks.

On August 5, 2004, Gerry Adams told the BBC that the Republicans needed to remove decommissioning "as an excuse" that prevented unionists from sharing power with them. The previous month he had told Powell that many of the IRA's weapons could not be decommissioned because they had been given to individuals for missions and never returned and individual members would not agree to decommission their weapons. So only those weapons that were centrally held could be decommissioned. Adams also hinted that Mickey McKevitt, the former IRA chief quartermaster, had taken many arms with him when he formed the Real IRA in late 1997.[36]

Partly as a result of this statement and the belief that it engendered that the IRA was finally ready to decommission, the two governments scheduled talks at Leeds Castle, site of Israeli-Egyptian talks in the summer of 1978, for mid–September to last for three days. On September 14 Sinn Fein complained to the press that it had found a British "bug" at Connolly House, the Sinn Fein headquarters in Andersontown, West Belfast. A second device had been found eight days earlier at the home of one of Adams's staff. It was an obvious ploy to "wrongfoot" the British as negotiations began. The summit was ostensibly called to discuss proposed DUP changes to the GFA. But because none of the other parties were willing to go along with this the two governments concentrated on trying to arrange an arms deal — guns for government. Paisley appeared to be in poor health at Leeds leading to speculation in the press about the succession prospects in the DUP.[37]

Paisley and Peter Robinson went to Dublin to meet with Bertie Ahern in late September 2004. These negotiations, which lasted for two and a half months, were the DUP's first experience with protracted negotiations. BBC security correspondent Brian Rowan told Paisley several times that the IRA would not allow photographs of decommissioning, information that Rowan had from his own Republican contacts. In October the two governments held proximity talks shuttling between Hillsborough Castle and the DUP office in Lisburn. The government civil servants shuttled back and forth to accommodate the Democratic Unionists's refusal to meet directly with Republicans before the IRA had decommissioned.[38]

There was some discussion of photographs being taken by the clergy witnesses (one Catholic priest and one Protestant minister that the IRA had agreed to permit witness the decommissioning) to show privately to skeptics. On November 22, Peter Robinson told Rowan that there would be no deal without photographs. McGuinness checked with his colleagues in the IRA and was told that this was impossible. On November 27, Paisley told a political rally in North Antrim, "The IRA needs to be humiliated and they need to wear their sackcloth and ashes not in a backroom but openly, and we have no apology for the stand that we are taking." Ian Paisley, Jr. later admitted that the DUP had realized that photographs were an insurmountable obstacle about two weeks before his father gave his "sackcloth and ashes" speech.[39]

Despite this obvious ploy to cancel any deal, Blair aide Jonathan Powell detected a new seriousness in Paisley at the Leeds Castle talks in September 2004. Paisley was intransigent on the issue of decommissioning because he thought that transparent decommissioning was needed in order to regain unionist confidence that was necessary for any deal to be successful. He told Blair, "If Sinn Fein were serious, it was clear then the DUP could do a deal. He wanted to see a peaceful Ulster before he passed on."[40]

Paisley's speech effectively put an end to the political initiative of the two governments as the IRA reacted in a predictable fashion. But the initiative did not end officially until December 8. The two governments published the positions of the two sides, revealing that they agreed on all matters except for verification for decommissioning. The publication of the papers was delayed one day because December 7 was Lundy Day in Ulster, and Paisley did not want inferences drawn about his positions.[41] Political analysts speculated at the time that Paisley had decided that he did not want to make a deal with Sinn Fein until after the Westminster election that would probably be held in the spring of next year. This would allow him to consolidate his party's status as the leading unionist party by presenting himself as the leader who had stood up to the Republicans or Sinn Fein/IRA as the DUP liked to say. Alex Atwood accused Sinn Fein of selling out the Belfast Agreement by agreeing to changes including a change in the status of the first minister and deputy first minister.[42]

The atmosphere in Belfast and the entire province was abruptly changed a month later by two events that was again put the IRA in both the spotlight and the docket and made Paisley's speech seem perfectly reasonable if not prophetic. On December 21, 2004, 26.5 million pounds sterling was stolen from the Belfast main branch of Northern Bank in what was the largest bank robbery in either British or Irish history to date. The police quickly concluded that the robbery fit the profile of previous IRA robberies — kidnapping of the families of two of the bank staff who were forced to open the vault. After stealing 14 million pounds in the first load, the robbers returned twice more to steal the remaining contents of the vault. Within days the Police Service of Northern Ireland had publicly pinned responsibility for the robbery on the IRA and claimed that at least four separate active service units had come together to pull off the robbery. The police simply did not believe that any other paramilitary organization or private gang had the organizational expertise to operate in this fashion. And the robbery was typical of a series of hostage-taking robberies earlier in the year in Northern Ireland that had resulted in 3.2 million pounds of losses. These took place even as Adams and McGuinness were negotiating at Leeds Castle. Gerry Adams was forced to go into spin mode and accused the police of operating in typical RUC fashion.[43]

The *Garda Siochana* recovered notes from the robbery in Cork in February during a police raid. New notes worth 50,000 pounds were found in the toilets at a police sports club in South Belfast after a tip from an anonymous source of drugs being located there.[44] The Northern Bank had changed the design on its bank notes shortly after the robbery thereby rendering the stolen money into so much fancy paper. The bank job led parties in the South to focus on the dangers posed by the IRA, and Justice Minister Michael McDowell of the Progressive Democrats was very outspoken in denouncing the threat posed by the Republicans. "The Provisional movement is dominated and has been dominated up till recently by one body and that is the Army Council of the IRA," said McDowell. "The IRA carried out those robberies, serious armed robberies, and had a separate fund-raising section. And the members of the Army Council must all have had knowledge of one kind or another of that campaign of robbery and violence and extortion which has kept the organization going. Gerry Adams and Martin McGuinness have been members of the Army Council throughout all of the relevant period we are talking about and it is inconceivable that as members of the Army Council they wouldn't know the finances of their own organization and what they are based on," opined McDowell.[45] The Progressive Democrats quickly became as much of a *bête noire* for Sinn Fein as the Democratic Left had earlier been in the 1990s. But others blamed Tony Blair as well. "The real bottom line is that the Prime Minister was prepared to sacrifice Northern Ireland. It didn't matter much what sort of circumstances the rest of us had to live in here, as long as there weren't bombs going off in London," claimed SDLP MP Alasdair McDonnell. "The ballot box and the Armalite has been replaced by the ballot box and the bank robbery," wrote former republican sympathizer Kevin Toolis. The proceeds would be used to fight Sinn Fein's plan for unification by separate elections.[46]

The robbery weakened the influence of those within the DUP, like Deputy Leader Peter Robinson, who supported a deal with Sinn Fein. It also led Dublin to take a harder line towards Sinn Fein after Irish intelligence reported to Taoiseach Bertie Ahern that the political leadership had known about the robbery plans. Blair was still unwilling to become firm with Adams and McGuinness.[47]

In late January 2005 Robert McCartney, a Catholic forklift operator from a republican family, was murdered in the street outside Magennis's Bar in the Markets area of Belfast. He was stabbed to death trying to protect a friend, who had his throat slashed, after the two tangled with four men, two of whom were IRA members and one of which thought that McCartney had made a rude gesture toward the man's girlfriend. After the stabbing the IRA men used their paramilitary expertise to forensically clean the bar of all traces of the crime. And they threatened the crowd inside if anyone talked to the police. There were at least two Sinn Fein candidates/activists in the bar at the time. The police found no cooperation from members of the public in their investigation. McCartney was survived by partner Bridgeen Hagans, the mother of his children, and four sisters. The five women made justice for their brother a personal crusade and went on a media blitz. They held interviews with the Ulster media, the Irish media, the British media and even the American media when President Bush invited them to the White House for the annual St. Patrick's Day party in 2005. Eventually Ms. Hagans and Paula McCartney were forced to move out of the Short Strand neighborhood of North Belfast due to intimidation. The IRA conducted its own investigation and offered to execute the guilty parties, but the five women said that all they wanted was for Sinn Fein to ask its members to cooperate with the police. This is something that Adams refused to do, but he did urge anyone with knowledge of the crime to discuss it with their attorneys.[48]

The robbery and murder had the combined effect of making IRA decommissioning more likely as Sinn Fein was under increased pressure from Dublin, London, and Washington to deliver. Richard Haass, the Bush administration man in Belfast, had gradually become charmed by Adams and softened his original hard-line approach. But his replacement by Mitchell Reiss, an academic specialist on North Korea, brought back the toughness. Reiss was given a free hand by the Bush administration and he convinced Bush to ban all politicians from the annual St. Patrick's Day party at the White House that year and invite the McCartney sisters instead in order to signal to Adams their displeasure.[49]

On May 6, 2005, the Westminster election was held resulting in a third term for Tony Blair and the Labour Party and a major shakeup in Northern Ireland. David Trimble lost his Upper Bann seat to David Simpson of the DUP by 5,298 votes after he had comfortably retained it in 2001. The Ulster Unionists were reduced to a single Westminster seat held by Lady Sylvia Hermon, wife of former RUC Chief Constable Jack Hermon, in North Down. North Down is distinct from the other constituencies located east of the Bann River in the Protestant unionist heartland. It has more in common with southern England than with Northern Ireland with its wealthy Bangor neighborhoods and small villages. It was the constituency that Robert McCartney had won a seat in a decade before in a by-election. It was the base of his UK Unionist Party and the only constituency in Northern Ireland where the Conservatives were competitive at the local level. And Hermon as an English lady married to a security figure was not a typical UUP candidate.[50]

The DUP ended up with nine seats from 33.7 percent of the vote compared with the UUP with one seat and 17.7 percent. Sinn Fein protected, but failed to dramatically advance, its lead over the SDLP by winning five seats and 24.3 percent of the vote compared to three seats and 17.5 percent for the latter party. Alliance was next with 3.9 percent of the vote and zero seats. In the local election held on the same day the DUP topped the poll with 29.6 percent of the vote and 182 seats, followed by Sinn Fein with 23.3 percent and 126 seats — a gain of 18 seats, the UUP with 18.0 percent and 115 seats and the SDLP with 17.4 percent and 101 seats — a loss of 16 seats. Alliance received 5.0 percent and 30 seats and all other parties were less than one percent of the vote each and in single digits for seats won. The UUP in only six years had gone from ten Westminster seats to one. The DUP had nearly reversed this process going from two to nine.[51]

Weeks before the election the Belfast Telegraph predicted that both the UUP and the SDLP would be reduced to a single seat. Why did the SDLP fare better than predicted? The SDLP, unlike the UUP, fought the election not as a province-wide election but in order to protect their turf in three separate constituencies. The UUP should have fought to protect its existing five seats but instead wasted resources on other constituencies that they did not have a hope of winning. The UUP still had a mindset of themselves as the established unionist party. The SDLP had popular candidates in its three seats: Mark Durkan in Foyle, Eddy McGrady in South Down, and Alasdair McDonnell in South Belfast, who benefitted from the two main unionist parties splitting the unionist vote. South Belfast is a very middle class constituency so Sinn Fein had little appeal there. The SDLP lost a seat in Newry and Armagh when Seamus Mallon retired and the seat went to Sinn Fein's Connor Murphy. But their pickup allowed them to keep their overall number of seats the same. Mark Durkan did a lot of canvassing in his constituency before the election to introduce himself to voters and he benefited from John Hume's popularity.[52]

The McCartney murder hurt Sinn Fein, slightly allowing the SDLP to guard its position and not lose further ground. The Northern Bank job probably did not hurt the party as republicans considered it another example of IRA daring-do that did not hurt anyone except for rich capitalists. The SDLP seemed to have already hit bottom in 2001–2003 and was on its way to recovery in 2005.[53] The UUP on the other hand was still in free-fall.

There are several explanations for this astounding defeat. First and foremost, unionist voters were punishing the UUP for the sins of Sinn Fein/IRA: the failure to decommission fully, the lies about the IRA's activities, the continued criminality of the IRA. Trimble was being blamed for failing to do what the British were unable or unwilling to do. The DUP tapped into unionist insecurities about the Republicans, about the British, and about Dublin. Paisley reassured voters that he had no intention of going into government with Sinn Fein.[54] Second, voters were tired of the squabbles within the UUP that had made it effectively dysfunctional as a party. Trimble was never ruthless enough for his own good in punishing dissenters. He was neither loved nor feared as a party leader—a very dangerous position to be in for any leader. He was "too much the fox, and not enough the lion." The party began to split into factions following the 2003 loss and Trimble began to lose touch with the party base. Third, the UUP had never actually lost an election before 2003 and the party was not a modern centralized election-winning machine as were the British and Irish parties. The party was based on its constituency branches and was not able to run a centralized campaign. The party never conducted a thorough post-election analysis after the Assembly election of what went wrong and right. Fourth, Trimble probably should have stepped down as party leader after the 2003 election as he was too easy a target for the DUP. This would have given a new leader a chance to build support before the election. Fifth, with Trimble no longer the first minister after October 2002 the party was not able to control the media's agenda.[55]

Three days after the election Trimble resigned as party leader at a press conference. He had recovered from his emotional defeat and was in a good mood. The press then began to speculate about the upcoming leadership contest, the first in a decade. Initially it appeared to attract heavyweight competitors as had the 1995 contest: John Taylor, Ken Maginnis, Sylvia Hermon, and Reg Empey. Maginnis announced his candidacy on May 18 and admitted that if he had won in 1995 he would not have done as good a job as Trimble did. He was essentially running as Trimble's successor. But Maginnis had recently lost a council election in Dungannon, which hurt his image as a winner. So by mid–June he had dropped out of the race. Lady Hermon's husband was suffering from Alzheimer's disease and she decided that she was not able to be both a caretaker to her husband and the leader of a party that needed rebuilding. Taylor decided he did not want the job at his advanced age. So when nominations closed on June 17 there were only three candidates: Empey, the culture and arts minister in the Assembly; David McNarry, a former Trimble aide; and Alan McFarland, an unknown former army officer. McNarry was eliminated in the first round of voting with only nine percent. Empey won in the second round 52.8 percent to McFarland's 47.2 percent, a total similar to that of many of Trimble's leadership challenges. Ulster Television's chief political correspondent Ken Reid did not even think that the leadership contest was worth covering in person. It was not an auspicious sign for the future of the party under Empey.[56]

Ulster unionist academic G. K. Peatling listed eight different explanations normally given for the collapse of the peace process between 2001 and 2004. First was a lack of skill by the sponsors in choreographing the process. Second was politicians deliberately misleading the public about the peace process. Third, the institutionalization of tribalism in the GFA led to intensification of the conflict. Fourth, liberal optimism in the possibility of ending the conflict was naïve. Fifth, unwise unilateral concessions to Sinn Fein led to loss of support for the process among unionists and led more nationalists to vote for Sinn Fein. Sixth, hostile attention to Republicanism by the media and the other parties and the two governments alienated Sinn Fein and the IRA. Seventh was the lack of integration of the province into the UK. Eighth was the lack of integration of the province into the Republic. The last two explanations are symptoms of the conflict and are in fact mutually exclusive. Peatling favors no single explanation for the collapse, but argues for a combination of the second, third, and fifth explanations. He argues that neither the nationalists — especially the Republicans — nor the unionists properly prepared their own public for the concessions that would be necessary to win the peace. As a result both unionists and Republicans felt that they had given up too much and received too little in return. He argues that the provisions on decommissioning were deliberately vague in order to reach an Agreement, but that the interpretation of the relevant clause by Unionists and Alliance was stone-cold sober compared to Sinn Fein's wild predictions about the GFA leading to a united Ireland in the near future. He also argues that the process was too focused on the Republicans, thereby putting Sinn Fein or even the IRA in the driver's seat.[57]

This author (Mitchell) is most sympathetic to the third and fifth explanations. While the Agreement reflected the sectarianism operating in the province it also had the effect of intensifying it. In the past the SDLP's attitude was that Alliance with its nonsectarianism was a "luxury that Northern Ireland could not afford."[58] The UUP seemed to echo this attitude. The result was an Agreement that favored initially the moderate sectarians at the expense of both the extremists and the nonsectarians. As the conflict failed to go away and the governments appeased the IRA, the extremists benefited at the expense of the moderates. Decommissioning was a necessary tradeoff in exchange for power sharing, a North-South dimension, and an early prisoner release. By not explicitly linking prisoner releases with decommissioning, the two governments allowed all the paramilitary organizations to avoid their obligations and thereby invite the Unionists to try and compel the Republicans to disarm. London never properly understood unionist fears and therefor pushed the unionists too far, too fast and were cavalier about their doubts about the process.[59]

On the same day that nominations closed for the UUP leadership contest, June 18, former IRA Shankill bomber Sean Kelly was returned to prison for violating the conditions for his early release under the GFA by order of NI Secretary Peter Hain. Republicans said that he had actually been a calming influence on the streets during sectarian riots after his release. He was the first Republican to be returned to prison. Several loyalists, most prominent among them being Johnny Adair of C Co. UDA, had been reinterned. Republicans interpreted his arrest and imprisonment as a form of pressure on Sinn Fein and the IRA to act on decommissioning. On July 27 Gerry Adams gave a copy of a statement to Hain that the IRA had ordered an end to its armed campaign and had ordered all volunteers to dump arms. This was similar to the order issued in May 1923 at the end of the Irish civil war by the IRA. Sean Kelly was released from prison that evening five weeks after having been reinterned.[60]

In the statement that the IRA issued it authorized its representative to engage with the Independent International Commission on Decommissioning (IICD) of General de Chastelain and for any decommissioning to be witnessed by two clergymen — one Catholic and one Protestant. The former IRA prisoner who read the statement for the recording given to the media had spent 21 years in prison before being one of the first prisoners released in 1998. Both the prime ministers, Ahern and Blair, accepted the IRA statement on its face. As a result, already in the summer of 2005 the British army began removing its presence from the province by taking down observation towers along the border. It announced that the Ulster battalions of the Royal Irish Regiment, Ulster's home guard unit and the successor to the infamous B Specials and

Ulster Defence Regiment, would be stood down. Hugh Orde, the commander of the new police service, told BBC reporter that decommissioning would affect the IRA's potential only in the short term, but that it would put pressure on other paramilitary organizations to decommission.[61]

In mid–September 2005 General de Chastelain suddenly disappeared for several days. There had been hints that the IRA was suddenly about to decommission its arsenal. The *Sunday Business Post* ran a piece by an independent defense consultant laying out what would be the easiest most practical methods of decommissioning and the best ways to publicize it in order to win widespread unionist acceptance that it had occurred and been complete. These latter suggestions appear to have been completely ignored by the IRA.[62] When he reemerged it was to announce that the IRA had finally completed its decommissioning obligation and that the method used was consistent with that called for in the Decommissioning Act of 1997. He further stated in his report that the quantity of weapons decommissioned was consistent with intelligence estimates of the IRA's arsenal provided to him by the British and Irish intelligence services. "Very large quantities of arms, which we believe include all the arms in the IRA's possession," had been decommissioned according to De Chastelain. "This can be the end of the use of the gun in Irish politics," he said optimistically. But he refused to give a detailed inventory of the weapons destroyed or a list of the places where the decommissioning took place. He said he had not asked to take photographs, as this had been rejected by the IRA in the past, and that the parties would just have to take his word on it. The two clergymen, the Rev. Harold Good, a former Methodist Church president, and Father Alec Reid, a Catholic priest who had been involved in facilitating the Hume-Adams talks, verified that this was true. One of the two said he had hauled sacks of arms as part of the decommissioning process and the other said he would be willing to stake his life on the IRA not having held any arms back. "We spent many long days watching the meticulous and painstaking way in which General de Chastelain went about his task of decommissioning huge amounts of explosives, arms and ammunition," said Good. "That was a very significant moment. The last of everything," he added. De Chastelain later ascribed the long period that it took before the IRA decommissioned to a process of getting to trust him and the IICD and that the peace process would deliver.[63]

Tony Blair and Bertie Ahern both announced that they believed that decommissioning had been completed, as did Washington. The State Department had its own man on the IICD, Andrew Sens. Reg Empey reacted to the news by calling on loyalist paramilitaries to follow the example of the IRA. He also said that the IRA must give up its criminality. Ian Paisley was noncommittal. He had groused about the unionists not being allowed to pick their own Protestant witness or to photograph. He was careful to raise just enough doubts that he could use them as an excuse for not going into government with Sinn Fein if he decided that he did not want this, but not enough to make a new Executive impossible in the future. Brian Rowan was convinced that it was inevitable that Sinn Fein and the DUP would eventually end up in government together. But UKUP leader Robert McCartney declared decommissioning to be irrelevant just as it was about to occur, because IRA criminality was much more insidious and dangerous. He congratulated Dublin on paying attention to this and said that Britain and the DUP were negligent. But even those without a political axe to grind had doubts. Journalist Alan Murray wrote that De Chastelain seemed to be much more concerned about not embarrassing Republicans than he was about convincing unionists. And Trimble biographer Henry McDonald claimed that the IRA had actually struck a secret deal with the two governments that would allow them to retain their handguns—many of them freshly imported from Florida—for personal protection and ethnic enforcement in their ghettoes. And the Ulster Volunteer Force began to even speak to its members about the possibility of a dialogue with Republicans, but not yet about decommissioning its own weapons.[64]

Many believed that by overreaching with the December 2004 Northern Bank robbery and the McCartney murder the following month, the Republicans had created the conditions—against their will—that finally brought about decommissioning. The three governments had put pressure on Adams who was finally able to triumph over the Provisional hardliners. Some might even allege that Adams had allowed the robbery to take place with this outcome in mind. But British academic and Trimble supporter Paul Bew believed that the governments had decided to put the onus for failure of the peace process on the DUP instead of on the Republicans. Decommissioning took place but without photographic evidence and assurances were probably given to Sinn Fein that the GFA would not be renegotiated as the DUP had demanded. The DUP wanted to end the d'Hondt method of mandatory power sharing.[65]

The week preceding the beginning of the final IRA decommissioning process in September 2005 witnessed some of the worst rioting in Belfast in decades. Loyalist mobs backed up by paramilitaries of the UVF ran amuck in East Belfast. The ostensible reason for the riots was the rerouting of a traditional Orange Order parade along the Shankill Road for seventy yards to avoid a small nationalist area in bordering Springfield in West Belfast. Unlike the Orange Order in Portadown, the Shankill Orange organizers had been involved in discussions with local residents. The Shankill is a traditional Protestant area surrounded by nationalist neighborhoods. So they felt they were being denied their rights in their own areas. But the real underlying reasons were wider: British concessions to Republicans following the IRA statement in July: the release of Sean Kelly, the demilitarization in South Armagh and elsewhere, and the scheduled disbandment of the RIR's Ulster units. But in reality there were other reasons for the riots. The organizers were hoping for the same sort of official recognition and appeasement that the Republicans had received for a decade. Too weak to win a stake in power sharing or even anything beyond a single Assembly seat in East Belfast in 2003, the PUP was losing its influence with the hardmen of the UVF. The UDA stayed out of the riots, which included North Belfast, Ballymenna, Ballyclare, Newtonabbey — any town with a loyalist population. The riots and the killing of five LVF members since April had finally led Peter Hain to declare the UVF to be off-ceasefire. Thus, it would not be eligible for any of the privileges afforded to paramilitary organizations that were still on ceasefire — like the IRA and the INLA.[66]

DUP MLA Diana Dodds, wife of MP Nigel Dodds, blamed the riots on government funding of loyalist areas that propped up the paramilitaries. "Over 80% of the Shankill votes DUP. They didn't vote for people with guns and the government needs to recognize that you cannot bypass the elected representatives. In many cases it is the people who cause the problems who get the funding," claimed Dodds. "There is no strategic plan. Central government piecemeal funds this, that and the other, but never within a strategic context. Funding is churned out to the community and in many cases they institutionalize paramilitarism while doing it." Sammy Duddy of the Ulster Political Research Group, the replacement for the defunct UDP, agreed with Alasdair McDonnell of the SDLP (quoted above). "This has come about because the government has been saying to the loyalists 'You have no clout; we are dealing with Sinn Fein and the Provisional IRA, who can threaten another Canary Wharf.' There is a feeling that they have the inside track with the government and Protestants don't," he said. "That being said, this rioting is only bringing grief to poverty stricken areas and it's the wrong way to go about anything. It's time to admit that the Orange Order has always used the paramilitaries as the big stick," he claimed. "They use them to police their parades through contentious areas. They use them as their army when it suits and then washes their hands if things turn out badly."

But Alex Benjamin, a Jewish Ulster Unionist official who moved to Northern Ireland in 1991, blamed the police for much of the violence. He claimed that the police initially failed to restrain the rioters and then acted provocatively and with overwhelming force. He claimed to have heard some police shout "Orange bastards" at some of the rioters. What Benjamin might have have witnessed was unprofessional but very human payback for organizations that had confronted the police and killed and wounded their colleagues since 1998. At least 115 shots had been fired by loyalists at the police, many into Land Rovers obviously intended to kill the occupants. Some 116 vehicles had been hijacked, many for use in barricades or to set on fire.[67]

The decommissioning by the IRA meant that the security forces would not have to worry about fighting on two fronts at the same time. But the rioting also limited the ability of the DUP to make any sort of deal with the Republicans in the near future if it felt so inclined. And the fact that Robert Commander, a friend of IRA murder victim Robert McCartney, was badly beaten by the IRA during the week of the riots gave them an excuse not to engage with Sinn Fein. In the wake of the riots the DUP presented its own demands. These included: a severance package for members of the Ulster battalions of the RIR, the replacement of the Parades Commission with a new body more oriented towards the right to march, more funding for loyalist areas, more unionists to be appointed to public bodies such as the Equality Commission, and parity of funding for Protestant festivals and cultural activities with funding for nationalist festivals and cultural activities.[68]

There were several issues still waiting to be resolved before devolved government could be restored to the province. First, the Republicans wanted a blanket amnesty for "on the runs" (OTRs)—IRA fugitives from justice who had either escaped from prison or had fled the province before they could be captured and tried. The British were inclined to grant this as an extension of the prisoner releases of the Belfast Agreement. But unionists and Alliance wanted a symbolic trial and conviction of any OTRs before their release. Second, the Republicans were still demanding implementation of some Patten reforms, notably regarding policing boards, before they were willing to publicly back the police as the DUP demanded. And Sinn Fein wanted to implement a scheme of "restorative justice" with local community boards deciding cases. The SDLP feared that this would amount to little more than a formalization of the IRA's punishment beatings or "turning the hood over to the hoods." Sinn Fein was also demanding an early devolution of security matters—policing and justice—to Stormont, which under the GFA were reserved for London.[69]

Even with decommissioning seemingly removed as a major issue, SDLP politician Sean Ferran was forecasting a bumpy short-term for politics in the province. He predicted that the DUP would deliberately call for more on decommissioning and criminality than the Republicans would be willing to give and that the Republicans in turn would deliberately give less than the Agreement obligated. "The danger can only be overcome if the governments stand strong for the agreement and put those who fall short of it under positive popular pressure." Journalist and former Stickie Liam Clarke advised the DUP to imitate Sinn Fein and never admit failures while presenting every concession granted to them as a major triumph. "The biggest problem facing unionism as it drifts towards 2006 is finding a new definition of success," wrote Clarke. He wrote that the unionist way was to always play a zero-sum game (like the Palestinians) and as a result to usually lose. Clarke was advocating in essence a better sort of spin management on the part of unionists.[70] This advice would have been just as relevant for the UUP, but most of its politicians did not want to listen to it because they were intent on ousting Trimble.

The year ended with a strange affair. The British quietly dropped the charges against the three individuals implicated in the "Stormontgate" spy ring affair of October 2002 on December 8. Soon afterwards Denis Donaldson held a press conference and with his Sinn Fein colleagues present calmly announced that he had secretly been a paid British agent for about two decades after having been compromised in his private life. He was possibly compromised or recruited after being arrested for traveling on a false passport on his return from a Hezbollah training camp in Lebanon in 1981. Donaldson told the press in Dublin, "The so-called Stormont-gate affair was a sham and a fiction. It never existed. It was created by Special Branch." Donaldson claimed that he was approached by the British in their first contact with him since 2002 and warned that his life was in danger. This might have motivated his sudden confession. Or one of his fellow "spies" might have wondered why the charges had suddenly been dropped. In any case Donaldson decided that this was a good occasion to end his double life and Sinn Fein was more than happy to exploit the situation. Adams alleged that the Stormontgate affair had been cooked up by "securocrats" in the British establishment to either save Trimble or to sabotage the peace process. But the affair also left the Republicans and the press wondering how many more British agents there were among Sinn Fein/IRA after the revelations about Donaldson and former IRA internal security deputy Joe Scappaticci in 2004. It also left both sides more suspicious of the other with their own conspiracy theories that fit existing prejudices.[71]

The two governments gave the DUP and Sinn Fein a rest of eight months before they again resumed the peace process. As the year opened the British government quietly dropped legislation to grant amnesty to "on the runs" after all the various parties objected to the legislation for various reasons. Donaldson was murdered by unknown assassins on April 4, 2006, at his secluded cottage in Donegal. Two days later the two governments held talks on the peace process. They decided to call the Second Assembly into session for its first session since the election of November 2003 on May 15. The parties would be given eight weeks to debate before a recess in July. They would then be given a further twelve weeks until November 24 to come up with a deal or the Assembly would be closed down permanently and all salaries to Assembly members would be cut off completely.[72]

DUP members made belligerent declarations that they could not be bribed and as a result not much was accomplished in the first eight-week session. When the parties convened Reg Empey announced that PUP MLA David Ervine would join the UUP Assembly group to give it an extra seat. This would have the effect of depriving Sinn Fein of one seat in the Executive and giving the UUP another seat. But after consulting a lawyer Speaker Eileen Bell of Alliance ordered the motion out of order. The reasoning was that the two parties had not campaigned as allies and there was nothing in the PUP's election literature to indicate any link with the UUP. In May the Northern Ireland Office announced plans to revamp local government in the province by reorganizing the 26 existing councils into seven "supercouncils" that just happened to be organized along ethnic lines. This would allow the DUP and Sinn Fein to carve up local government between them severely reducing the influence of the three centrist parties.[73]

In early October 2006 the International Monitoring Commission issued its most positive report to date on the IRA. It declared that many IRA structures had been dismantled, that the organization had no wish to return to war and that it could not sustain a prolonged campaign if it did return to violence. A month before, the UVF leadership told BBC correspondent Brian Rowan that "[w]e believe that the Provo war is finished. We believe that now it has turned to unarmed struggle.... We don't believe there is a will on their behalf to go back to war.... Our threat assessment is there is not the will nor the inclination."[74] A few days after the IMC issued its report, Ian Paisley, in his religious capacity as the moderator of the Free Presbyterian Church, held formal discussions with the head of the Catholic Church in Ireland, Archbishop Dr. Sean Brady at Armagh, the center of the Church for the island. From October 11 to 14, 2006, three days of intensive multiparty talks were held at a hotel in St. Andrew's, Scotland on the northeast coast of Great Britain. The summit ended with the two governments issuing a terse statement and an agreement that the DUP and Sinn Fein agreed to but did not sign. The agreement was essentially a timeline for resolving the policing issue and reconvening the Executive after new Assembly elections in March 2007. The DUP and Sinn Fein would meet in the Assembly on November 24 to elect a first and deputy first minister. Sinn Fein would then accept the PSNI as an acceptable police service and urge their supporters to cooperate with it. Elections would be held in March 2007 and then the Executive would be set up. It was the type of elaborate choreography that had failed repeatedly in the past because Sinn Fein or its Republican allies had not lived up to their commitments: in 1999, in 2000, and most spectacularly in October 2003.[75]

This time the choreography worked! On November 11, the UDA announced that it was "standing down" as of midnight and all of its intelligence would be destroyed and its arms put beyond use. Neither of the main paramilitary organizations ever decommissioned their weapons, but all claimed they were putting them "beyond use," whatever that meant.[76] On November 24 the shadow Assembly was converted into a full Assembly with the election of Ian Paisley as first minister and Martin McGuinness as deputy first minister. This was despite former UDA gunman Michael Stone breaking into Stormont. A brave security guard prevented him from harming anyone and he was wrestled to the ground. Despite a successful career as an artist, Stone craved publicity and wanted to be the hero of the rejectionist loyalists. He was returned to prison — probably for another decade or more. At the end of the year Sinn Fein announced that it would convene an *Ard Fheis* (party conference) to debate the policing issue. Adams prepared the ground carefully and in late January the *Ard Fheis* declared the party's full support for the PSNI. This was after Police Ombudsman Nuala O'Loan, the wife of a senior SDLP official, announced evidence that the RUC had colluded with loyalists in the killing of several Republicans by supplying them with intelligence and shielding them from prosecution. This was a sweetener before the *Ard Fheis*. Earlier that month David Ervine, the PUP's only remaining MLA, died after a massive heart attack. He was replaced by Dawn Purvis without a by-election being called.[77]

The Assembly election on March 7, 2007, resulted in both the DUP and Sinn Fein increasing their number of seats at the expense of their respective Unionist and nationalist rivals. The DUP received 36 seats, up six from 2003, with 30.1 percent of the vote. Sinn Fein won 28 seats, up four from 2003, with 26.2 percent of the vote. The SDLP came in third in terms of first preference votes with 15.2 percent, but fourth in terms of seats with only 16, down two. The UUP beat out the SDLP with 18 seats, down nine from 2003, but only 14.9 percent of first preferences. Alliance improved dramatically from 2003 with its vote up 1.6 percent to 5.2 percent for seven seats. Dawn Purvis managed to squeak into the Assembly with only .6 percent of the vote. She probably received significant numbers of lower preference votes from UUP and even Alliance voters in East Belfast. And there were two members of other parties — a Green and an independent.[78]

On March 26 Ian Paisley, Martin McGuinness and Gerry Adams met and agreed to set up an Executive on May 8, 2007. Paisley had pleaded that he needed time to prepared his supporters for power sharing with their traditional enemies. All was smiles at the press conference. This delay also allowed Paisley to claim that he would not allow the governments to dictate a timeline to him. The first hundred days of the new Executive were so pleasant and amicable that Paisley and McGuinness were dubbed the "chuckle brothers" by the frustrated or bemused media and a rival UUP MLA. Paisley liked to refer to McGuinness as his deputy in public, and McGuinness seemed content to be called by a shortened version of his official title, although in reality they are equals under the Agreement.[79]

So why did Ian Paisley reverse his entire political career, which consisted of opposition to any concessions to nationalists as well as republicans? He had opposed Terence O'Neill for his rapprochement with Dublin and his attempts to reconcile nationalists with Ulster Unionist rule through very minor reforms. He then forced out of office James Chichester-Clark, O'Neill's cousin, who succeeded him as UUP leader. He colluded with the mainstream of the UUP, to oppose the power-sharing Executive of Brian Faulkner and bring it down. Sinn Fein had not been a party to that power sharing government.[80]

London and Dublin had used a carrot and stick strategy of combining bribes and threats. London threatened to raise water rates in the province and make the residents pay a greater share of the administration of the province. Peter Hain told an English audience what did the trick in Northern Ireland, "When any politician knocked on their door canvassing they were greeted with the instruction to get into power whatever their differences and sort out the water charges. So after seven to eight centuries of conflict it all came down to water charges."[81] Both governments offered a combined package of aid as a "peace dividend," although many unionists thought that this was merely repackaging of the existing budget with little new. Dublin was offering to pay mainly for road repairs on main routes between the Republic and Northern Ireland. And there was the threat that devolution after decommissioning would lead to something approaching de facto joint government with Dublin having an active consultative role in the North that had ended with the GFA. This was the deciding factor for Peter Robinson. "Had the DUP not secured devolved government, the Direct Rule administration would have proceeded with an all-Ireland agenda and also imposed an Irish Language Act. Many people were concerned with Plan B and a greater role for Dublin in the affairs of Northern Ireland and undoubtedly over time that would have insidiously grown," explained Robinson. Although Paisley had earlier rejected similar reasoning when it was put forward by Trimble earlier in the decade. A year earlier unionist academic Dr. John Coulter had analyzed the factions in the DUP in an article in *The Blanket,* an online revisionist republican magazine, and predicted a possible move by the "modernist" faction led by Robinson to split off and form a new united unionist party with the UUP. This would occur if Paisley did not go into government with Sinn Fein. Opposed to the "modernists" are the "fundamentalists" led by Nigel and Diana Dodds and the "ultras" led by Jim Allister. Coulter had the Robinson camp numbering 16 MLAs to 12 for the "fundamentalists" and four MLAs for the "ultras." We may have to await the memoirs of one of the DUP leaders to find the reason why Paisley, grouped by Coulter with the "fundamentalists," decided to go with the "modernizers."[82]

Polling data had demonstrated that unionists wanted Paisley to go into government with Sinn Fein now that decommissioning had occurred. He could take credit for forcing the IRA to decommission as Trimble had attempted to do in October 2003. And he had even gotten them to accept policing. Paisley at age 80 had probably decided that he wanted to finally experience power and relish the prestige of being first leader now that the "heavy lifting" of decommissioning had finally been accomplished. According to biographer Ed Moloney, Paisley was also urged to go into government by his family. Both the Free Presbyterian Church and the DUP had been family enterprises run by Paisley's immediate family. His wife, Eileen, had gone into the House of Lords in May and she wanted her husband to pave the way to the succession by son Ian, Jr.[83] There was also the matter of a putdown to the Ulster Unionist establishment that had treated Paisley as a rude outsider unfit for power for thirty years. Not only had he prevented every Unionist leader from making peace with the nationalist minority, but he had now done so himself. The IRA, by disarming, had removed all the risk that Brian Faulkner and David Trimble had faced in their own failed peace attempts.[84] It was like Richard Nixon making peace with the Chinese and Soviet Communists in the early 1970s, Ronald Reagan doing the same fifteen years later, and Menahem Begin making peace with Egypt in 1979. The leader of the right could do what liberals could not.

Paisley in late 2006–early 2007 had essentially four choices. First, he could have simply pleaded ill health and advanced age and retired from politics. Few men his age were still active in democratic politics in the West— Shimon Peres of Israel being the main exception. Second, he could have remained in charge and continued a policy of opposition to Sinn Fein, Dublin and London. This would have been a return to his roots and he would have had support for this course from his core supporters. But he might have risked Peter Robinson, Nigel Dodds, and Jeffrey Donaldson splitting off to form a new unionist party, possibly in conjunction with the Ulster Unionists. Third, he could have blessed power sharing with the Republicans but allowed Peter Robinson or Nigel Dodds to become first minister. This would have been an imitation of what Gerry Adams and John Hume had done. In fact, many expected him to take this course. The fact that he ignored this course and took power himself, the fourth option, indicated that he probably wanted to change his role in Northern Ireland history. His role had always been a destructive one and he had never demonstrated any craving for power in the past. Paisley pledged to stay in office for a full Assembly term — four years. This seemed to indicate that he would retire at age 84. A fifth choice would have been to begin power sharing and retire after a short period — six months to a year — once he had assured that it was up and running. He could always retire at any point if his health deteriorates but he seemed full of energy and completely recovered from whatever illness ailed him in 2004.

Things seemed to have worked out just in time. In May 2007 Bertie Ahern was reelected to a third term as taoiseach. Sinn Fein, rather than doubling its caucus in the South to ten seats as it had confidently predicted, lost a seat in the Dail leaving it with four. But it did increase its overall share of the vote from 6.5 to 6.9 percent. Gerry Adams when he appeared in press interviews in the Republic before the election seemed uninformed about Irish politics. Sinn Fein abruptly reversed itself on a major economic policy — indicating that its policies were more opportunistic than principled. Although Fianna Fail's existing coalition partner, the Progressive Democrats, fared very poorly and Michael McDowell lost his seat, it was easily able to form a coalition with a few independent deputies.[85] Had this come about before the IRA decommissioned and Sinn Fein went into government, many in the Republican base might have began asking some probing and difficult questions about Adams's strategy for Irish unity.

In July 2007 the DUP finally began to follow the advice of Liam Clarke from two year earlier. The Rev. William McCrea published an article in the Belfast *News Letter*, the mainstream newspaper most sympathetic to the DUP, pointing out that the IRA had been defeated. Journalist Alex Kane wrote a piece confirming the analysis, but pointing out that this had been obvious for a rather long time. Kane also suggested that the article had been authorized by DUP headquarters.[86]

Epilogue

In September 2007 the Ulster press was full of news of three separate political stories that together promised a shakeup of politics in the province. First, Reg Empey, leader of the UUP, had agreed to hold discussions with the

DUP about a possible election pact for the next set of elections. With the two main unionist parties at last in basic agreement about the Agreement, the imperative was to form a united front so that neither McGuinness nor Adams could be elected first minister and to keep the number of nationalist seats at Westminster and on local councils to a minimum. Meanwhile Jim Allister had called a meeting of all of those DUP (or former DUP) councilors and prominent figures from his "ultra" faction who wanted to discuss forming a new party. A meeting was held at an Orange hall in the village of Moygashel in North Antrim with about fifty people in attendance. It was not a great beginning, but neither was the start of the Protestant Unionist Party in 1969 that two years later turned into the DUP.[87] The third story was the announcement by Bertie Ahern that Foreign Minister Dermot Ahern would be forming a committee to look at the possibility of Fianna Fail organizing on a 32-county all-Ireland basis. After 2001 there had been much speculation that the SDLP would have to eventually join with one of the parties from the South in order to survive. Pundits put the favorite in this race as Fianna Fail, as the Irish Labour Party could not do much for the SDLP and Fine Gael's ties with the party had diminished over the last twenty years. The only question was whether it would be merely an alliance or a full merger. Bertie said that the party would not plan on contesting Westminster seats. This left open the possibility that the SDLP might retain its name to run for the British parliament, but contest seats in the Assembly under the Fianna Fail label. Fianna Fail wanted to save the SDLP and the North from Sinn Fein and keep the Republicans busy up North so they would not be a threat in the Republic.[88]

If these mergers (or at least alliances) occurred the Big Four would then become the Big Three with their being a Unionist Party, Fianna Fail and Sinn Fein. If the SDLP disappeared and no party from the Republic came north to challenge Sinn Fein then there would be a return basically to the politics that existed from 1922 to 1968 when the UUP confronted the Nationalist Party. Except that Sinn Fein is much more formidable than the Nationalists ever were. Alliance would play the role of the tiny Northern Ireland Labour Party, which was active in Belfast from the 1940s to the 1970s. If there are two nationalist parties competing against a merged unionist party (possibly to be called simply the Unionist Party) it would be the mirror image of Ulster politics in the 1970s when there were two unionist parties but only one nationalist party, the SDLP. Then the SDLP benefited from unionist infighting and managed to win a number of seats particularly in the area west of the Bann River. If the situation reversed, unionists might look forward to winning a few — if not all — of those seats back. But in any case this promises to be the biggest change in Ulster politics in a quarter century. As of early 2010 neither merger has come about. The UUP had formed a formal election pact with the Conservative Party, with which it was allied from 1906 to 1986, and an informal election pact with the TUV (see below) in order to oppose the DUP. When the former pact was concluded in November 2008, the Tories had only one councillor, a UUP defector, in all of Northern Ireland.

On October 20, 2007, Paul Quinn, a 21-year-old truck driver from the village of Cullyhanna in South Armagh, was lured across the border to a farm in Co. Louth where he was set upon by a gang of men armed with iron bars and nail-spiked pieces of wood. When an ambulance arrived he was still alive and conscious but looked like a blob of jelly. He died in the hospital a few hours later. The family blamed local Republicans, former IRA men, who Quinn had had a run-in with on two separate occasions. Quinn had not learned the important survival lesson that slights from local thugs with IRA connections were to be tolerated. The Sinn Fein spin machine went into gear and blamed the killing on local criminals and said that Quinn was probably being killed over a diesel-smuggling dispute. But where this incident differed from previous incidents over the last decade was that there was more protest from local republicans than from the DUP. The DUP called for a thorough police investigation of the incident but said that it was of political significance only if the Republican leadership had given the order for the beating/killing. On the day of the funeral, Peter Robinson presented the Executive's new budget to the Assembly. What this illustrated was the true nature of the peace in Northern Ireland: power sharing would go on and paramilitaries would be tolerated as long as they killed only within their "own" communities. The 25-year Republican armed struggle had resulted in a partitionist solution that resembled Italy more than either the UK or the Republic.[89] Ulster continued to be a place apart.

Ian Jr. was implicated in an influence-peddling scandal and forced to resign as his father's top aide. This left his father vulnerable. Ian Sr. had faced opposition within the Free Presbyterian Church to his deal with the Republicans. They had not publicly repented for their past and so Paisley by associating with them had broken a prime principle of the church — non-association with unrepentant sinners. As head of the government he was also forced to implement nondiscrimination legislation for homosexuals that also went against church and party policy. A commission was formed within the church to look into the matter and it ruled by a slight majority (nine to seven) that Paisley could not hold both offices. In September 2007 Paisley lost a wider vote to stay on as moderator and was forced to step down. After 36 years the church had finally divorced itself from the party, thereby lessening the church's influence within the party.[90]

Using the scandal with Ian Paisley, Jr., as an excuse, Peter Robinson moved quickly with the backing of the full party to force Ian Sr. out as first minister and party leader. This occurred in early April 2008 as Northern Ireland prepared to celebrate the tenth anniversary of the signing of the Belfast Agreement. Paisley was forced to announce that he would retire in May. This gave him a year as first minister. And it allowed Robinson to begin the task of building a new secular modernized DUP. He would have to show that he was able to accomplish the task with his party that Trimble had failed at with the UUP. Robinson was expected to show a more detached, professional attitude towards Martin McGuinness than the "chuckle brothers" routine of his predecessor.[91]

Robinson like Trimble deferred to the International Monitoring Commission. He said that he would wait until the IMC had issued its report on the Quinn murder before making a decision as how to react. In late April 2008 the IMC ruled that the Quinn murder had not been sanctioned by the leadership of the IRA, but that past or present IRA figures had been involved. This gave Robinson sufficient cover to avoid a major showdown with Sinn Fein, while being able to pressure them.[92]

From June until November 2008 Sinn Fein boycotted the meetings of the Executive in protest of the DUP's refusal to allow for the devolution of policing and justice powers to Stormont. Sinn Fein had agreed that it would not take over the ministry and suggested that Alliance put up the minister. Alliance refused because it wanted to be the only opposition in a system that virtually had eliminated opposition through mandatory power-sharing. The DUP was reluctant to agree to a devolution of justice powers because early in 2008 its Member of the European Parliament Jim Allister split off to form his own party, Traditional Unionist Voice, based on traditional DUP ideology and the rural base of the party. Politics had triumphed, but had not yet been normalized.

The loyalist paramilitaries continued to devolve further into gangsterism as the Shoukri brothers, leaders of the North Belfast UDA — although officially expelled from that organization — followed the path of Johnny Adair. One of the brothers died of a drug overdose in late November 2008 and the other remained in prison. The lack of a centralized leadership in the UDA and UVF and their lack of clout on the political scene precluded decommissioning on their part. The guns were needed for robberies and protection rackets. But the loyalists were no longer either a political factor or a security problem, but rather simply a policing problem.

Suddenly in late June 2009 there were hints of major announcements to come from the loyalist organizations regarding decommissioning. On June 27, 2009, a senior UVF spokesman read a statement that said: "The UVF and the Red Hand Commando have decommissioned all their weapons." Reporters said this occurred at a military base in Northern Ireland during the weekend of June 13–14. At the same time approximately as the UVF statement the UDA issued a statement that it had begun the decommissioning process and would complete it in the near future according to a timetable agreed to between the IICD and the UDA. General de Chastelain, head of the IICD, would only confirm that the UVF and Red Hand Commando had carried out "major decommissioning" and that the UDA had begun decommissioning.[93]

The INLA had basically followed the same route as the loyalists after Omagh and concentrated on the drug trade. The IRA had virtually disbanded after 2005 but many former members remained involved in organized crime. Only the Real IRA remained in the liberation business, attempting to murder policemen throughout 2008 and finally succeeding with two artillery soldiers waiting deployment to Afghanistan in 2009. A few days later the CIRA killed a policeman responding to a distress call.[94]

Conclusion

Introduction

In this conclusion I would like to sum up as much as possible the lessons of the two cases, particularly as they relate to making peace in the Middle East, but for making peace elsewhere as well. In Italics I will state a lesson and follow it with plain text afterwards. I have chosen the cases I did, as they will relate to future peacemaking in the Middle East, but they might also be applicable for conflict resolution in other deeply-divided societies such as Cyprus, Macedonia, Bosnia, and others.

But first a quick summary of why in my opinion the Northern Ireland peace process was successful and the Oslo peace process was not. Northern Ireland had a number of conditions favorable to peace that were lacking in the Middle East. First, Northern Ireland had a prominent nationalist party, the SDLP, which eschewed violence and believed in change through consent. It was the SDLP that negotiated the Good Friday Agreement with the Ulster Unionists. Second, the republican community had grown tired of the armed struggle and so was not willing to support the dissident republicans in their desire to continue the "long war." Third, the IRA and INLA had been prevented from creating an unacceptable level of violence by the British army — the former was riddled with informers and the latter had been taken over by criminals and weakened by internal fighting and factionalism. After 1997 Sinn Fein was committed to winning as much as it could through the threat of violence but without actually returning to violence. Fourth, London as the sovereign in Northern Ireland was willing to put pressure on the unionists that Washington had been unwilling to impose on Israel and lacked the leverage to impose on the Palestinians. Fifth, the 9/11 terrorist atrocities actually worked in favor of the Northern Ireland peace process by cutting off much of the IRA's American funding while not having that effect on the Palestinians. This is because the Irish-American community is much more assimilated than the Palestinian or Muslim Arab communities in the United States. The Middle East also had a number of negative factors that were not present in Northern Ireland. First, was the continual intervention by outside powers to exacerbate the tensions and level of violence. Damascus and Tehran remain committed to this negative intervention through support of Hezbollah, Hamas and other Palestinian groups. Second, continued settlement and colonization of the West Bank by Israel led to a drop in Palestinian support for the peace process. The status quo to be negotiated was continually changing throughout the Oslo process. Third, the unstable political systems of both Israel and the Palestinians made it easy for extremists to disrupt the peace process. And topping the list off was that Northern Ireland had an effective mediation mechanism — *dual mediation* — and the Middle East did not.

Until 1997 the Middle East peace process was more advanced than the Northern Ireland peace process due to the Oslo accords. But in 1996 Israel experienced a change in government that lowered the prospect of a successful settlement, whereas the following year Britain and Ireland experienced changes of government that increased the odds of a settlement. By the time that Labor returned to power in 1999 trust had been eroded between Israel and the PLO and Labor was working from a smaller support base within the coalition. Because the public reaction to the Omagh bombing in August 1998 put an end to the dissident republican terrorist campaign, London and Dublin were able to negotiate an implementation of the Good Friday Agreement free from the threat of violence; whereas the implementation of the Oslo accords was always under the shadow of Islamist violence. In October 2000 Yasir Arafat and the PA effectively joined the Islamists on a permanent basis, something they had done temporarily in 1996 and 1997 before then. Although there was rioting in Belfast and a few murders within the republican and loyalist communities, the ceasefires remained largely intact while the two governments and the politicians worked out a solution to decommissioning. Once this occurred, a return of power sharing was only a matter of time.

The Lessons

Lesson One: The settler party(ies) involved in a failed peace initiative will pay a heavy price for such a failure and will be reluctant to undertake similar initiatives if it (they) survives.

In Israel the two parties of the "peace camp" (Meretz, Labor) have both lost at least two-thirds of their 1992 Knesset representation. Labor has gone from 44 seats under Rabin to 19 seats in 2003 and Meretz went from 12 seats to six. In 2009 they fell further to 13 and three seats respectively. The Center Party never recovered and fell apart as it had no real core ideology, but rather was a collection of ambitious political defectors from the two main parties. Barak has become a major convert to the skeptical camp. This was all fallout from the failure at Camp David 2000 and from the Al-Aksa Intifada.

In Northern Ireland the two sectarian center parties, the Ulster Unionists and the SDLP, are in the process of disintegrating. As I discussed in Chapter 7 both parties are now in the process of discussing mergers in order to survive in some form. Trimble was courageous and willing to jump first on two occasions but he became more skeptical over time of both Sinn Fein and Tony Blair. He managed to win reelection to both Westminster and the Assembly after the Belfast Agreement, but the UUP lost the elections to the Second Assembly and were nearly wiped out in the 2005 Westminster election. An election pact with the Conservative Party in early 2009 appears to have added little to the UUP's potential electorate and an independent observer has predicted their continued irrelevance long into the near future. Like the Labor Party it has an aging electorate with little new blood in the party.[1]

Lesson Two: Centrists make the peace and the extremists can then either break it or remake it.

In 1993 the Oslo peace was negotiated between the liberals within Labor and the liberals within Fatah. The peace became unglued in the mid–1990s because Arafat failed to honor the agreements that Abu Ala and Abu Mazen had negotiated with Israel and Netanyahu failed to carry out the spirit of the agreement negotiated by Labor. Settlements were not a helpful factor, but were not prohibited by the Oslo Accords. By the time Barak came into office in 1999 the atmosphere was already spoiled and he did not take this into account when he planned his strategy for dealing with the Palestinians.

The Belfast Agreement was mainly negotiated between the SDLP and the UUP with the paramilitary parties negotiating the security issues with the two governments. If the UUP had been required to negotiate with Sinn Fein in 1998 the Agreement probably would not have come about. If the DUP and the UKUP had remained in the negotiations after Sinn Fein came in in September 1997 the Agreement probably would not have come about. Anti-Agreement unionists, both within the UUP and outside of it, forced Trimble to continually put ultimatums to Sinn Fein over IRA decommissioning. The IRA refused to instill confidence in Republican intentions through either clear transparent declarations about their intentions or decommissioning. Finally after decommissioning occurred in 2005 the two governments were able to negotiate and pressure the two sides into a final agreement.

Today the centrists in the Middle East are Fatah and the nonparty independents on the Palestinian side and Labor, Kadima, and Meretz on the Israeli side. Meretz may not seem to be a center party within Israeli politics, but if one looks at Hamas on one side and the Likud and Israel Beitenu on the other, than the above-mentioned parties are all in the center. Labor took 29 years to go from largest party to second largest and another 29 years to go to third largest; it took only three years to go to fourth largest. If Fatah cannot be stabilized and Labor rebuilt, there will not be a Middle East peace for decades. Maybe Hamas and the Likud can make peace, but it will take decades and thousands more deaths for the two sides to be ripe for peace.

After the peace was saved in Northern Ireland and both Britain and Ireland began touting it as a model for peace in the Middle East and other regional conflicts, Israelis were quick to deny any lessons. The *Jerusalem Post* ran a background analytical piece denying any parallels.[2] Herb Keinon wrote that the IRA never advocated "bringing Ireland to London." This overlooks that for the Protestants Northern Ireland is their real home, even if they want it to be part of the United Kingdom rather than to be independent. The other point is that the IRA was never a religious organization with religious motivations, unlike Hamas. Zion Evrony, Israel's ambassador to Dublin, makes this same point in another article where he quotes from Hamas's charter.[3] But there are considerable parallels between the IRA and the PLO. Both are secular organizations with a large religious input into their subtext. Both fed off of ethno-religious rage. I feel almost certain that even if the PLO was still in charge in the Palestinian Authority the Israeli establishment would simply emphasize the lack of parallel between Northern Ireland and Israel. But I argue that the Ulster equivalent of Israeli withdrawal from the territories in the Israeli-Palestinian conflict is power sharing. Both are examples of compromise. In one conflict the solution is partition, in the other it is power sharing within the earlier partition. Maybe in the distant future Israel may pursue a consociational future with its own Palestinian minority. If that occurs, it can hopefully learn lessons from Northern Ireland's experience with the Belfast Agreement.

Lesson Three: Dual mediation involving two governments, each of which is the patron of one of the parties in the conflict, is an effective form of mediation. To be effective, however, both governments must mediate in a balanced fashion and protect the interests of their clients.

Arafat and other leading Palestinians blamed Washington for being too pro-Israeli. They felt that its mediation at Camp David was biased in favor of Israel. There is truth in this assertion. It could hardly be otherwise: Israel is a democracy; the Palestinian Authority is a corrupt authoritarian regime. During the Cold War Israel was our close ally in the region whereas the Palestinians were the clients of our enemy, the Soviet Union. Most Americans are Christians who share an affinity with the Jewish people and the Palestinians share the religion of those who attacked us on 9/11. Rather than artificially trying to make the United States more "even handed," Washington should adopt the mediation form successfully used in Northern Ireland and use Europe as a natural balance. The Europeans because of guilt over colonialism, sympathy for the Palestinians, and dependence on Middle Eastern oil are naturally more sympathetic to the Arab side. Using the Clinton parameters as a starting point Washington and Brussels could easily develop a Middle East version of the Downing Street Declaration as the basis of a future joint peace effort. Brussels has tried to inject itself into the Middle East diplomatic arena since the Venice Declaration of 1980. Europeans diplomats carefully monitored the Oslo peace process and a European representative was present at Taba in January 2001.

The Northern Ireland peace process took nearly fourteen years after the Downing Street Declaration to stabilize because Blair favored Sinn Fein over both of the centrist parties. After Major represented unionist interests well in the original Declaration and Blair made his pro-Union speech in 1997, Blair gradually developed a pro-Republican bias. This is most likely because he was intimidated by the IRA's intact arms and feared another Republican campaign on the British mainland. Englishmen and most Scotsmen do not regard the unionists to be real British, but rather some form of exotic Irishmen. They regard Northern Ireland as a colonial situation rather than a domestic one, whatever the legalities. Naturally they favored the safety of their own countrymen over that of Protestant Irishmen (whom many in Labour regarded as responsible for the conflict in the first place).[4] The DUP and some of the anti–Agreement Ulster Unionists expected this treatment by London from the beginning. After about two or three years of the Blair treatment, Trimble came to expect it as well.

Northern Ireland's peace process was ultimately successful because of the smooth transitions among governments in both Britain and Ireland. All prime ministers from both countries seemed to have an equal dedication to advancing the peace process. That Bertie Ahern and Tony Blair succeeded is mainly a tribute to their longevity in office and the fact that they came along after the peace process was already developing. The Northern Ireland Office and the Department of Foreign Affairs in the Republic provided the bureaucratic support and expertise necessary for the negotiations. The civil servants in these offices provided the continuity between administrations necessary for success.

The Northern Ireland peace process was also dependent on cooperation with a number of foreign governments who supplied key individuals: America (Mitchell, Haas, Reis), Canada (De Chastelain), and Finland (Holkeri, Ahtisaari). In addition the American and South African governments played a special role. Pretoria ran seminars to educate the participants about the dynamics and lessons of the South African peace process. Belfast has now returned the favor by conducting similar workshops for Israelis and Palestinians, Sri Lankans and Iraqis. Clinton played a role approaching that of a third sponsor of the peace process in March-April 1998 and on St. Patrick's Days for years afterwards.

For the Middle East friendly Arab governments can play similar roles mediating between the Americans and the Palestinians. Candidates for this role are Egypt, Jordan, and Saudi Arabia. Cairo for years played a role of mediating between Washington and the PLO from 1989 until 1995. Jordan often fronted for the Palestinians at peace summits because Israel refused to negotiate with the PLO. Saudi Arabia mediated between Fatah and Hamas in negotiating a united Palestinian government in 2006. That such a government failed was not Riyadh's fault.

Lesson Four: The peace process requires leaders both from the parties and the mediators who are dedicated to peace and willing to take risks for peace.

With each peace process there must be figures from both sides and among the mediators willing to take risks for the peace to succeed. In the Middle East it was the Oslo negotiators backed by Shimon Peres and Yitzhak Rabin on the Israeli side and Mahmoud Abbas (Abu Mazen) on the Palestinian side that were crucial. Peres's vision and commitment was crucial to the effort. But without the political credibility of Rabin the Oslo agreements never would have passed the Knesset. Peres had been a dove and "peacenik" since the late 1970s when Dayan's flight from Labor, Peres's work in the Socialist International, and the influence of his younger advisors such as Yossi Beilin and Uri Savir had an effect on him. Peres first had an opportunity to display this with the London Agreement with King Hussein in 1988. But the need to transfer from Jordan to the Palestinians as a negotiating partner tested his commitment.

Rabin and Barak were both initially skeptical about the peace process in general and about Arafat and the PLO in particular. But once they understood that it was in Israel's security interest and that there was no other reliable partner they committed themselves fully. Barak was probably influenced by the commitment of his mentor, Rabin, to the process. Both preferred to make peace with Damascus first as they regarded states rather than terrorist organizations to be the proper partners for peace.

Likewise Ahmed Qurei (Abu Ala) and Abu Mazen were dedicated. But on the Palestinian side Arafat was the sole decision-maker and what he decided was the Palestinian decision. Now Abu Mazen is in charge, but unfortunately he lacks his own domestic constituency in the territories to support the compromises that he would need to make for peace. Particularly compromises on the refugee issue. And with Hamas in charge in Gaza and in much of the West Bank, Abu Mazen is in no position to take great risks for peace.

Jordan's King Hussein also demonstrated a dedication to peace in the region over the years. He was active in trying to get Arafat to let him represent the Palestinians at an international peace conference during the early 1980s. Arafat agreed and then changed his mind. Hussein concluded the London Agreement with Peres in 1987 but then gave up attempting to negotiate on behalf of the Palestinians the following year. He cut his regime's ties to the West Bank. Hussein's greatest effort was when he showed up at the Wye Plantation Conference in 1998 shortly before his death. Dying of cancer he still took the time and the risk to his health to urge the parties to make peace.

David Trimble and John Hume were rightly awarded the Nobel Peace Prize for their roles in the Northern Ireland peace process. Hume took considerable risks in the early days of the peace process from 1988 to 1994. He was willing to sacrifice his own political future and that of his party in order to ensure that peace arrived in the province. One can validly question his wisdom in doing this, particularly after 1994, but not his sincerity. Trimble took considerable risks from 1998 to 2003 for peace. They eventually cost him his position as first minister and as party leader. But his party is still paying the price. Gerry Adams likewise took risks for peace — even greater risks because he was risking his life. But his conduct in selling the peace meant lying to all sides — to the IRA, to the SDLP, to the Unionists and to the two governments. For this reason and the failure of the IRA to decommission on time he did not win the Nobel Prize.

No American president has ever been reelected because he negotiated a peace agreement in the Middle East (or as a third-party mediator in any regional conflict). Nixon was forced to resign two months after Henry Kissinger negotiated the Syrian-Israeli separation of forces agreements. Ford failed to win election in November 1976 despite Kissinger having negotiated the Sinai II Interim Agreement. Carter failed to win reelection in 1980. The collapse of the Israeli-Lebanese peace treaty in 1983 did not prevent Ronald Reagan from winning reelection in 1984. George Bush the elder did not win reelection after organizing the Madrid peace conference in 1991 and restarting the Middle East peace process. Clinton's failure at Camp David did not prevent Al Gore from winning more votes than George W. Bush in 2000, but American pressure on Israel might have affected the vote in Florida. Presidents do not negotiate peace in the Middle East in order to get reelected; presidents get elected in order to negotiate peace in the Middle East and elsewhere where peace is in America's interest.

Likewise, Thatcher's negotiation of the Anglo-Irish Agreement in 1985 did not affect her reelection. Major started the peace process in Northern Ireland but failed to win reelection. The collapse of the Northern Ireland peace process in 2003-04 did not effect the 2005 Westminster election on the British mainland. Blair's diminished majority was due to his longevity not to anything he did in Northern Ireland. The one election where Northern Ireland possibly had an effect was in 2001, when the Belfast Agreement became a symbol of Blair's foreign policy and skills as a peacemaker and politician.

Blair devoted much of his workweek to Northern Ireland week in and week out for years. He did so not in order to win reelection but because he was personally committed to peace in Northern Ireland. This is because of his personal family background, his religious convictions, and his early experiences in the province as a prime minister.

In a similar fashion Jimmy Carter devoted much of his first two years in office from April or May of 1977 to late March 1979 to securing a peace treaty between Israel and Egypt. His Camp David summit in September 1978 was a big gamble with no guarantee that it would pay off in terms of a future agreement. He risked his political capital on it. There is every reason to believe that if he had been reelected in 1980 he would have devoted much of his second term to widening that peace with either a peace agreement between Israel and Jordan or between Israel and the Palestinians. One of the first books he wrote after leaving office was about peace in the Middle East. And he has written a second book on the subject, which earned him much criticism from conservatives and from the American Jewish community.[5]

Bill Clinton devoted as much effort on a weekly basis during the final six months of his presidency as Carter did in his first two years. Clinton was handicapped by the assassination of Rabin in November 1995, the election of Benyamin Netanyahu in 1996, and by Barak's decision to attempt to negotiate peace first with Syria rather than the Palestinians. Although he failed to mediate a successful peace agreement either between Israel and Syria or Israel and the Palestinians he did advance the peace process on both tracks. He also took a big gamble in July 2000 and unfortunately it did not pay off. His December 2000 Clinton Parameters will probably be the starting basis for any future Middle East mediation effort.

The Israeli-Palestinian peace process has largely languished and gone backwards since 2001 because President George W. Bush was unwilling to take a "hands-on" approach to it as Carter and Clinton had done. Bush has intermittently engaged — in 2003 with the road map and in 2007 with Annapolis — but then he left it to his secretaries of state and the parties involved. Without backing at the highest level diplomacy will founder and fail.[6] Since the Nixon presidency Middle East peacemaking has required the active involvement of the president in policy formulation and his support for the secretary of state. William Rodgers and Kissinger's shuttle diplomacy spoiled the Israelis and Arabs by getting them used to dealing with the American secretary of state.

Lesson Five: Political failure in another area can make a mediator more dedicated to mediating peace.

Clinton was much more dedicated to negotiating a peace agreement in his second term than he was in his first. And he was much more dedicated after his impeachment by the House of Representatives than he was before he had that black mark on his record. One might argue that this was due to circumstances on the ground in the Middle East as mentioned above, but Clinton seemed to demonstrate a perseverance and drive in 2000 that he lacked from 1995 to 1999. Could this have been because he believed that only a peace agreement in the Middle East would remove the stigma of impeachment from his historical legacy?

With Tony Blair it is harder to judge. He was dedicated to peace in the province throughout his decade in office. After March 2003 he had more incentive in terms of historical legacy to see that the Belfast Agreement remained intact than he had before. And that incentive continued to increase as things went bad in Iraq in 2004 and 2005 and continued to grow worse. The Good Friday Agreement is without question the greatest achievement of Blair's decade in office, whether one classifies it as a domestic policy achievement or a foreign policy win. Many in Britain — particularly in his own party — will continue to believe that Iraq far outweighs the peace in Northern Ireland in terms of Blair's legacy. But I am convinced that historians will not agree. There have been many colonial failures in Britain's history especially in the twentieth century. But Ireland was unique as an unresolved issue. Blair succeeded where Gladstone failed. Gladstone and Disraeli were the great

British prime ministers of the nineteenth century. Ireland was to Britain during the late nineteenth and twentieth centuries what the Israeli-Palestinian conflict was to the United States in the late twentieth century.

As 2007 developed Condoleeza Rice began to show an interest in making peace in the Middle East. There was speculation in Israel that this was because of her lack of achievement in other areas since becoming Secretary of State. Her main achievement as secretary has been to set the American intervention in Iraq on surer footing. But this still is not something that can be readily measured. As the first female black secretary she, even more than most secretaries of State, wanted to have something positive to show as a legacy. She wanted historians to be able to say that she helped advance the peace process — like Jim Baker, George Schultz, and Madeleine Albright — even if she had no agreements to her credit when she left office.

So future voters and pundits should keep this in mind when looking at presidents. It may be precisely because a president is flawed that he develops the energy, dedication, and desire to risk all for peace in the Middle East.

Lesson Six: The timing of mediation efforts is critical.

William Quandt wrote in the introduction of *Camp David: Peacemaking and Politics* that the best time for an American president to negotiate a Middle East settlement is during his second and third years of his first term. He is too busy being reelected during his fourth year and still learning the "lay of the land" during his first year. The next best time is during the first two years of his second term. By the end of his sixth year in office, most presidents are beginning to be perceived as lame ducks and are completely lame ducks during the eighth year. Both Clinton and George W. Bush waited until their final year in office to get serious about Middle East peace. George H.W. Bush laid the preliminary groundwork for a Middle East settlement with the Madrid Conference in his third year and then left the rest for a second term that he was never granted. So any opportunity must be seized and exploited as soon as it occurs.[7]

Lesson Seven: Negotiating peace in native-settler conflicts is difficult because of the nature of both sides.

Settler societies in small territories with limited immigration tend to be siege societies.[8] Whether this is called a "laager mentality," a "Masada complex," or a "bawn psychology," it is the feeling that one is surrounded by enemies and that one either has no external allies or that they are unreliable.[9] It is especially prevalent on the settler nationalist right. It is no accident that the founding myth or myths in Israel, Ulster, and white South Africa are all siege accounts: the Siege of Derry, Blood River, Masada, and Tel Hai, as is the story of the siege of the Alamo — a prime American political myth.[10] The slogan of unionist nationalism is "No Surrender!" As a result of this the settlers tended to discriminate against the natives and regard them as either actual or potential traitors.[11]

Because of this discrimination the natives regard the settler societies as "failed," "ungovernable," and the like. Liberation movements, especially those involved in armed struggles, tend to be maximalist in their goals. They normally do not want a compromise settlement but a complete victory whether that is a socialist South Africa, a restored Palestine, or a united Ireland. Often native liberation mythology speaks of a time before the colonial conquest as a golden age. There is a long litany of heroes from the resistance — from those who resisted colonial conquest to those who fell in the early stages of the present liberation struggle. When, after many years or decades of struggle, a situation of ripeness appears because both sides realize that they cannot win, but must compromise. When that occurs the settler electorate is usually divided over the wisdom of the peace process, often closely divided as in the cases of both Northern Ireland and Israel.[12] The native leaders making peace have usually not adequately prepared their followers for a compromise peace or for the scope of compromise necessary. This results in a leadership having to lie to both its supporters and its partners in peace. Terrorists often commit violations of the peace agreements. They fail to disarm, they arm in excess of the limitations in the peace agreement, and they commit terrorist attacks and murders, or fail to prevent others from carrying these out.

As a result of the intersection of these terrorist violations of the agreement and the closely divided settler electorate the support for the peace process soon disappears on both sides. The hard-line settler party (DUP, Likud) gains support and the leader of the peace camp must either sit by and watch this support continue to erode away or take actions against the other side. Such actions include border closures, sanctions "within" the agreement like Trimble's ban on Sinn Fein participation in North-South meetings, and finally resignation. In 2003–06 I believed that the main lesson of the Middle East peace process and Northern Ireland peace process might be that successful peace processes are impossible because of the above factors. Northern Ireland has demonstrated that it is not impossible just very difficult. Unless an American administration is willing to dedicate as much time and effort as Major and Blair did in Northern Ireland in cooperation with Reynolds, Bruton, and

Ahern, it has little chance of success. I believe that without joint American-European mediation there is also little chance of peace.

Lesson Eight: It is better to negotiate the terms of the peace agreement early in the process rather than waiting for the necessary trust to build up between the two sides later in the process.

Northern Ireland's peace process was ultimately successful because decommissioning was dealt with during the negotiations. The solution was a bit of a fudge, but a commitment was established that the unionists and the two governments could hold the Republicans to. In the Middle East this expected trust never developed because the enemies of peace on both sides were able to mobilize during the five-year period that was supposed to be used to develop trust. Each set of enemies was then able to exploit the failures on the other side to erode and destroy support for the peace process in its own nation. The Palestinian opponents used the expansion of settlements, settler violence, and Israeli closures of the territories to erode support. Israeli opponents used Palestinian terrorism and refusal to stick to the terms of the agreement to erode support. The peace process was nearly destroyed during the mid–1990s under Netanyahu. With Arafat as a partner the Oslo process was probably doomed in any case, but it might have fared better had the difficult issues been tackled up front.

Lesson Nine: In settler societies military politicians (i.e., former generals) have credibility that other politicians lack.

If Ken Maginnis had been a former major general rather than merely a former major he might well have saved Trimble. The Oslo peace process rested upon the credibility of the Labor Party's former generals — foremost among them Yitzhak Rabin, known by reporters as "Mr. Security," for his reputation with the public. In Israel it has been former generals who have sold peace agreements to the public from Moshe Dayan during the 1970 ceasefire agreement with Egypt to Dayan, Yigael Yadin, and Ezer Weizman in 1979 with the Egptian-Israeli peace treaty, to Rabin in the 1990s. But once a military politician loses his security reputation it is difficult to recover. This happened with Dayan in October 1973 due to the surprise Arab attack of October 6 and Dayan's panicked reaction during the early fighting, with Sharon in 1982 because of the disastrous consequences of the First Lebanon War, and with Barak in 2000. Sharon had to wait 18 years to recover his reputation and he recovered it thanks to Barak losing his reputation. Barak is attempting to recover his reputation now after a break from politics of six years. And he is rebuilding his reputation on the failure of Amir Peretz in the Second Lebanon War and by his own leadership during the Gaza war of 2008.

Lesson Ten: Paramilitary/terrorist organizations with no visible political support can upset the peace process at any time.

In addition to dissident organizations such as Hamas that have genuine support, peacemakers have to worry about the destabilizing effects of terrorist acts by terrorists with little or no visible political support. In Northern Ireland this meant all of the loyalist organizations except for the UVF and all the republican organizations except for the Provisional IRA. Only the PUP and Sinn Fein were popular enough to be represented in the Assembly, and the UDP only had four councilors at the local level. Many of these smaller organizations were populated by volatile personalities who did not like discipline imposed from above, particularly once they became addicted to drugs or alcohol. Examples of these are Johnny Adair in the UDA, Billy Wright in the UVF/LVF, Dominic McGlinchey and Dessie O'Hare in the INLA, and others. The only real way to deal with these individuals was to keep them under surveillance if released and lock them up as soon as it became clear that they were violating their early release conditions. The Real IRA could easily have ended the peace process by provoking a major loyalist reaction if they had not been so foolish as to set off a major bomb in a town with a population from both communities (Omagh). Had they continued to bomb only towns that were mainly Protestant they could easily have provoked a loyalist reaction that might have ended the process.

In the Middle East the Islamists were the danger and will be in the future. If in the future the peace agreement is not between Israel and Fatah/independents but rather with Hamas there could easily be dissident factions within Hamas to worry about as well as Islamic Jihad. A future Israeli-Hamas agreement could easily produce the growth of a "Real Hamas" or "Continuity Hamas." With the Palestinian Authority having responsibility for security in parts of the Palestinian territories it may be more difficult than in Northern Ireland to keep a watch on these individuals and organizations. Iran has used Islamist militias to battle the peace process supported by the established Sunni leadership. It can now rely on three different organizations to advance its interests: Hezbollah in Lebanon, Palestinian Islamic Jihad and Hamas in the West Bank and Gaza.

There is also a danger from extremist Israeli settlers on the West Bank deciding to end the peace process through an atrocity. Baruch Goldstein, an American immigrant belonging to the Kach movement, nearly ended the Oslo process in 1994 before it had really begun. The Kahanist movement will have to be carefully monitored during any future peace process to avoid a possible repetition of this incident.

Lesson Eleven: Deadlines cannot be rigid as opponents of peace will exploit this to end the process.

Deadlines or "goals" are rarely met for a variety of reasons. The Islamists learned early on that they could exploit these deadlines by setting off bombs that would lead to a closure of the territories and a freeze in negotiations. This had the effect of taking away time from the five-year goal for a final settlement as envisaged in the Oslo agreement.

Likewise, decommissioning goals were not met — mainly because the paramilitary organizations had no real intention of disarming. Once the prisoners were removed as leverage, the Unionists were forced to resort to various sanctions to force the Republicans to disarm. The sanctions were then used as excuses by Sinn Fein to put off the deadline. Sinn Fein argued that the two-year clock should start ticking with the setting up of the Executive in December 1999 rather than from May 1998. Sanctions on North-South meetings were used as an excuse not to decommission. Even the two governments' deadline for the creation of a new Executive in 2007 was not met. Deadlines should be treated as goals and leverage rather than as a rigid timeline.

Lesson Twelve: Peace processes involving terrorist organizations are built on lies, but must have a minimum level of truth to be sustained.

Those who murder and maim civilians in the name of a cause will not shrink at lying for that same cause. Gerry Adams and Martin McGuinness lied in the peace process about the activities of the IRA until they were able to persuade the IRA to decommission.[13] But pressure from Unionists was necessary to keep the governments and the terrorists honest. Both governments were willing to overlook quite a bit in the name of peace. Ruling on the viability of a ceasefire was more a political judgment about the ultimate intentions of a terrorist organization than it was about the current activities of that organization. Trimble had to walk a fine line between making Sinn Fein pay for each and every ceasefire violation and going along with the governments who were willing to put decommissioning on the back burner forever.

The Israeli leadership had to make similar judgments about Arafat and the PLO leadership. Arafat was a congenital — and poor — liar.[14] Ultimately Peres, Rabin, and Barak had to constantly evaluate whether or not Arafat could be persuaded to rein in the Islamist terrorists and whether or not he was willing to make concessions on crucial issues such as refugees and Jerusalem to match Israeli concessions. Peres was perhaps too visionary and not skeptical enough. Rabin was skeptical, but was assassinated before he could make a mature final judgment about Arafat's intentions. Barak matched Rabin's skepticism of Arafat and decided to test him at Camp David.

Lesson Thirteen: Mediators do not have to be neutral in the conflict, but they must keep a distance from the two sides.

Israeli political scientist Sa'adia Touval wrote in the early 1980s that neutrality was not necessary for successful mediation. In fact, partiality could often lead the other side to make concessions in order to win a reverse of alliances. Also, Kissinger demonstrated in the mid–1970s that a close connection in a regional conflict can be an asset as it will lead the other side to perceive that it gives the mediating power leverage.[15]

But unless the mediator is willing to engage with the other side or pressure his own side or both, he will be ineffective. Kissinger perceived that partial success in the Yom Kippur War by Sadat would give him an opportunity to negotiate a partial peace and a reversal of alliances. Jimmy Carter fell in "love" with Sadat but was still able to pressure him at Camp David I. Jim Baker was happy to pressure all the parties in order to convene a peace conference at Madrid in October 1991.[16] But Clinton was unwilling to pressure either Rabin or Barak. With Rabin he had little occasion to pressure before the assassination, but probably would have been unwilling to do so even if Rabin had lived, because he saw Rabin as a father figure.[17] Clinton befriended both Arafat and Barak, but was unwilling to seriously pressure either of them at the Camp David II summit. Neither side was afraid of displeasing the United States. Peace negotiator Aaron Miller thinks that if Washington had made clear to both Israel and Syria that a total Israeli withdrawal from the Golan was required and a Syrian gesture to Israel comparable to those made by Sadat and Arafat was required in exchange, than either an Israeli-Syrian peace treaty could have been salvaged or the process could have been ended much earlier. This would have allowed Barak much more time to negotiate with Arafat and possibly have left Arafat more cooperative.[18]

Likewise, George W. Bush had become much too close to Ariel Sharon. This was for a number of reasons. First Sharon showered him with attention when he visited Israel on a governors' tour in December 1998. Second, Clinton had briefed Bush during the transfer period that Arafat was responsible for the failure of Camp David II. Third, Bush was dependent on a pro-Israel evangelical Republican base for support. Fourth, Bush just was just not very interested in Middle East diplomacy — he wanted to be a war president and not a peace president. He wanted to finish the job that his father had left unfinished in 1991 by toppling Saddam Hussein. He did not see the peace process begun at Madrid in 1991 as part of that unfinished business. He briefly attempted to resuscitate the peace process in 2003 by making an end run around Arafat but Arafat easily foiled this. So he simply deferred to Sharon.[19]

Blair's bias has already been covered (Lesson Three). For this bias to be overcome, mediators must either be conscious of their own personal and national biases and be willing to overcome them or deal with the bias institutionally through *dual mediation*. Because the evangelicals are such an important constituency within the Republican Party and the Jews within the Democratic Party, an institutional solution seems best. The *realpolitik* attitude of Henry Kissinger, Zbigniew Brzezinski, and Jim Baker towards the Middle East now seems to be dead within the Republican Party, and probably within the Democratic Party as well.

The 2008 election illustrates the difficulty of this. Obama on the Democratic side and McCain on the Republican side were the candidates least affected by the pro-Israel bias of their respective parties. But McCain was forced to pander to the right to attract the support of Evangelical conservatives. And Obama ended up naming Hillary Clinton, the most pro-Israel Democratic candidate, as his Secretary of State following his election.

Lesson Fourteen: Although Israel can make peace on only one front or track at a time, it can negotiate on two or more. Such parallel negotiations can lead to breakthroughs.

The route to Damascus may be through Jerusalem and vice versa. Damascus was much more serious about negotiations in early 2000 and in 2007 when a breakthrough seemed possible in the parallel Palestinian track. Many Arab rulers are much more interested in a peace process than in actual peace. Arab rulers seem to want a military peace with Israel without normalization. Therefore, they are content when there is no immediate military threat to avoid negotiations. But the last Arab ruler to make peace with Israel will get the worst deal, or at least that is the fear. The Syrian and Palestinian leaderships can be played off against one another to Israel's benefit. So even when a peace agreement with the Palestinians appears unlikely, it may be in Israel's interest to revive negotiations in order to induce Damascus to be serious.[20]

But in doing this, both Israel and Washington must be able to conduct two tracks simultaneously. This means that Jerusalem must hold a ruling coalition together and Washington must have diplomats allocated to both tracks as well as plans for how to conduct the negotiations. Jerusalem cannot let it leak that it is not serious about either track. And a breakthrough on either track must be immediately exploited.

Lesson Fifteen: Unlike Northern Ireland, the Middle East peace process suffered from outside military pressures. But a sound regional policy can neutralize this factor.

For decades Arab countries had either directly intervened or intervened by proxy by sponsoring Palestinian fedayeen organizations. After the Iran-Iraq War, Iran got into the act by sponsoring the Islamists. Initially they supported only Islamic Jihad, but gradually they began to support Hamas as well, as Hezbollah convinced Hamas to accept Iranian aid. The Clinton administration attempted to leverage the peace process to gain leverage over both Iran and Iraq by gaining support among moderate Arabs in the region. The policymakers also understood that a peace process could prevent the outsiders from exploiting the conflict for their own ends. Thus Clinton attempted to run an integrated regional policy, as Nixon once had. Bush eventually experienced that this equation can work in reverse and the lack of a viable peace process hurt his policy in Iraq, Lebanon, and Afghanistan.[21]

Lesson Sixteen: Israel's franchise system produces weak coalitions that are incapable of making peace with the Palestinians.

Israel has a proportional representation list system under which the entire country is one big multi-candidate constituency of 120 members. Every government since independence has been a coalition government: most contain at least four parties and Arab parties are by tradition excluded from coalitions. This makes the coalition leader (Labor, Likud, Kadima) subject to blackmail by small right-wing or religious parties. For the last two decades no government has served out its term — most last between 2.5 and three years. This is much better than the average of eight months for governments in France's Fourth Republic or Italy's postwar governments. But France needed to change its system of government before it could make peace in Algeria and withdraw. Israel will need to reform its franchise system so that the overall number of parties represented in the Knesset is drastically reduced and so that the major parties are strengthened before it can make peace with the Palestinians. Because it lacks a Charles de Gaulle figure and figures like David Ben-Gurion and Yigael Yadin tried to reform the system and failed, it may require outside American pressure to accomplish this vital reform. Northern Ireland's PR-STV franchise system might make a good transplant in Israel.

So having considered all the lessons, what can we say about the likelihood of an Israeli-Palestinian peace agreement in the near future? First, the Anglo-Irish effort represents the minimum level of commitment and energy needed to succeed in peacemaking in a native-settler conflict like that in the Middle East. The United States must be willing to both share the burden and match the effort of John Major and Tony Blair. The initial period after the signing of the Good Friday Agreement from July 1998 to October 2002 illustrates how difficult it will be to make peace with the fragmented Israeli political system. From 1998 to 2003 there were up to seven separate unionist and loyalist political parties. Only after the consolidation that occurred in the election for the Second Assembly in November 2003 did a stable enough unionist polity emerge to allow the peace to be rescued. And this was only once the Republicans had met the minimal goals of the unionists — complete decommissioning vouched for by the IICD. During the failed portion of the Northern Ireland peace process I thought that the lesson from Belfast was that cheating by terrorist groups on agreements combined with a deeply-divided settler community would kill any hope of a final settlement. With the numerous outside actors like Iran with a vested interest in prolonging the conflict, and the Israeli coalition system, this may yet prove to be the main lesson from Belfast for the Israeli-Palestinian conflict.

The Israeli-Palestinian track is not yet ripe for peace and probably will not be ready for some time. This is because Hamas — and some elements in Fatah — still see the utility of armed struggle — Israeli intelligence has not penetrated the Islamist organizations to anywhere near the same level that British intelligence penetrated the IRA and INLA, not to mention the loyalists. Plus continuation of armed struggle seems to boost the electoral potential of the Islamist parties and radical nationalists as opposed to weakening them as was the case with Sinn Fein and the Irish Republican Socialist Party (the political wing of the INLA). The IRA took some 35 years from birth until it was ready to completely decommission. Fatah took about 46 years between its creation and its willingness to forego armed struggle in favor of purely political means. Hamas has only been in existence for two decades — it might take another decade or two until it or elements of it are willing to make the strategic decision to give up armed struggle. And then Israel will still have to cope with Islamic Jihad and irredentist Hamas elements while it makes peace with Hamas and Fatah. When it does, it should look for lessons not just from Oslo but from Belfast as well.

Until Hamas has taken the strategic decision to give up the military option or at least appears ready to do so, Israel should not be talking with the Islamists other than for the purposes of arranging prisoner exchanges and other routine matters for fear of accidentally prolonging the conflict by giving Hamas the wrong idea. That is at least one interpretation of the experience of British-IRA negotiations in the 1970s.[22]

Epilogue

As this book goes to press Northern Ireland has just weathered its biggest and most serious crisis since 2007. Since 2008 Sinn Fein has been pressing the DUP to agree to the devolution of justice and policing powers to a minister within the power-sharing executive to complete the new order. Sinn Fein wants this so that it can show its supporters that it has some control over these areas that were previously controlled first by the UUP-dominated Stormont parliament and then by the British through the Northern Ireland Office. Because unionists do not yet trust their Republican counterparts this has been very politically sensitive for them. Sinn Fein had agreed that it would not put forward a candidate for the ministry if the DUP promised the same — and most thought that the ideal compromise candidate would come from the non-sectarian Alliance Party. Originally Sinn Fein had set Christmas 2009 as a deadline for devolution or they would resign bringing down the Assembly. But the Sinn Fein leadership allowed this deadline to slip as the DUP was having problems due to the rise of the Traditional Unionist Voice (TUV) splinter party led by former DUP MEP Jim Allister.

January began with the announcement that the UDA had finally decommissioned all its weapons, except for those controlled by the breakaway South Antrim "Brigade" of the UDA. Simultaneously Gerry Adams was caught in lies about his relationship with his younger brother Liam Adams whose daughter Aine accused him of sexual molestation over several years. It was then revealed that Gerry Adams, Sr., an IRA figure in the 1940s, had sexually abused several of his children, but apparently not Gerry Adams. Gerry Adams claimed that he had warned several youth agencies that employed his brother about his brother's past. He also claimed that Sinn Fein had severed all contact with his brother starting in 1996. *Sunday Tribune* Northern editor Suzanne Breen established that this was false by examining old newspapers from the period. Because some of those accused on being child molesters had been knee-capped in the past by the IRA, it suddenly appeared that Adams's brother had received preferential treatment.

Then at the beginning of the second week in January a far more serious scandal broke. It was revealed that MP and MLA Iris Robinson, wife of First Minister Peter Robinson, had had an affair with a 19-year-old man (she is 59) and had used her influence to procure a government loan for him so that he could start a business. She had also kept 5,000 pounds of the loan for herself as a commission. When she confessed this to her husband he made her return the money. He also blamed her history of depression for the affair and made her resign her government positions once the word of the loan became public knowledge. He then stepped down temporarily as first minister so that his conduct could be investigated to see if he was in breach of ethics guidelines for not having promptly reported his wife. Arlene Foster, the former UUP rebel, temporarily took over as first minister. After a week he was cleared and able to return to his post.

The affair was very serious not only because it exposed the hypocrisy behind the DUP's evangelical preaching against homosexuals, but because if Peter Robinson would have been forced to step down as first minister, the deputy minister would also have had to step down and then the DUP and Sinn Fein would have had to appoint replacements. Sinn Fein could easily have refused to appoint a replacement forcing new Assembly elections just at the time that the DUP was also facing a Westminster election and plagued by the Robinson scandal. This gave Sinn Fein considerable leverage in the negotiations as it would be less punished by its electorate for the Adams family scandal than the DUP would be for "here's to you Mrs. Robinson" (which suddenly became a hit song on the province's airwaves). The DUP wanted a deal on parades — a replacement for the Parades Commission that ruled on controversial Protestant and Catholic parades. The DUP desperately needed some tradeoff for the devolution of policing and justice to show its voters that it was still boss.

The two prime ministers converged on Belfast as they had at times past throughout the peace process. A deadline was set for a deal and then the two governments would announce their own proposal if no deal were forthcoming. As with so many deadlines in the past it was allowed to slip and the bluff was called. Finally after ten days of crisis talks a deal was announced during the first weak of February and a twenty-page Hillsborough Agreement was signed. Devolution is set for April 2010 and there are guidelines for a solution to the parades issue through a new six-man working group that will author a new bill on parades by December 2010. There are also sections dealing with the smoother functioning of the Executive. But this could easily go wrong in the future — but at least the DUP and Sinn Fein can concentrate on the general election.

Epilogue

On February 9, 2010, the legislation allowing for decommissioning of arms without forensic examination of those arms for prosecution in possible crimes was allowed to expire. Before it did it was revealed that three more paramilitary organizations had decommissioned their weapons: the South Antrim UDA, the INLA and the Official IRA, which had declared a ceasefire in May 1972 without ever disarming. All the organizations on ceasefire — all the major paramilitary groups from The Troubles era — had decommissioned at the cost of 10 million pounds Sterling for the cost of the International Commission on Decommissioning to operate since 1997.

If David Ford or another Alliance candidate becomes the new justice and policing minister it will be Alliance's greatest prominence and influence since the collapse of the Sunningdale Executive in May 1974 — 36 years earlier. The Good Friday Agreement and St. Andrews Agreement and the entire peace process have really been "Sunningdale for some real slow learners." Under the d'Hondt system of ministry allocation the SDLP was next in line for a ministry and cried foul when Sinn Fein and the DUP appeared to be giving away its ministry.[1]

In the near future Peter Robinson is likely to be replaced as DUP leader by Nigel Dodds, who was influential in winning hardline support for the Hillsborough Agreement. Gerry Adams is also likely to be relegated to a more ceremonial honorary role within Sinn Fein to deal with foreign supporters. He fulfilled his role by winning support for peace from the IRA. He failed badly in the 2007 Irish election and Martin McGuinness has been Sinn Fein's leader within Stormont.

The events of January and February 2010 demonstrated that politics are still not "normal" in Northern Ireland by Western norms but that they are finally largely peaceful. The dissident republicans of the Continuity IRA and of two rival factions of the Real IRA remain a threat — they killed two soldiers and a policeman in May 2009. But the political climate for them is no more hospitable than it was for the IRA during its Border Campaign of 1956–62, which added a couple of new songs and martyrs to the republican arsenal but no progress toward a united Ireland. Northern Ireland remains a flawed model for conflict resolution in the Middle East (and elsewhere), but the best real one in existence.

Chapter Notes

Chapter One

1. See Thomas G. Mitchell, *Native vs. Settler: Ethnic Conflict in Israel/Palestine, Northern Ireland and South Africa* (Westport, CT: Greenwood, 2000) for a background to these conflicts and to the native-settler conflict theory that I used throughout this chapter.

2. Herman Giliomee and Jan Gagiano, *The Elusive Search For Peace: South Africa, Israel, and Northern Ireland* (New York: Oxford University Press, 1990).

3. Donald H. Akenson, *God's Peoples: Covenant and Land in South Africa, Israel and Ulster* (Ithaca: Cornell University Press, 1992).

4. Mitchell, *Native vs. Settler*, pp. 3–4.

5. The seven items compared were: settler politics and ideology, native liberation movements, (settler) liberal parties, native system parties, the armed struggles, settler terror, and splinter groups from both native and settler terrorist groups. The only comparison that was weak was that in the chapter on native system parties where I compared non–Israeli Palestinian Village Leagues in a failed internal settlement attempt to the SDLP in Northern Ireland and the mixed-race Labour Party and Zulu Inkatha Freedom Party in South Africa. This comparison was made because of the dual nature of Palestinians as both internal and external and because I felt that I lacked the time and money to properly research Israeli Arab parties of which I knew little; Mitchell, *Native vs. Settler*, pp. 126–27.

6. Thomas G. Mitchell, *Indispensable Traitors: Liberal Parties in Settler Conflicts* (Westport, CT: Greenwood, 2002).

7. Stephen Howe, *Ireland and Empire* (New York: Oxford University Press, 2000), pp. 169–228.

8. *Ibid.*, p. 221.

9. Donald H. Akenson, *Small Differences: Irish Catholics and Irish Protestants 1815–1922* (Montreal: Kingston, 1988).

10. Howe, *Ireland and Empire*, pp. 222–27. The three works are: Ian Lustick, *Unsettled States, Disputed Lands* (Ithaca: Cornell University Press, 1993); Michael MacDonald, *Children of Wrath: Political Violence in Northern Ireland* (Cambridge, MA: Polity Press, 1986); Ronald Weitzer, *Transforming Settler States: Communal Conflict and Internal Security in Northern Ireland and Zimbabwe* (Berkeley: UC Press, 1990).

11. Thomas G. Mitchell, "Israeli Politics as Settler Politics," *The Journal of Conflict Studies* Winter 2004 Vol. XXIV No. 2, pp. 135–54.

12. After researching the Turkish religious parties I found major differences because of the secular nature of the Turkish system, with the Turkish military playing the role of enforcer. I believe that the Turkish parties would be very similar to the Israeli parties without these enforced limits on what they can agitate for.

13. The United States has never had coalition governments, but has had periods of multiparty systems particularly from 1848 to 1860. South Africa had two coalition governments in the interwar period but both were two-party coalitions and very stable — in fact in the second the two parties merged after a year. Neither the U.S. nor South Africa has had religious parties on the Israeli model although both have had pious parties (the Northern Whigs and the Liberty Party in the U.S. and the National Party in South Africa).

14. The seven unionist parties were: the UUP, the DUP, the UKUP, the Northern

Ireland UP—a splinter from the UKUP—the Ulster Democratic Party, the Progressive Unionist Party, and the Independent Unionists—three Ulster Unionists who ran as independents in 1998.

15. This occurred with both the Rabin and Barak governments.

16. Because there is only this one short example of coalition governments in a peace process among settler societies to compare to Israel, for a better comparison one should look at the French Fourth Republic as it dealt with decolonization in Indochina and North Africa. France was able to leave Algeria only because it suffered a major defeat at Dien Bien Phu in 1954 and was unable to leave Algeria until after De Gaulle created the Fifth Republic.

17. See Ed Moloney, *Paisley: From Demagogue to Democrat* (Dublin: Poolbeg, 2007) for a history of both the church and the party. Paisley first ran for the Stormont parliament in 1969, founded the Protestant Unionist Party in 1970 and renamed it the Democratic Unionist Party in 1971.

18. Guy Ben-Porat, *Global Liberalism, Local Populism* (Syracuse: Syracuse University Press, 2006), pp. 183–90, 199–201, 216–17, 236, 266–67.

19. Guy Ben-Porat, "Introduction," in Ben-Porat, ed., *The Failure of the Middle East Peace Process?* (New York: Palgrave Macmillan, 2008), pp. 3, 4, 10–12.

20. *Ibid.*, p. 9.

21. Benjamin Miller, "The State-to-Nation Balance: A Key to Explaining Difficulties in Implementing Peace—The Israeli Palestinian Case," in Ben-Porat, ed., *The Failure*, pp. 39–69 especially pp. 50–56.

22. Jonathan Rynhold, "Realism, Liberalism and the Collapse of the Oslo Process: Inherently Flawed or Flawed Implementation?" in Ben-Porat, ed., *The Failure*, pp. 111–32 especially pp. 119–23.

23. Ben-Porat, "Conclusion: Implementing Peace Agreements," in Ben-Porat, ed., *The Failure*, pp. 259–65.

24. Many countries around the world have recognized Palestine as an independent country but it lacks the attributes of an independent state, and Arafat's constant threats to declare independence during the Oslo process are an indicator that his previous declarations should not be taken seriously.

25. The South West Africa People's Organization used mainly guerrilla warfare rather than terrorism in its armed struggle against the whites in Namibia. And SWAPO never spoke of abolishing South Africa.

26. I. William Zartman, *Ripe for Resolution: Conflict and Intervention in Africa* (New York: Oxford University Press, 1989), pp. 134–69 for an explanation.

27. For a short summary of the theory of internal settlements see the chapter in Thomas G. Mitchell, *Indispensable Traitors: Liberal Parties in Settler Conflicts* (Westport, CT: Greenwood, 2002). It is based on Mitchell's doctoral dissertation on internal settlements in Southern Africa.

28. John Bew, Martyn Frampton, and Inigo Gurruchaga, *Talking To Terrorists* (New York: Columbia University Press, 2009), pp. 252–59.

29. I. William Zartman and Sa'adia Touval, "International Mediation in the Post–Cold War Era" in Chester Crocker et al., *Managing Global Chaos* (Washington, D.C.: U.S. Institute of Peace, 1996), p. 446.

30. C.R. Mitchell, *The Structure of International Conflict* (New York: St. Martin's Press, 1981), p. 287.

31. Thus Egypt would not be a suitable mediator because it derives value from its role as a mediator between the U.S. and the Palestinians rather than from the conflict's resolution.

32. President Richard Solomon of the U.S. Institute of Peace in the foreword to Chester Crocker, Fen O. Hampson, and Pamela Aall, eds., *Herding Cats: Multiparty Mediation in a Complex World* (Washington, D.C.: U.S. Institute of Peace, 1999—hereafter *Cats*), p. x.

33. See note 10 for a history of the Irish question from the 1860s to 1922.

34. Jussi Hanhimaki, *The Flawed Architect: Henry Kissinger and American Foreign Policy* (New York: Oxford University Press, 2004), pp. 314–15, 326–30.

35. John Boykin, *Cursed Is the Peacemaker: The American Diplomat Versus the Israeli General, Beirut 1982* (Belmont, CA: Applegate, 2002).

36. Sa'adia Touval, *The Peace Brokers: Mediators in the Arab-Israeli Conflict, 1948–1979* (Princeton, NJ: Princeton University Press, 1982), pp. 10–19, 314–15, 325–31.

37. *Ibid.*, p. 18.

38. I. William Zartman, ed., *Elusive Peace: Negotiating an End to Civil Wars* (Washington, D.C.: The Brookings Institution, 1995), p. 341.

39. Crocker et al., *Cats*, p. 25.

40. Actually it was Dublin who issued the

invitation, but as the sovereign power in Northern Ireland (London) could have refused the invitation or refused to give Dublin an equal status.

41. John J. Mearsheimer and Stephen M. Walt, *The Israel Lobby and U.S. Foreign Policy* (New York: Farrar, Straus, and Giroux, 2008); and see Dan Fleshler, *Transforming America's Israel Lobby* (Washington, D.C.: Potomac Books, 2009) for arguments against some of the wilder charges made by the two.

42. Aaron David Miller, *The Much Too Promised Land* (New York: Bantam, 2008), p. 81.

43. Zartman, *Elusive Peace*, pp. 343–45.

44. *Ibid.*, p. 340.

45. See chapter seven for a more nuanced presentation of the motives.

46. Crocker et al., *Cats*, p. 21.

47. *Ibid.*, p. 22.

48. *Ibid.*, p. 4.

49. *Ibid.*, pp. 34, 39–40, 665, 674.

50. *Ibid.*, pp. 675, 456.

51. *Ibid.*, p. 692.

52. *Ibid.*, pp. 694, 698.

53. *Ibid.*, p. 695.

54. *Ibid.*, p. 684.

55. *Ibid.*, p. 679.

56. Arend Lijphart, *The Politics of Accommodation: Pluralism and Democracy in the Netherlands* (Berkeley: UC Press, 1968).

57. Lijphart, *Democracy in Plural Societies* (New Haven: Yale University Press, 1977).

58. Belgium and Switzerland. The divisions within Austria and the Netherlands were religious and ideological.

59. For a quick summary see Mitchell, *Indispensable Traitors*, pp. 131–35, and Timothy D. Sisk, *Power Sharing and International Mediation in Ethnic Conflicts* (Washington, D.C.: U.S. Institute of Peace Press, 1996).

60. John McGarry and Brendan O'Leary, "Consociational Theory and Peace Agreements in Pluri-National Places: Northern Ireland and Other Cases," in Ben-Porat, ed., *The Failure*, pp. 70–96.

61. Donald Horowitz, *Ethnic Groups in Conflict* (Berkeley: UC Press, 1985).

62. This line was quoted to me by Alliance leader John Alderdice in an interview in the summer of 1998. Alliance was very critical of the details of the power sharing arrangements of the Good Friday Agreement especially its ethnic classifications that left nonsectarian parties as second-class players.

63. See Sisk, *Power Sharing*, p. 70 for a table comparing the two approaches.

64. Kevin Boyle and Tom Hadden, *Northern Ireland: The Choice* (London: Penguin, 1994).

65. Their books include: *The Future of Northern Ireland* (1991); *Explaining Northern Ireland: Broken Images* (1995); *The Politics of Antagonism: Understanding Northern Ireland* (1996); and *The Northern Ireland Conflict: Consociational Engagements* (2004).

Chapter Two

1. On Madrid see Itamar Rabinovich, *Waging Peace: Israel and the Arabs 1948–2003* (Princeton: Princeton University Press, 2004), pp. 34–37.

2. Michael Bar-Zohar, *Shimon Peres* (New York: Random House, 2007), pp. 291–356, 415–24 on the Peres-Rabin relationship.

3. Begin was the leader of the Etzel pre-state underground and Shamir was one of the leaders of the Lehi underground. Shamir later served in the Mossad for a decade (1955–65) before joining the Likud in 1970.

4. Efraim Inbar, "Labor's Return to Power," in Daniel J. Elazar and Shmuel Sandler, eds., *Israel at the Polls 1992* (Lanham, Maryland: Rowman & Littlefield, 1995), pp. 27–41, and Gerald Steinberg, "A Nation that Dwells Alone? Foreign Policy in the 1992 Elections," in Elazar and Sandler, pp. 189–92.

5. This gridlock forced national unity governments in 1984 and 1988. There was a major gap in 1977, but that was because many Labor voters defected to the Democratic Movement for Change and then returned in 1981.

6. *Ibid.*, p. 21 the right out-voted the left by 7,000 votes.

7. *Ibid.*, pp. 37–39.

8. Shas was founded in 1983–84 as an ultra–Orthodox party concentrating on *mizrahi* Jews.

9. See Bar-Zohar, *Peres*, pp. 401–14 on the London initiative.

10. *Ibid.*, p. 426.

11. See Yossi Beilin, *Touching Peace: From the Oslo Accord to a Final Agreement* (London: Weidenfield & Nicholson, 1999), pp. 11–23, and Yossi Beilin, *The Path to Geneva* (New York: RDV, 2004), pp. 12–15, for his political background. Beilin discusses his grandfather in the prelude to Beilin, *My Brother's Keeper* (New York: 2000), and mentions him on *Path*, p. 11.

12. Beilin, *Touching*, p. 273.

13. On the Norwegian role in Oslo see Jane Corbin, *The Norway Channel: the Secret Talks that Led to the Middle East Peace Accord* (New York: Atlantic Monthly Press, 1994). This book emphasizes the Norwegian role as opposed to others that concentrate on the negotiations.

14. Beilin, *Touching*, pp. 72–73.

15. *Ibid.*, pp. 38, 70.

16. See Uri Savir, *The Process* (New York: Random House, 1998) for a discussion of the "official" rounds at Oslo and of the subsequent Oslo I and Oslo II negotiations in the Middle East.

17. David Makovsky, *Making Peace With the PLO* (Boulder, CO: Westview Press, 1996), pp. 86–94 for Rabin's analysis during Oslo.

18. Such as Abu Iyad who made contradictory statements in late 1988. On the Hussein-Arafat relationship see Michael Bar-Zohar, *Facing a Cruel Mirror* (New York: Charles Scribner's Sons, 1990), pp. 138–43.

19. These two are major themes in Barry M. Rubin and Judith C. Rubin, *Yasir Arafat: A Political Biography* (New York: Oxford University Press, 2003).

20. Bar-Zohar credits Beilin and the blazers and the Socialist Internationale for Peres's transformation from a hawk to a dove: Bar-Zohar, *Peres*, p. 346. Meretz didn't exist in the 1980s when the blazers came into being, but Mapam, Ratz and Shinui did and they all interacted with doves within Labor.

21. Efraim Inbar, *Rabin and Israel's National Security* (Baltimore: Johns Hopkins University Press, 1999) for details see pp. 1–57, 84–93, 104, 109, 114–18.

22. *Ibid.*, pp. 134–39.

23. On the unofficial talks see Beilin, *Touching*, pp. 61–84.

24. Beilin, *Touching*, p. 105.

25. Makovsky, *Making Peace*, p. 53; Savir, *Process*, p. 26; Samuel Segev, *Crossing the Jordan* (New York: St. Martin's Press, 1998), pp. 197–98.

26. Makovsky, *Making Peace*, p. 64.

27. Segev, *Crossing*, pp. 210–12, 214.

28. *Ibid.*, pp. 217–20; Patrick Tyler, *A World of Trouble* (New York: Farrar, Straus & Giroux, 2009), p. 411.

29. Bar-Zohar, *Peres*, pp. 447–50; Tyler, *World*, p. 402.

30. Savir, *Process*, p. 164.

31. *Ibid.*, pp. 98, 105, 137, 141 map.

32. *Ibid.*, pp. 165, 176; Makovsky, *Making Peace*, 94, 100.

33. Dan Kurzman, *Soldier of Peace: The Life of Yitzhak Rabin* (New York: Harper Collins, 1998), p. 469; Said K. Aburish, *Arafat: From Defender to Dictator* (New York: Bloomsbury, 1998), pp. 269–71.

34. Kachane was murdered by an Egyptian Islamist in New York in 1990.

35. Savir, *Process*, pp. 121–36; Dennis Ross, *The Missing Peace* (New York: Farrar, Straus, and Giroux, 2004), pp. 127–33.

36. Savir, *Process*, p. 135.

37. *Ibid.*, pp. 139–40; Ross, *Missing Peace*, pp. 135–36.

38. Aburish, *Arafat*, pp. 7–32, 71–76.

39. Savir, *Process*, pp. 177–78.

40. *Ibid.*, pp. 164–65.

41. On the Altalena incident see any biography of David Ben-Gurion, Menahem Begin, or Yitzhak Rabin. On Hamas terrorism see Rabinovich, *Waging Peace*, p. 68; Efraim Karsh, *Arafat's War* (New York: Grove Press, 2003), pp. 111, 113, 115.

42. Yossef Bodansky, *The High Cost of Peace* (Roseville, CA: Prima, 2002), pp. 109, 111, 132–34, 201; Karsh, *War*, pp. 6, 60–62, 110–15, 133–36. For film clips of Arafat speaking out repeatedly during the Oslo process in ways that counteract his commitments under the agreement see the film *The Trojan Horse* distributed by Sisu Home Entertainment and available for rental from Netflix. MEMRI is listed as a source of many of the images in the credits.

43. On the interactions between the three undergrounds see Menahem Begin, *The Revolt* (New York: Dell, 1978) and Dan Kurzman, *Genesis 1948: The First Arab-Israeli War* (New York: World, 1970). Amihai "Gidi" Paglin, the operations officer for Etzel, had a brother who was a senior figure in the Palmach. See Shlomo Ben-Ami, *Scars of War, Wounds of Peace* (New York: Oxford University Press, 2006), pp. 210–11 for Arafat's use of Islamist terrorism.

44. See Ben-Ami, *Scars*, pp. 208–10, 238, for the Jerusalem vs. Tel Aviv comparison. The other comparison is that of Begin's American-Israeli press secretary.

45. Kurzman, *Soldier of Peace*, pp. 473–75, 480; Bar-Zohar, *Peres*, pp. 453–56; Segev, *Crossing*, p. 255, 372; Savir, *Process*, pp. 252–54.

46. Aburish, *Arafat*, pp. 288–89, 291.

47. Leah Rabin, *Rabin: Our Life, His Legacy* (New York: G. P. Putnam, 1997), p. 19; Ross, *Missing Peace*, p. 193. Weizman had revealed to the press that Rabin had a "nervous breakdown" on the eve of the 1967 war dur-

ing Peres's contest with him for the party leadership and Likud used this in its election campaign in 1977.
48. Rabinovich, *Waging Peace,* p. 68.
49. Charles Enderlin, *Shattered Dreams* (New York: Other, 2002), p. 12.
50. Kurzman, *Soldier of Peace,* pp. 484–86, 497; Enderlin, *Dreams,* pp. 15–18.
51. Ben Caspit and Ilan Kfir, *Netanyahu: The Road to Power* (Secaucus, NJ: Birch Lane, 1998), pp. 210–16.
52. Kurzman, *Soldier of Peace,* pp. 6, 508–11; Enderlin, *Dreams,* pp. 3–4;
53. On Rabin's funeral see Kurzman, *Soldier of Peace,* pp. 513–16; Rabin, *Rabin,* pp. 20–22; Aburish, *Arafat,* p. 294.

Chapter Three

1. On the Stockholm back channel see Yossi Beilin, *Touching Peace: From the Oslo Accord to a Final Agreement* (London: Weidenfeld & Nicholson, 1999), pp. 141–89; Shlomo Ben-Ami, *Scars of War, Wounds of Peace: The Israeli-Arab Tragedy* (New York: Oxford University Press, 2006), p. 226; Itamar Rabinovich, *Waging Peace: Israel and the Arabs 1948–2003* (Princeton, NJ: Princeton University Press, 2004), pp. 71–72.
2. Rabinovich, *Waging Peace,* pp. 72–74; Patrick Tyler, *A World of Trouble* (New York: Farrar, Straus & Giroux, 2009), p. 448.
3. Ben Caspit and Ilan Kfir, *Netanyahu: The Road to Power* (Secaucus, NJ: Birch Lane, 1998), pp. 201–03.
4. Said K. Aburish, *Arafat: From Defender to Dictator* (London: Bloomsbury, 1997), p. 295; Efraim Karsh, *Arafat's War* (New York: Grove Press, 203), p. 121; Yossef Bodansky, *The High Cost of Peace* (Roseville, CA: Forum, 2002), p. 138; Dennis Ross, *The Missing Peace* (New York: Farrar, Straus, and Giroux, 2004), p. 261; Tyler, *World,* p. 449.
5. Rabinovich, *Waging Peace,* pp. 74–77; Ben-Ami, *Scars,* pp. 237–38; Michael Bar-Zohar, *Shimon Peres* (New York: Random, 2007), pp. 466–67; Ross, *Missing Peace,* pp. 256–57; Bill Clinton, *My Life: Vol. II The Presidential Years* (New York: Vintage, 2005), p. 327; Bernard Reich, *A Brief History of Israel, Second Edition* (New York: Checkmark, 2008), p. 189.
6. Guy Ben-Porat, *Global Liberalism, Local Populism* (Syracuse: Syracuse University Press, 2006), pp. 197–201.
7. Clinton, *My Life,* p. 313; Bodansky, *High Cost,* p. 146; Karsh, *War,* pp. 141–42; Rabinovich, *Waging Peace,* p. 87.
8. On Albright's background and the competition see Madeleine Albright, *Madame Secretary* (New York: Miramax, 2003), pp. 3–126, 216–20.
9. Aburish, *Arafat,* p. 299; Nir Hefez and Gadi Bloom, *Ariel Sharon* (New York: Random, 2006), p. 317.
10. Rabinovich, *Waging Peace,* pp. 80–81; Hefez and Bloom, *Ariel,* p. 302.
11. Charles Enderlin, *Shattered Dreams* (New York: Other Press, 2002), p. 43.
12. See Aburish, *Arafat,* on Arafat's early career; Karsh, *War,* p. 136.
13. Aburish, *Arafat,* pp. 306–08.
14. Ben-Porat, *Global,* pp. 189–190.
15. Aburish, *Arafat,* pp. 278–80; Ross, *Missing Peace,* pp. 275, 409.
16. Karsh, *War,* pp. 95–99; Aburish, *Arafat,* p. 315. The statement was on PA TV on Dec. 1, 1997.
17. *Ibid.*, pp. 100–01.
18. *Ibid.*, pp. 102–04. For a collection of film clips showing incitement against Jews and Israelis from Palestinian television, many involving young children, see the film *Israel and the War of Images* distributed by Sisu Home Entertainment and available for rental from Netflix.
19. Karsh, *War,* pp. 147–50; Rabinovich, *Waging Peace,* p. 99; Bodansky, *High Cost,* pp. 151–52; Tyler, *World,* p. 479.
20. Ross, *Missing Peace,* pp. 266–67.
21. Avi Shlaim, *Lion of Jordan: The Life of King Hussein in War and Peace* (New York: Knopf, 2008), pp. 564–65.
22. Ross, *Missing Peace,* pp. 269–322; Rabinovich, *Waging Peace,* pp. 103–04.
23. Karsh, *War,* p. 153; Shlaim, *Lion,* pp. 574–75.
24. Ross, *Missing Peace,* pp. 355–56; Albright, *Secretary,* pp. 294–98.
25. Albright, *Secretary,* pp. 298–99; Efraim Halevy, *Man in the Shadows* (New York: St. Martin's Press, 2006), pp. 164–77; Shlaim, *Lion,* pp. 578–80, 582; Avi Shlaim, *The Iron Wall* (New York: W. W. Norton, 2001), p. 577.
26. Shlaim, *Iron Wall,* pp. 565–67, 583. Yigal Allon was deputy premier under Eshkol and Meir from 1967 to 1974 and foreign minister under Rabin from 1974 to 1977; he was also a leading ideologue in labor Zionism during the 1960s.
27. Tyler, *World,* pp. 484, 488.
28. Rabinovich, *Waging Peace,* pp. 106–07,

110–13; Hefez and Bloom, *Ariel,* pp. 326–27.
29. On the summit see Albright, *Secretary,* pp. 306–18; Ross, *Missing Peace,* pp. 415–59; Clinton, *My Life,* pp. 464–70; and Tyler, *World,* p. 491. On Hussein's participation see Shlaim, *Lion,* pp. 595–98.
30. Enderlin, *Dreams,* p. 96; Beilin gives the figure of 8 in favor, 4 against and 5 abstained: Yossi Beilin, *The Path to Geneva* (New York: RDV Books, 2004), p. 80.
31. Enderlin, *Dreams,* p. 96–99, 102.
32. On Barak see Albright, *Secretary,* p. 474; Clinton, *My Life,* pp. 518, 533; Beilin, *Path,* pp. 47–49.
33. Bodansky, *High Cost,* pp. 221–23; Beilin, *Path,* p. 46; Clayton E. Swisher, *The Truth About Camp David* (New York: Nation Books, 2004), pp. 9–10.
34. Reich, *Brief History,* p. 194.

Chapter Four

1. Itamar Rabinovich, *Waging Peace* (Princeton, NJ: Princeton University Press, 2004), pp. 125–26.
2. *Ibid.*, pp. 126–27; Shlomo Ben-Ami, *Scars of War, Wounds of Peace* (New York: Oxford University Press, 2006), pp. 241–42; Dennis Ross, *The Missing Peace* (New York: Farrar, Straus and Giroux, 2004), p. 509.
3. Ross, *Missing Peace,* p. 591.
4. Rabinovich, *Waging Peace,* pp. 128–30; Ross, *Missing Peace,* pp. 510–17. *Time* ran a cover story on Syrian domestic politics in 1983.
5. See Itamar Rabinovich, *The Brink of Peace: The Israeli-Syrian Negotiations* (Princeton, NJ: Princeton University Press, 2002) for a complete explanation of the issues involved. Madeleine Albright, *Madame Secretary* (New York: Miramax, 2003), p. 475; Patrick Tyler, *A World of Trouble* (New York: Farrar, Straus, & Giroux, 2009), p. 501.
6. Rabinovich, *Waging Peace,* p. 134; Albright, *Secretary,* pp. 476–77.
7. Rabinovich, *Waging Peace,* pp. 24–26; William Quandt, *Peace Process,* 2nd Ed. (Berkeley: UC Press, 2001), pp. 177–204; Clayton E. Swisher, *The Truth About Camp David* (New York: Nation Books, 2004), p. 124.
8. Tyler, *World,* pp. 499–500.
9. Swisher, *Truth,* pp. 78–79.
10. *Ibid.*, pp. 90–109 on the run-up to Geneva; Martin Indyk, *Innocent Abroad* (New York: Simon & Schuster, 2009), pp. 273–75.
11. Swisher, *Truth,* pp. 112–23, 127–30; Ross, *Missing Peace,* pp. 573–90, and Albright, *Secretary,* pp. 478–82 for an alternate version.
12. Swisher, *Truth,* pp. 145, 173–82; Enderlin, *Dreams,* pp. 149–51; Ross, *Missing Peace,* pp. 617–19.
13. Rabinovich, *Waging Peace,* pp. 145, 150–51.
14. Swisher, *Truth,* pp. 214–15.
15. Enderlin, *Dreams,* pp. 147–49; Ross, *Missing Peace,* pp. 603–04, 613–17; Yossi Beilin, *The Path to Geneva* (New York: RDV Books, 2004), p. 144; Yossef Bodansky, *The High Cost of Peace* (Roseville, CA: Forum, 2002), p. 309.
16. Ross, *Missing Peace,* pp. 626–31, 637–38; Swisher, *Truth,* p. 229.
17. Bodansky, *High Cost,* pp. 265–83; 327–30; Swisher, *Truth,* p. 217.
18. Beilin, *Path,* pp. 151, 275.
19. Swisher, *Truth,* pp. 236–37, 239.
20. Albright, *Secretary,* pp. 483–84; Swisher, *Truth,* p. 234, Swisher interview with Albright.
21. Bodansky, *High Cost,* p. 314; Beilin, *Path,* pp. 156–57.
22. Albright, *Secretary,* p. 484; Swisher, *Truth,* pp. 225–27.
23. Swisher, *Truth,* pp. 219–20, 231–35; Bill Clinton, *My Life Vol II: The Presidential Years* (New York: Vintage, 2005), p. 592; Ross, *Missing Peace,* pp. 626–27, 649.
24. Quoted in Swisher, *Truth,* pp. 248–49.
25. Those wishing for such a lengthy detailed discussion should consult Ross, *Missing Peace,* pp. 650–711; Swisher, *Truth,* pp. 250–334; Albright, *Secretary,* pp. 484–93; Ben-Ami, *Scars,* pp. 248–64 passim; Robert Malley and Hussein Agha, "Camp David: The Tragedy of Errors," *New York Review of Books* Aug. 9, 2001; and Beilin, *Path,* pp. 157–67. There was also a special issue of *Jerusalem Report* on Camp David II published in July 2001.
26. The first term in parenthesis is the Hebrew term and the second the Arabic term, which translates as noble sanctuary.
27. Swisher, *Truth,* pp. 244, 260–61, 262, 274–76, 290; William B. Quandt, *Peace Process Revised Edition* (Berkeley, CA: University of California Press, 2001), pp. 348–49; Indyk, *Innocent,* p. 311; Tyler, *World,* p. 503.
28. For a summary of the phase strategy see Efraim Karsh, *Arafat's War* (New York: Grove Press, 2003), pp. 46–49, and Benjamin

Netanyahu, *A Place Among the Nations: Israel and the World* (New York: 1993).

29. See Quandt, *Peace Process*, p. 46; Rabinovich, *Waging Peace*, p. 11. Swisher shows his clear pro-Palestinian bias by accepting the Arab version of 242 and arguing that both Washington and Jerusalem refused to accept the terms of 242 because they did not accept the June 4, 1967 border.

30. Quandt, *Peace Process*, pp. 50–51 for the American positions; Netanyahu, *A Place*, for the Likud position; and Michael Brecher, *Israel's Foreign Policy System* (Yale: Yale University Press, 1973).

31. See previous chapter on Arafat. On Camp David I see Quandt, *Camp David: Peace Making and Politics* (Washington, D.C.: The Brookings Institution, 1986) or Quandt, *Peace Process*, pp. 197–203.

32. On Barak see Ben-Ami, *Scars*, pp. 253–54, 261; Beilin, *Path*, pp. 286–89.

33. Ross, *Missing Peace*, pp. 674–81.

34. *Ibid.*, p. 684; see Swisher, *Truth*, p. 111 for the full quote.

35. *Ibid.*, pp. 687–88.

36. *Ibid.*

37. *Ibid.*, pp. 693–94.

38. *Ibid.*, pp. 694–96; Barry Rubin and Judith Culp Rubin, *Yasir Arafat: A Political Biography* (New York: Oxford University Press, 2003), pp. 197, 227; see also Danny Rubinstein, *The Mystery of Arafat* (South Royalton: UK, 1995) for other examples of Arafat's specious claims, and Swisher, *Truth*, pp. 305–06 on the religious aspect.

39. Ross, *Missing Peace*, pp. 689, 703; Rabinovich, *Waging Peace*, p. 153; Beilin, *Path*, pp. 169; Ben-Ami, *Scars*, p. 275 on the refugee issue at Taba. Geneva was a non-binding peace treaty negotiated between members of Meretz and Labor on one hand and members of the PA including Yasir Abd Rabbu on the other.

40. This was by email when Rice was in charge of George W. Bush's foreign policy education team. The prediction was made following the election of Barak as prime minister and Clinton's impeachment. Indyk, *Innocent*, pp. 325–26, 373.

41. Indyk, *Innocent*, pp. 354–55.

42. Rabinovich, *Waging Peace*, pp. 156–58.

43. Ross, *Missing Peace*, pp. 751–53; Albright, pp. 496–97; Clinton, *My Life*, pp. 634–35; Indyk, *Innocent*, p. 370.

44. Ross, *Missing Peace*, p. 716.

45. Indyk, *Innocent*, pp. 346–53.

46. Bodansky, *High Cost*, pp. 307–08; Karsh, *War*, pp. 179, 180; Indyk, *Innocent*, p. 353.

47. Bodansky, p. 312; Karsh, *War*, pp. 177–78.

48. Bodansky, *High Cost*, p. 317; Karsh, *War*, pp. 178, 179.

49. Bodansky, *High Cost*, p. 321.

50. *Ibid.*, pp. 322–23.

51. *Ibid.*, pp. 323, 332–33; Karsh, *War*, p. 178.

52. Bodansky, *High Cost*, pp. 336–38.

53. Beilin, *Path*, p. 180; Rubin and Rubin, *Yasir Arafat*, pp. 204; Enderlin, *Dreams*, p. 285.

54. Bodansky, *High Cost*, pp. 242–347 passim. This is the gist of Bodansky chapters 12–16. The war never occurred, and was unlikely to occur, but that does not mean that Arafat did not believe that it would occur.

55. Ross, *Missing Peace*, p. 728; Nir Hefez and Gadi Bloom, *Ariel Sharon* (New York: Random: 2006), p. 344.

56. Bodansky, *High Cost*, pp. 351–52; Tyler, *World*, p. 508.

57. *Ibid.*, pp. 354–55; Hefez and Bloom, *Ariel*, pp. 344–45; Enderlin, *Dreams*, pp. 285–87; Beilin, *Path*, pp. 190–91; Rubin and Rubin, *Yasir Arafat*, pp. 203–05; Ross, *Missing Peace*, p. 731. Ross claimed that five rioters were killed — the only source who mentions any deaths — and the head of the Jerusalem police was knocked unconscious by a thrown rock. I think that he is confusing the riots from October 1990 with those a decade later.

58. Bodansky, *High Cost*, pp. 355–57, 366, 371; Beilin, *Path*, pp. 196–98; Rubin and Rubin, *Yasir Arafat*, pp. 206–07; Hefez and Bloom, *Ariel*, p. 347; Albright, *Secretary*, pp. 495–96, Ross, *Missing Peace*, p. 741.

59. Ross, *Missing Peace*, p. 746; Rubin and Rubin, *Yasir Arafat*, p. 212.

60. Tyler, *World*, p. 514; Ben-Ami, *Scars*, pp. 274–77; Beilin, *Path*, pp. 227–30; Indyk, *Innocent*, pp. 371–72. I find Ben-Ami's account to be more credible. See Enderlin, *Dreams*, pp. 351–57 for a summary of the points in dispute.

61. Ross, *Missing Peace*, p. 784; Rubin and Rubin, *Yasir Arafat*, p. 213; Swisher, *Truth*, pp. 403–05; Bush quote is from Indyk, *Innocent*, p. 379.

62. Rabinovich, *Waging Peace*, pp. 160–76; this author (Mitchell) puts Swisher in the revisionist category, Bodansky and Karsh in the determinist category, and Enderlin in the eclectic.

Chapter Five

1. For this part unionist in lower case refers to the wider unionist community or more than one unionist party, while Unionist refers to the Ulster Unionist Party. Likewise republican refers to the subset of physical-force nationalists that support the use of violence to bring about a united Ireland, while Republican refers to the Provisional Republican Movement consisting of the (Provisional) IRA and Sinn Fein. Loyalist refers to the unionist equivalent of republicans — those unionists prepared to use terrorism to prevent a united Ireland. It will be written only in lower case as both loyalist political parties had unionist as part of their titles.

2. Paul Dixon, *Northern Ireland: The Politics of War and Peace* (New York: Palgrave Macmillan, 2001), p. 226.

3. Thomas Hennessey, *The Northern Ireland Peace Process: Ending the Troubles?* (Dublin: Gill & Macmillan, 2000), pp. 54–66 for a detailed analysis of the Brooke-Mayhew talks.

4. Eamonn Mallie and David McKittrick, *The Fight For Peace* (London: Mandarin, 1997), pp. 97–108; 153–54; Henry McDonald, *Trimble* (London: Bloomsbury, 2001), pp. 120–21, 125; John Major, *John Major: The Autobiography* (New York: HarperCollins, 1999), pp. 438–39; Dixon, *Northern Ireland*, p. 231. For a shorter summary of the origins of the peace process than Mallie and McKittrick or Major, see Deaglan De Breadun, *The Far Side of Revenge* (Cork: The Collins Press, 2001), pp. 1–23.

5. Mallie and McKittrick, *The Fight*, pp. 29–42.

6. George Drower, *John Hume: Man of Peace* (London: Vista, 1996), pp. 50–51.

7. For a full discussion of these two different types see Thomas G. Mitchell, *Native vs. Settler: Ethnic Conflict in Israel/Palestine, Northern Ireland and South Africa* (Westwood, CT: Greenwood, 2000).

8. David McKittrick and David McVea, *Making Sense of the Troubles* (London: Penguin, 2001), pp. 40–61.

9. Brendan O'Brien, *The Long War: The IRA & Sinn Fein* (Syracuse: Syracuse University Press, 1995), pp. 20–21; McKittrick and McVea, *Making Sense*, p. 60; Tim Pat Coogan, *The IRA: A History* (Niwot, CO: Roberts Rinehart, 1994), pp. 277–92, 383–90; David Sharrock and Mark Devenport, *Man of War, Man of Peace: The Unauthorized Biography of Gerry Adams* (London: Pan, 1998), p. 245; Ed Moloney, *A Secret History of the IRA* (New York: W.W. Norton, 2002), pp. 540, 542.

10. Steve Bruce, *The Edge of the Union* (New York: Oxford University Press, 1994), pp. 98–107; Brian Rowan, *Behind the Lines: The Story of the IRA and Loyalist Ceasefires* (Belfast: Blackstaff, 1995), pp. 140–51.

11. Bruce, *Edge*, p. 154; McKittrick and McVea, *Making Sense*, pp. 326–27.

12. Michael Connolly, *Politics and Policy Making in Northern Ireland* (New York: Phillip Allan, 1990), pp. 98–114; Padraig O'Malley, *Uncivil Wars, Ireland Today* (Belfast: Blackstaff, 1983) for a detailed discussion of the Big Four. The best source on Alliance is Thomas G. Mitchell, *Indispensable Traitors: Liberal Parties in Settler Conflicts* (Westwood, CT: Greenwood, 2002).

13. McDonald, *Trimble*, pp. 121–28, 142–78; McKittrick and McVea, *Making Sense*, pp. 205–06. The best work on mainstream unionism is by Irish academic Feargal Cochrane, *Unionist Politics and the Politics of Unionism since the Anglo-Irish Agreement* (Cork: Cork University Press, 2001).

14. On the DUP see Ed Moloney and Andy Pollak, *Paisley* (Dublin: Poolbeg, 1994); Steven Bruce, *God Save Ulster!: The Religion and Politics of Paisleyism* (New York: Oxford University Press, 1986); and Clifford Smyth, *Ian Paisley: Voice of Protestant Ulster* (Edinburgh, 1987).

15. Sharrock and Devenport, *Man of War*, pp. 252–97; O'Brien, *Long War*, pp. 154–208. O'Brien provides an excellent analysis of the nationalist interparty political competition in the 1982–92 decade.

16. "As evidenced by his opposition to Sunningdale." Ed Moloney, *Paisley* (Dublin: Poolbeg, 2008), pp. 256–62.

17. Hume's definition also is consistent with that employed by this author in his doctoral dissertation on internal settlements in Southern Africa. An internal settlement is a settlement between the colonial or settler government and internal leaders of the native population that bypasses the external nationalists connected with the armed struggle. It is also on terms that are less than what the external nationalists are demanding. Sunningdale was an internal settlement. See Thomas G. Mitchell, *Black Faces, White Heads: Internal Settlements in Southern Africa* (Los Angeles: USC, 1990) or Mitchell, *Indispensable Traitors* for a short treatment of the idea.

18. Drower, *John Hume*, p. 113; Hennessey, *Northern Ireland*, pp. 24–26.
19. Major, *Autobiography*, p. 440; Rowan, *Peace Was Won*, p. 32; Tim Pat Coogan, *The Troubles* (Boulder, CO: Roberts Rinehart, 1996), pp. 339, 353.
20. See Connolly, *Politics*, pp. 71–86.
21. McKittrick and McVea, *Making Sense*, pp. 282–86, 299–300; Dixon, *Northern Ireland*, p. 230.
22. McDonald, *Trimble*, pp. 125–27.
23. Coogan, *Troubles*, p. 338; McKittrick and McVea, *Making Sense*, pp. 192–94; Major, *Autobiography*, pp. 443–44.
24. Mallie and McKittrick, *The Fight*, pp. 170–73, 177; Coogan, *Troubles*, p. 356.
25. Drower, *John Hume*, pp. 156–60; Coogan, *Troubles*, p. 335.
26. Dixon, *Northern Ireland*, pp. 231–32; *News Letter* Mar. 4, 1993; *Irish Times* Mar. 11, 1993 cited in Dixon.
27. McDonald, *Trimble*, pp. 129–30.
28. Brian Rowan, *How the Peace Was Won* (Dublin: Gill & Macmillan, 2008), p. 45. See pp. 39–61 for background on how the back channel fit into the peace process.
29. Mallie and McKittrick, *The Fight*, pp. 241–52; Major, *Autobiography*, pp. 431, 445–47; Rowan, *Peace Was Won*, pp. 60–61, 63–71; McKittrick and McVea, pp. 189–90 for a concise version.
30. McKittrick and McVea, *Making Sense*, pp. 195–96; Major, *Autobiography*, pp. 452–53.
31. See O'Brien, *Long War*, pp. 369–72 for a text of the Downing Street Declaration; Rowan, *Peace Was Won*, pp. 71–74.
32. Coogan, *Troubles*, p. 368.
33. See Conor O'Clery, *Daring Diplomacy* (Boulder, CO: Roberts Rinehart, 1997), pp. 193–99 for the visa controversy, and generally for a discussion of the American role during Clinton's first term; Roger MacGinty and John Darby, *Guns and Government: The Management of the Northern Ireland Peace Process* (New York: Palgrave Macmillan, 2002), pp. 113–15.
34. Coogan, *Troubles*, p. 401; Clery, *Diplomacy*.
35. Clery, *Diplomacy*, pp. 161, 165; Roger MacGinty and John Darby, *Guns and Government: The Management of the Northern Ireland Peace Process* (New York: Palgrave, 2002), pp. 116–17.
36. Sourcing will be provided later on when these events are discussed in more depth.
37. MacGinty and Darby, *Guns*, pp. 58–60.
38. *Ibid.*, pp. 117–18.
39. *Ibid.*, p. 120; George J. Mitchell, *Making Peace* (New York: Knopf, 1999), pp. 47–50, 69; De Breadun, *The Far Side*, pp. 25–26.
40. British academic Paul Dixon in his latest book, *The Northern Ireland Peace Process: Choreography and Theatrical Politics* (London: Routledge: 2008), argues that the visa fight was a phony fight trumped up in order to give the Republicans a phony victory.
41. Rowan, *Peace Was Won*, pp. 75–76; McKittrick and McVea, *Making Sense*, pp. 196–97; Bill Clinton, *My Life: Vol. II: The Presidential Years* (New York: Vintage, 2005), pp. 148–52; Major, *Autobiography*, p. 456. Adams's attendance at the conference brings to mind the attendance of former Official Sinn Fein Vice-President and IRSP founder and President Seamus Costello at a similar conference at Amherst University in Massachusetts in 1975 in which many people were impressed by his performance. This then begs the question of what Costello might have been able to achieve if he had not been murdered in 1977 in a feud with the Official IRA. Costello was in many ways a model for the future Adams, although Adams certainly has not acknowledged this. See Jack Holland and Henry McDonald, *INLA: Deadly Divisions* (Dublin, 1994) and O'Malley, *Uncivil*, for a note on the conference.
42. Mallie and McKittrick, *The Fight*, pp. 287–89.
43. Major, *Autobiography*, p. 457; Rowan, *Peace Was Won*, p. 86;
44. MacGinty and Darby, *Guns*, p. 112.
45. This is the central message of Moloney, *A Secret History*, pp. 423, 429, 432, 496–501; Mallie and McKittrick use the Totally Unarmed Strategy for the acronym.
46. McDonald, *Trimble*, pp. 132–33; Alastair Campbell, *The Blair Years* (New York: Alfred Knopf, 2007), p. 142.
47. Rowan, *Peace Was Won*, pp. 87–92, 112; McDonald, *Trimble*, p. 134; Moloney, *A Secret History*, pp. 424–27; Coogan, *Troubles*, p. 378; Clery, *Diplomacy*, pp.156, 158.
48. McDonald, *Trimble*, pp. 135–36.
49. Rowan, *Peace Was Won*, pp. 117–28.
50. MacGinty and Darby, *Guns*, p. 63.
51. *Ibid.*, p. 91.
52. *Ibid.*, p. 81; Graham Walker, *A History of the Ulster Unionist Party: Protest, Pragmatism, and Pessimism* (New York: Manchester University Press, 2004), p. 255.

53. The Irish Dail election of 2007 seemed to throw cold water on this strategy by seeming to indicate that Sinn Fein had hit a ceiling as a minor party in the Republic with five seats.
54. Mallie and McKittrick, *The Fight*, pp. 349–51; George J. Mitchell, *Making Peace*, pp. 10–11, 20–21, 25.
55. Mallie and McKittrick, *The Fight*, pp. 344–46; McDonald, *Trimble*, pp. 157–58.
56. McDonald, *Trimble*, pp. 142–48, 152.
57. *Ibid.*, pp. 149–52. For detailed background on the entire history of the controversy see Chris Ryder and Vincent Kearney, *Drumcree* (London: Metheun, 2001) especially pp. 103–27 on Drumcree I. Irish historian Ruth Dudley Edwards, a key Trimble advisor, wrote a book on the Orange Order that is friendlier to the Order. The Loyal Orders consist of the Orange Order, the Apprentice Boys, and the Royal Black Preceptory. All three are unionist marching groups similar to the Ancient Order of Hibernians in Ireland and the United States.
58. McDonald, *Trimble*, pp. 153–58; Dean Godson, *Himself Alone* (London: Harper Perennial, 2004), pp. 150–55.
59. Major, *Autobiography*, pp. 479–83.
60. George J. Mitchell (hereafter simply Mitchell), *Making Peace*, p. 26.
61. Mitchell, *Making Peace*, pp. 29–38; Mallie and McKittrick, *The Fight*, p. 362.
62. McKittrick and McVea, *Making Sense*, pp. 208–13; Moloney, *A Secret History*, pp. 440–41; Clery, *Diplomacy*, pp. 245–46; Clinton, *My Life*, p. 309.
63. Major, *Autobiography*, pp. 488–89; Moloney, *A Secret History*, p. 444; McKittrick and McVea, *Making Sense*, pp. 209, 213.
64. See Coogan, *Troubles*, p. 417.
65. MacGinty and Darby, *Guns*, p. 92; Toby Harnden, *'Bandit Country'* (London: Hodder & Stoughton, 1999), pp. 251–54.
66. McDonald, *Trimble*, pp. 168–69, 249; McKittrick and McVea, *Making Sense*, p. 212; Walker, *A History*, p. 254.
67. Mitchell, *Making Peace*, pp. 46–57.
68. *Ibid.*, pp. 58–59; McKittrick and McVea, *Making Sense*, pp. 210–11; Ryder and Kearney, *Drumcree*, pp. 170–72; MacGinty and Darby, *Guns*, p. 155.
69. McDonald, *Trimble*, pp. 170–74; Godson, *Himself Alone*, pp. 239–42.
70. Johnstone Brown, *Into the Dark: 30 Years in the RUC* (Dublin: Gill & Macmillan, 2005), pp. 140–44, 153. Monaghan was the county seat of the county by that name that bordered on Northern Ireland and was part of the original province of Ulster.
71. Guy Ben-Porat, *Global Liberalism, Local Populism* (Syracuse: Syracuse University Press, 2006), pp. 216–17, 228, 230, 233, 236.
72. Moloney, *A Secret History*, pp. 458, 462–63; Liam Clarke and Kathryn Johnston, *Martin McGuinness: From Guns to Government* (London: Mainstream, 2001), pp. 220–21; McKittrick and McVea, *Making Sense*, p. 215.
73. Moloney, *A Secret History*, pp. 454–55.
74. Campbell, *Blair*, pp. 215–17.
75. Moloney, *A Secret History*, pp. 461, 463–64; Clarke and Johnston, *Martin McGuinness*, p. 224.
76. Campbell, *Blair*, pp. 222–24.
77. Mitchell, *Making Peace*, pp. 109–11; Clarke and Johnston, *Martin McGuinness*, pp. 226–27. A good summary of the process of restoring the ceasefire can be found in De Breadun, *The Far Side*, pp. 24–61. There are discrepancies between the dates Mitchell gives for the swearing-in of the Sinn Fein delegation (Sep 9) and that Clarke and Johnston give for the trip to America (Sep 6). Obviously one of the authors is mistaken.
78. Clarke and Johnston, *Martin McGuinness*, p. 220.
79. Moloney, *A Secret History*, pp. 476–78.
80. *Ibid.*, p. 479; McDonald, *Trimble*, pp. 179, 187; Godson, *Himself Alone*, p. 294; McKittrick and McVea, *Making Sense*, list the bombing as the work of the Continuity IRA.
81. Moloney, *A Secret History*, p. 289; "Warning over new terrorist threat," *BBC Northern Ireland Online* Feb. 7, 2000; MacGinty and Darby, *Guns*, p. 95.
82. McDonald, *Trimble*, pp. 176–77, 184; Godson, *Himself Alone*, pp. 273–74; Campbell, *Blair*, p. 204.
83. McDonald, *Trimble*, pp. 180–82; Walker, *A History*, p. 260. For O'Callaghan's complete back story see Sean O'Callaghan, *The Informer* (London: BCA, 1998).
84. Clarke and Johnston, *Martin McGuinness*, p. 223; Mitchell, *Making Peace*, pp. 129–37; McKittrick and McVea, *Making Sense*, pp. 218–19.
85. Mitchell, *Making Peace*, pp. 139–42; Godson, *Himself Alone*, p. 322. For a good summary of the peace talks from October 1997 to late March 1998 see De Breadun, *The Far Side*, pp. 92–110.
86. McDonald, *Trimble*, p. 193; Godson, *Himself Alone*, p. 323.
87. McDonald, *Trimble*, pp. 195–96.
88. Mitchell, *Making Peace*, p. 144; John

Rentoul, *Tony Blair, Prime Minister* (London: Warner, 2001), p. 403.

89. De Breadun, *The Far Side*, p. 112; Gerard Murray and Jonathan Tonge, *Sinn Fein and the SDLP* (New York: Palgrave Macmillan, 2005), p. 213.

90. This is based on interviews conducted with Paul Bew, Gary McMichael, and various Alliance leaders in Belfast in the summers of 1998 and 2001. Mitchell, *Making Peace*, p. 62; De Breadun, *The Far Side*, pp. 111–41 for daily summaries from April 3 to 10; Stephen Farry, "An Alliance Perspective," in Jorg Neuheiser, Stefan Wolff, eds., *Peace At Last?* (New York: Berghahn, 2002), p. 29.

91. Farry, "Alliance," pp. 30–31; MacGinty and Darby, *Guns*, pp. 61, 70.

92. Rentoul, *Tony Blair*, pp. 405–08; Clinton, *My Life*, p. 418, 423; McDonald, *Trimble*, pp. 201–07.

93. Hennessey, *Northern Ireland*, pp. 126–39; Jonathan Powell, *Great Hatred, Little Room: Making Peace in Northern Ireland* (London: The Bodley Head, 2008), p. 103.

94. Mitchell, *Making Peace*, pp. 152–80 for a detailed discussion of the final two weeks of negotiations; De Breadun, *The Far Side*, pp. 111–41 for daily summaries from April 3 to 10. McDonald, *Trimble*, pp. 209–10.

95. McDonald, *Trimble*, pp. 208–09; Rentoul, *Tony Blair*, p. 407; William Quandt, *Peace Process* (Washington, D.C.: The Brookings Institution, 2001), pp. 169–70, 234–35; Powell, *Great Hatred*, p. 104.

96. Campbell, *Blair*, pp. 292, 295, 297.

97. McDonald, *Trimble*, p. 214; Godson, *Himself Alone*, pp. 357–59; Frank Millar, *David Trimble: The Price of Peace* (Dublin: Liffey, 2004), pp. 62–63.

98. Millar, *David Trimble*, pp. 63–72.

99. Campbell, *Blair*, p. 295.

100. The exact number of seats in the Executive was not specified in the GFA, but there were six departments run by the British government in NI. Initially there were six full ministers and four deputy ministers chosen. But this could be increased to 12 resulting in a 4:3:3:2 split.

101. Coogan, *Troubles*, p. 361.

102. Hennessey, *Northern Ireland*, p. 98.

103. There are several detailed analyses of the Belfast Agreement. The best are probably contained in John McGarry and Brendan O'Leary, eds., *Comparing Northern Ireland* (New York: Oxford University Press, 2004), which has several pieces looking at the Belfast Agreement as a consociational agreement and comparing it with other consociational arrangements. The best short analysis is probably by Thomas Hennessey, *Northern Ireland*, pp. 172–96. He is a British academic historian specializing in Northern Ireland.

104. Rentoul, *Tony Blair*, pp. 408, 418; Mitchell, *Making Peace*, p. 181; *Washington Post* April 11, 1998 quoted in MacGinty and Darby, *Guns*, p. 122.

Chapter Six

1. Jonathan Powell, *Great Hatred, Little Room: Negotiating Peace in Northern Ireland* (London: The Bodley Head, 2008), pp. 113–15.

2. Alastair Campbell, *The Blair Years* (New York: Alfred Knopf, 2007), pp. 290, 300; Ian S. Wood, *Crimes of Loyalty: A History of the UDA* (Edinburgh: Edinburgh University Press, 2006), pp. 227–28; Henry McDonald, *Trimble* (London: Bloomsbury, 2001), pp. 227, 229.

3. Powell, *Great Hatred*, p. 116.

4. On the "garden center Prods" and the project see Frank Millar, *David Trimble: The Price of Peace* (Dublin: Liffey, 2004), pp. 28–54

5. Roger MacGinty and John Darby, *Guns and Government: The Management of the Northern Ireland Peace Process* (New York: Palgrave, 2002), pp. 147, 150.

6. See McDonald, *Trimble*, pp. 218–40; Dean Godson, *Himself Alone* (London: Harper Perennial, 2004), pp. 362–70; and Deaglan De Breadun, *The Far Side of Revenge* (Cork: The Collins Press, 2001), pp. 150–61; Powell, *Great Hatred*, p. 115.

7. David Vance, *Unionism Decayed* (UK: Author House, 2008), p. 62; Guy Ben-Porat, *Global Liberalism, Local Populism* (Syracuse: Syracuse University Press, 2006), p. 256.

8. Ben-Porat, *Global*, pp. 247, 250.

9. McDonald, *Trimble*, p. 241. McDonald cites a Coopers and Lybrand poll for his figures. Jonathan Tonge, *The New Northern Irish Politics?* (New York: Palgrave Macmillan, 2005), p. 59 cites an article for the higher figure; MacGinty and Darby, *Guns*, pp. 178–79.

10. Campbell, *Blair*, p. 304.

11. De Breadun, *The Far Side*, p. 163; MacGinty and Darby, *Guns*, p. 70. The authors say five but they forgot about the United Unionists as UUP MPs running as independents termed themselves.

12. McDonald, *Trimble*, pp. 249–50; Godson, *Himself Alone*, pp. 377–78.
13. Interview with Alex Atwood of the SDLP in Belfast in August 1998.
14. Wood, *Crimes of Loyalty*, pp. 239–41; Jim Cusack and Henry McDonald, *UVF* (Dublin: Poolbeg, 1997), pp. 350–51.
15. Vance, *Unionism*, pp. 90, 92–93, 96; the DUP appeared on a platform with LVF leader Billy Wright in 1996.
16. De Breadun, *The Far Side*, p. 284.
17. David McKittrick and David McVea, *Making Sense of the Troubles* (London: Penguin, 2001), pp. 309–10.
18. Liam Clarke and Kathryn Johnston, *Martin McGuinness: From Guns to Government* (London: Mainstream, 2001), p. 234.
19. MacGinty and Darby, *Guns*, p. 99; for background see Colin McInnes, "A farewell to arms? Decommissioning and the peace process," in Michael Cox et al., eds., *A Farewell to Arms? From "Long War" to Long Peace in Northern Ireland* (New York: Manchester University Press, 2000), pp. 78–92 and Eamonn Mallie and David McKittrick, *The Fight For Peace* (London: Mandarin, 1997).
20. John Rentoul, *Tony Blair, Prime Minister* (London: Warner, 2001), p. 412.
21. McDonald, *Trimble*, p. 156; Maginnis had 117 votes to Willie Ross's 116 votes. Taylor was the runner-up to Trimble with 333 votes to Trimble's 466 in the final round.
22. This is based on a reading of commentary on Ulster politics from the Ulster, British, and Irish presses from 1998 to 2007 on *www.nuzhound.com*, *www.belfasttelegraph.com*, and *www.irishnews.co.uk*.
23. PR-STV gives a voter the same number of votes as places in the multi-candidate constituency. In NI this meant six votes. If the candidate for the first preference of a voter had already received the minimum level of votes to be elected the voter's second preference was counted and so on until the vote was used towards a candidate who had not yet been elected. This way, provided a party carefully controlled its number of candidates in a constituency and urged voters to divide their votes between the party's candidates in that constituency along a geographic basis, no votes were wasted. Jonathan Tonge, *Northern Ireland: Conflict and Change*, 2nd ed. (London: Longman, 2002), p. 192.
24. Millar, *David Trimble*, pp. 119–20.
25. *Ibid*.
26. See Godson, *Himself Alone*, p. 377 for a discussion of transfer votes; Vance, *Unionism*, pp. 114–15.
27. Alliance was competitive in East Belfast, South Belfast, East Antrim, South Antrim, North Down, and Strangford constituencies. The Women's Coalition was competitive only in South Belfast — where it deprived Alliance of its traditional seat in 1998 — and in North Down. The common feature of all of these constituencies was that they were urban with middle class neighborhoods. Alliance's Stephen Farry lost to Monica McWilliams in South Belfast in 1998, but beat Jane Morris out of her seat in North Down in 2002. In 2001 the author suggested to a NIWC activist that the two nonsectarian parties should engage in heated debates and name-slanging, etc. so as to attract media attention for the benefit of both. I was told that such attacks were unpopular with women. The NIWC's two elected MLAs received media attention during the Weston Park negotiations in July 2001, but the party was otherwise ignored by the media as Alliance had traditionally been. For the media Ulster politics is a two-party competition in each of the two communities.
28. Chris Ryder and Vincent Kearney, *Drumcree* (London: Methuen, 2001), pp. 268–69; De Breadun, *The Far Side*, p. 166.
29. *Ibid*., pp. 270–78; McDonald, *Trimble*, p. 257; Godson, *Himself Alone*, p. 384.
30. Wood, *Crimes of Loyalty*, pp. 232–33.
31. A series of UVF bombs exploded on a single day in Dublin and Monaghan in the Republic in 1974 killing more people, but that was the work of at least three bombs.
32. De Breadun, *The Far Side*, pp. 168–72; McKittrick and McVea, *Making Sense*, pp. 223–25; McDonald, *Trimble*, pp. 258–61; Godson, *Himself Alone*, pp. 386–90, 393–94. Information on the dissident republicans was gleaned from a reading of news articles over the years on *www.nuzhound.com* and is ultimately based upon what the intelligence services leak to the press or comes out in criminal trials.
33. Campbell, *Blair*, pp. 310, 317.
34. McDonald, *Trimble*, p. 268; Campbell, *Blair*, pp. 321, 336; Ben-Porat, *Global*, p. 252.
35. McDonald, *Trimble*, pp. 272, 277–79, 281–83; Godson, *Himself Alone*, pp. 401–03.
36. McDonald, *Trimble*, p. 275; Godson, *Himself Alone*, p. 409.
37. Campbell, *Blair*, pp. 372–75.
38. De Breadun, *The Far Side*, pp. 232–38.
39. Campbell, *Blair*, pp. 410, 412.

40. McKittrick and McVea, *Making Sense*, pp. 313–14; McDonald, *Trimble*, pp. 299–300.
41. Godson, *Himself Alone*, p. 468; McDonald, *Trimble*, p. 306.
42. McDonald, *Trimble*, pp. 305–06; Campbell, *Blair*, pp. 417–19.
43. Ryder and Kearney, *Drumcree*, pp. 309–10.
44. Vance, *Unionism*, pp. 119–32.
45. For Trimble's explanation of how the policing debacle came about see Millar, *David Trimble*, pp. 86–105.
46. McDonald, *Trimble*, pp. 307–14.
47. MacGinty and Darby, *Guns*, p. 81; Clarke and Johnston, *Martin McGuinness*, p. 239.
48. Millar, *David Trimble*, p. 114; Rentoul, *Tony Blair*, p. 413; McDonald, *Trimble*, p. 309.
49. *Ibid.*, pp. 317–24; De Breadun, *The Far Side*, pp. 278–98; Clarke and Johnston, *Martin McGuinness*, p. 240.
50. Godson, *Himself Alone*, pp. 534–37.
51. De Breadun, *The Far Side*, pp. 299–301; MacGinty and Darby, *Guns*, p. 110.
52. Wood, *Crimes of Loyalty*, pp. 233–39.
53. *Ibid.*, pp. 239–43.
54. De Breadun, *The Far Side*, pp. 302–15; McDonald, *Trimble*, pp. 330–31; McKittrick and McVea, *Making Sense*, p. 228; Godson, *Himself Alone*, pp. 564–81. McDonald confuses the date of suspension with the date of Trimble's letter, conflating the two.
55. Clarke and Johnston, *Martin McGuinness*, p. 243.
56. McKittrick and McVea, *Making Sense*, p. 317; Godson, *Himself Alone*, pp. 597–98; McDonald, *Trimble*, p. 335; Millar, *David Trimble*, p. 182.
57. McDonald, *Trimble*, pp. 332–33.
58. Godson, *Himself Alone*, p. 596.
59. *Ibid.*, pp. 600–01; Clarke and Johnston, *Martin McGuinness*, pp. 246–47.
60. De Breadun, *The Far Side*, pp. 344–57; Campbell, *Blair*, p. 451.
61. Godson, *Himself Alone*, p. 619; MacGinty and Darby, *Guns*, p. 165; Campbell, *Blair*, p. 452.
62. De Breadun, *The Far Side*, pp. 359–60.
63. Godson, *Himself Alone*, pp. 601–16; McDonald, *Trimble*, pp. 338–41. McDonald gives dates of May 20 for the UUC meeting and May 22 for restoration, but De Breadun and McKittrick and McVea (p. 317) give the later dates.
64. Ryder and Kearney, *Drumcree*, pp. 325–34; McKittrick and McVea, *Making Sense*, pp. 318–19.
65. Colin Crawford, *Inside the UDA: Volunteers and Violence* (London: Pluto, 2003), pp. 211–13; Wood, *Crimes of Loyalty*, pp. 247–49.
66. McKittrick and McVea, *Making Sense*, p. 320; McDonald, *Trimble*, p. 342; Crawford, *Inside the UDA*, p. 214; Wood, *Crimes of Loyalty*, pp. 251–53.
67. Wood, *Crimes of Loyalty*, pp. 254–58, 263; McKittrick and McVea, *Making Sense*, p. 321.
68. Wood, *Crimes of Loyalty*, pp. 265–74.
69. Crawford, *Inside the UDA*, p. 214; Wood, *Crimes of Loyalty*, p. 278; interview with UDP leader Gary McMichael in July 2001.
70. Wood, *Crimes of Loyalty*, pp. 275, 279–83.
71. Crawford, *Inside the UDA*, pp. 215–17; Wood, *Crimes of Loyalty*, pp. 288–92, 298, 300.
72. McDonald, *Trimble*, p. 343; Godson, *Himself Alone*, pp. 624–25; ; G. K. Peatling, *The Failure of the Northern Ireland Peace Process* (Portland, OR: Irish Academic Press, 2004), p. 75.
73. Godson, *Himself Alone*, p. 629.
74. *Ibid.*, pp. 633–35; McKittrick and McVea, *Making Sense*, p. 321; Campbell, *Blair*, p. 484; Tonge, *Conflict and Change*, p. 212.
75. On Reid see Godson, *Himself Alone*, pp. 637–38.
76. Campbell, *Blair*, pp. 489–90.
77. Vance, *Unionism*, p. 113.
78. "Westminster General Election (NI) 7 June 2001," *CAIN* (Conflict Archive on the Internet) *Web Service*.
79. "Local Government Elections (NI) 7 June 2001," *CAIN Web Service*.
80. Godson, *Himself Alone*, pp. 654–70.
81. *Ibid.*, p. 676.
82. *Ibid.*, pp. 671–72. Both the *Daily Telegraph* and the *Sun* made this suggestion.
83. *Ibid.*, pp. 677–81.
84. The author was present in Belfast during the summer of 2001 and during the summer of 1998.
85. Godson, *Himself Alone*, pp. 685–88.
86. Ed Moloney, *A Secret History of the IRA* (New York: W. W. Norton, 2002), p. 491.
87. *Ibid.*, pp. 491–92, Godson, *Himself Alone*, pp. 693–94; Peatling, *The Failure*, p. 80.

88. Godson, *Himself Alone,* pp. 695–98; Peatling, *The Failure,* p. 79; Millar, *David Trimble,* p. 183 and the author's discussions with Alliance members in the summer of 2001.
89. Godson, *Himself Alone,* p. 699; Tonge, *Conflict,* 268.
90. Godson, *Himself Alone,* pp. 710–11; Brian Rowan, *The Armed Peace* (Edinburgh: Mainstream, 2003), pp. 18–19, see pp. 15–32 for a detailed account of the affair.
91. Peatling, *The Failure,* pp. 81–83.
92. Godson, *Himself Alone,* pp. 728–32.
93. Brian Rowan, *How the Peace Was Won* (Dublin: Gill & Macmillan, 2008), p. 1.
94. This is based on a daily reading of the Northern Ireland press during the time of his exposure and of his murder. See Henry McDonald, "IRA informers still living in fear," *The Observer* Sep. 9, 2007. McDonald claims that his murderers were Republicans from east Tyrone and Derry acting without official sanction.
95. See Paul Bew, "Shadowy alliance haunts Stormontgate," *Yorkshire Post* Dec. 22, 2005, reprinted in Paul Bew, *The Making and Remaking of the Good Friday Agreement* (Dublin: Liffey, 2007), pp. 128–31; Rowan, *Peace Was Won,* pp. 2–3, see pp. 1–36 for a very detailed account of the Stormontgate affair.
96. Godson, *Himself Alone,* pp. 733–34.
97. Powell, *Great Hatred,* pp. 209, 235; Rowan, *Peace was Won,* p. 65–66.
98. Rowan, *Peace was Won,* p. 63.
99. Stephen Farry, "An Alliance Perspective on the GFA," in Jorg Neuheiser and Stefan Wolff, eds., *Peace At Last?* (New York: Berghahn, 2002), pp. 35, 36, 40–43.
100. Stefan Wolff, "The Peace Process Since 1998," in Neuheiser and Wolff, *Peace at Last?* pp. 227, 230.
101. "Carrots and Capitulation—Mandelson on Blair, *The Guardian* Mar 14, 2007; P. Bew, "The Long Good Friday, " *Literary Review* May 2008, both quoted in John Bew, Martyn Frampton, Inigo Gurruchaga, *Talking To Terrorists* (New York: Columbia University Press, 2009), p. 258.

Chapter Seven

1. This chapter of the Northern Ireland case makes use of numerous newspaper articles downloaded from the Newshound site (*www.nuzhsound.com*). The dates listed are the dates when the article was posted on the site rather than the journalist's dateline. So anyone checking the endnotes may have to look a day or two earlier than the date listed.
2. Dean Godson, *Himself Alone: David Trimble and the Ordeal of Unionism* (London: Harper Perennial, 2004), p. 740.
3. *Ibid.*, pp. 720–23.
4. *Ibid.*, pp. 745–46, 750–51; Peter Stothard, *Thirty Days: An Inside Account of Tony Blair at War* (New York: HarperCollins, 2003), pp. 210–16, 219–28 on the summit.
5. Godson, *Himself Alone,* pp. 754–60; Jonathan Tonge, *The New Northern Irish Politics?* (New York: Palgrave Macmillan, 2005), pp. 128, 260.
6. Godson, *Himself Alone,* pp. 765–66.
7. *Ibid.*, pp. 767–68.
8. *Ibid.*, p. 770; G. K. Peatling, *The Failure of the Northern Ireland Peace Process* (Portland, OR: Irish Academic Press, 2004), p. 88.
9. Godson, *Himself Alone,* p. 776.
10. *Ibid.*, pp. 778–790.
11. Frank Millar, *David Trimble: The Price of Peace* (Dublin: Liffey, 2004), pp. 172–73.
12. "Assembly Election (NI) Wed. 26 Nov. 2003," *CAIN Web Service,* pp. 1–2; Peatling, *The Failure,* pp. 106, 257.
13. David Vance, *Unionism Decayed* (UK: Author House, 2008), pp. 114–16.
14. Millar, *David Trimble,* pp. 183–85.
15. Godson, *Himself Alone,* pp. 799–800.
16. Vance, *Unionism,* p. 113.
17. Arlene Foster, the daughter of former party officer Sam Foster, and Noah Beare.
18. *Ibid.,* p. 802.
19. "Analysis: The nationalist dilemma now facing the SDLP," *Belfast Telegraph Digital* Feb. 6, 2004; "Options keep on shrinking for Trimble and the SDLP," *Irish Independent* Jan. 28, 2004.
20. See Thomas G. Mitchell, *Native vs Settler: Ethnic Conflict in Israel/Palestine, Northern Ireland, and South Africa* (Westwood, CT: Greenwood, 2000) for amplification on this theme. It is also a theme in the writings of Conor Cruise O'Brien. The South African peace process had the support of only about half of South Africa's Afrikaners making F.W. de Klerk vulnerable to the same sort of pressures as with Trimble, but his opponents were much more disorganized due to the death of their leader in April 1992 and the splintering of the Conservative Party.
21. Consociational theory is based on four European cases: Austria, Belgium, the Netherlands and Switzerland. Only two of these, Belgium and Switzerland involved ethnic

divisions. See Arend Lijphart, *Democracy in Plural Societies: A Comparative Exploration* (New Haven: Yale University Press, 1977).

22. The biggest theorist of consociational democracy is Dutch-American political scientist Arend Lijphart at the University of San Diego. His two biggest supporters for its application to Northern Ireland are John McGarry and Brendan O'Leary, both originally from the province. Its biggest critic is integrationist theorist Donald Horowitz at Duke University School of Law. See John McGarry and Brendan O'Leary, *The Northern Ireland Conflict* (New York: Oxford University Press, 2004), for a detailed discussion of the GFA by its supporters and critics. See also Tonge, *New Northern*, pp. 31–58, 255–65.

23. Jonathan Powell, *Great Hatred, Little Room* (London: The Bodley Head, 2008), p. 236.

24. Mark Devenport, "Parties roll up sleeves for review," *BBC News* Jan. 23, 2004; Jack Holland, "Paisley's orange crush," *The Irish Echo Online* Jan. 23, 2004; Paul T. Colgan and Pat Leahy, "DUP's new cardinals vie for power," *The Sunday Business Post Online* Dec. 8, 2003; Henry McDonald, "The retiring kind," *The Observer* Feb. 9, 2004; Eric Waugh, "Unforgiven by unionists for bringing the republican cuckoo into the nest," *Belfast Telegraph Digital* Feb. 12, 2004; Steven King, "On a par with Parnell? It's too early to judge Hume's place in history," *Belfast Telegraph Digital* Feb. 12, 2004; Suzanne Breen, "Hume wise to walk before a fall," *News Letter* Feb. 5, 2004; John M. Brown, "Hume to step down after 24 years as an MEP," *Financial Times* Feb. 5, 2004. Charles S. Parnell was a Protestant landlord who championed the rights of nationalists as head of the Irish Party in parliament in the 1880s. He was brought down by an adulterous affair with a supporter and finally died of a heart attack in 1891. John Redmond was Parnell's successor as leader of the Irish Party and he won home rule for Ireland in 1914, but it was delayed until the end of WWI. By then Sinn Fein had replaced the Irish Party as the leading nationalist party because Redmond made the mistake of supporting the British war effort. Parnell is well remembered by Irish historians, while Redmond is not.

25. "European Election (NI) 10 June 2004," *CAIN Web Service*; Brian Rowan, *Paisley and the Provos* (Belfast: Brehon, 2005), p. 57.

26. Thomas Harding, "'Execution kidnap' fuels fears over IRA ceasefire," *Daily Telegraph* Feb. 23, 2004; Jim Dee, "Beating incident may damage new chance for peace," *Irish Times* Feb. 23, 2004; Henry McDonald, "'Pub brawl' four now held as political prisoners," *The Observer* Mar. 7, 2004; Ed Moloney, *Paisley: From Demagogue to Democrat?* (Dublin: Poolbeg, 2008), pp. 410–11.

27. "Adams angry at 'kidnap' claims," *BBC News* Feb. 23, 2004; Noel McAdam, "Tohill abduction dogs political negotiations," *Belfast Telegraph* Feb. 25, 2004; Matthew Tempest, "Trimble calls for exclusion of Sinn Fein," *The Guardian* Feb. 24, 2004; Gerry Moriarty and Mark Hennessy, "Paisley to demand decision on IRA ceasefire," *Irish Times* Feb. 23, 2004; Gerry Moriarty, "Taoiseach to raise Tohill incident with McGuinness," *Irish Times* Feb. 25, 2004; Simon Doyle, "Litany of ceasefire breaches," *Irish News* Feb. 24, 2004.

28. Devenport, "Parties"; John Devine, "DUP proposal for assembly without ministers rejected," *Irish Independent* Feb. 9, 2004; Angelique Chrisafis, "DUP reveals plan to restore devolution," *The Guardian* Feb. 9, 2004; Peter Robinson, "The DUP plan for devolution," *Belfast Telegraph Digital* Feb. 9, 2004; "Viewpoint: DUP's plan still has real potential," *Belfast Telegraph Digital* Feb. 10, 2004.

29. Roy Garland, "Courageous DUP is finally facing realities," *Irish News* Feb. 10, 2004.

30. Brian Rowan, "Analysis: UDA 'must win trust,'" *BBC News* Feb. 25, 2004.

31. Gary Grattan, "Lost generation for UUP: claim," *Belfast Telegraph Digital* Jan. 25, 2004; "Trimble rejects 'step down' call," *BBC News* Feb. 27, 2004; "Ex-UUP leader calls for change," *BBC News* Mar. 8, 2004; Dominic Conningham, "Trimble determined to stay on as UUP leader," *Irish Independent* Mar. 9, 2004; Susan McKay, "Ex-Burnside aide 'stalks' Trimble," *Sunday Tribune* Feb. 23, 2004; "Trimble secures UUP leadership," *BBC News* Mar. 27, 2004.

32. "Comment: More Unites Than Divides The Risk-Takers," *News Letter* Feb. 11, 2004.

33. "Agreement talks 'in trouble,'" *BBC News* Mar. 13, 2004; Ciaran KcKeown, "Talks Must End If SF Is Not Tackled," *News Letter* Mar. 16, 2004.

34. Jim Cusack, "control the IRA," *Irish Independent* Mar. 14, 2004; Chris Thornton, "Research casts doubt over aide's prison article claim," *Belfast Telegraph Digital* Mar. 20, 2004; "Play By The Rules, MLA Suggests To Sinn Fein," *News Letter* Mar. 19, 2004; Tom

Brady, "Republican identity 'usurped by criminal Provos,'" *Irish Independent* Mar. 13, 2004; Suzanne Breen, "Sinn Fein Silence on Scappaticci," *News Letter* Mar. 19, 2004; "Stakeknife," *Wikipedia* accessed on Sep. 27, 2007. See Greg Harkin and Martin Ingram *Stakeknife: Britain's secret agents in Ireland* (Madison: University of Wisconsin Press, 2004).

35. Mark Devenport, "Setting a faster pace?" *BBC News* Mar. 13, 2004; Peatling, *The Failure*, p. 259.

36. Powell, *Great Hatred*, p. 246.

37. Rowan, "Analysis," pp. 60–61, 65, 68–69.

38. *Ibid.*, pp. 75–76, 79, 81.

39. *Ibid.*, pp. 92, 99–100, 102.

40. Powell, *Great Hatred*, p. 251.

41. Moloney, *Paisley*, p. 421. Lundy was a Scottish professional soldier during the siege of Derry in 1688 who was prepared to surrender the city to its Irish besiegers and has since been a hate figure for Protestants and synonym for traitor.

42. This is based on press speculation in articles at the time on the Newshound site (*www.nuzhound.com*); *Ibid.*, p. 113.

43. *Ibid.*, pp. 116–18; Kevin Toolis, "The Adams-McGuinness technique: rob banks to buy your way to power," *Times Online* Sep. 22, 2005.

44. *Ibid.*, pp. 122–23.

45. Toolis, "Adams-McGuinness."

46. *Ibid.*

47. Moloney, *Paisley*, pp. 422–25.

48. Rowan, "Analysis," pp. 133–37; this is also based on press coverage on Newshound from January to April 2005;

49. Moloney, *Paisley*, pp. 427–30.

50. Michael Kerr, *Transforming Unionism: David Trimble and the 2005 General Election* (Dublin: Irish Academic Press, 2006), pp. 130, 132; author interview with Alliance MLA Eileen Bell in 1998 who is from North Down. McCartney, an attorney and former UUP member, is not to be confused with the Republican murder victim with the same name. McCartney polled only 734 votes in 2005 in the council election; Vance, *Unionism*, p. 115.

51. "Local Government Elections (NI) Thurs. 5 May 2005," (*www.ulst.ac.uk*); Rowan, "Analysis," p. 23; Kerr, *Transforming Unionism*, p. 184.

52. (*www.ulst.ac.uk*); Kerr, *Transforming Unionism*, pp. 183–84.

53. Kerr, *Transforming Unionism*, p. 166; Rowan, "Analysis," p. 23.

54. Moloney, *Paisley*, p. 436.

55. Kerr, *Transforming Unionism*, pp. 148–56.

56. *Ibid.*, pp. 174–200.

57. Peatling, *The Failure*, pp. 90–144 especially pp. 90–123.

58. An Alliance member attributed this quote to Alex Atwood of the SDLP in a conversation with the author in 1998.

59. Peatling, *The Failure*, pp. 147, 218. See Jonathan Powell, *Great Hatred, Little Room* (London: The Bodley Head, 2008), pp. 234–35, 311–12 for evidence of this cavalier British attitude towards Trimble.

60. Rowan, "Analysis," pp. 27–31.

61. *Ibid.*, pp. 36, 38, 42–43, 46.

62. Declan Power, "Decommissioning: How it will happen," *The Sunday Business Post Online* Sep. 18, 2005.

63. Rowan, "Analysis," pp. 158–59; Gerri Peev, "General hails end to Irish politics' gun era," *The Scotsman Online* Sep. 27, 2005; Brian Rowan, *How the Peace Was Won* (Dublin: Gill & Macmillan, 2008), pp. 87–89.

64. Peev, "General hails"; Robert McCartney QC, "Opinion: The decommissioning debate," *Belfast Telegraph Digital* Sep. 18, 2005; Alan Murray, "The stark truth is that the IRA hasn't gone away," *Irish Independent* Sep. 27, 2005; Henry McDonald, "Republicanism is history," *The Guardian* Sep. 27, 2005; Rowan, *Peace was Won*, pp. 160, 195, 198.

65. Paul Bew, "Test of wills as pressure now grows on DUP to act," *Irish Independent* Sep. 27, 2005, reprinted in Bew et al., *Talking To Terrorists*, pp. 126–28.

66. Jenny McCartney, "Belfast blazes, so out comes the tripe," *Sunday Telegraph Online* Sep. 18, 2005; William Graham, "Loyalist violence has been ignited but unionist hearts are left cold," *Irish News* Sep. 18, 2005; Jim Cusack, "Belfast burns as exclusion of loyalists returns to haunt both governments," *Irish Independent* Sep. 18, 2005.

67. Liam Clarke and Jason Johnston, "Focus: Back to the future," *Times Online* Sep. 18, 2005; Alex Benjamin, "Police were deliberately provocative, says witness," *Times Online* Sep. 18, 2005.

68. Jenny McCartney, "Belfast blazes"; Liam Clarke, "DUP power offer as IRA seals arms," *Times Online* Sep. 18, 2005. Neither Moloney nor Powell even mention the riots in their accounts, indicating that they considered them to be of little importance.

69. Paul Bew, "Shadowy alliance haunts Stormontgate," *Yorkshire Post* Dec. 22, 2005,

in Bew et al., *Talking To Terrorists*, pp. 128–31.

70. William Graham, "Forecast poor for NI politics SDLP warns," *Irish News* Oct. 14, 2005; Liam Clarke, "The DUP should emulate Sinn Fein and play a smarter game," *Times Online* Oct. 30, 2005.

71. Bew, *Yorkshire Post*, Dec. 22, 2005; "Court proceedings against three men accused of spying for the IRA at Stormont are dropped," 8 Dec 2005, *Timeline: Northern Ireland's road to peace* BBC Northern Ireland Website; Alan Cowell, "British Agent Tells (a Bit) of Years Undercover in Ulster," *The New York Times* Dec. 23, 2005; Kevin Sullivan, "Tale of Espionage Marks a 'Bizarre' Turn in N. Ireland," *Washington Post* Dec. 18, 2005; Mark Devenport, "After 'Stormontgate' where's the trust?," *BBC News* Dec. 11, 2005. Scappaticci was unmasked as a British agent by former British agent "Kevin Fulton" in 2004 and though he vigorously denied the allegation he eventually fled to Italy, where his father had emigrated from decades earlier.

72. Entries from 11 Jan. 2006; 4 Apr. 2006 and 6 Apr. 2006 from the *Timeline*, BBC Website.

73. "Stormont assembly sits for first time since its suspension in 2002," *Timeline*, BBC Website,15 May 2006; Patrick Murphy, "Exposing the myths of power sharing 'existence,'" *Irish News* May 29, 2006.

74. Rowan, *Peace Was Won*, p. 158.

75. "St. Andrew's Agreement," *Wikipedia* accessed on Sep. 25, 2007; Henry McDonald, "Paisley hails 'miracle' of Sinn Fein's police talks," *The Observer* Sep. 30, 2007.

76. Rowan, *Peace Was Won*, p. 159.

77. Entries from 24 Nov. and 28 Dec. 2006, 8 Jan., 22 Jan. and 28 Jan. 2007 on the *Timeline*, BBC Website.

78. "Assembly Election (NI) 7 March 2007," CAIN (*www.ulst.ac.uk*).

79. Martina Purdy, " 'Chuckle brothers' enjoy 100 days," *BBC News* Aug. 16, 2007.

80. On Paisley's early career see Ed Moloney and Andy Pollak, *Paisley* (Dublin: Poolbeg, 1994) and Steven Bruce, *God Save Ulster!: The Religion and Politics of Paisleyism* (New York: Oxford University Press, 1986).

81. Gareth Gordon, "Hain is 'gone but not forgotten,'" *BBC News* Jul. 1, 2007;

82. Barry White, "Little to be gained from short term shock tactics," *Belfast Telegraph Digital* Jul. 11, 2007; Alex Kane, "Unionism won't survive on just an Assembly headcount," *News Letter* Sep. 1, 2007; John Coulter, "DUP Analysis," *The Blanket* (*www.lark.phoblacht.net*), accessed on June 23, 2006.

83. Moloney and Pollak, *Paisley*, pp. 448–49.

84. *Ibid.*, pp. 514–16.

85. Dean Godson, "Warning for Britain as Irish voters snub Adams," *Daily Telegraph* May 28, 2007; Michael Brennan, "Back to the drawing board for Sinn Fein after poll setback," *Irish Independent* May 28, 2007.

86. William McCrea, "The united Ireland bubble has well and truly burst, *News Letter* Jul. 19, 2007; Alex Kane, "William McCrea is right 'the IRA has been defeated,'" *News Letter* Jul. 28, 2007.

87. This eventually became the Traditional Unionist Voice party.

88. "A political deal ... or has unionism lost its way," *Belfast Telegraph* Sep. 21, 2007; "Viewpoint: Allister and co have nothing to offer," *Belfast Telegraph* Sep. 22, 2007; Stephen King, "Party merger moves have one thing in common — keep Sinn Fein out," *Irish Examiner* Sep. 26, 2007; Tom McGurk, "The SDLP would welcome the sight of a Fianna Fail lifeboat," *The Sunday Business Post* Sep. 23, 2007; Tom Kelly, "To merge or not to merge is the question for SDLP," *Irish News* Sept. 25, 2007.

89. Jenny McCartney, "Paisley and McGuinness chuckling in power," *Sunday Telegraph Online* Oct. 28, 2007; Jim Cusack, "SF denials on savage killing fall on deaf ears," *The Independent* Oct. 28, 2007; Colm Heatley, "Quinn murder causes south Armagh split," *Sunday Business Post* Oct. 28, 2007; Suzanne Breen, "Fatal attack on Paul Quinn was 'ordered by Provisional IRA,'" *Sunday Tribune* Oct. 28, 2007.

90. Moloney, *Paisley*, pp. 499–511.

91. See Mark Devenport, "Cooler style of patient Robinson," *BBC News Northern Ireland* April 15, 2008 and the Newshoud site in early April 2008 for details. Moloney's biography was published in early 2008 before the coup occurred.

92. "IRA leadership not involved in Quinn killing," *The Irish News Online* April 30, 2008.

93. David McKittrick, "Northern Ireland loyalists get rid of their weapons," *The Independent on Sunday* June 28, 2009; and Greg Moriarty, "De Chastelain confirms major UVF disarmament," *Irish Times* June 29, 2009. Also based on other articles from the Newshound website (*www.nuzhound.com*) accessed in late June 2009.

94. This is based on a daily reading of the NI press on *Newshound*.

Conclusion

1. David Vance, *Unionism Decayed* (UK: Author House, 2008), pp. 141–42.
2. Herb Keinon, "Analysis: Why the N. Ireland comparison doesn't fit," *Jerusalem Post Online Edition* Aug. 13, 2007.
3. Zion Evrony, "Hamas is not the IRA," *International Herald Tribune* Aug. 31, 2007.
4. See John McGarry, "Comparing Northern Ireland," in John McGarry and Brendan O'Leary, *The Northern Ireland Conflict* (New York: Oxford University Press, 2004), pp. 140–41; Michael Ancram MP, "Fading the Line in the Sand," *Belfast Telegraph Digital* Sep. 21, 2005.
5. The two books are *The Blood of Abraham* (1985) and *Palestine: Peace Not Apartheid* (2006). On Carter's motivation see Aaron D. Miller, *The Much Too Promised Land* (New York: Bantam, 2008), pp. 157–62; this is based on interviews with Carter and his colleagues in the administration.
6. See Mark Matthews, *Lost Years: Bush, Sharon and Failure in the Middle East* (New York: Nation Books, 2007); Charles Enderlin, *The Lost Years* (New York: Other Press, 2007); and Miller, *The Much Too Promised Land*, pp. 321–62 for a detailed critique of the Bush Arab-Israeli policy.
7. Martin Indyk, *Innocent Abroad* (New York: Simon & Schuster, 2009), pp. 397, 401–02.
8. Not all settler societies are siege societies. Australia and Canada were never siege societies. Colonial America ceased to be a siege society after the French and Indian War. New Zealand, if it ever was a siege society, was not one after the 1860s.
9. Laager is Dutch for camp and refers to the camps of the Voortrekkers (pioneers) within barriers made of circled wagons and thorn bushes between the wheels. This was during the Great Trek of 1835–1845. Masada was the site of a siege by the Romans from 70 to 73 AD after the Jews revolted in 66 AD and Jerusalem was conquered in 70 AD. Bawn refers to the stone towers surrounded by low walls that the Ulster Scots built during the Ulster Plantation during the early 17th century.
10. Masada has been used by the IDF since the mid-1960s and by Zionist youth groups before that to inculcate this siege mentality. For the use of this see the beginning and end of the TV miniseries *Masada* from 1981. Tel Hai and Betar, another siege from roughly the same era as Masada (135 AD vs. 73 AD), were used by the Herut Party to foster a right-wing expansionist ideology. The Day of the Covenant, related to Blood River, was a national holiday in apartheid South Africa.
11. For a discussion of this see Thomas G. Mitchell, *Native vs. Settler: Ethnic Conflict in Israel/Palestine, Northern Ireland, and South Africa* (Westwood, CT: Greenwood, 2000); Donald H. Akenson, *God's Peoples* (Ithaca: Cornell University Press, 1992), pp. 3–5, 263–345.
12. It is the native question that divides "left" from "right" in settler societies. See Mitchell, *Native vs. Settler*, and Thomas G. Mitchell, *Indispensable Traitors: Liberal Parties in Settler Conflicts* (Westwood, CT: Greenwood, 2002) for a discussion of the roles of both liberal and conservative parties in settler societies.
13. On Adams's lying see Jim Cusack, "SF denials on savage killing fall on deaf ears," *The Independent* Oct. 28, 2007.
14. On Arafat's reputation for prevarication see Efraim Halevy, *Man in the Shadows* (New York: St. Martin's Press, 2006), pp. 125, 128. Halevy, the Mossad director under Netanyahu and Sharon, considered Arafat to be divorced from reality.
15. Sa'adia Touval, *The Peace Brokers: Mediators in the Arab-Israeli Conflict 1948–1979* (Princeton, NJ: Princeton University Press, 1982), introduction.
16. Miller, *The Much Too Promised Land*, pp. 178–79, 197, 202.
17. Martin Indyk, *Innocent Abroad* (New York: Simon & Schuster, 2009), p. 175.
18. Miller, *The Much Too Promised Land*, pp. 250–52, 285–87, 309–11.
19. *Ibid.*, pp. 321, 323–24, 348–53; Matthews, *Lost Years*, pp. 18–23, 271–73; Enderlin, *The Lost Years*, pp. 2, 160, 215.
20. Indyk, *Innocent Abroad*, pp. 413–14.
21. *Ibid.*, Part II, pp. 147–238, and Part I, pp. 30–43 for details.
22. John Bew et al. *Talking to Terrorists* (New York: Columbia University Press, 2009), pp. 39–57.

Bibliography

The Oslo Process

Aburish, Said K. *Arafat: From Defender to Dictator.* New York: Bloomsbury, 1998.
Albright, Madeleine. *Madam Secretary: A Memoir.* New York: Miramax, 2002.
Bar-Zohar, Michael. *Facing a Cruel Mirror.* New York: Charles Scribner's Sons, 1990.
———. *Shimon Peres: The Biography.* New York: Random House, 2007.
Beilin, Yossi. *The Path to Geneva: The Quest for a Permanent Agreement 1996–2004.* New York: RDV, 2004.
———. *Touching Peace: From the Oslo Accord to a Final Agreement.* London: Weidenfeld & Nicolson, 1999.
Ben-Ami, Shlomo. *Scars of War, Wounds of Peace.* New York: Oxford University Press, 2006.
Ben-Porat, Guy. *Global Liberalism, Local Populism.* Syracuse: Syracuse University Press, 2006.
———, ed. *The Failure of the Middle East Peace Process?* New York: Palgrave Macmillan, 2008.
Bew, John, Martyn Frampton, and Inigo Gurruchaga. *Talking to Terrorists.* New York: Columbia University Press, 2009.
Bodansky, Yossef. *The High Cost of Peace.* Roseville, CA: Prima, 2002.
Clinton, Bill. *My Life: The Presidential Years,* Vol. II. New York: Vintage, 2005.
Elazar, Daniel, and Shmuel Sandler, eds. *Israel at the Polls, 1992.* Lanham, MD: Rowman & Littlefield, 1995.
Enderlin, Charles. *Shattered Dreams.* New York: Other, 2002.
Halevy, Efraim. *Man in the Shadows.* New York: St. Martin's Press, 2006.
Hefez, Nir, and Gadi Bloom. *Ariel Sharon.* New York: Random House, 2006.
Horowitz, David. *Still Life with Bombers.* New York: Alfred Knopf, 2004.
Inbar, Efraim. *Rabin and Israel's National Security.* Baltimore: Johns Hopkins University Press, 1999.
Karsh, Efraim. *Arafat's War.* New York: Grove Press, 2003.
Kurzman, Dan. *Soldier of Peace: The Life of Yitzhak Rabin.* New York: HarperCollins, 1998.
Makovsky, David. *Making Peace with the PLO.* Boulder, CO: Westview, 1996.
Miller, Aaron David. *The Much Too Promised Land.* New York: Bantam, 2008.
Peres, Shimon. *Battling for Peace.* New York: Random House, 1995.
———. *The New Middle East.* New York: Henry Holt, 1993.

Quandt, William B. *Camp David: Peace Making and Politics.* Washington, D.C.: Brookings Institution, 1986.
_____. *Peace Process,* rev. ed. Washington, D.C.: Brookings Institution and University of California Press, 2001.
Rabin, Leah. *Rabin: Our Life, His Legacy.* New York: G. P. Putnam's Sons, 1997.
Rabinovich, Itamar. *Waging Peace: Israel and the Arabs 1948–2003.* Princeton: Princeton University Press, 2004.
Reich, Bernard. *A Brief History of Israel,* 2d ed. New York: Checkmark, 2008.
Ross, Dennis. *The Missing Peace.* New York: Farrar, Straus and Giroux, 2004.
Rubin, Barry, and Judith C. Rubin. *Yasir Arafat: A Political Biography.* New York: Oxford University Press, 2003.
Savir, Uri. *The Process.* New York: Random House, 1998.
Segev, Samuel. *Crossing the Jordan: Israel's Hard Road to Peace.* New York: St. Martin's Press, 1998.
Shlaim, Avi. *The Iron Wall.* New York: W.W. Norton, 2001.
Swisher, Clayton. *The Truth About Camp David.* New York: Nation Books, 2004.

The Northern Ireland Peace Process

Bew, John, Martyn Frampton, and Inigo Gurruchaga. *Talking to Terrorists: Making Peace in Northern Ireland and the Basque Country.* New York: Columbia University Press, 2009.
Bew, Paul. *The Making and Remaking of the Good Friday Agreement.* Dublin: The Liffey Press, 2007.
_____, Henry Patterson, and Paul Teague. *Between War and Peace: The Political Future of Northern Ireland.* London: Lawrence & Wishart, 1997.
Bruce, Steve. *The Edge of the Union.* New York: Oxford University Press, 1994.
Campbell, Alastair. *The Blair Years: The Alastair Campbell Diaries.* New York: Alfred Knopf, 2007.
Clarke, Liam, and Kathryn Johnston. *Martin McGuinness: From Guns to Government.* London: Mainstream, 2001.
Clinton, Bill. *My Life: The Presidential Years,* Vol. II. New York: Vintage, 2005.
Coogan, Tim Pat. *The IRA: A History.* Niwot, CO: Roberts Rinehart, 1994.
_____. *The Troubles: Ireland's Ordeal 1966–1996.* Niwot, CO: Roberts Rinehart, 1996.
Cox, Michael, Adrian Guelke, and Fiona Stephen, eds. *A Farewell to Arms? From "Long War" Long Peace in Northern Ireland.* New York: Manchester University Press, 2000.
Crawford, Colin. *Inside the UDA: Volunteers and Violence.* London: Pluto, 2003.
Cusack, Jim, and Henry McDonald. *UVF.* Dublin: Poolbeg, 1997.
De Breadun, Deaglan. *The Far Side of Revenge.* Cork: The Collins Press, 2001.
Dixon, Paul. *Northern Ireland: The Politics of War and Peace.* New York: Palgrave Macmillan, 2001.
Drower, George. *John Hume: Man of Peace.* London: Vista, 1996.
Godson, Dean. *Himself Alone.* London: Harper Perennial, 2004.
Harnden, Toby. *"Bandit Country."* London: Hodder and Stoughton, 1999.
Hennessey, Thomas. *A History of Northern Ireland.* New York: St. Martin's Press, 1997.
Hume, John. *A New Ireland.* Niwot, CO: Roberts Rinehart, 1996.
Kerr, Michael. *Transforming Unionism: David Trimble and the 2005 General Election.* Dublin: Irish Academic Press, 2006.
MacGinty, Roger, and John Darby. *Guns and Government: The Management of the Northern Ireland Peace Process.* New York: Palgrave Macmillan, 2002.

Major, John. *John Major: The Autobiography.* New York: HarperCollins, 1999.
Mallie, Eamonn, and David McKittrick. *The Fight for Peace.* London: Mandarin, 1997.
McDonald, Henry. *Trimble.* London: Bloomsbury, 2001.
McGarry, John, and Brendan O'Leary. *Explaining Northern Ireland.* Cambridge, MA: Blackwell, 1995.
_____. *The Northern Ireland Conflict.* New York: Oxford University Press, 2004.
McGartland, Martin. *Fifty Dead Men Walking.* London: Blake, 1997.
McKittrick, David, and David McVea. *Making Sense of the Troubles.* London: Penguin, 2001.
Millar, Frank. *David Trimble: The Price of Peace.* Dublin: The Liffey Press, 2004.
Mitchell, George J. *Making Peace.* New York: Knopf, 1999.
Moloney, Ed. *Paisley: From Demagogue to Democrat?* Dublin: Poolbeg, 2008.
_____. *A Secret History of the IRA.* New York: W. W. Norton, 2002.
Murray, Gerard, and Jonathan Tonge. *Sinn Fein and the SDLP.* New York: Palgrave Macmillan, 2005.
Neuheiser, Jorg, and Stefan Wolff, eds. *Peace at Last?* New York: Berghahn, 2002.
O'Brien, Brendan. *The Long War: The IRA and Sinn Fein, 1985 to Today.* Syracuse: Syracuse University Press, 1995.
O'Clery, Conor. *Daring Diplomacy.* Boulder, CO: Roberts Rinehart, 1997.
O'Doherty, Malachi. *The Trouble with Guns: Republican Strategy and the Provisional IRA.* Belfast: Blackstaff, 1998.
Peatling, G. K. *The Failure of the Northern Ireland Peace Process.* Portland, OR: Irish Academic Press, 2004.
Powell, Jonathan. *Great Hatred, Little Room: Making Peace in Northern Ireland.* London: The Bodley Head, 2008.
Rentoul, John. *Tony Blair: Prime Minister.* London: Warner, 2001.
Rowan, Brian. *The Armed Peace: Life and Death After the Ceasefires.* Edinburgh: Mainstream, 2003.
_____. *Behind the Lines: The Story of the IRA and Loyalist Ceasefires.* Belfast: Blackstaff, 1995.
_____. *How the Peace Was Won.* Dublin: Gill & Macmillan, 2008.
_____. *Paisley and the Provos.* Belfast: Brehon, 2005.
Ryder, Chris, and Vincent Kearney. *Drumcree.* London: Methuen, 2001.
Sharrock, David, and Mark Devenport. *Man of War, Man of Peace: The Unauthorized Biography of Gerry Adams.* London: Pan, 1997.
Stephens, Philip. *Tony Blair: The Making of a World Leader.* New York: Viking, 2004.
Stothard, Peter. *Thirty Days: An Inside Account of Tony Blair at War.* New York: HarperCollins, 2003.
Tonge, Jonathan. *The New Northern Irish Politics?* New York: Palgrave Macmillan, 2005.
_____. *Northern Ireland: Conflict and Change,* 2d ed. London: Longman, 2002.
Walker, Graham. *A History of the Ulster Unionist Party: Protest, Pragmatism, and Pessimism.* Manchester University Press, 2004.
Wood, Ian S. *Crimes of Loyalty: A History of the UDA.* Edinburgh: Edinburgh University Press, 2006.

Index

Abbas, Mahmoud 32, 49, 55, 70, 74, 80, 87, 207, 210, 211
Abu Ala *see* Qurei, Ahmed
Abu Mazen *see* Abbas, Mahmoud
Adair, Johnny 153–54, 158–59, 160, 217
Adams, Gerry 93, 99–100, 102, 108, 116, 120, 131, 139, 140, 146, 148, 150, 166, 171, 182, 183, 185, 190, 198, 200, 211, 218, 225–26, 227
African National Congress 1, 5, 56
Ahern, Bertie 120, 127, 129, 130, 144, 147, 174, 184, 186, 191, 200, 209, 216
Akenson, Donald 6
Al-Aksa Intifada: course 86–87; preparations for 83–85; start 86
al-Assad, Hafiz 66–68
Albright, Madeleine 53, 214
Alderdice, John 102, 127, 141, 148
Al-Hashemi, King Hussein 58, 66, 211
Alliance Party 98, 105, 121, 126, 141, 142, 148, 163, 166, 167, 169, 175, 176, 181, 187, 189, 190, 196, 197, 201, 227
Allister, Jim 179, 199, 225
Anglo-Irish Agreement 15, 95, 98, 212
Arafat, Yasir 10, 11, 27, 34, 52, 54–57, 87, 206, 209, 210, 211, 216, 219, 220; and Al-Aksa Intifada 83–86; at Camp David 74, 77–79, 80; in Oslo process 36–37, 40, 43
Articles 2 and 3 (Irish Constitution) 100, 130, 153
Ayalon, Ami 65

Baker, James 10, 17, 27, 214, 219
Barak, Ehud 48, 51, 52, 62, 63, 64, 68–69, 70–72, 84, 207, 210–11, 212, 216–17, 219; and Al-Aksa Intifada 81, 85–87; at Camp David 75, 77–78, 80; Syrian negotiations 65, 66–68; and Taba 87
Barghouti, Marwan 70, 83
Beilin, Yossi 30–32, 35, 49
Ben-Porat, Guy 8, 9, 51
Bew, Paul 124

Blair, Tony 109, 120–21, 123, 132, 135, 138, 144–46, 148, 162, 165, 168, 172–73, 178, 186, 191, 209, 212, 213, 215, 220; and Ahern, Bertie 144; and Good Friday Agreement 126, 129, 130; *see also* Sinn Fein; Trimble, David
Bono 133
Brooke, Peter 93–94, 103
Bruton, John 113, 215
Burnside, David 174, 180–81
Bush, George H. W. (41) 87, 211, 220
Bush, George W. (43) 87, 88, 172, 212, 219, 220

Cahill, Joe 105, 110
Camp David Summit (1978) 74
Camp David Summit (2000) 20, 71–82, 83; effects 88–89; issues 79–82; procedures 74, 77–79; reasons for 71; reasons for failure 74–75
Chichester-Clark, James 99
Christopher, Warren 36, 52
Clinton, Bill 22, 37, 49, 51, 58, 59, 60, 61, 62, 65, 68, 210, 212, 213, 220, 221; at Camp David 71, 72, 74, 78, 79; Clinton parameters 20, 80, 81; in N. Ireland peace process 105, 106, 110, 128, 161
Colombia Three 155, 164–65
colonization 5
Combined Loyalist Military Command 104, 111, 121
consociationalism 23–24, 177–78
Continuity IRA 12, 123, 125, 144, 149, 204, 227
Craig, William 99
Currie, Austin 95
Cyprus 3, 205

Dahlan, Mohammed 40, 77, 83
de Brun, Bairbre 152
de Chastelain, Jon 107, 115, 151, 154, 175, 190–91, 210
decommissioning (of arms) 112–13, 127,

137–39, 145, 147, 151, 154, 156, 168, 169, 183–84, 190, 191–92, 206–08, 218, 227; IRA and 183–84, 190, 191–92; UDA, UVF and 227; *see also* Social Democratic and Labour Party
Democratic Unionist Party (DUP) 1, 11, 12, 13, 98; and decommissioning 189, 194, 195; and GFA 134, 135, 180; and peace process 111, 114, 121, 161, 162, 166, 171, 174, 175, 176; and Sinn Fein 225–26; and UUP 181, 187–88
de Rossa, Proinsas 113
Dodds, Nigel 98, 152, 177, 178, 193, 199, 200, 227
Donaldson, Denis 167–68, 195
Donaldson, Jeffrey 94, 106, 125, 127–28, 135, 137, 155, 164, 166, 174, 176, 199
Downing St. Declaration 104–05, 108, 209
Drumcree 114, 118–20, 124, 133, 142–43, 148–49
dual mediation 16, 18, 22, 206, 208–10
Dublin 103, 106, 107, 108, 112, 137, 139, 146, 147, 154, 156, 172, 181, 186, 188, 198, 199, 206, 211, 218, 222
DUP *see* Democratic Unionist Party
Durkan, Mark 140, 152, 166, 188

elections: Assembly (1998) 135–36; Assembly (2003) 171, 175–76; Assembly (2007) 197; Forum 117–18; Westminster (2001) 162–63; Westminster (2005) 187–88
Empey, Reg 94, 140, 152, 153, 181, 189, 196
Erekat, Saeb 55–56, 69
Eretz Israel (Land of Israel) 28
Ervine, David 136, 175
Etzel (Irgun Zvai Leumi) 44

FAFO 31
Faulkner, Brian 99, 128, 199
Fianna Fail party 95, 201
Fine Gael party 95, 102
Fitt, Gerry 95
FitzGerald, Garret 95
Ford, David 181, 227
Frameworks Document 113

Golan Heights 67–68
Goldstein, Baruch 39, 218
Good Friday (Belfast) Agreement (GFA) 125–30, 138, 177, 180, 183, 184, 206, 208; Referendum 131–34
Gore, Al 106, 212
Graham, Alistair 134

Hagana 44
Hamas 42, 50, 208, 217, 221, 222–23
Harris, Eoghan 124, 145, 150
Heads of Agreement 125
Hebron 39
Hirschfeld, Yair 31
Holkeri, Harri 115
Horowitz, Donald 23–24

Howe, Stephen 6
Hudaibiya 43
Hume, John 93, 94, 96, 99–100, 140, 141, 146, 161, 178–79, 211; Hume-Adams dialogue 93, 99–100
Husseini, Feisal 31

IICD 146, 157, 170, 204, 227
IMC 172, 174, 203
INLA 12, 98, 111, 117, 124, 127, 144, 159, 179, 205, 217, 227
Irish Republican Army (IRA) 96, 101, 102, 108, 109–10, 112; and peace process 116–17, 121, 137, 138, 147, 148, 151, 156, 158, 159, 166–70, 172–73, 174, 179, 182, 189, 190–92, 194–96; *see also* Sinn Fein
Islamic Jihad 42, 217, 221, 223
Israeli Labor Party 28–29, 66–67, 206–07, 216, 221
Israeli-Palestinian conflict 6–13

Kadima 208, 221
King Hussein 58, 66, 211
Kissinger, Henry 16, 21, 34, 211, 213, 219

Lake, Tony 105
Larson, Terje 31
Lehi 28, 44
Leverage 19
Levy, David 53, 54, 62, 67, 71–72
Lijphart, Arend 22–23
Likud Party 28–29, 46, 51, 53–54, 64, 67, 208, 215, 221
Lipkin-Shahak, Amnon 38
London 103–05, 106, 107, 108, 112, 137, 139, 146, 147, 154, 156, 172, 181, 198, 199, 205, 206, 211, 218, 222
Loyalist Volunteer Force 146, 158, 217
Lustick, Ian 6

MacDonald, Michael 6
Maginnis, Ken 94, 101, 106, 114, 120, 135, 140, 149, 216
Major, John 100, 103, 104, 108, 130, 212, 215
Mallon, Seamus 102, 140, 141, 145, 148, 154, 161, 187
Mandelson, Peter 151, 154, 155, 156, 159, 162, 169
Mansergh, Martin 102
Mayhew, Patrick 94, 102, 112
McCartney, Robert (UKUP) 187, 192; murder 186–88
McDowell, Michael 182, 185, 200
McGarry, John 23, 24
McGimpsey, Chris 95, 101, 140, 152
McGimpsey, Michael 95, 101, 140, 152
McGuinness, Martin 11, 12, 103, 108, 139, 140, 148, 152, 156, 171, 182, 185, 218; in GFA negotiations 116, 120; and Paisley, Ian 177, 178, 197, 198

McKevitt, Michael 122
mediation theory 14–22
Meretz 29, 51, 72, 206–07
Miller, Benjamin 8–9
Mitchell, Chris 15
Mitchell, George 53, 86, 106, 107, 115, 210; as GFA talks mediator 125–26; Mitchell Commission 115–16; Mitchell Principles 116, 122; in review process 151
Mofaz, Shaul 65
Molyneaux, James 11, 94, 99, 108, 109, 113–14, 181
Mowlam, "Mo" 132, 145, 148, 151, 154
Mubarak, Hosni 43, 58, 66

National Religious Party 29
natives 5, 12
Netanyahu, Benyamin "Bibi" 40, 46, 51–54, 58, 60, 61, 62, 63, 207, 212, 216
Nixon, Richard 15, 16, 211, 213
Northern Bank robbery 185–86
Northern Ireland Unionist Party 13, 135
Northern Ireland Women's Coalition 135, 141, 142, 163, 166

O'Callaghan, Sean 124, 158, 159
Official IRA 96–97, 99, 159, 227
O'Leary, Brendan 23, 24
Omagh bombing 143–44, 217
O'Neill, Terence 99
Orange Order 132, 134, 143, 148–49
Oslo process 30–37, 205–07, 216, 218; Oslo I 37–40; Oslo II 41–46

Paisley, Ian, Jr. 184, 199, 202
Paisley, Ian, Sr. 98, 99, 108, 156, 162, 168, 171, 172, 177, 178, 183, 191, 197, 198, 199–200, 202–03
Palestine Liberation Organization (PLO) 19, 28, 31, 32–37, 206, 207–08, 210, 219
Palestinian Authority 38, 41, 43–44, 54–57, 206
Palestinian refugees 9, 80
partitionist settlement 10, 208
Patten Commission 149–51
Peres, Shimon 12, 28–30, 34, 35–37, 37–39, 47, 48–50, 51, 210, 219
Powell, Jonathan 156, 167, 168, 173
power sharing, power-sharing settlement 10, 177–78, 208
Progressive Unionist Party 97, 118, 128, 135, 136, 161, 175, 193, 217
Provisional IRA *see* IRA
PSNI (Police Service of NI) 149, 179, 180, 185, 193–94, 195, 196
Pundak, Ron 31

Qurei, Ahmed 31, 36, 55, 70, 74, 77, 207, 211

Rabbu, Yasir Abd 56, 69
Rabin, Yitzhak 12, 28–30, 33–35, 37, 38, 39, 42, 210–11, 212, 219; assassination and funeral 47
Rabinovich, Itamar 88
Rajoub, Jibril 85, 86
Rashid, Mohammed 77
Real IRA 122–23, 125, 144, 183, 204, 217, 227
Reid, John 159, 162, 164, 168
Reynolds, Albert 100, 103, 104, 105, 106, 110, 215
Reynolds, Lee 113–14
Robinson, Peter 98, 108, 134–45, 152, 171, 172, 177, 178, 184, 186, 199, 200, 202, 226–27
Rodgers, Brid 118
Ross, Dennis 17, 36, 58, 67, 71, 84
Ross, William 106
Royal Ulster Constabulary 98, 100, 109, 149, 151, 161
Rynhold, Jonathan 9

Scappaticci, Freddy 182–83, 195
settlements 11, 54, 69
settlers 5, 12
Sha'ath, Nabil 38, 55–56
Shamir, Yitzhak 27–28
Sharon, Ariel 60, 61, 85–86, 87, 216, 219–20
Sher, Gilead 70, 88
Shoukri, Andre 160
Shoukri, Ihab 160
siege mentality 2
Singer, Yoel (Joel) 32
Sinn Fein 98, 101, 109, 111–12, 117, 120–22, 125–26, 128, 131, 135, 136, 146, 148, 154, 165, 168, 171–73, 175, 178, 180, 184, 187–89, 194, 195–97, 200, 202, 207, 215, 216, 218, 225–26
Social Democratic and Labour Party 93–95, 96, 98, 126, 133, 135–37, 140, 145, 156, 161, 166, 171, 175, 181, 184, 190, 194, 197, 201, 205, 207, 211
Soderberg, Nancy 105, 110
Spring, Dick 113
Stone, Michael 131–32
Strand 1 94, 125–26, 128, 129–30
Strand 2 94–95, 125–26, 128, 130
Strand 3 94, 125–26, 129
Sunningdale 95, 133
Swisher, Clayton 88, 89
Syria 67–68, 212, 219, 220–21

Tanzim 70, 83, 87
Taylor, John 140, 147
terrorism: Palestinian 42, 44–45
Tohill, Bobby 179–80, 183
Touval, Sa'adia 17, 219
Trimble, David 11, 94, 98, 106, 109, 114, 115,

119, 132, 137, 139, 140, 141, 145, 146, 148, 150, 154–56, 158, 161–64, 166, 168, 171–74, 175, 181, 188, 195, 199, 207, 209, 211, 215–16, 218; in GFA talks 120, 123, 126, 128; *see also* Blair, Tony; Democratic Unionist Party; Sinn Fein

UKUP 118, 121, 134–35, 175
Ulster Defense Association (UDA) 97, 102, 104, 131, 143, 153–54, 158–61, 204, 227
Ulster Democratic Party 97, 118, 125, 128, 135, 136, 161, 217
Ulster Unionist Council (UUC) 137m 149, 151, 155–56, 158
Ulster Unionist Party (UUP) 13, 94, 98, 111, 113, 132, 135–36, 139–40, 146–47, 150, 154, 161–64, 166, 172, 175, 176, 180, 181, 187–89, 193, 195, 196, 197, 201, 205, 207, 209, 211, 218
Ulster Volunteer Force (UVF) 97, 104, 111, 119, 136, 143, 203–04, 217
United Nations 2

Washington 172, 191, 209–10, 221
Washington Talks 28, 32
Weitzer, Ronald 6
Weizman, Ezer 45
Wright, Billy 119, 124, 158, 217
Wye River Summit 60, 61

Yassin, Ahmed 59
Young, Oran 21

Zionism, Zionists 8, 10, 31, 32

www.ingramcontent.com/pod-product-compliance
Ingram Content Group UK Ltd.
Pitfield, Milton Keynes, MK11 3LW, UK
UKHW041936140426
5217IPUK00014B/504